# Teaching Social Skills

## Social Skills

*to*

## Students

*with*

## Visual Impairments

# Teaching
# Social Skills
*to*
# Students
*with*
# Visual Impairments

*From Theory to Practice*

**Sharon Z. Sacks** and **Karen E. Wolffe**
Editors

**AFB PRESS**

American Foundation for the Blind

Printed in the United States of America

Library of Congress Cataloging-in-Publication Data

Sacks, Sharon.
  Teaching social skills to students with visual impairments : from theory to practice / Sharon Z. Sacks and Karen E. Wolffe.
    p.   cm.
  ISBN 978-0-89128-882-4

  1. Children, Blind—Education—United States.   2. Children with visual disabilities—Education—United States.   3. Social skills—Study and teaching—United States.   4. Social intelligence—Study and teaching—United States.   I. Wolffe, Karen E.   II. Title.
  HV1664.S63S33 2005
  371.91'1482—dc22

                                                              2005026078

Photo credits: J. Richard Russo, cover (both), pp. xv, 118; L. Penny Rosenblum, pp. 48, 328, 476.

The American Foundation for the Blind—the organization to which Helen Keller devoted her life—is a national nonprofit devoted to expanding the possibilities for people with vision loss.

We dedicate this textbook to our partners in life, our husbands,
Rick Sacks and Terry Hirsh,
who have spent endless hours supporting us and encouraging us
through all of our professional endeavors.
We admire and love you.

# Contents

# Acknowledgments

We are most appreciative of those who helped in the development and production of this text. Without their continued support and patience, this endeavor would not be a reality. First, we would like to thank our families for their care and understanding while we spent numerous hours engaged in writing and editing tasks. They provided us with the time and space needed to produce an informative and useful resource.

The staff at AFB Press and the American Foundation for the Blind has guided us through every aspect of the book's development. We especially want to acknowledge Natalie Hilzen, Director and Editor in Chief of AFB Press, for her editing expertise, as well as Ellen Bilofsky and Rebecca Burrichter for their efforts toward ensuring the book's timely production, including copy-editing and design expertise. Their professionalism is truly valued.

This text could not have been completed without the dedication and expertise of our chapter authors, Lizbeth Barclay, Jane Erin, Susan LaVenture, Judith Lesner, Sandy Lewis, Ann MacCuspie, Penny Rosenblum, Rosanne Silberman, and Mary Zabelski. Their knowledge of social skills instruction and cutting-edge research has added to the depth and breadth of the book. We also wish to extend a special thank you to Richard Russo, former Director of the California School for the Blind Assessment Center, and Penny Rosenblum for the photos used in the text.

Finally, we wish to thank all of our students with visual impairments for allowing us to learn from them. Through our work with students who are blind or visually impaired we have been able to design interventions and strategies that can foster social competence and self-advocacy—keys for life success.

# Foreword

In the early 1990s, the urgent concerns of parents and teachers about the quality of educational services for students with visual impairments in this country coalesced around a national grassroots movement that became known as "The National Agenda." As a result, a groundbreaking document entitled *The National Agenda for the Education of Children and Youths with Visual Impairments, Including Those with Multiple Disabilities* was published in 1995 to outline vital educational goals and serve as a blueprint for national advocacy efforts. Among the key concepts advanced was that of the expanded core curriculum, which described essential instructional areas for students who are visually impaired. An essential component of the expanded core curriculum is social skills instruction. When one considers the fact that the curriculum includes areas of learning that sighted children primarily obtain in a spontaneous manner, through vision, it should be no surprise that social skills instruction is high on the list of unique educational needs for blind and visually impaired students.

During the development of inclusive education, in which students with visual impairments were placed in regular classrooms in their communities rather than in more separate settings such as residential schools for blind students, it was assumed that these students would learn social interaction skills naturally, in the give-and-take environment of regular classrooms. Yet research, literature, and anecdotal accounts suggest otherwise. Blind and visually impaired students who do not receive regular, systematic instruction in social skills are at high risk of becoming social isolates in their regular classrooms.

Authors like Ann McCuspie, T. D'Allura, and many others continue to remind us that the acquisition of social skills does not happen naturally for most blind and visually impaired students. In fact, the sequential, meaningful teaching of social skills requires a teacher with significant knowledge of the impact of vision loss on the effective development of social skills.

I fear that it is not a lack of an understanding of need, nor a lack of curriculum materials that prevents most blind and visually impaired students from receiving this instruction. It is more likely that it is a lack of time that precludes the opportunity for teachers of students with visual impairments to focus on the development of social interaction skills.

In the past, Sharon Sacks and Karen Wolffe have contributed in very significant and practical ways to our awareness of the need for this instruction, and they have provided very effective curriculum materials for the teaching of social skills. Now they have surpassed their previous accomplishments by compiling a major contribution to the literature. These two educators and scholars have produced an up-to-date and definitive book on the learning of social skills by blind and visually impaired students. I have learned to expect no less from these exceptional professionals. The critical importance of this book cannot be overstated.

Recently I have challenged our profession to consider three solutions to the thorny issue of social skills instruction:

1. Accept the status quo and assume that most blind and visually impaired students will graduate from high school with very few skills to equip them for assimilation into a sighted world.

2. Learn and grow from the literature and the curriculum materials we have, and make the teaching of social skills a higher priority for instruction. Consider the possibility that learning social skills might be as important as learning to read.

3. Partner with schools for blind students, because most of these schools are now concentrating on teaching the expanded core curriculum, and there exists a wonderful opportunity to learn social skills because teachers at these schools in fact have time to teach these critical areas of learning.

With the completion of *Teaching Social Skills to Students with Visual Impairments*, Sacks and Wolffe have restored my confidence that the best solution to our challenge is option number 2. In this publication they have provided educators and other concerned parties with the knowledge and the tools to teach social skills and the urgent message of the vital importance of doing so. Now it is up to the rest of us to apply what we have learned from this invaluable new resource.

Phil H. Hatlen, Ed.D.
*Superintendent*
*Texas School for the Blind and Visually Impaired*

# Introduction

In 1992 the American Foundation for the Blind published the first text on social development and social skills training for students with visual impairments. Although some research in this area had been undertaken prior to the early 1990s, there was no collected body of knowledge that addressed the significance of this issue. Many family members and teachers of students with visual impairments had observed the frequent social isolation and awkwardness experienced by the majority of visually impaired children, including those attending school in mainstream or integrated settings. Parents as well as professionals recognized the importance of teaching social skills and sought strategies to assist youngsters in developing friendships, as well as interacting effectively in school, community, and ultimately work and independent living environments. In 1992 *The Development of Social Skills by Blind and Visually Impaired Students: Exploratory Studies and Strategies* (edited by Sharon Sacks, Linda Kekelis, and Robert Gaylord-Ross) began to lay a foundation and set a precedent reflecting the realization that social skills had, in fact, to be actively and deliberately taught.

Today, social skills instruction has become accepted as an integral part of best practice in educating students who are blind or visually impaired. Yet teachers and families alike continue to grapple with how these strategies can be implemented in a time when the focus of education is directed toward academic success and data-based decision making. Goal 8 of the *National Agenda for the Education of Children and Youths with Visual Impairments, Including Those with Multiple Disabilities* stipulates that all students who are blind or visually impaired, including students with additional disabilities, will receive specialized assessment and instruction in a range of disability-specific areas, including social skills. Given this mandate it seems logical that a text rich in strategies-based interventions would benefit professionals and families.

*Teaching Social Skills to Students with Visual Impairments: Theory to Practice* expands upon the knowledge base and provides a compendium of intervention strategies to support and enhance the acquisition of social skills in children and youths with visual impairments. While we have tried to emphasize the practical applications of teaching social skills, we believe strongly that theory and research provide an excellent framework for practice. Theory provides the basis for practice; research allows us to test to determine the effectiveness of interventions or instruction based on theoretical perspectives. Without understanding social development theory, it would be difficult to justify or rationalize social skills instruction. Likewise, the paucity of research that is based on social development theory in the field of blindness and visual impairment has placed us at a disadvantage in the larger disability community. Too often in our discipline, we design interventions or methods of instruction based on what has worked in the past rather than selecting successful methodology based on theory and research.

The four parts of this text reflect this viewpoint. Part 1, Personal Viewpoints, addresses social skills from a first-person perspective. The second part, Theories of Social Development, examines how theory seeks to explain social development and influences assessment and practice. The Elements of Social Success, Part 3, ties personal perspectives and theory to actual practice. Finally, Part 4, Intervention and Practice, offers numerous examples and models for teaching social skills to students who are blind or visually impaired, including those with additional disabling conditions.

We strongly believe that the acquisition of social skills is the key to later success for students who are blind or visually impaired. Without a repertoire of acceptable social behaviors, students may be at risk for social isolation and a life of dependence as a result of their inability to get and maintain employment. Teaching social skills is one of the more important curricular areas in which teachers and families must work to achieve positive student outcomes. We hope that the strategies and interventions included in this text will promote greater inclusion of these skills in the educational curriculum for children and youths who are visually impaired. The true significance of social skills is perhaps nowhere better characterized than by Helen Keller, who said, "Walking with a friend in the dark is better than walking alone in the light."

# Personal Viewpoints

How do children become social beings, comfortable with themselves and with others? The process is a complex developmental phenomenon, influenced by numerous factors. Among them is the child's constant observation and imitation of the social behaviors of the people who are part of his or her daily life. When a child is unable to observe the surrounding world, the information and input fueling social development can be fragmented, confusing, and incomplete. As a result, providing the child with specific information, direct instruction, and opportunities for interacting as a social being and helping the child develop skill and a level of comfort in social interactions becomes critical. Families of children who are visually impaired, early interventionists, and teachers, therefore, play a pivotal role in helping these children acquire social finesse.

Before exploring theoretical models of social skills or interventions that promote social competence for students with visual impairments, it is instructive to view how the development of social skills has influenced the lives of individuals with visual impairments and their families, using a qualitative approach. The chapters in Part 1 present a personal view of how social skills are acquired and developed from childhood and adolescence into adulthood from the perspective of a child (now an adult) with a visual impairment and that of parents who have raised children who are visually impaired. The personal perspective is a vitally important one, providing insight into the way in which children with visual impairments experience the world and people around them and the elements that promote and support the social evolution of these children. We hope that beginning the text with personal perspectives will allow the reader to appreciate that teaching social skills is more than just a matter of concepts and theories. The anecdotes and illustrations throughout Part 1 bring social skills to life through the eyes of those who have lived and experienced what it means to be visually impaired seeking connection in a sighted world.

While it is not always easy to describe one's personal experiences, the importance of sharing perspectives from an individual who is visually impaired and from parents of students who are blind or visually impaired is enormous. These first two chapters set the tone for this book by providing a personal viewpoint, something generally omitted from most educational texts dealing with social skills instruction. We believe that starting out with a personal focus will help underline the need for and importance of social skills instruction for students with visual impairments. Each chapter describes in detail how the child's socialization was promoted in the home, school, and community. Anecdotal illustrations provide many examples of how social skills are learned and nurtured.

Sacks begins her chapter by describing several tenets necessary for students with visual impairments to achieve social competence. She illustrates how these tenets applied to her own social development. Throughout the chapter, she reflects upon her social experiences with her family, school friends, and colleagues. The emphasis on family and teacher support is woven throughout.

In the second chapter, three parents describe the journeys they have taken to support their children's social development. Each story has a different focus. One story illustrates how social skills were taught and expected in a child who was blind. The second story examines the socialization of an adolescent who has low vision. The third describes the socialization process for a student who is visually impaired with additional disabilities. Each parent describes her early experiences with teaching and advocating on behalf of her child and offers insight into the relationship between family support and social development. These parents emphasize the importance of partnerships between parents and professionals and recognize the diversity among families and their children in teaching social skills.

# CHAPTER 1

# The Development of Social Skills: A Personal Perspective

## Sharon Z. Sacks

S cholarly textbooks rarely offer a personal point of view. The information provided is generally based on theoretical perspectives, systematic research, and best practices. This text is no different. The editors hope to provide a compendium of literature, timely research, and practical interventions related to social skills development and instruction for students with visual impairments. However, we also believe that much can be learned through sharing of personal experiences and anecdotal information.

Thus, by sharing my own personal perspective in this chapter, we aim to bring understanding to the process by which individuals with visual impairments learn and acquire social skills throughout their lives with the support of family, friends, and professionals. I hope that professionals and families will gain greater sensitivity toward the personal dreams of persons with visual impairment encountered in acquiring social skills.

The challenge I faced in writing this chapter was to carefully balance scholarly rhetoric and an autobiographical memoir. It was not easy to share my innermost feelings and to write about my own personal experience of the socialization process; nor was it easy to ask family, friends, and colleagues to share their perspectives about my social development and the subsequent experiences encountered throughout my childhood, adolescence, and adulthood. However, through these personal examples and illustrations I hope professionals and families will gain new insights regarding the socialization of students with visual impairments. My experiences may be unique. They cannot reflect the diversity of students with visual impairments served in educational programs today. Many of these students may have additional disabilities or they may come from socially or linguistically different backgrounds. However, the lessons learned through my experiences at home, in school, and in the community may benefit others and help to provide a rationale for continued intervention by professionals and families. Key issues for the successful socialization of students who are blind or visually impaired, such as school placement, family involvement, and early intervention by trained professionals, are discussed with examples throughout the chapter.

## CRITICAL CONCEPTS

It is essential for professionals and families to understand the process by which students with visual impairments acquire and learn social skills. These individuals are pivotal in helping students to acquire and maintain a repertoire of social skills. They also provide the valuable information and feedback that is so important in the development of positive social behavior in students with visual impairments.

Subsequent chapters will focus on the development and assessment of social skills; others will provide an array of intervention strategies to support students toward acquiring a repertoire of socially competent behavior. This information is intended to assist teachers, families, and students, but this is not a cookbook. Each student who is blind or visually impaired is an individual, and as such, his or her educational program must be designed with care and consideration for individual differences and abilities.

The following tenets provide a foundation for professionals and families to draw upon when designing interventions and strategies for teaching social skills. These principles provide a framework for discussion as well as a conceptual framework for the ideas and concepts presented throughout this text.

- The acquisition and maintenance of socially appropriate behavior is typically mediated by vision for sighted individuals. Much of what is learned socially is acquired through imitation and modeling.

- Students with visual impairments do not acquire skills and behaviors through incidental learning, as sighted children typically do.

- The acquisition of social skills by students with visual impairments is not learned naturally, but through the support of significant others in the student's life.

- Students with visual impairments require routines and experiences that promote opportunities for hands-on activities and real-life tasks.

- Family members of students with visual impairments must view the acquisition and maintenance of social skills as important, and promote socially competent behavior in all environments in which the student participates.

- For students and adults with visual impairments, the process of using social skills effectively requires persistence and physical energy to maintain competent social behavior. This process requires that the student who is blind or visually impaired use all senses as well as cognitive skills, to figure out the social situation. For example, when a person who is blind is in a large group, figuring out the members of the group takes skill and integration of one's cognitive and sensory abilities.

- Acquiring and learning social skills is an ongoing process for persons with visual impairments.

- Families and educators must work in tandem to promote and establish the expectation of socially competent behavior from their students with visual impairments.

## THE IMPORTANCE OF FAMILY SUPPORT

For all students with visual impairments the influence of family support and nurturing is essential. Whether a child is born with a severe visual impairment or acquires it as a young child, parents, siblings, and extended family members provide the foundation for the acquisition of social skills. The home environment provides a natural context for the socialization process. It is the first place where children learn routines, family rituals and customs, and develop a sense of inner security and safety.

My own family's influence on my social development stemmed from a strong sense that I was an integral part of the family unit. My parents seemed to have clear expectations for me. Even though my premature birth was not expected, and the diagnosis of retinopathy of prematurity was a grave shock and concern to my parents and other family members, they welcomed my birth and expected me to be part of all family activities, participating to the best of my ability. I was included in family outings and day-to-day routines and was disciplined when my social behavior was inappropriate. I learned quickly that expectations were the rule not the exception.

While my parents had no formal training and relatively little support from professionals, they instinctively created a stimulating and rich home environment for me. They interpreted the visual world by describing objects and activities in my world. Because I was a second child, I was treated like my brother. I spent much of my time involved in family activities. If the family was watching television, I was on the floor on a blanket with my brother. Toys and people came into my physical circle. My parents constantly interacted with me with verbal cues, tickling, touching, and genuine loving. They directed my visual cues to faces and actions in my environment. At mealtimes, I was included in the events around the kitchen table. I was given food to taste and encouraged to respond verbally when I liked or disliked a food item or activity. As an older infant and toddler, I spent a lot of my waking time on the go. I was a regular presence at Cub Scout meetings, Little League games, and outings in the park.

My brother, six years my senior, created an active home environment for my family. His friends were a part of the home milieu. Pretend games (cops and robbers) and active sports (kickball and softball) took place in our backyard. I was in the midst of all the activity and fun. Conversations with my brother indicate that he perceived me as being no different than him. "When my friends came over, they just accepted you. They thought of you as my little sister, and tolerated your getting in the way. I never felt sorry for you because Mom and Dad never felt that way" (personal communication, January 2002).

Family support and participation in the social development process is critical during early school experiences, but it is also an essential component during adolescence. Parents, and particularly older siblings, can assist in providing opportunities for greater responsibility and autonomy. This delicate balance between nurturing and letting go promotes greater levels of independence and interdependence. Family members and professionals must work together to find ways for students who are blind and visually impaired to learn the skills involved in typical teen experiences: flirting, hanging out, going to the mall, dating, and dressing in the "in" clothing. As in the formative years, during adolescence those close to students with visual impairments must interpret the visual world and understand and accept the teen culture. They must provide the information and orchestrate experiences that help the students achieve greater integration with both their blind and sighted peers.

For example, learning to apply makeup during the middle school years was an important part of my daily routine as a young adolescent. My mother, and later my sighted friends, helped me learn how to apply eyeliner and mascara without making a mess. Until I became proficient, my mother applied the makeup daily.

In addition to activities with other students with visual impairments, my parents facilitated my participation with sighted peers in after-school activities, youth groups, and other school organizations. They willingly transported me to dance and swim lessons. They encouraged me to join scouting and youth groups. In junior high and high school I participated in school service organizations with many after-school commitments. Even when my friends began to drive, my parents supported the use of public transportation and encouraged independent travel.

## PROMOTING SOCIAL INTERACTIONS

For most people, early social development is acquired through imitation and modeling (Warren, 2000). Sighted infants and toddlers learn about their world through observation and visual cues from others in their environment. Children who are blind and visually impaired require that the world be brought to them. Students with visual impairments cannot be expected to acquire a repertoire of social skills through incidental learning. Family members and teachers often need to physically model and demonstrate a range of social behaviors or exchanges in various contexts before a student can integrate these concepts into practical applications.

My mother instinctively understood the importance of providing early social experiences for me. Because our family was surrounded by a large circle of friends, children of all ages were always available. However, my mother had to encourage me to reach out to others. She modeled social greetings ("Say hello" or "Can I play?") and pushed me to try new activities (playing on the swings or slide in the park). She made every effort to help me "look" at an individual when speaking to him or her. For example, when I greeted my grandparents at their apartment each week, she would remind me to "Say hello to Grandma and Grandpa," and she would position my body in the direction of their faces. She also reinforced the concept of an erect head position, by pointing out that I needed to "look at Grandma."

When we participated in play programs, she facilitated opportunities for sharing and communication ("Let's go on the merry-go-round with the other children. I'll stay with you."). A park program provided many varied opportunities for "messy play"; finger painting and playing with clay alongside peers often stimulated pretend play and make-believe scenarios.

Although my vision was very limited, I picked up visual cues that helped me learn to imitate actions and gestures from peers. I also learned to use auditory cues to help determine the nature of my social experience. For example, I learned to identify people by memorizing their voices and by identifying their general body features (color and length of hair, body stance, and type of walk). My parents and other family members introduced many of these skills. By being placed in a variety of social situations, it became natural for me to pick up on these cues and practice them in real contexts.

My family recognized that I enjoyed having stories read to me and that I liked to dance and sing with music. They sought out activities that promoted these interests. My mother and I attended the story hour at the local library. I participated in a movement and music class through the park district. Each of these experiences helped me to become more interactive with both peers and family members.

My mother always brought the social world to me. She encouraged me to reach out to other children and to participate in a range of activities. Throughout these early social experiences, there was always the expectation that I would act in a socially appropriate manner. For example, as a preschooler I poked my eye, especially when I was tired or bored. My parents found times when I was not engaged in eye-poking to provide verbal reinforcement about "how pretty I looked." When I was engaged in eye-poking, they provided a simple cue—"Sharon"—which reminded me to take my fingers away from my eyes.

Perhaps the most challenging aspect of creating interactive social experiences was the continuous education my parents had to impart to others. My parents became my greatest advocates. They provided information about my visual impairment, allayed fears and stereotypes about my disability, and convinced early educators that I could participate along with sighted children in a school or recreational setting. In particular, parents of sighted children were concerned about safety and liability issues and wanted to make sure that their children would receive as much attention and support from the teacher as I did.

Despite these challenges, my family was fortunate to find a preschool teacher who believed strongly in educating all children. She encouraged my participation in the preschool program and created a learning environment that was organized and structured, yet nurtured curiosity and active learning. She encouraged socialization through play, creative dramatics, music, and storytelling. In her attempt to include me in the social milieu of the preschool setting, she encouraged interaction with other young children. She modeled appropriate social behavior and expected me to participate as an equal. I was never excluded from an activity, and I was always encouraged to try new experiences. I learned that if I didn't try, I wouldn't have the opportunity to learn new things or to experience new adventures. As a result, I became a risk taker, which in and of itself created new challenges for my teachers and my family.

## DEVELOPING A STRONG IDENTITY

The diagnosis of a severe visual impairment or blindness can be devastating for families, particularly if they hold stereotypic views about the potential of persons who are blind. If family members lack experience with people who have disabilities, they may not only be uncomfortable around a child who is blind or visually impaired, but may also treat the child as if he or she were a sighted child who simply lacked vision. Such attitudes on the part of family members or even some professionals may prevent families from fostering a strong sense of self in the child who is blind or visually impaired. Early intervention programs, staffed by educators trained to work with students with visual impairments, can assist students in developing a strong and positive self-identity. Professionals can also facilitate greater communication and collaboration among those who are closest to the child.

For example, my preschool teacher worked together with my teacher of visually impaired students and immediate family to ensure that I would develop a positive self-image. During these early years, I felt no different from my sighted age-mates. I don't think I understood that I had a visual impairment perhaps or that I saw differently than others. I never felt isolated or alone. I was never teased or ridiculed by the children in my preschool class or in my neighborhood. While my parents had already established social contacts with my classmates' parents, they, too, felt welcomed. The preschool teacher assumed the leadership role on behalf of my parents. She answered questions about my disability, and acted as a support to my mother when concerns arose.

For many students with visual impairments, entrance into the more formal educational settings of kindergarten or the primary grades poses new challenges. The larger school environment may not be as welcoming or as willing to accommodate the individual needs of the student who is blind or visually impaired. The structure of school itself focuses on more academic pursuits, with less emphasis placed on affective education. As a result, students with visual impairments may not have opportunities to develop their own unique set of attributes or values that relate directly to their visual impairment. Instead of feeling that blindness is an integral part of them, many students learn to view themselves as inadequate or incapable of achieving an array of skills.

While I recall functioning well in the classroom environment, physical activities were much more difficult. I lacked the agility to throw and catch a ball, jump rope, or maneuver around the climbing equipment. There were many more children to contend with in the elementary setting, and they moved faster than in the preschool environment. As a result, I tended to play with one or two children rather than in large groups. Also, I tended to gravitate toward activities that were less physically active: swinging on the swings, building with blocks, and chatting with classmates. My kindergarten teacher did not actively encourage or promote social interactions in free-play situations. She tended to monitor each activity directly intervening only if students' safety became an issue.

As the school environment became more academic, I began to recognize differences in how I approached schoolwork and social activities. At the same time, my sighted classmates began to perceive me as slower and less competent. I vividly remember being teased about wearing glasses in kindergarten. I also remember having great difficulty in completing worksheets. The teacher moved so rapidly through the assignment that I could not locate the correct row or set of items on the page. After that incident, classmates began to call me "four eyes" and "blindy." Some students began to distance themselves from me, particularly on the playground. I simply had no strategy to deal with my first experience of taunting. I could not understand the change in my peers' behavior, nor could I find ways to combat the isolation I experienced at such a young age.

Because academics were such a priority throughout my educational career, my teachers of students with visual impairments did not view social skills as a priority. They spent little time helping students communicate about their visual impairment to others. There were few opportunities to meet and interact with blind adults or to participate in activities with other students who were blind or visually impaired. However, Saturday and summer day-camp programs sponsored by the local agency for persons who are blind helped to nurture a strong sense of identity and provided numerous opportunities to encounter challenging activities. Relationships with other blind and visually impaired children established a strong social network. Even though many of the other students in these programs did not attend the same school or live close to my home, I looked forward to seeing them or talking to them on the telephone.

Experiences in a special class for students with visual impairments with minimal mainstreaming during my elementary school years (the only option for educational placement at that time) also helped to strengthen my sense of identity as a person with a visual impairment. Although I traveled a long distance from my home to school each day, I valued the friendships I developed with peers who were blind or visually impaired. The program for students with visual impairments featured relatively small classes (8–12 students in a class, two grades per class) and a combination of academics and activities to enhance socialization. For the most part the teacher of visually impaired students provided the majority of the educational curriculum. Minimal mainstreaming into the general education classroom occurred for social studies, some for science activities, music, and special assemblies. As students progressed through the elementary grades, greater time was spent in the general education classroom depending on the students' academic abilities and levels of independence and socialization.

Group activities, such as painting a Thanksgiving mural or creating pottery for holiday gifts for family members, enhanced our ability to work together, to share materials and supplies, and to feel good about a finished product. Even though the teacher of visually impaired students did not focus on specific social skills instruction or allocate time to help students deal with their individual visual impairments, it was clear that she had high expectations for students' performance and created a classroom environment that was organized, structured, and highly nurturing.

## PROMOTING HANDS-ON ACTIVITIES AND REAL-LIFE EXPERIENCES

For students who are blind or visually impaired to achieve high levels of social competence, they must have opportunities to participate in activities and experiences that promote social inclusion with both blind and sighted age-mates. Families and teachers of students with visual impairments cannot assume that these experiences will occur naturally or that the student will engage with others without consistent support or intervention. Professionals and family members working with these students must interpret the nuances and intricacies of the social culture of children and teens. These caring adults need to be aware of the games, conversation topics, language, and dress of specific age groups, and they must be committed to teaching these skills and to finding effective strategies to ensure that the student experiences success within home, school, and community environments.

While incidental learning influences how students with visual impairments acquire a repertoire of social skills, it is also important to consider the general level of motivation and desire students possess when engaged in social experiences with peers and adults. Some children who are blind or visually impaired prefer solitary play and choose not to be involved with others. Some students may want to engage in social activities with peers, but are afraid of the unknown and are dependent on adults to mediate their social world. Students who have not had early experiences that promote exploration and curiosity or a willingness to take risks may be more reticent than others.

In the safety of my home, I was encouraged to learn new games and participate in activities that facilitated social interactions with peers. My parents recall that it was my own desire to achieve and to be part of a group that prodded them into action. I vividly remember spending time with my brother learning to play "two square" and "wall ball." My mother spent hours teaching me how to jump into a moving jump rope. I spent every afternoon practicing these games so I could participate with my sighted peers. I was *determined* to be part of the social milieu. Learning to ride a bike without training wheels was a real challenge. My father and brother took turns racing beside me to keep the bike upright while I peddled madly down the street. After weeks of struggle and bruised body parts, I mastered the art of bike riding. It was an accomplishment for the entire family.

Throughout my childhood and adolescence, I was expected to complete chores around the house and assume responsibility for my own belongings. For example, I helped to prepare dinner each night, cleared and washed the dishes, and kept my bedroom organized and clean. As a teenager, I secured jobs babysitting neighbors' children and working in a dress shop stocking merchandise and gift wrapping packages. I received an allowance and was paid for employment. I learned early on that earning money provided me with opportunities to make choices and decisions about money management. I quickly learned that there was a strong connection between the value of work and the level of autonomy and control that earning money provides.

I also learned that reciprocating for assistance from others was important. Even as a young child, my family encouraged me to give to others by sharing toys and games or helping peers with schoolwork. As a teenager I volunteered as a candy striper at a local hospital, assisted in an elementary school classroom, and was a camp counselor for local day camp programs. These experiences helped to focus my attention on others and to teach the importance of giving to others rather than always receiving.

## MANAGING DIFFERENCES

One of the most essential ways in which families and professionals can assist students with visual impairments in developing a strong social identity, is to help them understand and communicate their visual disability to others. When students feel comfortable and at ease with their visual impairment, they will gain greater acceptance and approval from peers and adults with whom they interact. Providing information, even at the most basic level, allays the fears of others and answers their questions of curiosity and concern. This is particularly true for students with low vision, who may seem to look and function like a sighted person, but require adaptations and specialized equipment to master academics, travel independently, or be employed in the community. Students who are able to explain to others how they perceive the world and how they function in it may encounter less social isolation because these explanations reflect a positive self-image. Students who choose to hide or mask their visual impairment may encounter awkward or uncomfortable situations in which they are perceived by others as incapable or incompetent.

While the self-contained nature of my elementary school educational program provided a sound academic foundation for later school success, the sighted students at the school perceived those of us in the program for visually impaired students to be "different." Teachers viewed themselves as providers of subject-matter curricula, and very little time was spent helping the two groups to get to know or to learn more about one another. As a result, many of the students with visual impairments (myself included) were subject to teasing and ridicule by our sighted peers. I keenly remember the exclusionary comments and experiences: "You can't play with me, you can't see the ball," or "I don't want you on our team, you're dumb." Sometimes students' actions were more covert. Instead of teasing, or name-calling, they walked away or ignored our overtures to be included in group activities and games. Neither the teacher of students with visual impairments nor the general education teacher was prepared to effectively change attitudes and actions. The students who were blind and visually impaired in my class did not have strategies that would help them thwart this type of behavior.

While my parents worked hard to lay the groundwork for successful social experiences outside of school (such as selling candy for Camp Fire Girls, performing in dance recitals, and participating in religious school programs), they, too, felt uncomfortable talking about my visual impairment. It was not until my adolescence, when I pressured my ophthalmologist to explain my visual impairment to me, that I began to incorporate my blindness as a distinct part of my self-identity. Nonetheless, I did not develop ways to communicate to others in my daily life about my visual impairment until adulthood, when I developed various strategies on my own and gained confidence from the positive feedback I received from colleagues and friends. For example, in my adolescent years, I never discussed my visual impairment with friends unless I was confronted with a question. As a young adult in college, I began to explain my visual impairment to roommates and friends. I realized quickly that they responded positively to my attributes as an individual and that the visual impairment was simply a piece of my identity. Because I received such positive feedback, I began to speak more openly and easily about my vision loss.

## LEARNING THE RULES OF SOCIALIZATION

Many of the social behaviors learned in society are acquired incidentally. This is especially true for skills that are learned visually and for which no verbal feedback is required. Social exchanges can be communicated through a nod, a physical gesture, or a facial expression. Students who are blind or visually impaired may have greater difficulty learning these subtle behaviors because they are mediated so strongly by visual feedback from others. Because students are more dependent on parents, professionals, and peers to interpret and model visual behavior at socially appropriate times and in specific social situations, it is incumbent upon those close to them to communicate the importance of using specific social behaviors and following certain social rules according to the appropriate context. Without this knowledge, students are at a disadvantage in successfully developing positive social relationships.

While my experiences with visually impaired peers in school and in recreation programs enhanced my level of social confidence, interacting with sighted peers was much more complex. Much of what sighted peers did to engage socially was accomplished through nonverbal communication (facial expressions, gestures, body stance) and unspoken social rules. These social nuances made it difficult to become part of peer groups, especially as students moved from elementary to secondary school programs. Even though I used my vision effectively to travel independently or to complete school assignments, I had to depend on my auditory and cognitive skills to absorb all of the social rules in my environment. I worked extremely hard to fit in and to be part of the sighted community. I dressed like my peers, worked with family to learn the games my peers played, and became familiar with popular music and cultural groups of that time. I used a lot of physical and emotional energy to grasp the rules of my peer culture. But it wasn't until high school and college that I connected with a group of sighted peers who shared my interests and values. I continually worked throughout my adolescence and into adulthood to develop these skills. My strong desire to win acceptance and achieve a high level of social status encouraged my continued persistence in acquiring skills in this area.

## THE INFLUENCE OF ROLE MODELS AND MENTORS

Students who are blind or visually impaired often seek peers and adults who have a similar visual impairment so that they can share their experiences with one another. Since most students with visual impairments are educated in their local communities, they may have limited opportunities to meet and interact with others like themselves. While it is important to learn skills that will enhance social contacts with sighted peers and colleagues, it is equally important to develop relationships with people who are blind or visually impaired. Sharing strategies to enhance social interactions and discussing practical ways to gain entry into groups or to maintain conversations within group contexts supports and enhances the socialization process. Exchanging anecdotes about humorous or embarrassing social experiences brings some levity to issues that are generally considered sensitive and personal. It is important for visually impaired students to learn that they are not unique in experiencing awkward social situations. Older students or adults who are blind or visually impaired can add the perspective of experience.

Role models and mentors can help to facilitate social growth and acceptance of a visual impairment by answering questions about how specific social situations were handled or by providing techniques for initiating specific social behaviors or actions. One of the most successful role model and mentoring programs for students with visual impairments is the CareerConnect Web site sponsored by the American Foundation for the Blind (www.afb.org/CareerConnect). CareerConnect matches blind and visually impaired students with employed adults who are blind or have low vision. Students not only gain access to valuable career information, but also have the opportunity to meet and establish relationships with successful visually impaired adults. (See the Resources section for more information.)

Although I had many opportunities to interact and develop friendships with peers who were blind and visually impaired, my contact with adults who are blind had been mostly limited to my rehabilitation counselor. It was not until late adolescence, through the assistance of one of my teachers of visually impaired students, that I was able to actually meet a professional woman who was blind. She was a psychologist and career counselor. She was also savvy and articulate. She had her own car and a driver to transport her from appointment to appointment. She answered my numerous questions about appearance, dating, educational goals, and career opportunities. Even though our relationship was brief, it made a lasting impression on the way I perceived my future goals.

As a college student I sought out opportunities to work with and develop social relationships with other disabled students by organizing a disabled students union on campus. I also participated in the state consumer organization of the blind as a student member. These experiences helped to enhance my feelings of self-worth and ultimately create a strong identity as a person with a visual impairment.

# MASTERING THE ART OF SOCIAL COMPETENCE

Developing and maintaining a set of socially competent behaviors and skills is a continuous process for students with visual impairments. Strategies for acquiring and maintaining social relationships are introduced and initiated during childhood and adolescence but they require hard work and commitment. Often, students with visual impairments do not recognize the value of learning these skills, although, once learned, they are used frequently throughout a child's school years. However, it is in adulthood when the skills learned as a child become most meaningful and useful. Successful adults who are blind or visually impaired acknowledge that they constantly refine and improve their social skills. They recognize that there is a strong connection between social competence and social integration into the workplace and the community. The more success persons with visual impairments have with social contacts, the more willing they are to place themselves in situations in which their social abilities are challenged.

As a person with a visual impairment, I am continually learning to refine and enhance my social skills. I depend on those close to me—family, colleagues, and friends—to provide me with the necessary information for success in a variety of social situations. I have learned to ask questions to obtain information that will help me interpret non-verbal cues and social nuances that are typically acquired visually. Throughout my adult years, I have placed myself in situations where I must interact with groups of sighted and blind individuals on many different levels: professional situations, casual encounters with acquaintances and friends, and in my home life as a wife and mother. In every situation that I encounter, I have used some form of social skills to enhance current relationships and gain access to others.

For example, as my children began to develop friendships with other children their age, I needed to demonstrate my social competence with the parents of their friends. Not only did I have to explain the nature of my visual impairment to them, but I had to make them feel confident that I was capable of caring for their children during play dates or school field trips. I learned that I could be an equal participant in all aspects of my children's lives. While I was unable to drive, destinations on public transit became a real treat for my children and their friends. I organized field trips for all of the students using buses and the Bay Area Rapid Transit system.

Another important aspect of developing social competence in my adult years was learning to make light of situations in which I was at a disadvantage visually (for example, seeing facial expressions at a distance). I have learned to speak openly and honestly about my visual impairment, emphasizing the positive aspects. For example, I tell people that I have no fear of skiing down steep snow-covered hills because I can't see the expanse or difficulty of the hillside. Finally, I have learned to laugh at the mistakes I have made in numerous social situations, like greeting a person who turns out not to be the individual I expected, and have found strategies to combat embarrassing situations.

## CONCLUSION

The acquisition and utilization of social skills for students who are blind or visually impaired is an individual journey that is influenced by family support, early learning experiences, and developmental abilities and skills. How students learn and acquire social skills is an individual process and is unique to each student's situation. The personal anecdotes woven in this chapter reflect my own life experiences and are not meant to represent guidelines for all students with visual impairments. Students who are blind or visually impaired are a diverse group and require individualized techniques and strategies for learning social skills. While expectations of families of visually impaired children may be similar to those of my family, parents and other caregivers are faced with numerous challenges. It is not uncommon for both parents to work outside the home, and children with visual impairments often spend after-school time with child care providers or other family members who may not be familiar with the ways in which children with visual impairments develop social skills. Many families come from culturally and linguistically diverse backgrounds in which English is not the primary language spoken in the home. As a result, the social rules and customs may be different. It is also important to note that the majority of students with visual impairments exhibit additional disabilities. Creating social skills activities and strategies for instruction may be different for these students; it may require additional support of personnel from other disciplines.

I hope that by sharing my experiences, readers will gain greater insights into the social skill development of students with visual impairments. Regardless of additional disabilities and differences in family structure and background, it is critical for professionals and family members alike to recognize that teaching social skills to students who are visually impaired is a conscious and deliberate process that develops over time and that these skills cannot be learned through incidental experiences alone.

I also hope that my experiences will help readers appreciate the interface between research and practice. Although some information in this text may reflect cutting-edge research and methodology, the focus is on practical approaches and strategies that can be used to ensure that students who are blind or visually impaired will acquire the social skills needed to interact with competence and self-assurance.

## REFERENCES

Warren, D. H. (2000). Developmental perspectives: Youth. In B. Silverstone, M. A. Lang, B. P. Rosenthal, & E. Faye (Eds.), *The Lighthouse handbook on vision impairment and vision rehabilitation, Vol. 1* (pp. 325–337). New York: Oxford University Press.

# CHAPTER 2

# A Family Perspective on Social Skills Development

Susan LaVenture, Judith Lesner, and Mary Zabelski

Families and caregivers play a pivotal role in helping to promote socialization. They are the first and possibly the most important advocates a child can have throughout his or her development. How a family accepts a child's visual impairment can have a tremendous impact on the social and emotional development of the child.

There are many causes of visual impairment in children. Some children are born with a medical or genetic eye conduction causing congenital blindness or visual impairment, while other conditions may develop later from disease, accidents, or unusual environmental circumstances. Today, over 50 percent of children born with visual impairments have additional disabilities. Whatever the cause, each family deals with the diagnosis of a visual impairment in its own way, ranging from complete acceptance to denial, from discomfort to rejection. Some

This chapter is dedicated to Cara Dunne Yates, who passed away, after a long bout with cancer, on October 20, 2004.

parents view the diagnosis as "God's will." Some go about their daily lives with little interruption, while still others undergo a long period of grief or mourning. The range of reactions also apply to extended family members. Cultural or religious values can influence how a family accepts and copes with their child's diagnosis. When the family views the diagnosis in a positive way, opportunities for the child to develop a strong sense of self and experience positive interactions with others are more likely.

One common reaction among parents of newly diagnosed children is a strong sense of grief or loss as they realize they do not have the "perfect" child they had hoped for and that their child may have a permanent disability. The loss of dreams held for the child's future can engender a variety of feelings, such as sadness, fear, and anger. Often families have had little or no exposure to children or adults with visual impairments and do not understand that their child can learn, grow, and lead a rich and full life. Feelings of isolation, also common, are often compounded because immediate family members, neighbors, friends, local doctors, and schools also are often unfamiliar with visual impairment and its impact on the family. Families need to be referred, as soon as possible, to early intervention specialists who can offer a program for students with visual impairments. Teachers in such programs can help families to understand how blindness or severe vision loss affects the child's overall development, particularly in the area of social skills. Teachers can also introduce families to strategies and interventions that promote socialization and interactions with others.

Teachers of students with visual impairments and other specialists play a key role in providing resources and information to parents regarding specialized social skills curricula and materials designed for students who are blind or visually impaired. Teachers of students with visual impairments are often best positioned to orchestrate and encourage parents to interact with other families of children with visual impairments. These professionals are equipped to facilitate networking among new families and families with older students who are blind or visually impaired. These opportunities provide encouragement for new parents by allowing them to observe how other families function in their lives at home, in school, and within the community.

It is also very important for families to meet and know adults who are blind or visually impaired so that they can understand that having expectations for their child—now and in the future—is both realistic and a critical part of the child's development. When parents partner with teachers of students with visual impairments and other specialists, positive alliances emerge. Networking with other parents allows families to seek out valuable resources and organizations for the blind and visually impaired. These opportunities ultimately affect the children's social development and later success with employment and independent living.

Once the family has come to understand and accept their child's visual impairment or blindness, they can have a positive impact on how the child accepts his or her condition. The family's expectations for their child's progress and goals also greatly influence the child's self-confidence. But total family acceptance and adjustment to a child who has visual impairment or blindness is the ideal, and life is not always that simple. Individuals and families are different and they process their emotions and the events in their lives differently. Some families may never learn to accept their child's condition; some families may never have access to resources or the people who could help them. That said, we do know that with family acceptance and involvement, relationships with friends, and access to positive role models in a child's life, it is likely that a child who is blind or visually impaired will develop a strong sense of acceptance and social competence.

This chapter seeks to contribute to readers' understanding of the importance of family support and involvement in the socialization process for students with visual impairment. But professionals who work with students with visual impairments and blindness also need to be aware of the differences that exist among families with respect to their level of acceptance, involvement, and understanding of the social development process. By sharing examples, stories, and experiences from three different parents' perspectives, we hope to increase readers' sensitivity toward families and their individual journeys, as well as to offer strategies to enhance students' social skills.

## THE FAMILY'S ROLE IN ENCOURAGING SOCIAL SKILLS

The family plays one of the most significant roles throughout a child's development, so family life is a natural setting for social development in children. Raising a child who has a visual impairment does not need to stop the normal, everyday functions of a family's social life; having a child who is blind or visually impaired could even be considered to make the family experience more interesting and challenging.

Encouraging social skills in children can begin at birth when parents, siblings, grandparents and close friends begin communicating with an infant verbally, by touch, and by trying to make eye contact.

Parents can play a key role in facilitating social interactions within the family unit. It is important for parents to find ways to include their child who is blind or visually impaired in the daily routines of the family. The visually impaired child needs to be involved in caring for his or her own personal needs, sharing in chores around the house, and taking responsibility for appropriate social behavior. Because children with visual impairments may need additional assistance with completing daily tasks, it is essential for family members to strike a balance between helping too much and providing too little support.

Interactions between siblings can play a very important role in bringing normalcy to the social development of the child who is blind or visually impaired. Siblings have a great knack for being direct with each other and telling the truth when no one else dares to be honest, about "unmentionable" characteristics or habits. Siblings, also, are gifted at trying to keep their brothers or sisters on an equal playing field when vying for parents' attention and preventing them from receiving special treatment. Parents need to recognize the areas in which each of their children need special guidance and support.

Sometimes family members may need to describe or interpret social nuances, whether in the family or community setting, such as body language or other behavior that would typically be learned through visual observation. As students begin to interact with peers in school and community settings, parents and extended family members play a critical role in assisting the child with interactive play and nurturing relationships between the child and his or her peers. By modeling appropriate language and play skills, parents help their child to invite interaction with sighted youngsters. If the visually impaired child is to develop positive social relationships, parents and extended family will need to bring the social world to the child.

As students with visual impairments move through school and adolescence, parents and family members continue to play an important part in the socialization process. Parents can encourage participation in groups and clubs, such as chorus, scouting, swim team, or drama. Siblings can help to give their brother or sister information about popular games or movies, clothing styles, and age-appropriate conversation topics. It is essential that the family promotes and nurtures an attitude that encourages interdependence and self-advocacy. These elements, along with acceptable social skills, are critical for success as an adult.

# PARENTS' STORIES

In each of the following stories, a parent of a visually impaired child recounts the role of the family in the child's social development. Each parent describes different ways in which she encouraged positive social development in her child. Cara's mother actively promoted the use of social skills by her totally blind daughter, who attended a variety of public school programs from her early years through adolescence. Alex's mother offers examples of how her son showed his strong self-esteem and acceptance of his visual impairment through his sense of humor and through understanding the science of his diagnosis of retinoblastoma, a rare infant eye cancer. Jacob's mother describes her experiences in raising her son, who is visually impaired with additional disabilities. An advocate and professional who also has years of experience in supporting parents and students through her position as a residential supervisor at a specialized school for the blind shares her suggestions for encouraging independence. It is important to note that while each student described in these stories has a different level of visual impairment, from totally blind to excellent use of vision in one eye, the acquisition of social skills has been influenced by family support, partnerships with teachers, and the development of self-advocacy skills.

# CARA'S STORY

## THE EARLY YEARS

As a parent, I recognized early on that socialization was a critical part of Cara's overall development. I realized that in infancy Cara needed to develop reciprocal social relationships with family members and friends. When my daughter was a toddler, my relatives and family wanted to protect her and keep her safe from harm. Although I was inexperienced as a parent and looked to my family and friends for assistance, I sometimes felt that their attitudes toward her were not very positive. I thought of my daughter as a very bright, active inquisitive toddler who needed opportunities to play and explore the environment. Diagnosed with retinoblastoma (retinal cancer) at 16 months of age, she completely lost the sight in one eye shortly afterwards. Despite the fact that her vision continued to decrease, I was amazed at her interest in the toys and people around her. Her medical treatment included radiation, chemotherapy, and cryotherapy, and she had completely lost sight in both eyes by the time she was 5.

Since I could not resume my full-time job because of Cara's illness and the need to spend time with her, I took a part-time job as a preschool teacher. I brought my daughter with me to school every day. This situation turned out to be an ideal opportunity for Cara and me. We started at the preschool when she was 2½, and she stayed as a full-time student until I enrolled her in a special public school program when she was 3½. She was able to enjoy the benefits of playing, learning, and developing socially with peers of her own age. The children did not understand what a visual impairment is and did not perceive her as being different from them. Plus, I was present to facilitate and guide her through the games, free-play activities, use of the playground equipment, story time, and lunch and snack time with the other children. She learned to take turns, share, and help with clean-up. Most of all, I learned that despite her visual limitations, she was more like the other children than different. I knew that for her to be able to interact socially with her peers, she would have to participate in the same activities they did. I was in a position to engineer that, and it worked!

As Cara grew and moved into the public school preschool program for children with visual impairments and then into the early grades with her sighted peers. I would invite some of the neighborhood children to our house to play. In this way, I could subtly supervise and facilitate the activities, explaining to her what she missed visually. Sometimes, I took the children to the park, where I could assist her if needed. I also taught her to ride a two-wheel bicycle, purchasing the smallest bike available so she could plant her feet firmly on the ground, push off, and catch herself as needed. She was riding without training wheels before some of her friends of the same age. I think that this helped her to feel socially in tune with the other children.

From the time she was little, Cara was very much interested in doing the same things the other children were doing, whether it was climbing trees, riding bikes, swimming, or playing in a group. If there were no children around for her to interact with, I acted as her friend. Since she could not see the other children who were playing near her in our neighborhood, she couldn't seek out friends on her own. So I explained to her what was happening in small group situations and gave her opportunities to touch and feel the toys or objects that the other children were using. I showed her how to play the games, describing how the other children participated. To help her understand what the other children were doing or the objects they were playing with, I provided a running narrative of their actions. I also found small models of large items that children talk about, things like airplanes, fire engines, farms, chimneys, and other objects that sighted children often learned about by looking at pictures. Whenever possible, I tried to expose Cara to the real experiences of exploring a fire engine or visiting a farm.

Cara's experiences in the preschool with sighted peers had helped her to develop social skills and close relationships with other children. However, I realized that the regular preschool program, although meeting some of her social needs, could not provide the pre-academic and pre-braille skills that she needed to compete with the other children educationally. She would not be able to master the skills that the other preschoolers would learn, such as visually identifying and tracing numbers and letters and coloring within the lines, as her sight declined. She needed a specialized preschool program to give her the basic academic skills she needed as a visually impaired student, as well as mobility skills for safe travel within her immediate environment. This meant traveling to a school outside of the neighborhood within our local public school district.

It was especially important for me to make sure that Cara had the opportunity to play with other children after school and on weekends since she was not able to meet neighborhood friends at school. I invited her friends over to play and arranged activities, facilitating the group so that she could take part in the games they were playing. I organized trips to the zoo, parks, and local fast-food restaurants with my friends who had small children. I also suggested games that she knew how to play or places that she was familiar with for these outings.

## SCHOOL EXPERIENCES AND SOCIALIZATION

In elementary school, Cara spent time each day in the resource room for students with visual impairments where she worked on basic braille reading and math skills and had opportunities to interact with other students who were blind or visually impaired, although she was in the general education classroom with her sighted peers for most of the school day. This was a very positive opportunity, giving her a peer group with some similar issues and friends who could discuss their visual impairments, empathize, strategize, and receive and offer advice. Because of these opportunities, she did not feel like she was different. In fact, there were 20 students who were blind or visually impaired in her school. With the support of the teacher of students with visual impairments, these students participated in school assemblies and other schoolwide social events (holiday programs or dance festivals, for example). The program allowed these students to share their feelings and experiences about being blind or visually impaired in a safe and caring environment, and it allowed Cara to develop friendships with sighted as well as visually impaired peers.

## SPORTS AND RECREATION

Engaging in sports provided another social opportunity for my daughter. Throughout her elementary and high school years, Cara always wanted to participate in regular gym activities. Although I felt that some of her gym teachers would have preferred that she sat out or attended an adaptive physical education class instead, my husband and I always made sure that she was included in the regular gym program. We had observed the social benefits of these experiences and felt strongly that Cara should be included. Often, this meant that one of us had to approach the gym teacher in the beginning of the school year to discuss her participation in the regular activities. As parents, we could offer helpful suggestions. Some of her teachers were very creative, finding other students to run with her and assist her on the rings and ropes.

In high school she participated in softball, volleyball, and other activities. Sometimes it required some adaptations because by then she was totally blind. In volleyball, for instance, she became the "permanent server" on her team. The team would rotate around her as she stayed in the serving position. In softball, the other girls figured out ways to call out the pitches and run the bases with her when the gym teacher couldn't come up with a plan. These experiences helped her to be a part of the group and helped the students to accept her as one of them.

Because I had taught her to ride a two-wheel bike at an early age and we taught her to ski when she was very young, she was able to participate in typical athletic activities that made her feel good about her sports abilities. Feeling good about athletic accomplishments is one way of enhancing self-esteem and developing better social skills. Her classmates began to think of her as a talented athlete, not as a poor blind girl.

## NURTURING INDEPENDENCE

Children who are blind or visually impaired need to feel that they are a part of the family by contributing to daily chores and routines. They need to have roles, domestic responsibilities, and assigned chores, just like everyone else, even if they need assistance to participate. When Cara was very young, she had to put her toys away, set the table, and take the garbage out. There are always ways we can adapt a chore with a little assistance from another family member. A friend's son, who is blind and has multiple disabilities, also takes out the garbage, but his brother or sister walks alongside him, making sure that he gets to the garbage can in the yard and makes it back to the house without wandering off.

Cara liked to walk the dog with us and eventually learned to give the dog a bath in the bathtub. (Charlie was a small poodle!) I think that this early experience with a dog helped her to realize that she could handle a dog guide and take care of it properly as an adult. Eventually these small domestic responsibilities can lead to a mastery of chores, making a child feel important and needed within the normal family unit. Factors such as regular participation in family routines can enhance a child's feelings of social worth.

Cara also helped her aunt with her baby cousins, learning to change diapers and dress and play with them. Eventually, as she got older, a friend who liked the way she interacted with her cousins asked Cara to babysit for her own two small children. The kids loved having her as a babysitter because of the way she played with them and gave them attention. Through her babysitting, she earned some spending money and felt like other young teenagers with their first jobs. Recently, as a young woman, she became a mother herself. If she hadn't had those positive opportunities to take care of other children, perhaps she would never have chosen to have a baby of her own.

The ability to undertake a small domestic chore can become a critical step toward independence in later years. I taught my daughter how to use the washer and dryer when she was in elementary school. I did this out of necessity because we had to load the wagon and walk down to the Laundromat to do the laundry. She helped me to sort the clothes, measure the soap, and load the washers and dryers. This skill became very important later on. When she was in high school, she was too busy with homework to learn new domestic tasks. But when she went to college she already knew about sorting clothes and operating the washer and dryer. We put braille labels on the laundry machines at school so she could operate them independently. In her freshman dorm, some of the young men (who had never before operated a washer or dryer) asked her to help them with their laundry. This opened up opportunities for social contacts and made her feel important.

## NURTURING SELF-ESTEEM

There are several external factors that affect the development of self-esteem in all children. Peer pressure, competition, desire for acceptance, and fear of the future make it difficult for most students, blind or sighted, to get through their school years feeling confident and secure. These factors may have even greater bearing on children who have some kind of disability. Feeling that others perceive them as different makes it difficult to feel good about themselves—the essence of self-esteem.

One avenue to consider for nurturing self-esteem is offering students opportunities to help others. Given their visual limitations, many people offer to help them, but there are ways in which parents and professionals can encourage these students to help others. For example, when Cara was home from college on a break, she brought her dog guide, Hayley, to a grade school where several other children who were blind or visually impaired could meet her. The students asked Cara many questions and she demonstrated how to use the dog, explaining that first she had to be a good cane-user and traveler. She offered those students a positive role model and gave them hope in recognizing that they, too, could become independent travelers in the future. After that visit, Cara told me how much she wanted to help other children through her own personal experiences.

Parents' attitudes are also very important to our children, and they become aware of them at a very early age. If parents tend to feel sorry for their visually impaired children and do everything for them, it interferes with their ability to feel good about themselves. Parents need to let their children know that they have confidence in them and their abilities; encourage them to try new things, whether cooking, playing an instrument, participating in sports, or doing a required task in the home; give them many opportunities to practice; and compliment them for trying.

## TEACHING SOCIAL ETIQUETTE

Becoming aware of social etiquette is another aspect of developing social skills. Because so much of social etiquette is learned incidentally, children with visual limitations often miss a lot of the visual clues and communications that others take for granted. Information about proper social etiquette can best be conveyed if parents and teachers provide information about specific behaviors in relevant social settings. For example, when she was younger, Cara had the habit of engaging in some inappropriate behaviors, such as flapping or twiddling her hands and jawing (moving her mouth from side to side). At first my husband and I would point out how silly her behavior looked and tell her to stop. I found that repeatedly saying "Stop twiddling" or "Don't do that" only made her defiant and persist in the behavior. Eventually, I stopped telling her what was wrong with her behavior and started focusing on the behaviors of other children. I would tell her that I noticed how a particular student was rocking or holding her head down and how the other children would stare at her. At times when she wasn't rocking or flapping her hands, I would tell her how attractive she looked or how socially appropriate her behavior was. This really seemed to work. In fact, the more descriptions I provided about other children's expressions and behavior, the more she began to understand social behavior issues. The more I complimented her about her own use of appropriate social behaviors, the fewer her inappropriate mannerisms became.

As Cara grew into the teen years, she became more self-conscious about her appearance and how others perceived her. I used to study how other teens dressed at school and describe the new fashion or the latest hairstyle, shoe style, or jewelry item. She realized that when she looked nice or received positive comments from others, she was accepted by her peers. I also would share with her my observations about other girls who dressed in a sloppy or unstylish manner and how the other students might react to her. By giving her this observational feedback about other teens, I was able to get her attention without giving her any negative criticism or feedback about herself.

## FRIENDSHIP

During the teen years, peer interaction is usually more important than interaction with parents and families. Many teens who are blind or visually impaired feel socially isolated because they don't feel like they belong. It is critical for teenagers to establish friendships and participate in social activities outside the school environment. When my daughter was in the eighth grade, she was very lonely. Although she had both sighted and visually impaired friends at school, she didn't have any friends in the neighborhood. Her two best neighborhood friends had moved. Her moods changed rapidly: one minute she was angry and unhappy, and the next, if a friend happened to call, she was deliriously happy. As a parent, I thought I was going to lose my mind! As I talked to other parents, however, I came to realize that this behavior is quite typical of teens, whether they are blind or sighted. However, it is harder to find a solution with a child who is visually impaired and may have a limited ability to travel independently or seek out new friends.

When Cara entered high school, the situation changed. Her orientation and mobility instructor had taught her to walk to school independently using her cane. The high school was about a mile away from our house. I had arranged for two of her acquaintances to accompany her to school. This arrangement didn't work out because I had contrived this situation and it was awkward. However, while walking home from school that first week, she met another girl who lived around the corner, and they quickly became fast friends. Over the course of her freshman year, she met two other girls who became good friends. These friendships made all the difference in the world to her, as she developed her own teen social life with these quiet, studious girls who had similar likes and dislikes. They shared lots of secrets, about crushes on the telephone and spent a lot of time together during the summer.

Friendships are particularly important during the teen years. Had Cara been unable to find friends in the neighborhood, I would have had to explore other programs that could encourage her social skills. As she was an only child, we were fortunate that she found and kept such good friends.

## DATING

While in high school, Cara did not date much. She would go to occasional parties and talk about some of the boys at school who she liked, but she never really had more than one or two dates. When senior prom time came around, she went through typical teen angst: she really wanted to go, but was not invited by the boy she had a secret crush on. Instead, she was invited by a boy whom she "detested," and finally arranged to go with someone else. She got caught up in the magic of prom night and her focus was not about her date, but only the dance itself, the music, and how everyone complimented her dress. A few days later, her secret crush wrote in her yearbook how "beautiful" she had looked on prom night. His comment made her day (and probably the rest of her year!). I was so glad that she was able to participate in the social experience of the prom.

## DRIVING AND SOCIALIZATION

An interesting thing happened while Cara was in her last years of high school. In our state, all high school students are required to take driver's education classes. Since my daughter is totally blind, I thought that she would be exempt. I discussed it with her teacher of visually impaired students and, finally, with the principal, and was told the course was a graduation requirement for all students. The previous year, parents of another student who was blind challenged the requirement in the state courts and lost! So, as much as we felt that this requirement was ludicrous, we had to go along with it.

Surprisingly, the driver's education class turned out to be a positive experience. Cara took and aced the theoretical, rules-of-the-road part of the class, although she was excused from actually driving. She learned about auto safety and driving rules and requirements, and, again, was able to feel just like the other students in her class. When it came time for the driving test, she asked a couple of classmates if they would take it for her. Many of the boys wanted to take the test in her place and acted as if it was the most normal thing in the world! Everyone got a good laugh out of this situation.

## CONCLUSION

Because of the friendships Cara developed over her childhood and adolescence, she was not afraid to meet new people and enter new social situations. Although she was somewhat quiet, she always had friends and enjoyed socializing. Looking back, I am confident in saying that it is never too early to encourage social interaction with other children. Providing hands-on opportunities to participate in everyday sports activities, play groups, and neighborhood programs gave Cara the self-assurance to engage in the same social situations as her sighted peers. Teaching her household skills and giving her responsibilities allowed her to feel as capable as her friends. Together, these early opportunities led Cara to develop self-esteem and self-confidence.

# ALEX'S STORY

## DEVELOPING STRONG SELF-ESTEEM

My third child was diagnosed with retinoblastoma, a rare infant eye cancer at 10 months of age. When he was born, Alex looked like a healthy Gerber baby; he ate well, slept well, and had an easygoing temperament. When he was diagnosed, our family was devastated; this malignancy was life-threatening and would leave him blind if left untreated. Alex had one eye immediately removed to save his life, and he subsequently underwent five years of medical treatment to control the small tumor in his remaining eye. His enucleated eye was replaced with a prosthetic eye. The vision in his remaining eye was stable and helped him to develop motor and language skills. His residual vision also assisted him in picking up incidental visual cues around him.

Growing up, Alex was the youngest, competing with his older brother and sister. He had a very natural upbringing, and we treated him like his siblings. In our household, as parents we had the same expectations for Alex as we did for his siblings: to take responsibility for his personal hygiene, to keep his bedroom and clothing in order, and to participate equally in household chores such as cooking, cleaning, and outdoor yard work. In raising the children, I would praise them when I observed special efforts or talents; but if they did not show any effort or follow through, they were reprimanded. Alex experienced the same consequences and discipline as his brother and sister.

Even though Alex wears a prosthetic eye, he is a very handsome young man. Throughout his childhood, I reminded him of his good looks at opportune moments. For example, when he was dressed up for a special occasion, I would comment on how photogenic he was. With positive praise and acceptance of Alex's visual impairment from his parents and siblings, Alex showed signs of a strong sense of self at a very young age. He seemed to accept the absence of his missing eye quite well, even with a sense of humor at times. When he was very young, playing in the sandbox, some of the neighborhood children heard about his "fake eye" and pleaded with Alex to show it to them. He easily popped out his eye and displayed it proudly. The only sad part was that the eye fell out of his hand and got lost it in the sandbox. The kids and I had to go digging to find it!

One day in elementary school, Alex came home from school with a few extra dollars. I asked him where he had gotten the money. He replied that some boys on the school bus asked him to take his eye out, and he said he would if they paid him. Even today as a young man, 17 years old and 6'2", Alex will talk to new friends and acquaintances about his visual impairment at the beginning of their relationships. He says he prefers mentioning his visual impairment right from the start to break the ice. Then he feels much more at ease as they get to know one another. Alex says he also uses this same technique for dating.

## SPORTS AND OTHER ACTIVITIES

As Alex was growing up we encouraged him to participate in sports and other activities, as we had with his sighted brother who is 16 months older. The boys were very close, and achieved similar developmental milestones. They competed with one another in a variety of social situations; they both were Boy Scouts, joined Little League baseball teams, played basketball at the local YMCA, and participated on school sports teams and in other extracurricular activities. Alex currently plays on his high school's varsity basketball team.

My role as Alex's parent was to fill out the necessary medical information and special considerations forms. I also spent time educating coaches and club organizers about Alex's visual impairment; they needed to have contact information for his ophthalmologists along with his pediatrician in case of a medical emergency or eye injury. Even though Alex wears protective safety glasses while participating in sports activities, as his parent I still worry about his safety and possible loss of his remaining vision. I firmly believe, however, that being overprotective and holding him back from participating, in spite of the risks, would deprive him of having these normal experiences that are so important to him.

## ENCOURAGING PARTICIPATION IN DRIVING

Alex is fortunate to have enough remaining vision to be able to drive legally. The rite of passage of getting his driver's license was particularly important to Alex as it provided him with a sense of independence and control over his life. He wanted desperately to live and act like his peers, and driving provided a social outlet for Alex that is not always available to others with visual impairments. We encouraged him to take driver's education, study, and take his exam to receive his driver's license. We also researched where to get reading material and information about driving with low vision, which helped him to make decisions about what adaptations he might need, given the scope of his visual impairment. Alex learned to use special techniques, such as moving the head from side to side to monitor the road, and adaptations, such as a wide-angle rearview mirror and outside rearview mirrors. We also put Alex in touch with other drivers who had low vision so he could compare notes and gain some additional information based on their experiences. I know that encouraging Alex to drive is the right thing to do, as it is a milestone for him. As much as I worry about his safety, I don't share that with him, because I do not want to discourage him in his quest for independence.

## DATING

We have always encouraged Alex to be open about his visual impairment. Throughout his formative years, we discussed the nature of his vision loss and openly communicated with friends and family about his diagnosis. As a result, Alex feels very comfortable talking to others about his visual needs. He discusses his visual impairment when he first meets a girl that he likes, before any dating begins. He gauges how much he discloses based on the girl's response. Responses have ranged from standoffish and uncomfortable to curious and open. Often, girls want to know what happened and how much he can see. Alex is willing to answer questions and discuss his visual impairment if the other person is interested. Alex's physical appearance and witty personality have helped him to attract friends, particularly girls. He is at ease with himself and can laugh at his visual impairment. He is also very concerned about how he looks. He always chooses to wear clothing that is in style or "cool," which helps him to feel part of the culture of his sighted peers.

## ACCEPTANCE OF VISUAL IMPAIRMENT

When Alex was undergoing medical treatment for retinoblastoma, I wanted to know the most current medical information about this disease. In my search, I began collaborating with the ophthalmologists, researchers, and geneticists to gather information and make it available to my family. Because of my interest in this eye disease, I developed strong relationships in the medical community. As part of my collaboration, I am asked to speak to Harvard and MIT medical students about retinoblastoma and its impact on the family. When my children were very young, I would bring them with me to classes. During this time, Alex started to develop familiarity with the terminology used to describe his visual impairment. Because he was an outgoing and bright youngster, he began to ask pointed questions about his eye disease.

When Alex was 8 years old, on the way home from one of these lectures, he began to ask questions about the genetics of retinoblastoma. I recognized then that Alex could become an active participant in this activity. By age 10, Alex was answering questions from the medical students during the question-and-answer period of the lecture. The audience loved him. When he spoke about his visual impairment, he showed a great sense of humor about his eye disease and himself. Through this experience he developed poise and social competence. He learned skills such as making eye contact and turn taking while answering questions. He also learned how to make others feel at ease when discussing his own visual impairment. He shared experiences that were funny, yet powerful, and helped the medical students to view him as the well-adjusted child that he is.

## CONCLUSION

I believe that our family's openness to discussing and learning about Alex's disease has helped him have a greater understanding and acceptance of his medical condition, his visual impairment, and himself. As Alex moves on to college next year, he will use these skills to advocate for himself with professors and peers. He will use his knowledge about his visual impairment to communicate to others his unique educational and social needs. Most important, Alex will use his social competence to develop strong and lasting relationships with others.

# JACOB'S STORY

## ENCOURAGING SELF-ESTEEM

Jacob's birth was a traumatic one. Initially, he and I both required a great deal of medical intervention. I realized that despite Jacob's multiple disabilities, including cerebral palsy and visual impairment, ensuring appropriate social behavior and developing friendships would be extremely important. I believe that the basis for developing social competence begins with a strong sense of self-esteem, and this process starts with the parents. Children must feel valued in order to value themselves. Unfortunately, most sighted people who discover their child is blind know very little about blindness; nor do they know any individuals who are blind or visually impaired. Thus, they often feel that there is no hope for a real life for their child. The parents' fears and preoccupation with the child's loss of sight make it difficult for them to impart a sense of self-worth to the child.

I was determined that this would not happen to Jacob. Because of my years of experience in working with children who were visually impaired and my friendships with adults who were blind, I did not share the general notion that life is impossible for a person who is blind. I knew and knew of many extremely capable and independent adults who were blind.

It was always very important to me that other people perceive Jacob as a wonderful human being, and I worked hard at helping friends and family observe his attributes and strengths. He was a cute baby, but exhibited motor and language disabilities along with his visual impairment. Some people saw these disabilities as a burden and they made comments that were negative and hurtful. Because of their candor, I realized what Jacob was going to be up against his entire life.

The recognition made me determined to help him to find ways to demonstrate his abilities to others and change their perceptions. When friends and family made comments that focused on this "burden," I redirected their comments by showing how cute and capable Jacob was as an infant and toddler.

From early on, we were very open about Jacob's disabilities, answering questions as they arose. When Jacob was older, we helped him acquire the skills he needed to answer questions about both his visual impairment and his cerebral palsy in a direct and open manner. As early as preschool, Jake was able to tell other children about his vision loss. He explained why he couldn't talk clearly or why he had trouble moving. When activities were hard for him or he couldn't do them at all, we made it clear to him that this was because of his disabilities. We talked to Jacob about the other things he could do easily and never attributed his lack of success to being lazy or lack of trying. It was important for us to acknowledge to Jacob that some tasks—such as getting dressed when he was young—were harder and took longer for him than it did for other children.

We also worked very hard to make sure that Jacob experienced successes and was seen as a valuable person. I made sure that Jacob was part of the social milieu of his classroom. For example, for many years I made elaborate Passover and Hanukkah parties for Jacob's elementary school classes, which were great hits. I also made sure that he was acknowledged for his achievements. For instance, the PTA in the elementary school did a walkathon every year to raise money for the school. Students who raised the most money or who walked the farthest were honored at an assembly and were given prizes. Each year Jacob raised the most money for his class, giving him recognition for something other than his disabilities. Every time Jacob won an award or brought home an excellent report card, we expressed great pride and excitement. We decorated the house with his medals, certificates, and artwork. I continually recited his accomplishments in front of him to anyone who stood still long enough to listen.

We tried to help Jacob view his disabilities in a positive light and were particularly sensitive to people feeling sorry for him. For example, when he was about 4 years old, we were getting off a plane and he was teetering along. One of the flight attendants said, "Oh, look, he's so tired he is wobbling." I laughed and said, "Oh, that's how he always walks. He has cerebral palsy." She was taken aback, but I wanted Jacob to know that his condition was not something shameful that was to be hidden. I wanted him to feel proud of himself and the skills he had, but I also wanted him to learn how to deal with negative attitudes toward his disabilities. At about that same period, he and I were shopping at a supermarket and he was, as usual, talking his head off loudly. In the aisles, we kept passing a mother with a son who was about the same age. Every time they passed us, he asked his mother, "Why does that boy talk so funny?" She kept ignoring his question, so after about the third time, I turned to the boy and said, "He talks like that because he has cerebral palsy." The mother glared at me, took her son's hand, and ran away. I wanted to model for Jacob the language he could use to explain his disabilities.

Because Jacob has quite a bit of usable vision, it was hard for him to understand why we referred to him as visually impaired. I wanted him to be knowledgeable about his visual impairment and understand how this part of his disabilities affected his overall identity as a person. He kept insisting that he could see. His peers at school, who were blind, had difficulty navigating around the classroom and playground. He didn't perceive himself as blind. To help him understand how much he could see, I started asking him when he could see certain things. For example, if we were in the mall, walking toward the bookstore, I would stop and say, "Can you see the book store sign? It's blue." He would say no, and we would walk on. By the fourth or fifth time I asked, he would be able to see it. Then I would remind him that I could see it the first time. By giving him this frame of reference, Jacob began to understand the scope of his visual abilities.

I also used a direct approach to help Jacob understand the impact of his other disabilities. Often Jacob pretended that his physical disabilities would go away. Even when he was young, he would tell me that he would outgrow his disabilities; I insisted he would not (crying on the inside the entire time). I kept insisting that he would always have them but would learn to deal with things better as he grew older. While this strategy may have seemed harsh, I believe that being honest and forthright helped Jacob to develop a strong self-image.

Because the world can be particularly difficult for children with disabilities and because parents also have our limits, I decided that Jacob needed a professional to help him deal with what he was going through. I was so emotionally involved and devastated by the rejection he was experiencing in school that I couldn't give him the help he needed. Jacob has been in counseling at various times since he was 8 years old. His counselor helped Jacob to view himself as a capable and successful individual and helped him with strategies to combat teasing and ridicule from peers. By partnering with the counselor, we assisted Jacob in finding ways to feel good about himself and to focus his attention on activities and groups that nurtured his self-esteem.

## DEVELOPING SOCIAL RELATIONSHIPS

The younger our children are, the more involved parents tend to be in their social relationships. This is true of the typically developing child as well as the atypically developing one. Parents generally arrange their young child's social life and keep up a steady stream of directions on appropriate manners and conduct. As children get older, they become increasingly independent in arranging their social lives and in following the norms of their peer group.

Since students with visual impairments often are perceived as different or "other" by their peers, the transition to managing their own social relationships does not always flow smoothly. Students with visual impairment have fewer opportunities to observe what is considered "normal," to understand body language, and even to recognize people. They are frequently regarded as standoffish because they do not return waves, make eye contact, or greet people by name. Despite our continued suggestions and modeling to help him respond in such situations, Jacob will still not admit it when he doesn't recognize someone who is greeting him. We have gotten him to at least respond to people, even if he doesn't know who they are. As a young adult, Jacob does a lot of public speaking. He has learned, through trial and error, that it is important to acknowledge others with a smile or wave, even if they are unfamiliar.

As Jacob entered school and became part of the community, we recognized the importance of his developing social relationships. We encouraged the development of social relationships in two ways. First, we found every possible appropriate organization that was of interest to Jacob and helped him to join and participate. He joined the Boy Scouts, participated in swimming activities, and enjoyed hiking and camping with his peers from his class for students with visual impairments. He became familiar with children in the neighborhood, and began to make his own choices about which ones he wanted to spend time with. Even though there were periods when Jacob had no close friends, he was still involved with peers and participating in activities that were age-appropriate and fun. It took time, effort, and money to accomplish this, but we felt it was essential to Jacob's development.

Second, we continually reminded Jacob that much of the rejection and isolation he was facing was the result of societal attitudes toward disabilities and was not caused by his behavior. This concept took a long time for him to fully assimilate. In the long run, I think it has made coping with prejudice much easier for him.

During those early years, Jacob did encounter a few children who accepted him with all his differences. These children genuinely appreciated him as an equal. They enjoyed his sense of humor and shared interest in the same games and activities. They thought of him as a "neat" kid who happened to have disabilities. Although Jacob had warm, reciprocal friendships with adults, his relationships with his peers were frequently less successful. While Jacob had a few friends throughout his school years, he had to work hard to maintain these relationships. For example, when Jacob entered kindergarten, at the same public school where he had been in the preschool program for children with visual impairments, I feared he would be rejected by his classmates and wouldn't have any friends. Much to my relief, that did not happen. He became friends with a group of about five or six boys who played together, ate lunch together, and visited one another's homes. I was thrilled.

This idyllic situation lasted until he entered second grade, at which point the boys and girls stopped playing with each other, and the boys all began playing only games that involved motor skills. Because of Jacob's disabilities, he was unable to participate in these kinds of activities. Although Cub Scouts, adapted bowling (using guide rails or a ramp to roll the ball), special Little League, and summer camp programs for students with visual impairments supplied social activities, nothing made up for the exclusion Jacob encountered. I believe that this rejection has affected Jacob's entire life and that he still bears scars from those years. Although we worked with the teacher for students with visual impairments and the general education teachers, no specific interventions were attempted.

Jacob's isolation lasted until fifth grade, when Jasper entered his life. Although new to the school and in fourth grade, Jasper soon became Jacob's best friend. Having a real friend to talk to and hang out with at lunch made a tremendous difference in Jacob's life and social development. They enjoyed the same activities and accepted one another for their unique attributes.

Despite Jacob's friendship with Jasper, we knew that middle school would be a challenge both socially and emotionally. We recognized that Jacob was somewhat immature for middle school, but we also wanted him to excel academically. We decided to enroll Jacob in the local school for the blind for a year of specialized instruction. In this setting, he became part of a social group of five boys with visual impairments. He thrived; in this environment, he was no longer the "different" child. He stayed over in the dorm for Boy Scout meetings and other special events. He went to other students' homes for weekends or they stayed with us. It was a great year for Jacob. He became more independent and felt capable of tackling the stresses of a large middle school environment. Providing this year for Jacob was one of the best things we did. When he returned to the middle school the next year, however, it was socially a disaster. Jacob felt isolated; he was teased by his peers. He received little support from the classroom teachers at the school and was not included in school activities unless he advocated for himself.

When we started looking at high schools, we wanted to find an environment in which Jacob could thrive socially and feel that he was a part of the school community. Although the resource room for students with visual impairments was at a large urban high school, we found a small alternative high in our school district. With fewer students, the staff and students all knew one another. Jacob did not have to keep explaining himself to new students or teachers. Jasper, Jake's good friend, also went to the same school. This friendship helped Jacob to gain entry into social groups and learn the social rules of the school environment. Jacob participated in student government, attended social events at the school, and was a graduation speaker. The students and faculty helped Jacob to realize that he was likeable and that he could have genuine friends; these experiences really affected the course of his life.

## LETTING GO: DEVELOPING AUTONOMY AND SOCIAL INDEPENDENCE

Learning to be independent and acquiring competent social skills go hand in hand. One cannot be independent, or even interdependent, without the ability to interact effectively with peers and adults. For students who are blind or visually impaired, this process does not happen easily. These skills are not innate; all of us learn slowly over time, with considerable practice, the skills needed to move away from home. We leave for short times, then longer times, and finally strike out on our own.

The process of separating from parents begins early, with toddlers' first forays away from their parents, and demonstrates the child's need and desire for autonomy and a separate sense of self. With children who are visually impaired, however, the process of separation often takes on a different form. Many children who are blind or visually impaired begin to walk later than their sighted peers and are less secure in their mobility. Rather than holding them back from running off, parents and caretakers often have to encourage them to explore and to move around on their own. As they get older, these children often lack the freedom of exploration that bicycles, and later, cars, provide.

Frequently, too, they lack the encouragement of a peer group to separate emotionally from their families. The role of the parents often becomes as much pushing as pulling.

It is vital that parents of students with visual impairments realize the necessity for our children to separate from us. We must be prepared to let go and, if necessary, to push the child out of the nest a bit, knowing that without undergoing the process of separation, the child can never achieve real independence. We also need to continually speak to our children about the time when they will be grown up and living on their own to encourage them to perceive themselves as people who will be independent. Sometimes the next step they need to take toward independence scares us silly but we need to take a deep breath and let them go.

One of the earliest steps we took to nurture independence and social interaction for Jacob was to leave him with friends, relatives, and babysitters for longer and longer periods. It allowed Jacob to experience both separation and reunion. He learned that being away from us was fun and that we would return. He also learned to interact and play with family friends, and he enjoyed time with his favorite babysitters, who brought new toys and games to add to his experience.

When Jacob was 4 years old and in preschool, everyone in the visually impaired program in our school district went off on an overnight trip to a local camp. Jacob's preschool teacher for students with visual impairments asked me if he could go. I said certainly, but I doubted that he would want to, and suggested that she ask him. Jacob came home from school the next day excited about the trip he would be going on with his class. As the trip approached, I kept waiting for him to change his mind. When my husband took him to the meeting point, we agreed that if Jacob was at all apprehensive not to insist that he go. We had already told his teacher that if he got homesick she could call us day or night and we would come to get him. Well, off he went and he never looked back. That was the beginning of a long series of overnight camping and ski trips with the program for students with visual impairments. During these trips, Jacob learned to make choices and he had experiences with caring for himself and meal preparation. He learned that he could be on his own without the constant support of his parents.

The next step was summer camp. We started out at a family camp run by the Foundation for the Junior Blind when Jacob was about 8 years old. The experience was wonderful for his independence. It was the first time that he went any distance on his own, going from the cabin at the top of the canyon down to the dining room at the bottom, with us watching from above. It marked the beginning of his independence. We went to this camp as a family for two years, before Jacob went off on his own to Kids Camp there and later Teen Camp. He developed many friendships with the students he met there, maintaining contact by telephone.

Another important milestone for Jacob was learning to travel independently. Orientation and mobility (O&M) skills played a tremendous part in Jacob's achieving independence. I believe that the more O&M skills students master, the more confident they will become and the easier it will be for them to gain more and more independence. The year that Jacob spent at the California School for the Blind working on his travel and independent living skills was wonderful for his mobility. As part of the program there, students learn the skills of shopping at a small shopping strip and are granted a "license" to go to the strip mall when they are ready. A school-run shuttle bus drops the students off at a designated area and picks them up at the same place 45 minutes later. Students must master money and time skills as well as learn how to get around in the shopping area. It also provides students with opportunities to practice their social skills through making purchases and asking for assistance. Jacob loved being able to shop on his own and he soon received his "license." Although my husband was a bit reluctant, he accepted the fact that Jacob was out there in the real world on his own. He really saw the benefit when Jacob started to bring home dinner for the two of them from the delicatessen!

It is vital for the social development of children who are blind or visually impaired to experience being out on their own whenever possible (without parents or teachers). Depending on a student's disability, the experience may occur at different times and in different ways. Some students may never be able to travel totally on their own, but may be able to go out with someone who acts as the facilitator for the trip. It is important for the student to be the decision maker, determining the how, where, when, and what of the trip.

Jacob initially didn't show much aptitude for getting around on his own and there were some real questions as to whether or not he could become an independent traveler. However, we all persevered and one day it all came together. In that process, he has learned to be a good problem solver. One day he got lost in San Francisco and learned quickly that people on the street who are drunk are not great sources for accurate directions. On another occasion on a trip back from San Jose, the cabdriver took him to the wrong train station. By effectively asking for assistance and using his problem-solving skills, he was able to figure out an entirely different route home than the one he had originally planned. I believe the keys to his progress in this area were the excellent O&M instruction provided by our school district and the specialized school for the blind, our family's encouragement about his getting out on his own, and his own willingness to take risks even when he feels scared. One other boost to his independence was certainly the existence of cell phones, the most marvelous invention for students who are blind or visually impaired and their parents.

Another aspect of independence is making decisions. Decision making must be learned from an early age, and the only way to learn is through practice. From the time that Jacob was very young, we encouraged him to make decisions: Do you want canned pears or applesauce for dessert? Do you want hot or cold cereal for breakfast? Do you want to wear jeans or shorts? As he got older, we broadened the kind of decisions that he was expected to make to include decisions about his own activities. To allow children to make decisions, however, parents need to be able to accept whatever decision they make. Unless they have the full freedom to decide among the alternatives being offered, they are not making a decision. If you ask a child, "Do you want to ____?" you must be prepared to accept, "No" as an answer.

Parents also need to be able to stand back and let their child make poor decisions. When Jacob started getting an allowance, he had total control over how he spent it. I watched him save up for toys he saw advertised on TV, buy them, and discover that they didn't live up to his expectations. Doing this allowed him to make $10 mistakes and learn from them, rather than waiting until he had more money to learn from more expensive mistakes.

Now Jacob is in college, living in an apartment on campus. He buys his own food, decides what classes he is taking, and manages his own money, balancing his checkbook and paying his bills. He is really living on his own. All the effort that we—our family, his caregivers and teachers, and Jacob himself—have put into helping him become independent has paid off.

## CONCLUSION

Writing about Jacob's history has made me relive some of it. As I look back, my greatest fear has always been that he wouldn't have friends and he would be lonely. I have been and still am more concerned about that than anything else in his development. I believe, based on my own life experiences and the joy and pleasure I have received from my friends and my social life, that social skills and the subsequent ability to make and keep friends are the most important factors in achieving a rich and full life.

Unfortunately, the development of social skills is an area about which professionals still know disappointingly little. Until recently, it has barely been discussed at IEP meetings. Often, when I brought up these kinds of issues about Jacob, I was met with sympathy but with very little professional knowledge or few strategies that might deal with social issues. I firmly believe that if children who are blind or visually impaired are to become independent and flourish as fully functioning adults, parents and professionals need to learn a lot more about empowering them with the skills needed to make friends and have a satisfying social life.

## CONCLUSION

Children who have visual impairments or blindness have unique issues in developing social skills. The successful development of these skills is impossible without the guidance and support of parents and other family members. Teachers of students with visual impairments can provide valuable instruction in social skills, but if there is little or no follow-through from the family, significant social growth may be difficult to achieve.

This chapter offers a glimpse into the lives of three families, each of whom has a child with a visual impairment. We hope that through our shared experiences, readers have gained a better understanding of the family's role in the social development of children who are blind or visually impaired. For professionals, whether veterans or new to the field, these stories demonstrate the importance of family involvement in the socialization process. The partnership and collaboration between families and professionals is so vital in helping visually impaired children to develop age-appropriate social skills. While families have diverse backgrounds, each with their own special customs and values, we hope that professionals can embrace each family free from their own biases or values. We look to you for your knowledge and expertise and hope that you can acknowledge and respect our beliefs, ideals, and input.

For parents, we hope you will recognize the significance of your role in the positive development of social skills for your child who is blind or visually impaired. You can seek, facilitate, and offer life experiences that will help your child accept his or her visual impairment, encourage friendships and other social relationships, and guide them socially through the school years into adolescence and adulthood.

This chapter has provided examples of practical ideas and strategies to enhance the social skills of students who are blind or visually impaired. We have shared the joys and obstacles our children have encountered in their quest to develop socially competent behavior. We are proud of their accomplishments and continue to strive for their independence as young adults. We hope that sharing our personal stories will help and support other families and professionals in their quest to ensure positive social experiences for students with visual impairments.

# Theories of Social Development

W hat can theory tell us about how children who are visually impaired become socially skilled individuals, how they learn to behave appropriately with others, and how they become capable of engaging in successful and satisfying interpersonal relationships? Part 2 looks at how children develop the behaviors necessary to interact and communicate with each other. Each chapter focuses on different age groups—one discussing children in their early years and the other adolescence—but they both examine the primary developmental issues relevant to each age.

Social development theory provides a framework for understanding the socialization process for students who are blind or visually impaired. These perspectives offer models that relate directly to practice. Although theory is often viewed as somewhat abstract, each of the chapters that follow provides examples that link theory to practice. These "Theory to Practice" boxes help identify the connection between the two. The authors believe that such linkage will allow professionals to make instructional decisions about teaching social skills to students with visual impairments based on sound theoretical models rather than tradition and habit.

Moreover, this sections sheds light on the social development process for each student described in the previous section, and suggests how social skills models are used as a means to determine intervention. These theoretical perspectives will contribute to an understanding of how the personal stories and examples provided in the preceding chapters demonstrate the validity of theory and its relevance to the teaching of social skills to students with visual impairments.

In Chapter 3, Sacks defines social skills using three different conceptual models. Examples of how each definition might be applied to students with visual impairment are included. Theories of social development are presented, illustrating the practical applications of each. Examples to illustrate the use of each model or theory are provided to connect abstract concepts to real-life situations.

Wolffe evaluates social development theory in relation to the social development needs of adolescents with visual impairments in Chapter 4. She reviews the research on the effects of visual impairment on adolescent development and discusses the influence of family and peers on the development of relationships and interdependence for students who are blind or visually impaired.

# CHAPTER 3

# Theoretical Perspectives on the Early Years of Social Development

## Sharon Z. Sacks

Both public and specialized school programs for children with visual impairments have traditionally emphasized the importance of acquiring a requisite set of academic skills. Although recent studies clearly demonstrate weaknesses in social competence and preparation for adult life among students with visual impairments (Wolffe, 2000; Sacks & Silberman, 2000; Sacks, Wolffe, & Tierney, 1998; Sacks & Wolffe, 1998; Wolffe & Sacks, 1997; Wolffe, 1999), the prevailing philosophy among educators continues to focus on direct instruction of academic content, academic tutoring, and instruction in communication skills

Portions of this chapter have been adapted, with permission of the publisher, from Sharon Zell Sacks, "The Social Development of Visually Impaired Children," in S. Z. Sacks, L. S. Kekelis, and R. J. Gaylord-Ross (Eds.), *The Development of Social Skills by Blind and Visually Impaired Students: Exploratory Studies and Strategies* (New York: American Foundation for the Blind, 1992), pp. 3–11.

(Wolffe, Sacks, Corn, Erin, Huebner, & Lewis, 2002). According to Hatlen (1980), this perspective, voiced as early as 1929 by Meyer, a prominent educator of students with visual impairments, dominated the educational field and directed the course of mainstream practices for almost 80 years.

Many students who graduated from mainstream school programs in the 1960s, 1970s, and 1980s did not acquire the skills necessary to function with independence in the community. Even with the passage of the Individuals with Disabilities Education Act (IDEA) in 1990, which established mandates for the initiation and implementation of transition planning and transition programs and included activities to promote job readiness and work experiences, activities of daily living, and social skills instruction, students with visual impairment continue to remain at risk for social isolation and reduced skill-appropriate employment opportunities.

Hatlen (1996) argued that students who are blind or visually impaired require a set of unique educational skills in addition to the general core curriculum. These specialized skill areas, referred to as the expanded core curriculum, are unique to the student's visual impairment and require direct instruction by a teacher of students with visual impairments. While these teachers acknowledge that teaching activities of daily living, social skills, career development, adaptive technology, orientation and mobility (O&M), and other functional skills is essential, their ability to include these topics in the curriculum is limited by time constraints, increased caseload size, and other educational priorities established by the IEP. In addition, many teachers of students with visual impairments are less clear about their students' developmental differences and how vision loss may affect the acquisition and maintenance of a requisite set of social skills and other functional abilities. Reardon and Sacks's (1985) hierarchy of nonacademic skills stresses the importance of acquiring a repertoire of socially acceptable behaviors and skills to attain greater independence and increased feelings of self-worth. Without a foundation in socially based skills, higher order skills (daily living skills, leisure skills, work skills, and academic pursuits) remain isolated components that students who are blind or visually impaired do not necessarily transfer to other contexts with peers, especially in inclusive and integrated settings.

This chapter provides definitions of social skills that can be applied to practice by teachers, parents, and other professionals. Understanding the theoretical nature of social development is the foundation for a better understanding of the unique sequence of social development for students who are blind or visually impaired.

# DEFINITIONS OF SOCIAL SKILLS

For those involved in the lives of students with visual impairments to teach social skills effectively, it is important to understand the typical social development process for young children who are sighted as well as for those who are blind or visually impaired. Although Warren (1994) contends that the developmental sequence for children who are blind or visually impaired should not be compared to that of typically developing children, recognizing the sequences and understanding social development theory as it relates to visual impairment is useful in designing intervention strategies. Before theoretical perspectives can be addressed, however, it is important to clearly define social skills so that there is consistency in terminology and perspective.

Social skills are a set of behaviors or series of actions that all human beings use to interact or to communicate with one another. These skills are bound by societal rules that are created by a community or culture. Social skills can be as basic as establishing eye contact with others or as complex as interpreting when to join a group. Sequences of social skills teach us to initiate greetings, for example, and help us to make sense of facial expressions or other nonverbal cues. Although some professionals believe that social skills can be learned by manipulating a person's social environment (for example, by providing modeling and feedback), others argue that the acquisition of social skills is based on an individual's personality type.

The following sections describe three perspectives for defining social skills: the trait or maturational model, the molecular or component model, and the process or systems model. Although these models were initially created for other populations (people with severe cognitive disabilities or emotional and behavioral disabilities), and as such are not directly applicable to individuals with visual impairments, the perspectives offered provide a framework for defining social skills in a variety of ways. Each model is defined and examples are provided to illustrate how each perspective can be applied in evaluating the social skills needs of students who are blind or visually impaired.

## THE TRAIT OR MATURATIONAL MODEL

The trait or maturational model assumes that skillful social behavior is predetermined and embedded in one's personality structure. Gesell (1928) believed that the sequence of human development, including social development, was determined by biological and evolutionary history. In other words, this model suggests that the acquisition of social skills is based on genetic makeup and personality type. It assumes that a child is born with certain behavioral structures that remain constant over time. This model has not been widely used or accepted by practitioners or theorists because it has not been proven empirically (McFall, 1982). If applied to the socialization of students with visual impairments, this model would attribute the passive or egocentric behavior exhibited by some students to a part of their personality makeup and assume that no action or intervention could elicit change.

Although this definition of social skills may not be widely used by practitioners, it has some application in that children do have different personalities. Some children with visual impairments are more shy and retiring than others. Conversely, there are students who have outgoing personalities and who exhibit risk-taking attributes, traits that enhance their opportunities to engage socially with peers and adults. When defining a visually impaired student's needs in the area of social skills and designing specific interventions, it is important to consider his or her specific personality traits.

## THE MOLECULAR OR COMPONENT MODEL

In the molecular or component model, social skills are considered to be observable units of learned verbal and nonverbal behaviors that when combined can foster successful interactions in specific situations (Foster & Ritchey, 1979; Hersen & Bellack, 1977; McFall, 1982). As Kelly (1982, p. 3) notes, "individuals use [these skills] in interpersonal situations to obtain or to maintain reinforcement from their environment."

The majority of social skills training interventions are based on this perspective. Specific behaviors are targeted for training because they have been identified by the community or culture as important or critical in promoting positive social relationships. In this model, what is considered socially skilled behavior is determined by teachers, family members, and other service providers. Hence, there is great variability in the selection and definition of behaviors targeted for intervention. In addition, the observation, measurement, and evaluation of social behaviors over time and across settings may be inconsistent because of personal bias or cultural values that influence what is considered socially acceptable behavior. For example, in Western society establishing eye contact is an essential part of a social greeting. In other cultures, however, establishing eye contact between an adult and child in a social interaction is frowned on.

When using this model to define social skills, it is critical that those involved in the process of assessment and intervention clearly define and communicate the targeted social behaviors that require intervention. Clearly defining appropriate social behaviors for a given social situation is particularly important for students who are blind or visually impaired. For example, when teaching a child who is blind about personal space, that concept must be clearly defined and modeled.

## THE PROCESS MODEL

The process model (sometimes called a "systems" model) assumes that social skills are components of specific actions (looks or nods, for example) or sequences of behaviors that create specific encounters, such as greetings or joining a group in play. The process model asserts that the use of social behaviors is contingent on rules that have been established by the society in which the person lives (Argyle, 1980; Trower, 1982). According to Trower (1982, p. 418), "such components are learned by experience or observation, retained in memory in symbolic form, and subsequently retrieved for use in the construction of episodes." This approach promotes the utilization of goals to attain a set of socially appropriate behavioral skills; it relies on one's ability to perceive both the physical environment and the internal needs of others. By using this model, an individual can monitor the immediate situation and evaluate his or her behavior in that situation in relation to external feedback (verbal or nonverbal) from others and an internal assessment (cognitive representational or logical thinking) (Argyle and Kenden, 1967). The process model includes the following components:

*Perceptions of other people:* The ability to respond effectively to another's needs or desires.

*Taking the role of others:* The ability to not only recognize another's feelings, but to understand what the other person is thinking or feeling.

*Nonverbal accompaniments of speech:* The ability to acquire appropriate proximity and orientation during an interaction through a combination of verbal and nonverbal cues. (Such elements are highly contingent upon sight and hearing.)

*Rewards:* The ability to acknowledge and reinforce a person's social behavior or initiations, through a smile or head nod, for example.

*Self-presentation:* The ability to send cues to another person to indicate one's role, status, or identity.

*Situations and their rules:* The ability to obtain the meaning of a given set of rules that govern the structure of a specific encounter (this may be accomplished through visual feedback if the rules are intricate).

*Sequence of interactions:* The ability to arrange a series of verbal and nonverbal cues in a certain order to obtain a positive outcome.

The process model has had limited utility for students with visual impairments because so much of what is involved in using this model assumes the use of vision. For example, the ability to monitor a social situation involves the integration of visual abilities and auditory and cognitive skills. Without vision, it is difficult to perceive another person's actions or feelings, and mediation and interpretation by another person may be required in order to do so. Furthermore, limited exposure to different types of environments or individuals means limited opportunities to experience or acquire first-hand knowledge about the social rules of various interactive situations. For example, students who are blind or visually impaired may blurt out answers to questions in a classroom setting instead of raising their hands because they have not observed the behavioral sequence of others or been taught the applicable classroom rule.

While each of the models defines social skills in different ways, they provide perspectives that may enable educators and families to initiate a range of interventions. Sacks & Silberman (2000) have proposed a framework for understanding the acquisition of social skills by students who are blind or visually impaired. They believe that there are three levels of socialization that persons with visual impairments may encounter.

The first level, *awareness*, presupposes that students have an awareness of their social environments and that they use individual social behaviors to make sense of the social world. Generally this level would apply to very young children who are blind or visually impaired or to students with multiple disabilities who are beginning to use isolated social behaviors (such as smiles, gestures, simple phrases, and words) to express interactive intent.

In the second level, the *interactive* level, students use their past experiences to begin to combine social behaviors with effective communication to influence various social encounters and exchanges across home, school, and community settings. Students learn to effectively integrate individual social behaviors into more complex social exchanges.

In the third level, the *evaluative* level, students with visual impairments not only effectively utilize a range of social behaviors in a

## Figure 3.1

# Hierarchy of Social Skills

### LEVEL I—AWARENESS

Self identity + Social awareness

=

Behavioral social skills

### LEVEL II—INTERACTIVE

Awareness of other people's needs + Strategies for positive interactions

=

Interactive social skills

### LEVEL III—EVALUATIVE

Interpretation of social situations + Awareness of social needs of others +
Strategies to enhance social competence

=

Cognitive social understanding

*Source:* Reprinted with permission from S. Z. Sacks & R. K. Silberman, "Social Skills," in A. J. Koenig & M. C. Hollbrook, Eds., *Foundations of Education, Vol. 2: Instructional Strategies for Teaching Children and Youths with Visual Impairments* (2nd ed.; New York: AFB Press, 2000), p. 621.

variety of contexts, they also begin to evaluate and modify their social behavior as a result of how their social interactions affect others. Usually children and adults who are blind or visually impaired and who are also quite socially competent have learned to integrate a repertoire of social behaviors and interactions to influence how others perceive them. This framework is presented graphically in Figure 3.1.

# THEORIES OF SOCIAL DEVELOPMENT

Before professionals can begin to design effective social skill interventions for students with visual impairments, a solid theoretical base is essential. Without such a foundation, it is difficult to justify the application of certain techniques and strategies. Too often practitioners rely on familiar interventions without really considering the conceptual framework behind them. The following discussion evaluates five theories of social development: psychoanalytic, social identification, critical periods, social learning, and cognitive structural. Each theory is evaluated for its practical application to the development of social competence and appropriate interactive skills in students with visual impairments. Issues related to social growth and development are also discussed to provide a more comprehensive perspective. Table 3.1 provides a summary of each social development theory and examples of how each theory can be applied to students with visual impairments.

## PSYCHOANALYTIC THEORY

Psychoanalytic theory emphasizes the centrality of the parent-child relationship in the child's early development. Its major proponents are Freud (1905/1974; 1924/1974; 1930/1974), Sullivan (1953), and Erikson (1963, 1959/1980).

According to Freud, socialization occurs when the child resolves a series of internal conflicts with the parent of the same sex, based on biological needs. Resolution of these conflicts, in Freud's view, is an ongoing process. He believed that human development is based on basic instincts that are influenced by a dynamic structure or model called the psyche. These interdependent structures (the id, the ego, and the superego) play a significant role in helping the child to move through a series of developmental stages, resolving internal conflicts and sexually based drives toward the opposite-sexed parent, and ultimately achieving a healthy sense of self. Since in Freud's view the child establishes a strong sense of identity through the parent-child relationship, peer relationships play a minimal role. According to Freudian theory, the child must resolve the parent-child conflicts at each stage of development in order to progress to the next level; the focus on peer support is de-emphasized until late childhood and adolescence. (See "From Theory to Practice: Freud's View.")

Sullivan (1953) diverged from Freud's perspective by emphasizing the importance of peer relationships. Sullivan believed that for adolescents to develop solid relationships with others, they first need to develop empathy for the perspectives of others through the growth of close friendships and intimacy. Sullivan suggested that when peer relationships are prevented, there are "evidences of a serious defect in personal orientation" (1953, p. 262). (See "From Theory to Practice: Sullivan's Perspective.")

**TABLE 3.1**  Overview of Social Development Theories

| Model | Description of Model | Unique Differences for Students with Visual Impairments | Implications for Practice |
|---|---|---|---|
| Psychoanalytic Theory | A model popularized by Freud, Sullivan, and Erikson, this theory emphasizes the importance of the parent-child relationship in early development and is based on a person's need to satisfy basic instincts. | Young children with visual impairments may be more dependent on adults to mediate and interpret their social world.<br><br>Families may be more reluctant to allow their child to explore and have opportunities to explore the environment. | Early intervention is critical in helping families to promote social interactions, attachment between parent and child, and experiential learning.<br><br>Early support from a teacher of students with visual impairments can encourage families to initiate social play and exploration by their visually impaired child. |
| Social Identification Theory | Durkheim believed that early family experiences set the stage for successful social experiences with peers and teachers. This model emphasizes the importance of allegiance to a student's classmates and teachers. | Students with visual impairments need social experiences with both peers who are blind and peers who are sighted.<br><br>The variety of activities in which a visually impaired student might participate may be different depending on whether the experiences involve other students who are visually impaired or sighted students. For example, play between blind children might be more solitary, such as listening to music. | Teachers and families of children who are visually impaired must be aware of and teach the social rules of both blind and sighted peer groups.<br><br>Play skills, including games and physical activities, must be taught throughout a student's educational career. |

*(continued)*

**TABLE 3.1**  *(continued)*

| Model | Description of Model | Unique Differences for Students with Visual Impairments | Implications for Practice |
|---|---|---|---|
| | | | Families must provide opportunities for students who are blind or visually impaired to engage in clubs and organizations that are specifically for students with visual impairments as well those that include students who are sighted. |
| Critical Periods | Harlow and Harlow believed that there are critical times in which specific social experiences must occur in order for growth and development to take place in a sequential manner. If these experiences or interactions do not occur naturally, the student is susceptible to isolation and withdrawal. Their initial findings were based on experiments done with primates. | While no empirical findings document a similar effect for students who are blind or visually impaired, research continues to acknowledge that visually impaired students often have weak social interactions with sighted age-mates and lack genuine peer relationships with this group. | This theory suggests the importance of early social interactions with peers. Teachers, parents, and others can provide experiences that promote social interactions through facilitated play, the introduction of play groups for young children who are blind or visually impaired, and varied and meaningful hands-on experiences with the physical and social environment. |

*(continued)*

**TABLE 3.1** *(continued)*

| Model | Description of Model | Unique Differences for Students with Visual Impairments | Implications for Practice |
|---|---|---|---|
| Social Learning Theory | This model, based on the work of Skinner and Watson, assumes that social behaviors can be learned and reinforced through manipulation of the student's environment. Theorists believe that when a stimulus (such as food) is provided, there is usually a response (the food is eaten), and behavior is reinforced (the person appears happy or satisfied). | Students with visual impairments can acquire a wide variety of social skills based on this theory, but the instructional model must be structured and consistent. It is important for anyone who uses this theory when working with students who are blind or visually impaired to provide consistent feedback and practice in natural contexts. | This model relies heavily on visual observation. It is important when using this model that teachers and family members provide verbal and physical feedback to elicit the appropriate response and immediately follow it with some sort of tangible reinforcement. Ongoing feedback and reinforcement of specific social behaviors is essential. |
| Cognitive-Structural Theory | This model is based on Piaget's theory of social development. Piaget believed that peers facilitate social growth and that children learn social rules through role-taking experiences with adults and peers (such as complimenting others or sharing toys with peers). He emphasized the importance of the child taking control over his or her social environment, without dependence on adults. | Students who are blind or visually impaired may be very dependent on adults to mediate their environments. Students may not have opportunities to interact with peers on a regular basis. They may have little or no experience with play conventions or social interactions with peers. Students may have few opportunities to make choices or decisions. | Families need to be provided with resources and activities to help their young child who is blind or visually impaired to gain experiences with peers. Students with visual impairments need to be given opportunities at a very early age to make choices and decisions without adult manipulation. Families and teachers need to provide opportunities for students with visual impairments to have chores and responsibilities. |

# From Theory to Practice

## FREUD'S VIEW

The influence of early attachment between parents and infants who are blind or visually impaired would be particularly important in Freud's view. Because many young children who are visually impaired do not always initiate social behavior or respond to social cues from their parents (such as smiles or touches), it is critical for families to learn strategies that can enhance a positive reciprocal relationship. For example, instructional personnel can help families understand that pairing a verbal cue with a tactile cue when engaging with a young child who is blind may help the child anticipate the interaction.

# From Theory to Practice

## SULLIVAN'S PERSPECTIVE

Based on Sullivan's perspective, it would be important for young children who are blind or visually impaired to be given a variety of opportunities to engage in activities that promote exploration and play with other children. These opportunities encourage young children to learn to interact with others in a socially appropriate manner. They learn to share toys, take turns during games, and acknowledge and recognize others apart from themselves and their immediate families. Through consistent modeling from family members and teachers, they learn the social rules involved in social situations. Too often, students who are blind or visually impaired are not expected to interact with others or encouraged to develop self-advocacy skills. As a result, many students who are blind or visually impaired have not had the requisite experiences to engage successfully with others and are not sensitive to others' needs and thus find themselves isolated from their peers.

Erikson (1963, 1959/1980) took a more modernistic view regarding psychoanalytic theory. He de-emphasized the importance of the relationship between biological needs and sexual drive and focused on the child's ability to establish a strong sense of self. In Erikson's view, children must experience parental control and support to advance through his eight stages of development from early infancy through adolescence, into adulthood and old age. (See Chapter 4 for more details concerning Erikson's model.) Although the family remains the child's central focus, in Erikson's view, children gain a greater sense of autonomy and independence through interactions with peers and experiences in varied environments.

Tait (1972), Fraiberg (1977), and Warren (1984) applied Erikson's model of development to young children with visual impairments. They concluded that while the first two levels of Erikson's model (trust versus mistrust and autonomy versus shame and doubt) were relatively equal in terms of the development of both sighted and blind students, differences emerged when children began to engage in exploratory activities. Their research documents their conclusion that young children with visual impairments are likely to be totally dependent on others to construct and integrate the external environment into a realistic, meaningful world. Fraiberg noted that without intervention, it is difficult for parents of young children who are blind to

# From Theory to Practice

## SOCIAL ACTIVITIES

Research suggests that it is incumbent upon educators and families to promote activities that enhance social interaction skills and encourage the use of socially appropriate language on an ongoing basis. For example, it would be important for families and educators to participate in activities such as play groups or structured classes like "Gymboree," or "Mommy and Me" music groups where young children learn to interact with peers. These experiences also allow families and professionals to model appropriate social language and behavior in a variety of settings, for example, during mealtime, waiting in line to use play equipment, or asking to share crayons and paint during an art activity.

create an environment that fosters positive social interactions and physical stimulation. Ferrell (2000), in her longitudinal studies of early development of children with visual impairments, found differences in the sequence of developmental milestones and delays in development, particularly in the areas of motor, self-care, and socialization. (See "From Theory to Practice: Social Activities.")

## SOCIAL IDENTIFICATION THEORY

In Durkheim's (1925/1973) model of moral development, early familial experiences are the basis for later social development. Durkheim believed that while the family provides the structure for developing values and establishing a solid sense of self, it is the school experience and identification with the classroom teacher and classmates that promotes a well-defined social identity. In other words, the classroom teacher facilitates activities that foster team spirit and competition, group cohesiveness, and the internalization of an allegiance to society through the development of rules and group organization.

Given what is known about the developmental sequence of children with visual impairments (Ferrell, 2000; Warren, 1994) and the differences that emerge in the way these students master their physical and social environments, it might be difficult for these students to establish a strong allegiance to any one group since their exposure to a range of activities and experiences is limited. Also, because students with visual impairments are dependent on family members and other adults to provide information and mediate the physical environment, they may be directly influenced by the values and thoughts of adults rather than by their peers.

Durkheim's focus on the selection of group allegiance is a particular drawback for students with visual impairments. If a student is to learn social rules and values from peers and classmates, with which group does the child who is blind or visually impaired identify—sighted classmates, classmates who are blind or visually impaired, or both? One would suspect that visually impaired students who had experiences only with sighted peers would show allegiance and social identification with sighted individuals. If opportunities to interact with persons who are visually impaired were therefore limited, students might view blindness more negatively than if they had more experience with other visually impaired students. Conversely, if students only interacted with peers who were blind or visually impaired, then their perceptions of social norms and values might be very different from those of sighted agemates. (See "From Theory to Practice: Opportunities for Interaction.")

## From Theory to Practice

### OPPORTUNITIES FOR INTERACTION

Providing opportunities for students to interact with both peers who are sighted and those who are blind is essential. This experience allows students who are visually impaired to learn the social rules and mores of the sighted world and at the same time provides opportunities to gain a strong sense of identity with persons who are similar to them. For example, families may find it beneficial for their children to attend summer camps and enrichment programs for youngsters who are blind or visually impaired. These programs promote a sense of independence and self-worth in young people with visual impairments, critical elements in fostering the development of social competence as an adolescent or young adult.

## CRITICAL PERIODS THEORY

Harlow and Harlow's (1962) studies of primates demonstrated the importance of peer interaction in social development and substantiated the influence of so-called critical periods—time frames in which an individual must learn particular behaviors that are crucial to integrating more advanced stages of development. In their experiments, Harlow and Harlow found that when primates were deprived of peer contact, even if they were given contact with their mothers, their social adjustment as adults was delayed. Although there are no empirical data to substantiate a similar effect among children who are visually impaired, observations of interactions between students with visual impairments and their sighted age-mates indicate limited social interactions (for example, joining in group activities) and weak maintenance of relationships with classmates (Sacks & Gaylord-Ross, 1992; Sacks & Wolffe, 1998; Sacks, Wolffe, & Tierney, 2000; Wolffe & Sacks, 1998). Although many factors, such as lack of early parental attachment, limited early intervention experiences, and additional neurological disabilities, may contribute to delays in age-appropriate socialization, there is no documented research that substantiates the effects of incomplete critical periods on the social development of students with visual impairments. (See "From Theory to Practice: Working with Families.")

# From Theory to Practice

## WORKING WITH FAMILIES

For young children who are blind or visually impaired to develop and demonstrate positive social relationships with peers, they must develop prosocial behavior with family members and relatives. Therefore, it would be important for a teacher of students with visual impairments to work in the home with families, helping them to develop strategies to enhance social interactions, such as face-to-face contact.

## SOCIAL LEARNING THEORY

Social learning theory is based on the principles of behavioral learning theory (stimulus, response, reinforcement, and generalization). Proponents of this model believe that behavior can be modified or changed by manipulating the environment. If the introduction of certain stimuli (such as food, verbal cues, or physical prompts), elicits a specific, positive response, a reinforcement (such as food or praise) is given to assist the student in learning the correct response or action. Bandura (1977, 1979, 1986, 1989); Bandura and Walters, (1963); and Skinner, (1938, 1957, 1976) clearly demonstrated in their research studies that children's behavior is directly influenced by positive and negative stimuli and that positive change can occur through appropriate modeling and feedback.

Initial research on social skill interventions that employed behavioral techniques used adults as trainers to model appropriate social behavior in a variety of contexts (Kelly, 1982). While this strategy may be effective for young children in home settings, it proved to be less effective when children began to interact with peers. The power of peer interaction and peer modeling strongly affects the long-term socialization of children. Mischel (1966) demonstrated that children learn gender-related behaviors (such as playing with dolls or pretending to be action heroes) by observing, imitating, and modeling same-sex peers.

The concepts of social learning theory have widespread application with training tools for use with students with visual impairments. Since students who are blind or visually impaired cannot observe others' social behavior, they do not easily imitate it; they therefore require physical modeling, verbal feedback, realistic reinforcement of

# From Theory to Practice

## SOCIAL GREETINGS

Teaching students with visual impairments to initiate a social greeting using the constructs of social learning theory may include

- describing the appropriate way to greet another person
- modeling the behaviors used in a social greeting (such as making eye contact, keeping appropriate body space, and waiting for a lull in the conversation to start talking)
- allowing the student to try the greeting sequence
- providing verbal and physical feedback (for example, saying "I liked the way you smiled at John before saying hello," coupled with a pat on the shoulder)
- practicing the greeting
- using it independently in a real situation

their performance, and consistent instruction to reinforce behaviors that depend on vision. (See "From Theory to Practice: Social Greetings.") Sacks and Gaylord-Ross (1989) compared students with visual impairments who received a teacher-directed intervention to learn how to generalize and maintain a set of social skills with those who received only peer mediation and support. In both situations behavioral techniques were used for training, reinforcement, and generalization of learned social behaviors. The authors clearly documented the greater influence of peers in the learning process. (See Chapter 7 for more details about the use of peers in the development of social skills for visually impaired students.)

## COGNITIVE-STRUCTURAL THEORY

In cognitive-structural theory (Piaget, 1926/1959, 1932/1965), interactions with peers are necessary for social and cognitive growth. Piaget makes a clear distinction between adult and child interactions. In Piaget's view, adults establish a level of control and authority over children by setting rules and sanctions. However, the influence of peer input establishes a set of rules and contingencies that are mediated through play and cooperation. Through peer interaction, children move from a protected environment influenced by adult demands to a world where children are more autonomous and establish greater levels of independence.

According to the cognitive-structural model, the social development of students who are blind or visually impaired may be limited by the students' slower physical and motor development. When students do not have the skills to explore the world around them, they are at a disadvantage in being able to make contact with others. Also, because of their reliance on the perceptions of a sighted mediator to help them make sense of the environment and engage with others in social exchanges and play experiences, they are highly dependent on the choices and social biases of the adults who mediate their world. Thus, if the adults who control and mediate their social environment do not give them opportunities to establish a locus of control within their homes, schools, and communities and offer opportunities to make choices or take risks, students are less likely to develop accurate judgments about their social environment and the individuals with whom they interact. (See "From Theory to Practice: Encouraging Independence.")

# From Theory to Practice

## ENCOURAGING INDEPENDENCE

Given the nature of the cognitive-structural theory, it is important that students with visual impairments, from a very early age, be encouraged to make choices and decisions with as much independence as possible. Families and teachers need to help students learn to take responsibility for their behaviors and their personal belongings. For example, young children who are blind or visually impaired may be expected to put away their toys after playing with them, or may be given choices regarding food during mealtime or games during playtime. Older children can begin to anticipate a specific social situation and apply problem-solving skills to their response. For example, if a student with a visual impairment is subject to teasing on the playground because he or she missed catching a ball, the student needs to think about how to respond; for example, whether to ignore the teasing, laugh at the teasing, or respond with an angry negative outburst.

# STAGES OF SOCIAL DEVELOPMENT

Although we may view the social development of children with visual impairments through the perspective of various theoretical models, it is necessary to keep in mind that development is also based on the individual nature of each child and the demands of the child's specific environment. As children with visual impairments develop and mature, it is important to recognize that their capabilities are also shaped by the expectations and experiences encountered in their environment.

The impact of vision loss on social development is particularly critical because for typically developing children the process of learning social skills and developing relationships with others depends so much on the use of vision. For example, when young children who are blind or visually impaired do not use eye contact, initial bonding with caregivers may be in jeopardy because a reciprocal relationship may not develop. A visual impairment can also greatly affect a child's ability to develop spatial concepts or a basic understanding of personal physical boundaries. Because children who are blind or visually impaired often have no concept of personal space, they may find it difficult to physically locate individuals without support from others; it is likewise not uncommon for them to approach or face a person too closely. Both situations may cause a sighted peer or adult to move away or retreat from the interaction.

Warren (1994) provided a strong rationale for applying an approach using individual differences to evaluate the development of children with visual impairments. He wanted to move beyond comparing the development of sighted children with children who were visually impaired by examining the differences among children with visual impairments in how they acquire a repertoire of skills and developmental milestones. Ferrell (1997) corroborated Warren's individual differences approach and explained how vision loss may affect learning and development. "Children with blindness and visual impairment learn differently, for no other reason than the fact that in most cases they cannot rely on their vision to provide information. The information they obtain through their other senses is inconsistent, fragmented, and passive. It takes practice, training, and time to sort all of this out" (p. v).

All aspects of development, especially experiences with the physical world, influence the social development of children with visual impairments. In particular, development in the areas of cognition, motor skills, and language affect interactions with others. At birth an infant, whether blind or sighted, has no social consciousness. However, as children begin to develop socially, it is important to consider the following questions: How do children emerge with a repertoire of interactive abilities and skills related to their individual and group social experiences? How does the influence of vision loss affect social development and the ability to form lasting social relationships?

To answer these questions, it is useful to review the social development process for children who are blind or visually impaired. It is important to recognize that, of all the developmental processes, socialization is most strongly influenced by the interrelationship of cognitive, motor, and linguistic development. Factors such as the child's temperament, the family's acceptance of the child's visual impairment, the child's environment, and the influence of cultural values on the child's development also need to be considered. The following sections describe the socialization process for children with visual impairments and demonstrate how other aspects of development influence this process.

## IDENTITY

An infant's acquisition of identity and self-concept is enabled through the emergence of cognitive abilities. A strong sense of self is dependent on at least a rudimentary understanding of the distinction between oneself and others in the environment. Understanding that the self is separate from others is essential; it lays the groundwork for developing relationships with peers and adults and, in later years, in establishing values and beliefs.

A child's sense of identity is reinforced and mediated by the experiences and demands encountered throughout development. Parents, other family members, educational professionals, and friends play a significant role in how children perceive themselves and their abilities. According to Coopersmith (1967), self-concept, or sense of identity, is framed by the way in which children master their environment and by the way they meet life's demands.

For students with visual impairments, establishing a strong sense of self involves numerous factors, including the child's cognitive abilities and skills, the family's understanding and acceptance of the visual impairment, society's perception and acceptance of persons who are visually impaired, and the child's motivation and desire to interact with the environment and with others. According to Tuttle and Tuttle (1996), while these factors may contribute to social isolation, dependence, egocentric behavior, and immaturity among students who are blind or visually impaired, they should be regarded as potential influences on development rather than absolutes or generalities.

Additional factors, such as the type and amount of visual loss, additional disabilities, and opportunities to interact with parents and siblings (holding, touching, and cuddling), may influence a child's ability to establish a basic sense of identity. For example, by 1 month of age, sighted infants are initiating social interactions with others through smiles and gestures. They quickly develop an awareness of themselves as interactive beings. By 3 months, the sighted infant reinforces parents' smiles with vocalizations. Infants who are blind or visually impaired perceive their world initially through sounds, movement, and some visual feedback (depending on the child's visual status). They are dependent on others to mediate their physical and social worlds. Routine activities such as changing a diaper or feeding a bottle must be paired with an anticipatory verbal or tactile cue to allow infants with visual impairments to understand the action and to establish daily routines and a sense of trust. The natural give and take between infants and their parents and caregivers must be stimulated through holding, touching, and massage. A sense of self-identity for the child who is visually impaired can be established early on by verbalizing the infant's perceived behavioral intent—saying, for example, "Oh, you're crying because you don't like that loud noise," or "Let's see if sitting this way makes you happier." With these strategies, the parent or caregiver helps the child to establish some control over the environment and recognize that his or her actions or behaviors can produce change.

## ATTACHMENT

As infants grow and develop, scope of their interactions becomes more limited. Initially, infants may establish relationships with many adults, who maintain their level of safety and security. However, as children begin to master their physical and social environments by reaching out to others and exploring their social world, they become less willing to interact with individuals who are not part of their daily lives. By 6 to 9 months of age, children who are sighted are often selective about their social interactions. Usually their interactions are limited to familiar individuals (parents, siblings, and caregivers).

Warren (2000) believes that vision loss alone may not affect the attachment process for infants who are blind or visually impaired, but that the parents' emotional response to their child's visual impairment may influence how they interact with their baby. For example, babies who are blind or visually impaired often do not initiate prosocial vocalizations (babbling and cooing) because they are listening to the sounds in their environment and waiting for someone (usually a parent) to make the initial contact. Parents and caregivers may feel disappointed or alarmed if there is no reciprocal response. Also, the type and nature of social interactions between the parent and child needs to involve more physical contact (touching paired with a verbal cue) than nonverbal cues (smiles and gestures) alone. When parents do not use this kind of strategy for their interactions or the baby's responses do not produce intrinsic reinforcement for the parent or caregiver, the attachment process is jeopardized.

## REACHING, GRASPING, AND MOVING

Both infants who are sighted and those who are visually impaired initially react passively to touching objects brought to them. They instinctively curl their fingers around the object or place the object in their mouths to obtain feedback. However, once young children begin to move and to explore the environment, unique differences exist between infants who are sighted and those who are blind or visually impaired. The introduction of a visual stimulus makes a sighted child instinctively reach out to grasp the object, food, or person. Sighted children are intrinsically reinforced by visual stimuli. Establishing eye contact, for example, provides immediate feedback between the sighted infant and his or her parents. When babies with visual impairments begin to roll over, sit, or crawl, they must be encouraged to reach out and move. Without the pairing of an auditory, tactile, or visual cue, the child has no immediate motivation to move, to explore, or to respond interactively. In fact, for many young children with visual impairments, the introduction of a new toy, food item, or person may have a negative effect. The child may withdraw because the stimulus is unfamiliar or may appear threatening if the child is not prepared for its introduction.

Once sighted babies are able to sit (6 months) or crawl (6 to 8 months), they become interactive with their social world. They begin to play interactive games with their parents ("patty cake" or "this little piggy"), and recognize the purpose of toys and objects in familiar settings. By the end of their first year, sighted babies generally are walking and beginning to imitate daily tasks such as eating with utensils, drinking from a cup, or playing with pots and pans. Their desire to explore and experiment with the function of toys, furniture, and familiar objects in the home or child care environment is expanded because of their newfound mobility. Often, toddlers with visual impairments must be coaxed into exploring their environment. These children are less likely to spontaneously explore their world unless parents and significant others provide structure and cues (visual, auditory, or tactile) that encourage them to explore and to interact with objects and people in a meaningful way. When young children with visual impairments are given very specific parameters to explore, they become familiar with the settings in which certain activities occur, and they look forward to the consistency of routines within those settings. Their desire to move and explore is heightened when they are familiar with the environment and have been introduced to toys, objects, and people.

## Social Communication

According to Warren (2000), there is no doubt that vision plays a significant role in the development of preverbal and linguistic communication. During the preverbal stage of language acquisition, eye contact between parent and child is important in establishing a social link that facilitates communicative intent. Without visual feedback, the interplay between infants who are visually impaired and their caregivers may be misinterpreted. For example, if an infant who is blind quiets every time he or she hears a familiar voice, the parents may interpret the child's behavior as disinterest in engaging in the interaction.

Parents of young children with visual impairments cannot rely on visual feedback to interpret communicative intent of the child. They must learn to use alternative cues that the child provides to establish social communication. For example, when parents and caregivers learn to interpret the meaning of vocal utterances or certain physical postures, such as cooing to mean enjoyment or clenching of fists to mean fear or displeasure with an activity, then they can react appropriately; the communication between parent and child is effective. Parents can facilitate turn taking and reciprocal interactions through the modeling of language and communicative intent. For example, if a baby who is visually impaired squeals and kicks his or her feet when put in a high chair, the parent could respond with a verbal cue, "Oh, you must be so hungry. Here comes your food."

While there may be subtle differences in the manner in which young children with visual impairment acquire language and use it in various contexts (Timmins, 1997), the general developmental sequence of language for children with visual impairments is similar to that of sighted children. According to Lueck, Chen, and Kekelis (1997) blind and visually impaired children express their first words around the same time as sighted children. How blind children use words and interpret their meaning in different social and environmental contexts may be different, however. For example, young children who are blind often use words as labels, rather than as a means of describing something. For example, a child might play with an object and call it a train but not be able to describe its function. Because their experiences outside of their own world often are limited, the social language of children who are blind may reflect these more ego-centered experiences. Children with visual impairments may have difficulty using pronouns correctly. For example, they may refer to themselves in the third person rather than using "I" or "me." Also, young children with visual impairments may ask many more questions about their experiences in their social world to help bring meaning to abstract ideas or concepts.

Timmins (1997) and Rogow (2000) recognized that the acquisition of language for students who are blind or visually impaired is strongly influenced by the severity of the child's visual impairment, the presence of additional disabilities, and the quantity and quality of social experiences that the child is exposed to throughout his or her early years. When families and educators learn to interpret behavioral cues or early linguistic intent as social communication, the child's ability to interact with others improves. When the focus of early language development is experiential, the child's ability to use and understand the meaning and function of words increases with every opportunity to engage in a variety of social situations. The connection between the pragmatics of language and the socialization process for young children with visual impairments is essential. Learning the give and take of social communication, either through verbal expression, gestures, or augmentative communication modes, can facilitate positive social interactions and enhance the development of appropriate peer relationships in home, school, and community settings.

The development of social skills for students with visual impairments is highly influenced by the integration of cognitive, linguistic, and motor skills. The quantity and quality of experiences the child encounters with other children and adults also influence the acquisition of social skills for these students. The acquisition of play skills provides the basis for successful social encounters in elementary and secondary school environments as well as in subsequent work and living arrangements. While each child is unique, and visually impaired children may demonstrate delays in certain aspects of play, particularly if they have additional disabilities, educator and families should be familiar with the typical stages of play for sighted children in order to understand more fully how vision loss affects socialization. Fazzi (2002) explains that two variables must be considered when evaluating children's play: first, whether or not the child is playing alone or with others, and second, how the child is using toys in play. She identifies the following sequence in the development of play as well as different types of play (Fazzi, 2002, pp. 193–194):

- Solitary play—also called solo play, when children play alone, show little interest in other children at play, and do not attempt to play with others
- Parallel play—when children play alongside or near other children with either similar or different toys or items; some interest in what the other children are doing is noted
- Cooperative play—when children are actively playing with others in an organized, give-and-take fashion

The following terms describe how children interact with and use toys and objects in their play:

- Manipulative play—when children are engaged with toys or objects primarily through exploration, such as mouthing or banging (for example banging a spoon on the floor to hear the sound it makes, or pushing buttons on a battery-operated toy to make lights flash or music play)
- Functional play—when children use toys or objects in the way in which they are intended during play (for example, pretending to drive with a toy car or pretending to cook with a toy saucepan)
- Symbolic play—when children pretend that an object is another object in their play scenario (pretending that cotton balls are scoops of ice cream or that a laundry basket is a boat)
- Dramatic play—when children assume fantasy roles in their play scenarios (for example, pretending to be a doctor or a cat)

This play sequence can assist families and teachers of students with visual impairments in determining when specific interventions might be appropriate. For example, if a preschooler who is blind seems to be engaged in solo play, then adults might want to facilitate or model parallel play by having a sighted child in the same play activity or by having an adult use words and actions to play with the child.

For many young children with visual impairments, particularly children with additional disabilities, acquisition of play skills may be much slower than for sighted peers, or it may develop in a different sequence. For example, a child who is blind may be able to engage in parallel or even cooperative play by using expressive language, but the child's use of toys or objects within the play setting may be at a manipulative or functional level of play, particularly if the child has had limited exposure to a variety of social experiences. When play situations are structured and facilitated by adults or peers in the child's immediate environment, the child is more likely to engage in a socially appropriate manner. The use and function of play skills does not automatically occur for children with visual impairments. Consistent practice in learning how to play may be needed throughout the preschool, elementary, and middle school years for students with visual impairments to gain social acceptance and acquire interactive relationships with sighted peers. Specific strategies to initiate social play for young children who are blind or visually impaired are described in Chapter 10.

As students with visual impairments move from early intervention programs to elementary and middle school environments, they will need to continue to develop interactive skills with peers and adults. These skills include making social initiations, turn taking, using social etiquette, joining and sharing in group activities, and learning typical games and activities of school-age students. It is also essential for these students to develop decision-making skills and to have opportunities to make choices in their daily lives. Families and teachers must have realistic expectations regarding young people's socialization and require them to act in a socially acceptable manner at home, in school, and in the community. Being able to interpret social situations and understand how their own behavior affects others is critical for students with visual impairments as they progress into adolescence and young adulthood.

## CONCLUSION

Although theoretical perspectives may sometimes seem unnecessary to those who provide direct services to students with visual impairments, this framework lays the foundation for understanding why the acquisition of social skills is so critical for students with visual impairments. Theory also provides a knowledge base that can be used to design and implement effective intervention strategies. Both the integration of developmental milestones and the relationship of theory to practice are particularly important in the area of social development.

Learning to play, to share toys, and to interact effectively with family members, teachers, and peers are essential skills that lay the foundation for later social competence. The integration of cognitive, linguistic, and motor development may influence the way in which social skills are learned. The partnership between family, caregivers, educators, and other support personnel is essential if social skill instruction is to be consistently maintained throughout a child's educational career. It is the responsibility of all parties who provide support to the student who is blind or visually impaired to model appropriate social behavior, provide experiences that enhance interactive play and socialization, and structure opportunities that allow students to practice an array of social skills strategies across settings. The chapters that follow provide numerous examples of how social skills are assessed, taught, and infused into the many experiences students with visual impairments encounter throughout their school years.

# REFERENCES

Argyle, M. (1980). Interaction skills and social competence. In P. Feldman & J. Orford (Eds.), *Psychological problems: The social context* (pp. 123–150). Chichester, England: John Wiley & Sons.

Argyle, M., & Kenden, A. (1967). The experimental analysis of social performance. In L. Berkowitz (Ed.), *Advances in experimental social psychology* (Vol. 3, pp. 58–98). New York: Academic Press.

Bandura, A. (1977). *Social learning theory*. Englewood Cliffs, NJ: Prentice Hall.

Bandura, A. (1979). *Principles of behavior modification*. New York: Holt, Rinehart, & Winston.

Bandura, A. (1986). *Social foundations of thought and action: A social cognitive theory*. Englewood Cliffs, NJ: Prentice Hall.

Bandura, A. (1989). Social cognitive theory. *Annals of Child Development, 6*, 1–60.

Bandura, A., & Walters, R. H. (1963). *Social learning and personality development*. New York: Holt, Rinehart, & Winston.

Coopersmith, S. (1967). *Antecedents of self-esteem*. San Francisco: W. H. Freeman.

Durkheim, E. (1973). *Moral education: A study in the theory and application of the sociology of education*. (E. K. Wilson & H. Schnurer, Trans.). New York: Free Press. (Original work published 1925.)

Erikson, E. H. (1963). *Childhood and society* (2nd ed.). New York: Norton.

Erikson, E. H. (1980). *Identity and the life cycle.* New York: Norton. (Original work published 1959.)

Fazzi, D. L. (2002). Social focus: Developing social skills and promoting social interactions. In R. L. Pogrund & D. L. Fazzi (Eds.), *Early Focus: Working with young children who are blind or visually impaired and their families* (2nd ed.) (pp. 188–217). New York: AFB Press.

Ferrell, K. A. (1997). What is it that is different about a child with blindness or visual impairment? In P. Crane, D. Cuthbertson, K. A. Ferrell, & H. Scherb (Eds.), *Equals in partnership: Basic rights for families of children with blindness or visual impairment* (pp. v–vii). Watertown, MA: Perkins School for the Blind and the National Association for Parents of the Visually Impaired.

Ferrell, K. A. (2000). Growth and development of young children. In M. C. Holbrook & A. J. Koenig (Eds.), *Foundations of education: Vol. 1. History and Theory of Teaching Children and Youths with Visual Impairments* (2nd ed.; pp. 111–135). New York: AFB Press.

Foster, S. L., & Richey, W. L. (1979). Issues in the assessment of social competence in children. *Journal of Applied Behavior Analysis, 12,* 625–638.

Fraiberg, S. (1977). *Insights from the blind.* New York: Basic Books.

Freud, S. (1974). Civilization and its discontents. In J. Strachey (Ed. & Trans.), *The standard edition of the complete psychological works of Sigmund Freud* (Vol. 21, pp. 64–145). London: Hogarth Press. (Original work published 1930.)

Freud, S. (1974). The dissolution of the Oedipus complex. In J. Strachey (Ed. & Trans.), *The standard edition of the complete psychological works of Sigmund Freud* (Vol. 19, pp. 173–182). London: Hogarth Press. (Original work published 1924.)

Freud, S. (1974). Three essays on the theory of sexuality. In J. Strachey (Ed. and Trans.), *The standard edition of the complete psychological works of Sigmund Freud* (Vol. 7, pp. 123–231). London: Hogarth Press. (Original work published 1905.)

Gesell, A. (1928). *Infancy and human growth.* New York: Macmillan.

Harlow, H. F., & Harlow, M. K. (1962). Social deprivation in monkeys. *Scientific American, 207*(5), 1–10.

Hatlen, P. H. (1980). Mainstreaming: Origin of a concept. *Blindness,* (Annual, American Association of Workers for the Blind, Washington, DC), 1–8.

Hatlen, P. (1996). The core curriculum for blind and visually impaired students, including those with additional disabilities. *RE:view, 28*(1), 25–32.

Hersen, M., & Bellack, A. (1977). Assessment of social skills. In A. Ciminero, K. Calhoun, & H. Adams (Eds.), *Handbook for behavioral assessment* (pp. 509–554). New York: John Wiley & Sons.

Individuals with Disabilities Education Act, 20 U.S.C. SS § 1400 et seq. (1997).

Kelly, J. A. (1982). *Social skills training: A practical guide for intervention.* New York: Springer.

Lueck, A. H., Chen, D., & Kekelis, L. S. (1997). *Developmental guidelines for infants with visual impairments*. Louisville, KY: American Printing House for the Blind.

McFall, R. M. (1982). A review and reformulation of the concept of social skills. *Behavior Assessment, 4*, 1–33.

Meyer, G. F. (1929). Some advantages offered children in day school classes for the blind in the public schools. *Outlook for the Blind, 22(4)*, 9–15.

Mischel, W., (1966). A social learning view of sex differences in behavior. In E. E. Macoby (Ed.), *The development of sex differences*. Palo Alto, CA: Stanford University Press.

Piaget, J. (1959). *The language and thought of the child* (M. Gabain, Trans.). New York: Humanities Press. (Original work published 1926.)

Piaget, J. (1965). *The moral judgment of the child* (M. Gabain, Trans.). New York: Free Press. (Original work published 1932.)

Reardon, M. P., & Sacks, S. Z. (1985, March). Social skills training: Foundation for functional learning. Paper presented at the meeting of California Transcribers and Educators of the Visually Impaired, San Francisco.

Rogow, S. M. (2000). Communication and language: Issues and concerns. In B. Silverstone, M. A. Lang, B. P. Rosenthal, & E. E. Faye (Eds.), *The Lighthouse handbook on visual impairment and vision rehabilitation* (pp. 395–408). New York: Oxford University Press.

Sacks, S. Z., & Gaylord-Ross, R. J. (1989). Peer-mediated and teacher-directed social skills training for visually impaired students. *Behavior Therapy, 20*, 619–638.

Sacks, S. Z., & Gaylord-Ross, R. J. (1992). Peer-mediated and teacher-directed social skills training for blind and visually impaired students. In S. Z. Sacks, R. J. Gaylord-Ross, & L. S. Kekelis (Eds.), *The development of social skills by blind and visually impaired students: Exploratory studies and strategies* (pp. 103–132). New York: AFB Press.

Sacks, S. Z., & Silberman, R. K. (2000). Social skills. In A. J. Koenig & M. C. Holbrook (Eds.), *Foundations of education: Vol. 2. Instructional Strategies for Teaching Children and Youths with Visual Impairments* (2nd ed.; pp. 616–652). New York: AFB Press.

Sacks, S. Z., & Wolffe, K. E. (1998). Lifestyles of adolescents with visual impairments: An ethnographic analysis. *Journal of Visual Impairment & Blindness, 92*, 7–17.

Sacks, S. Z., Wolffe, K. E., & Tierney, D. (1998). Lifestyles of students with visual impairments: Preliminary studies of social networks. *Exceptional Children, 64*, 463–478.

Skinner, B. F. (1938). *The behavior of organisms: An experimental analysis*. New York: Appleton-Century-Crofts.

Skinner, B. F. (1957). *Verbal behavior*. New York: Appleton-Century-Crofts.

Skinner, B. F. (1976). *Walden two*. New York: Macmillan.

Sullivan, H. S. (1953). *The interpersonal theory of psychiatry*. New York: W. W. Norton.

Tait, P. (1972). The effects of circumstantial rejection in infant behavior. *New Outlook for the Blind, 66,* 139–151.

Timmins, S. (1997). *Early development in children with severe visual impairment: Needs assessment for kindergarten and strategies for remediation* (2nd ed.). Ottawa, Ontario, Canada: Ottawa/Carlton Program for Students with Visual Impairments.

Trower, P. (1982). Toward a generative model of social skills: A critique and synthesis. In J. P. Curran & P. M. Monti (Eds.), *Social skills training.* New York: Guilford Press.

Tuttle, D., & Tuttle, N. (1996). *Self-esteem and adjusting with blindness* (2nd ed.). Springfield, IL: Charles C Thomas.

Warren, D. H. (1984). *Blindness and early childhood development* (2nd ed., rev.). New York: American Foundation for the Blind.

Warren, D. H. (1994). *Blindness and children: An individual differences approach.* Cambridge, England: Cambridge University Press.

Warren, D. H. (2000). Developmental perspectives: Youth. In B. Silverstone, M. A. Lang, B. P. Rosenthal, & E. L. Faye (Eds.), *The lighthouse handbook on visual impairment and vision rehabilitation* (pp. 325–337). New York: Oxford University Press.

Wolffe, K. E. (1999). *Skills for success: A career education handbook for children and adolescents with visual impairments.* New York: AFB Press.

Wolffe, K. E. (2000). Career education. In A. J. Koenig and M. C. Hollbrook (Eds.), *Foundations of education: Vol. 2. Instructional Strategies for Teaching Children and Youths with Visual Impairments,* (2nd ed.; pp. 679–719). New York: AFB Press.

Wolffe, K., & Sacks, S. Z. (1997). The social network pilot project: A quantitative comparison of the lifestyles of blind, low vision, and sighted young adults. *Journal of Visual Impairment & Blindness, 91,* 245–257.

Wolffe, K. E., Sacks, S. Z., Corn, A. L., Erin, J. N., Huebner, K. M., & Lewis, S. (2002). Teachers of students with visual impairments: What are they teaching? *Journal of Visual Impairment & Blindness, 96(5),* 293–304.

# CHAPTER 4

# Theoretical Perspectives on the Development of Social Skills in Adolescence

Karen E. Wolffe

Adolescence, in many ways, appears to be a phenomenon of modern Western society—a culture that indulges its youths with an extended time for education and growth unheard of even a century ago, when children as young as 10 years old were often expected to assume adultlike responsibilities at home and in the community. There is one aspect of adolescence, however, that is common to all cultures, social classes, and historical eras—the biological phenomenon (Anderson & Clarke, 1982; Dasberg, 1983; Fenwick & Smith, 1996; Tanner, 1962; Weiner, 1970; Wolffe, 2000). Blindness and visual

Portions of this chapter have been adapted, with permission of the publisher, from Karen E. Wolffe, "Growth and Development of Youths with Visual Impairments," in M. C. Holbrook & A. J. Koenig (Eds.), *Foundations of Education: Vol. 1. History and Theory of Teaching Children and Youths with Visual Impairments* (2nd ed.) (New York: AFB Press, 2000), pp. 135–160.

impairment do not have an impact on this biological phenomenon; however, lack of vision can and often does affect the psychosocial development of adolescents.

This chapter reviews several models of human development that are based on research concerning adolescents and young adults who do not have disabilities. It then presents an overview of both biological and social development during adolescence, including consideration of the impact visual impairment may have on these processes. Research studies that have dealt specifically with the impact of visual impairment on social development in adolescence are detailed, and this discussion leads to a final section that examines a critical developmental process in young people's lives: the evolution from dependence to independence and, finally, to interdependence. Activities and strategies for teachers, related service personnel, and family members who want to help adolescents with visual impairments develop positive social skills are presented in Chapter 12.

Although the inclusive ages presented by writers and researchers in the definition of adolescence tend to change over time and across cultures and social classes, for the purposes of this discussion, adolescence is considered as the period in an individual's life from approximately 10 or 11 years old to between 18 and 22 years of age.

## MODELS OF HUMAN DEVELOPMENT

There are four major theoretical models for typical developmental sequences of children: the maturational model, the psychoanalytic model, the behavioral model, and the cognitive-developmental model (Bee, 1997; Dworetzky, 1981; Salkind, 1985). Although some theories explain or try to predict behavior based on environmental factors, others emphasize the interaction between the environment and an individual's genetic makeup. An overview of basic differences between these theoretical models and the implications for practitioners are presented in the following sections and are summarized in Table 4.1.

### MATURATIONAL MODEL

Developmental psychologists who support the maturational model consider hereditary or biological factors to be of paramount importance in an individual's development. The model proposes that an individual's innate biological strengths and weaknesses are more influential in

**TABLE 4.1**  An Overview of Models of Human Development

| Models | Maturational Model | Psycho-analytic Model | Behavioral Model | Cognitive-Developmental Model |
|---|---|---|---|---|
| Assumptions | Development is determined by biological factors. | Development is based on a person's need to satisfy basic instincts. | Development occurs as a person learns from his or her environment. | Development is contingent on the modification of a person's cognitive structures over time. |
| Implications for practitioners | Importance of biological determinants and how children are reared. | Impact of early parent-child relationships on personality development. | Understanding of behavioral analysis, modification of behavior, and extinction of maladaptive behavior. | Understanding of cognitive processes and how to engage children in appropriate tasks to match their developmental level. |

*Source:* Reprinted from Karen E. Wolffe, "Growth and Development in Middle Childhood and Adolescence," in M. C. Holbrook and A. J. Koenig, Eds., *Foundations of Education, Vol. 1: History and Theory of Teaching Children and Youths with Visual Impairments* (2nd ed.) (New York, AFB Press, 2000).

a person's life than nurturing or the impact of the environment. Two leading proponents of this theory were Arnold Gesell (1928, 1946, 1956) and Konrad Lorenz (1958, 1965), both of whom were strongly influenced by Darwin's studies of biological evolution. Gesell's studies of twins, which compared the effects of nature (heredity) and nurture (environmental factors), greatly influenced mid- to late-20th-century child-rearing patterns, most notably through its incorporation in the work of Dr. Spock (Gesell & Thompson, 1929, 1941; Salkind, 1985).

Adherents of the maturational model assume that a child's basic social makeup is genetically determined. Therefore, a child who is shy or outgoing behaves in ways that are, in essence, ordained by his or her genetic makeup. This is not to imply, however, that the developmental psychologists and instructional personnel who follow this model do not believe that professionals and families can make a difference. They would argue that how children are brought up aggravates or subverts their inherited traits—that good child rearing encourages the healthy development of children. If a child is inherently shy or outgoing, these theorists would say that these natural traits can be positively affected by adult nurturing—not eliminated, but any negative consequences can be minimized by guidance and caring from significant adults.

## PSYCHOANALYTIC MODEL

Underlying Freud's psychoanalytic model, introduced at the beginning of the 20th century, is the basic assumption that human development consists of distinct components (dynamic, structural, and sequential) that are influenced by a continual need for gratification. In this model, Freud (1905) defined the dynamic component as the psyche or the mind, which he characterized as fluid and energized. The structural component of the model consisted of the id, ego, and superego, three separate but interdependent psychological structures. The sequential component of the model involved development through different stages (oral, anal, phallic, latency, and genital) that correspond to erogenous zones of the body. Freud believed that people encounter psychological conflicts (weaning, toilet training, attraction to the opposite-sex parent, development of ego defenses, and mature sexual intimacy) at each of these stages and that these conflicts have to be resolved for people to become healthy adults (Salkind, 1985).

Many modern psychoanalytic theorists have gravitated to the work of Erikson, who de-emphasized the centrality of the sexual drive (Erikson, 1963, 1959/1980). Although Erikson shared many of Freud's assumptions, he focused on a gradual emergence of self-identity rather than sexual drive as the primary motivation for growth and development. He proposed the following eight psychosocial stages, five of which occur in childhood:

- Basic trust versus mistrust (birth to 1 year)—at this stage children bond with their primary caregiver and realize that they can make things happen.
- Autonomy versus shame, doubt (2–3 years)—at this stage children engage in motor skills to make choices and are toilet trained; they learn control but may develop shame if skills training is not handled well.
- Initiative versus guilt (4–5 years)—at this stage children organize activities around goals and become more assertive; conflict with same sex parents may lead to guilt.

- Industry versus inferiority (6–12 years)—at this stage children are absorbed in learning cultural mores, and acquiring academic and tool-usage skills.

- Identity versus role confusion (13–18 years)—at this stage youths adapt to the physical changes of puberty, make career choices, achieve a sexual identity, and clarify values.

- Intimacy versus isolation (19–25 years)—at this stage people form intimate relationships, marry, and start families.

- Generativity versus stagnation (26–40 years)—at this stage individuals raise children, perform life work, and prepare the next generation.

- Ego integrity versus despair (40+ years)—at this stage people integrate the earlier stages and accept their basic identity.

Psychoanalytic theory emphasizes the critical importance of the early years of a child's life and focuses attention on the need for positive emotional support from caregivers. Psychoanalysts underscore the impact of good parenting and positive family relationships in the lives of children. The difficulty with this model remains its lack of empirical evidence to support the theorists' hypotheses (Bee, 1997).

Although proponents of the psychoanalytic model insist that a person's development is contingent upon the individual's need to satisfy his or her basic instincts, they believe that parent-child relationships can facilitate or inhibit a child's movement through the proposed psychosocial stages. Adherents to this model support parents and families in their efforts to react positively to children as they move through these stages. They discourage punishment of behaviors that they see as natural consequences of child development: toileting mishaps, conflicts with same-sex parent, overt expressions of sexuality in puberty such as masturbation, and so forth. Perhaps most important, from a social skills perspective, is the recognition by psychoanalysts of the importance of self-identity and the expectation that self-identity emerges gradually as children and youths mature.

## BEHAVIORAL MODEL

The behavioral model was introduced in the early part of the 20th century with Pavlov's work on what is known as classical conditioning. In his most famous experiment, classical conditioning occurred when a dog learned a new behavior (salivating) in response to the pairing of an unconditioned stimulus (food) with a previously neutral stimulus (a bell). In time, the dog salivated at the sound of the bell without seeing food (Pavlov, 1927). The dog was already programmed (innately) to salivate at the presentation of food, which is considered an unconditioned response. Salivating at the sound of the bell was the conditioned response. Classical conditioning involves attaching an old response to a new stimulus.

Behaviorists view development as a function of learning that proceeds according to certain laws or principles (Skinner, 1938, 1957, 1976; Bandura, 1977, 1979, 1986, 1989). The human being is seen as reactive rather than active, and behavior is considered a function of its consequences. If the consequences of a given behavior are good or positive, then the behavior is reinforced and will likely continue. On the other hand, if a behavior is punished or ignored, then the behavior will likely diminish or be extinguished.

The behavioral model is mechanistic; it assumes that the environment is more important in development than one's hereditary attributes. The adherents to this model believe that children's behaviors are modified or learned over time with both positive and negative reinforcement. Extensive scientific study by those who support this model has shown the power of different kinds of reinforcement schedules, with intermittent reinforcement as the most powerful. Consistent or scheduled reinforcement occurs when a behavior is reinforced at specified times; for example, rewarding a child who gets to school on time every day over the course of a semester. Intermittent reinforcement occurs when a behavior is reinforced, but not always and not on any particular schedule; for example, rewarding a child who greets a teacher every other day during the first month of the semester, once a week on any day during the second month of the semester, and any time during the last weeks of the semester. The child is more likely to continue greeting the teacher in this scenario because he or she is waiting to be reinforced rather than expecting reinforcement at a scheduled time. Arguably the greatest contributions of the behaviorists have been an emphasis on scientific study of behavior, systematic analysis of behavior, specific techniques to modify deviant behaviors, and encouragement of programmed instruction (Salkind, 1985).

Behaviorists believe that children's social behaviors are not a consequence of innate traits, but are learned from others in their environment and can be changed, positively or negatively, by external forces (reinforcement). They adhere to the notion that children's behaviors are malleable and can be affected by modeling or instruction coupled with reinforcement. They also believe that negative social behaviors (misbehaving) can be changed by ignoring or punishing the behavior. They believe that negative social behaviors tend to emerge and are maintained as a consequence of a child receiving either positive or negative attention or reinforcement. In order to positively apply behavioral techniques, instructional personnel need to define the weak or negative behavior they are trying to modify and determine what reinforcers are maintaining the behavior; then, they can change the behavior by either positively reinforcing the behavior they want to see in the old behavior's stead or ignoring it.

## COGNITIVE-DEVELOPMENTAL MODEL

The cognitive-developmental model (Piaget, 1932, 1952, 1977) stresses the individual's active rather than reactive role in the developmental process. Cognitive-developmentalists believe that development occurs in a series of qualitatively distinct stages and that the stages always follow the same sequence, but not necessarily at the same chronological time for all people. The stages are considered hierarchical, and the later stages subsume the characteristics of earlier stages; what children learn in earlier stages is used to develop more complex and mature sensorimotor schemas for use in later stages. Schemas are often loosely defined as concepts or a "complex of ideas." However, Piaget uses the term to denote the action of categorizing in some particular mental or physical fashion (Bee, 1997).

In this model, the four proposed stages of development are as follows:

- Sensorimotor (birth to 18 months)—at this stage, the child responds to the world almost entirely through sensory and motor schemas, operates entirely in the present and without intentions, and has no internal representation of objects.
- Preoperational (18 months to approximately age 6)—at this stage, the child begins to use symbols and language emerges, engages in pretend play, exhibits egocentrism, and can perform simple classifications, but cannot understand that two amounts that look different can be the same (conservation).
- Concrete operational (from approximately age 6 to age 12)—at this stage, the child discovers strategies for exploring and interacting with the world and masters internal schemas that enable him or her to perform mathematical functions, categorize objects and entities into related groupings, and perform feats of logic.
- Formal operational (from approximately age 12 onward)—in this final stage, the youngster is able to apply complex mental operations

to ideas and thoughts as well as to objects and experiences, and exhibits deductive reasoning.

Piaget believed that children actively participate as they develop an understanding of the world in which they live. He believed that babies are born with a small repertoire of basic sensory schemas such as tasting, touching, looking, hearing, and reaching and that they develop mental schemas over time, such as categorizing. According to Piaget, children shift from the simplistic schemas of infancy to increasingly complex mental schemas through the processes he termed assimilation, accommodation, and equilibration. Assimilation is the process of absorbing an experience or an event into a schema—connecting the concept to whatever other concepts are similar. Accommodation is a complementary process that necessitates changing a schema due to the assimilation of new information—it is the reorganization of thoughts. Equilibration is the means by which children achieve balance in their lives between what they know and what they are in the process of learning.

Although some of Piaget's ideas have been called into question and errors have been identified in his theory—such as his description of the timing of cognitive skills development—his notion of the child as actively engaged in constructing an understanding of his or her world has been widely accepted (Bee, 1997). Another important outgrowth of Piaget's work is the emphasis by contemporary developmental theorists on qualitative change—how an adolescent approaches a problem or a task is not only faster but qualitatively different than how a baby, toddler, or child approaches a similar problem or task.

Piagetian or cognitive-developmental theorists believe that children's behaviors can be changed or modified, but only when they are mature enough to grasp the concept (or cognitive structure) that the adult is trying to teach them. In other words, these theorists believe that children respond to their environment and the people in it contingent upon where they are in their own developmental process. For example, the adherents to this model expect children under the age of 6 years old to act in an egocentric fashion and would insist that to try to change such behavior is developmentally inappropriate and bound to be unsuccessful.

Although there are adherents of all four models of development, there is no consensus in the field of human development that one model is better or more accurate than another. Psychologists working with children and youths borrow from the array of models and consider the interaction between nature and nurture as the real answer to the question of how children develop (Bee, 1997).

# BIOLOGICAL ONTOGENY

The physical development process, or biological ontogeny, is the one given in the lives of adolescents, with or without disabilities. Biological periods are used for the basis of classification in the following discussion of adolescent development because their occurrence in nature is unequivocal. Three adolescent biological periods are identified: early, middle, and late. Each of these periods is described briefly, and concerns for youths with visual impairments are introduced.

*Early adolescence.* During this biological period, pubescent changes in physical structure begin. For girls, these physical changes include the appearance of pubic, underarm, and body hair; the production of underarm perspiration; breast development; and menstruation. For boys these changes include growth of pubic, underarm, body, and facial hair; development of underarm sweat glands; growth of the testes, darkening of the skin of the scrotum, lengthening and thickening of the penis, and onset of ejaculation; and deepening of the voice. Although these physical changes often begin in late elementary years, they continue through middle school and often extend into the high school years. It is important to note that for girls these changes occur, on average, two years earlier than for boys. Early adolescence typically occurs between 10 and 13 years old (Steinberg, 2002).

*Middle adolescence.* This period is most often referred to as puberty; it is the period of the most rapid physical change, typically occurring between 14 and 18 years of age (Steinberg, 2002). Perhaps the greatest physical changes occur during middle school or junior high school. For many young people this period of time is truly a physical transition from childhood to adulthood. Many young women reach physical maturation between the ages of 14 and 15 and young men between the ages of 15 and 16, while they are in high school. In essence, they attain the basic physical characteristics (vocal range, size, and appearance) that will be in evidence through maturity.

*Late adolescence.* Modest changes in stature and internal neural-biological states continue to occur and stabilize during this period, which is generally considered to take place roughly between the ages of 19 and 22 years old (Steinberg, 2002). In this period, the highest levels of coordination of physical action systems (sensorimotor integration and capabilities for reproduction) and cognitive capabilities are attained (Cairns, 1986; Fenwick & Smith, 1996; Wolffe, 2000).

Although these physical changes and growth milestones are usually the same for youths with and without visual impairments, parents and caregivers need to be aware of how visually impaired youngsters experience and react to these changes. (See "Theory to Practice: Physical Changes in Adolescence.") In early adolescence, youngsters with visual impairments need to receive private instruction from their parents or teachers in grooming and hygiene needs relevant to their changing bodies. For instance, girls need to be prepared for their menstrual cycle and understand the tools available to them for personal management (the different sizes and types of sanitary napkins, panty liners, tampons, and so forth). Both girls and boys may desire and need instruction in shaving. They may also want to explore the variety of body deodorants (powders, roll-on sticks, and the like) and other personal hygiene accoutrements (perfumes, after shave, makeup, blemish cover-up and medications). By middle adolescence, young adults need to be well aware of the "birds and bees" and all that such instruction implies: an awareness of their own sexual drives; how different people release their sexual drives (masturbation and intercourse); differences in sexual orientation (heterosexual, homosexual, asexual); the formal and informal or slang expressions that refer to body parts and sexual activity; how to protect oneself from sexually transmitted diseases and unwanted pregnancies; and so forth. Late adolescence is the time for helpers and caregivers to see whether the young adults can apply what they have learned and intervene only when they need assistance. At all stages of adolescence, it is important for those working with and caring for youngsters with visual impairments to encourage them to ask questions and to answer their questions honestly and without making value judgments. (Numerous resources for teaching sex education to children and youths are listed in the Recommended Readings section of this book.)

## SOCIAL ONTOGENY

When it comes to changes in social development, or social ontogeny, the experience of major ecological events (interactions between people and the environment) and social events in early and middle adolescence may differ significantly for young people with visual impairments. For youngsters without disabilities, such changes generally include opportunities to move about in their neighborhoods and

# Theory to Practice

## PHYSICAL CHANGES IN ADOLESCENCE

For youngsters with severe visual impairments, it is important for their caregivers, family members, and those who work with them to help them understand that the physical changes that they experience in adolescence are a normal part of physiological development. They need to be told how the children around them are changing physically and how those changes mirror what is happening to them. They need to know that other teenagers are also likely to be struggling with growth spurts, mood changes, acne, and the other trials and tribulations of puberty. Some changes will be fairly overt: voice changes and physical changes in height and weight; however, the more subtle changes, such as coping with skin problems or acquisition of facial and body hair, will not be easily determined without feedback from others with good vision.

communities with less supervision from their parents and other adults, to make independent and often heretofore forbidden purchases (for example, trendy clothing, movies, games, music, and makeup), and, in general, to have greater independence (although freedom of movement and sexual standards are typically more restricted for girls than for boys). For typically developing children, this pattern is accepted and expected.

The situation is often different for adolescents with visual impairments, however. Caregivers are often reluctant to allow them the same freedom of movement because of safety concerns; parents or other caregivers may feel less than confident in their children's orientation and mobility (O&M) techniques or may simply feel that these children are particularly vulnerable without good vision in such a fast-paced and car-mad world. Many visually impaired adolescents (and their primary informants, parents or caregivers) are unaware of what items are trendy and coveted by other youngsters, so they don't even think about expanding their ability to purchase such items. Without some input from a sibling or a same-sex friend from school, these youngsters may not know what they are missing, because they don't see what their peers are wearing or how they decorate their faces or hair. To determine what items are sought after among preteens and teens can require considerable work on the part of both the visually impaired youngsters and their caregivers.

As typically developing children begin to mature in early adolescence, they place greater emphasis on their social relationships with peers than on their relationships with parents and other adults. There is a shift from adult-child relationships, which are asymmetrical or vertical relationships, to child-peer relationships, which are symmetrical or horizontal relationships. Asymmetrical relationships are complementary, while symmetrical relationships are reciprocal (Cairns, 1986; Hartup, 1981, 1992, 1996). In asymmetrical or complementary relationships, one partner (typically the parent or caregiver or other adult) has greater knowledge and social competence than the other partner (the child). On the other hand, in symmetrical or reciprocal relationships, the partners are equivalent in general knowledge, age, or social prowess.

Many youngsters who are visually impaired may not shift into these symmetrical relationships as quickly as their sighted peers and may remain deeply involved in asymmetrical relationships with adults. Visually impaired students tend to receive more adult involvement at school than their sighted peers, in part as a result of the nature of their disabilities and their need for instruction in disability-specific areas (O&M, braille, use of optical devices, and so forth). In addition, there are frequently instructional aides provided for many visually impaired students in mainstream classes. Thus, students who are blind or visually impaired tend to have easy access to and involvement with myriad adult service providers that are not in the lives of their sighted peers, with the result that they generally have more adult-child relationships than is typical for teenagers. This prolonged period of adult-child interaction or involvement in asymmetrical relationships can be detrimental to youngsters with visual impairments because they may become dependent upon adults and their complementary exchanges of information with them (in other words, having adults tell them what to do and how to respond to social situations) rather than learning how to engage with their same-aged peers and share social messages and values that differ from those conveyed by adults.

As they move into middle and late adolescence, young people without disabilities gain even greater freedom because they learn to drive and begin to have access to cars. During this period, it is also common for many sighted youngsters to begin to work, at least part-time. Being unable to drive is an issue that is often emotionally upsetting for teenagers with visual impairments, creating not only an inconvenience but also the potential for additional social isolation. Getting a driver's license is often thought of as a "rite of passage" for young people in Western society, and being physically restricted from this process imposes considerable hardship on teenagers with visual impairments (Chase, 1986; Corn & Rosenblum, 2000; Corn & Sacks, 1994; Erin & Wolffe, 1999; Lowenfeld, 1971; Wolffe, 2000). Driving is an important milestone in the developmental process, and youngsters who will not be able to drive need support from their families and friends to participate actively in social and vocational activities. In addition, these youngsters need to learn how to negotiate and solve transportation challenges that will only increase with the demands of adult responsibilities.

A significant social characteristic of middle and late adolescence among typically developing adolescents is a sharp delineation between their interaction strategies for same-sex and opposite-sex relationships. Although they continue to use groups for social contact and interaction, there is a growing tendency toward forming more enduring sexual pairs. There is also a concerted movement away from the birth-family system; adolescents expend far more effort to influence and impress peers and other people who are outside their families (Steinberg & Morris, 2001). It is important to note that there are also gender differences in the friendships developed during middle and late adolescence. Girls tend to be more expressive with their friends, placing more value on frankness, sensitivity, trust, loyalty, and exclusiveness. Boys tend to be more instrumental with their friends (interested in doing things with tools or instruments rather than delving into feelings), placing greater value on giving and sharing materially and engaging in activities based on common interests (Camarena, Sarigiani, & Petersen, 1990).

The emphasis on developing relationships outside of the familial system entails the expectation that young adults with visual impairments can and will attract partners of the opposite or, in some instances, same sex. However, this developmental milestone may also prove difficult for many teenagers because of an underlying assumption of Western society, which communicates the message that being intact physically is critical to life satisfaction. The most popular young adults are often those who look most attractive and who have no apparent cosmetic flaws. This notion of a "perfect" body causes many adolescents significant duress. Sighted youngsters spend an inordinate amount of time in front of their mirrors, scrutinizing their appearance.

They gain and lose weight as they judge themselves to be too skinny or too fat to fit the "body perfect" image; they paint their faces and dye their hair, tattoo and pierce their body parts, and make an effort to dress differently than adults and younger children as they emulate popular musicians, athletic superstars, and film characters. Adolescents experiment with matching their body and appearance to the current popular image of "body perfect" (Elkind, 1984; Fenwick & Smith, 1996; Wolf, 1991; Wolffe, 2000).

Without good, functional vision, it is difficult to engage in this kind of experimentation with appearance and self-image. Young people with visual impairments may have trouble discerning how their appearance fits the social norm, unless someone with good vision is willing to give them honest feedback. If youngsters have any kind of overt cosmetic flaw, such as damaged eyes or facial scarring, the task of fitting the "body perfect" mold becomes nearly impossible. Often children with cosmetic flaws are teased at school and at play, contributing to a poor body image, which in turn affects their self-esteem. Even without overt cosmetic flaws, any deviation from the norm (which is manifested by having an intact physical self, including fully functional eyesight) may be perceived negatively by both the teen with the visual impairment and his or her age-mates, with a negative impact on self-esteem (Tuttle & Tuttle, 1996).

Positive self-esteem is the first internal capacity or resource for developing social competence (Peterson & Leigh, 1990). Studies dealing with the impact of visual impairment on self-concept and self-esteem have been contradictory (Beaty, 1991, 1994; Head, 1979; Hurre, Komulainen, & Aro, 1999; Meigan, 1971; Tuttle & Tuttle, 1996). The studies consistently indicate, however, that visually impaired young people who have positive support from their families and strong peer networks have higher levels of self-esteem than those without such supports (Hurre, Komulainen, & Aro, 1999; Kef, 1997; Rosenblum, 1997; Wolffe & Sacks, 1997; Wolffe, 2000). (See Chapter 5 for a more in-depth discussion of self-esteem.)

In addition to cosmetic or surface appearance, the way young people present themselves overall is a significant issue in adolescence. Teenagers often affect certain ways of walking, sitting, standing, and posturing that are indicative of how they feel, how they want to be seen, and how they see themselves. In some cases, their movements and mannerisms may identify them as belonging to specific cliques or social groupings. Certainly, how they walk or move through space tells those around them about their comfort level and how well they "fit in" to the social milieu. Children who are congenitally blind or severely visually impaired may have difficulty conforming to such socially appropriate behaviors. For example, those youngsters may have skipped early developmental stages (for instance, the critical crawling stage), leading to the development of noticeable differences in gait, posture, and fluidity of movement (Ferrell, 1986). In addition, the tendency of some visually impaired students to engage in stereotypic mannerisms, such as rocking, eye poking, or flicking their hands will tend to negatively influence their sighted peers (MacCuspie, 1996). Such observable differences between sighted and visually impaired youngsters are likely to cause difficulties for the visually impaired youths who are trying to "fit in." Teenagers do not necessarily conform to the adult world in which they live, but they conform avidly to the teenage world they aspire to join. This means that the behaviors and mannerisms that they adopt must fit the behaviors and mannerisms demonstrated by their friends or those they wish to join, because anything that sets someone apart from the strictures of those cliques or groups is likely to be disdained. One useful strategy that teachers, parents, and other caring adults can use to help youngsters with visual impairments navigate the challenges of adolescence is described in "Theory to Practice: Fitting In."

To this point in the chapter, the discussion has centered around adolescent development with an examination of possible biological and social implications in adolescence for youths with visual impairments. To better understand the overall impact of vision loss on the development of children and adolescents with visual loss, the following section explores a number of pertinent research studies.

# RESEARCH ON VISION LOSS AND DEVELOPMENT

Researchers investigating the impact of blindness or severe vision loss on child development describe evidence of both similarities and differences in the early development of children who are blind or have low vision and those who are fully sighted (Deitz & Ferrell, 1994; Ferrell, 1996a; Ferrell, 2000; Fraiberg, 1977). Initially, there appears to be little if any difference in the physical development of infants from either group. However, as babies grow up, differences emerge. Blind

# Theory to Practice

## FITTING IN

Professionals and family members working with adolescents and young adults who are visually impaired to develop social competence need to have some familiarity with current teen culture and trends if they are to help these youngsters to be comfortable and "fit in" at school and in the community. One of the most useful strategies is to observe and interview fully sighted youngsters of a similar age. In such an interview, a 13 year old without disabilities explained his impression of what it takes to fit in his school environment (T. McDaniel, personal communication, December 2003):

- wearing the correct clothes
- listening to what and who other students are talking about
- participating in extracurricular activities, such as band
- engaging in socially acceptable activities outside of school, such as garage bands
- paying attention to the classroom teacher (not being disruptive)
- treating other students with consideration

The young man also shared his list of what he considered "trendy" among his peers:

- instant messaging
- video game stations and handheld games
- all games and activities imitating "Xtreme" sports
- music
- television
- movies
- sports equipment such as bicycles and skateboards
- general activities, such as hanging out at the mall, jamming with other teenagers, and ogling at "suped-up" cars

Such lists will vary over time as well as from community to community and from youngster to youngster, but the essence of the activity is to determine what is considered trendy in the visually impaired youngster's own community. Concerned adults can interview sighted peers such as members of the immediate or extended family, young people in the neighborhood or with whom they attend religious or civic activities, or the children of friends and relatives. When selecting subjects for an interview, it is important to consider youngsters who are in the same age range, attend the same or similar schools, and who are the same gender as the student of concern. Although observations can also help adults evaluate what things and activities are trendy, one-on-one interviews seem to provide the most in-depth information.

babies frequently are delayed in walking, reaching, and pulling up. As infants and toddlers grow, the differences between blind and sighted children seem to increase albeit only significantly when multiple disabilities are present (Ferrell, 1996a; 2000). Longitudinal studies (such as the Canadian follow-up study detailed later in this section) give empirical evidence that these differences dissipate and may well disappear over the life span of an individual (Freeman, Goetz, Richards, & Groenveld, 1991).

Age at onset of visual impairment is also a significant factor that how it affects development. The older the child is when vision loss occurs, the more likely it is that the child will have acquired basic psychomotor skills through visual channels; therefore less delay in development of those skills will be evidenced. Conversely, the earlier the onset of visual impairment, the greater the effect will be on all areas of a child's development, including spatial awareness, mobility, non-verbal communication, personality, and general information. Making up for early developmental deficits is qualitatively and quantitatively different from restoring or substituting for abilities that a person has acquired (Freeman, 1987; Scholl, 1986).

By adolescence, many of an individual's behaviors and patterns are in place. However, the developmental process does not end at a particular age; in fact, many developmental milestones are achieved during adolescence. A limited number of studies have examined the impact of vision loss on adolescent development; a number of the most recent ones are described in the sections that follow.

## CANADIAN FOLLOW-UP STUDY

An important study to mention in reference to adolescent development is the Canadian follow-up study reported on by Freeman and his colleagues (Freeman, Goetz, Richards, & Groenveld, 1991). This was a follow-up of a 1973–74 study of young children who were legally blind (Jan, Freeman, & Scott, 1977) to determine the status of those same individuals as adults; 69 of the 92 individuals in the original study also participated in the follow-up study. With the exception of cognition, the longitudinal follow-up study looked at the same variables as the original study: social-emotional functioning, health, vision, mannerisms, and family. Highlights of the researchers' findings follow:

- Just over half (54.5 percent) of the 57 participants who could be questioned on the subject of marriage and sexuality reported having had a romantic relationship.

- With the exception of a few participants who had multiple disabilities, almost all stereotypic mannerisms had disappeared from the individuals in the sample. Some participants shared that they still engaged in their mannerisms when they were alone; however, they understood the negative social effect of mannerisms on sighted people. None of the participants credited any systemic treatment program with having helped them eliminate their behaviors; most indicated that they had stopped the behavior because family and friends had told them that their mannerisms were unacceptable.

- Many of the participants took more than the typical four years to complete their secondary school programs.

- Thirty-nine percent of the participants were employed (46.7 percent of the men and 32.7 percent of the women).

- Seventy-one percent of the sample participated in some regular sports or physical fitness program.

The researchers point out that most of these young adults were doing remarkably well without the help of sophisticated and systematic intervention; in fact, they were performing better than anticipated. However, the researchers were unable to locate the original control group for comparisons, making conclusions difficult to draw. In addition, many of the original participants with low vision refused to acknowledge their visual differences and tended to "pass" as normally sighted individuals. The researchers noted their participants' reports of social isolation, especially during the junior high school, and suggested that there might well be some benefit to developing interactive programs to improve the social skills of both blind people and sighted people when they deal with visually impaired people. The benefit of such a program might well be a decrease in this reported isolation.

## SOCIAL NETWORK PILOT PROJECT STUDY

In the mid- to late 1990s, researchers in the United States undertook a series of studies called the Social Network Pilot Project (SNPP), in which they examined how adolescents with visual disabilities, both blind and with low vision, compared to their sighted peers in major life areas (Sacks & Wolffe, 1998; Sacks, Wolffe, & Tierney, 1998; Wolffe & Sacks, 1995, 1997). Low vision was defined as vision impaired to the point that students were listed on special education rosters as visually impaired, but were not functionally blind. In other words, their primary learning modality was through vision rather than touch. The results are summarized in the following sections.

Students with visual impairments who participated in the project reported no other disabling conditions and were functioning close to grade level. However, due to the limited number of participants who completed the project (48 dyads consisting of young people and their parents), it is important not to overgeneralize the results, but rather to consider them as *possible* indicators of adolescents' behaviors.

### Academics

Students who were blind and students who were sighted reported receiving grades of As and Bs, while most of the students with low vision were making Bs and Cs. The greatest differences among groups in the academic area were sources of help with homework and where students studied. Blind students reported receiving help from six sources: parent, sibling, friend, tutor, paid reader, and volunteer. Students with low vision reported receiving help from four sources: parent, sibling, friend, and tutor. Although one-fifth of the sighted students reported receiving no assistance, those who did receive help identified three sources: parent, friend, or tutor.

The other difference between the sighted and the visually impaired students was where they studied. Only students who were blind or had low vision reported studying in classroom settings and with the guidance of a teacher. All groups reported studying at home, in the public library or school library, and at the homes of friends.

## Employment

Although the vast majority of the students (88 percent of the blind students and 94 percent of those who had low vision or were sighted) had worked for pay, the most significant difference among the students was how they had obtained their jobs. While 81 percent of sighted students reported finding their own jobs, only 31 percent of low vision students and 19 percent of blind students did likewise. For the most part, teachers and counselors were responsible for finding jobs for the students with visual impairments. Another difference was the kind of work students were doing. The majority of blind students (75 percent) had clerical jobs and worked at school. By contrast, the sighted students worked outside the school environment and evidenced a more even distribution of work activities (tutoring, teaching private lessons, babysitting, and working in retail establishments).

## Activities of Daily Living

When performing money management, time management, and personal management tasks, students with visual impairments were similar to their sighted counterparts. The most obvious differences among the participants were in the home management area: performing household chores, grocery shopping, cleaning, cooking, and general housekeeping responsibilities. Students with low vision reported having the least amount of responsibility for performing home management tasks, and blind students reported having only slightly more responsibility. Sighted students reported having considerably more responsibility at home than students with visual impairments. The greatest discrepancies occurred in activities centered on cooking, helping with yard work, and simple clothing repairs.

Both parents and students were asked what kinds of assistance they anticipated would be necessary for youths to live independently in the future. All participants anticipated an ongoing need for financial assistance into the foreseeable future. However, financial assistance was the only kind of assistance the students without visual disabilities and their parents expected them to need. On the other hand, 50 percent of the parents of students with visual impairments anticipated that their children would need financial assistance, as well as assistance with household and personal management tasks and transportation. Blind students likewise felt they would need assistance in all areas identified; students with low vision felt they would need assistance in all areas except personal management.

## Social Activities

According to the reports of both students and parents, the sighted students in this sample were the most active socially. The types of social interactions that took place after school were differentiated by the students' degree of vision loss. Sighted students and their parents reported that these students spent their time almost exclusively with friends and only occasionally with parents or siblings. By contrast, the majority of visually impaired students and their parents reported that they spent their time after school alone. Only 25 percent of students who were blind or had low vision reported that they spent time after school with friends. Overall, students with low vision appeared to be involved in the fewest activities and were the least likely to be in social situations that involved lots of other people.

## Use of Time

When researchers looked at how the students were spending their time, they found noticeable differences among the participants in the length of preparation time students needed for activities. Participants who were blind or had low vision tended to take longer to prepare for activities than sighted participants.

There were also differences among the groups in terms of their friendship networks and their levels of interaction within their friendship networks. Overall, participants who were blind or had low vision reported fewer social interactions than did the sighted participants. Students with low vision reported greater amounts of time devoted to sleeping than either blind or sighted students. Students with low vision were engaged in the most passive activities (watching television, listening to the radio, reading, playing a musical instrument alone, and the like); blind students were somewhat less so. The sighted students were the least involved in passive leisure activities.

The SNPP, although limited in size and intended solely as a pilot project, provided empirical documentation of the similarities and differences in lifestyles and social support systems between adolescents with visual impairments and their sighted counterparts. In summary, the results indicated that students who were blind or had low vision tended to be on fairly equal footing with their sighted peers in academic achievement and nearly so in activities of daily living. The two areas of greatest discrepancy in evidence were employment and social skills. With restricted access to vocational opportunities and a tendency to gravitate to passive rather than active social pursuits, youngsters with visual impairments need additional supports or intervention in these areas to be fully integrated into their communities.

# RESEARCH ON SOCIAL SKILLS AND ADOLESCENTS WITH VISUAL IMPAIRMENTS

Current research on social skills and youngsters with visual impairments has addressed their ability to form and maintain best friendships (Rosenblum, 1997, 1998) and relationship building in general (Kef, 1997, 1999). Other researchers have investigated how professionals and sighted classmates in academic environments can promote the social inclusion of youths with visual impairments, including those with multiple disabilities (Goetz & O'Farrell, 1999; MacCuspie, 1996). Researchers have also studied how college students with visual impairments perceive their social integration (Hodges & Keller, 1999) and the relationship between social networks and the employment of college graduates who are blind or have low vision (Roy, Dimigen, & Taylor, 1998). In addition, researchers have looked at the impact of physical activity on the acquisition of a positive self concept (Grønmo & Augestad, 2000), the relationship between parenting styles and self-esteem (Cardinali & D'Allura, 2001), effects of physical features associated with albinism on the self-esteem of African American youths (Gold, 2002), the relationship between social support and self-esteem (Huurre, 2000; Huurre & Aro, 1997; Huurre, Komulainen, & Aro, 1999), and differences in the lifestyles of students with low vision, students who are blind, and students who are sighted (Wolffe & Sacks, 1997; Sacks & Wolffe, 1998; Sacks, Wolffe, & Tierney, 1998).

A few research projects have looked at specific aspects of social awareness and social behavior in children and youths with visual impairments. For example, Kaufman (2000) looked at the clothing-selection habits of teenage girls who are sighted and those who are blind, while Frame (2000) and Sharkey et al. (2000) studied the relationship between visual impairment and gestures, and Kim (2003) investigated the effects of assertiveness training on enhancing social skills. Other researchers have looked at the acquisition of social skills by youngsters from other countries and cultures (Grønmo & Augestad, 2000; Huurre, 2000; Kef, 1997; Kroksmark & Nordell, 2001; Sharma, Sigafoos, and Carroll, 2000). The following sections provide a brief review of the findings from the most significant of these recent studies.

## RELATIONSHIP BUILDING AND SOCIAL INTEGRATION

Rosenblum's (1997, 1998) studies on the ability of teenagers with visual impairments to form and maintain best friendships found that although these adolescents had best friends, they tended to have fewer friends overall than their friends with vision. As in research with nondisabled adolescents (Camarena, Sarigiani, & Petersen, 1990; Duck, 1988, 1991), the females in Rosenblum's study had more best friends than did the males. The friends (visually impaired and sighted) identified in these studies were similar to one another in gender, ethnicity, age, and life experiences. An interesting finding is that the activities the friends reported doing together were no different than those of other adolescents whose friendships did not include visually impaired students: talking on the telephone, visiting one another's homes, attending school and extracurricular activity events, and sharing hobbies. However, for approximately half the dyads studied, the friends felt that the visual impairment negated some of the things that the friends could do together, such as attending films or engaging in team sports. The young, visually impaired people in Rosenblum's study identified the initial meeting of a potential friend as the greatest challenge to developing personal relationships. The difficulty these youngsters reported in making friends is consistent with findings in a Finnish study of adolescents (Huurre & Aro, 1997; Huurre, Komulainen, & Aro, 1999; Huurre, 2000).

In one of the most ambitious studies to date, Kef (1999) analyzed data collected on 354 Dutch adolescents between 14 and 24 years old. All the subjects had visual impairments; 19 percent were blind, 18 percent were severely visually impaired, 63 percent were moderately visually impaired; and 58 percent had stable eye conditions. Fifty-three percent of the participants were male and 47 percent were female. Kef's study focused on the ability of the youths to build and maintain relationships, the makeup of their social networks, and their sources of social and emotional support.

Kef determined that the visually impaired subjects had slightly smaller networks than those of sighted individuals in their age range: an average of 15 network members versus 20 for the sighted youngsters. The factors that she found could predict the size of her subjects' social networks were type of vision problem (stable versus progressive disorder) and age; younger subjects with stable disorders tended to have smaller networks. The largest subgroup within the networks of the visually impaired participants consisted of friends (28 percent), followed by close family members (26 percent), and extended family members (18 percent). Thirteen percent were people they knew from school or work, 6 percent were club members, 5 percent of the individuals in their networks were reported to be professionals, 3 percent were neighbors, and 1 percent were members of their living group.

The study participants noted that 24 percent of their friends were other visually impaired people. Although friends made up the largest sector of the personal networks of young people with visual impairments, 60 percent of the participants stated that they wished for more sighted friends and more opportunities to do things with sighted peers. Of concern was Kef's finding that 8 percent of the visually impaired adolescents stated that they had no friends. Although this rate is lower than the 18 percent in an earlier study (Walther, 1994, cited in Kef, 1999) who reported that they had no friends, it is still more than reported in Kef's sighted control group (3 percent).

Overall, Kef's study evidenced far more positive than negative psychosocial characteristics when compared to earlier studies of visually impaired adolescents (Cowen, Underberg, Verrillo, & Benham, 1961; Eaglestein, 1975; Jan, Freeman, & Scott, 1977; Van Hasselt, 1983). The majority of young people in Kef's study had friends and positive support networks that closely approximated the networks of sighted youths, albeit the networks of the visually impaired group were smaller. Her results parallel those of Huurre and Aro (1998), who investigated the psychosocial development of Finnish adolescents with visual impairments (details of this study appear later in this chapter). The young people in Kef's study seemed to be faring reasonably well in adolescence, with friends and family providing the bulk of their social support, as is the case with sighted adolescents. Although the networks of the visually impaired adolescents were smaller than those of the sighted control group, their networks were still diverse. The greatest single concern seemed to be the lack of dating experiences among the adolescents with visual impairments.

MacCuspie's (1996) qualitative study of visually impaired Canadian students focused on the social impact of the inclusion of these students in mainstream academic environments. Although MacCuspie studied elementary school students, her findings have relevance for those working with teenagers and young adults. For example, she found that within the context of the elementary school culture, opportunities for interaction between children with visual impairments and their sighted peers were significantly fewer than those among children without disabilities. Without such opportunities to interact, children with visual impairments are at risk for not establishing friendships. If students with visual impairments leave elementary school without having established friendships and feelings of social acceptance there, it seems likely that they will experience even greater difficulty doing so in the less socially structured milieu of secondary and postsecondary settings.

MacCuspie also determined that the inclusion of students with visual impairments into regular classrooms did not result in positive social skill development; in fact, visually impaired students faced a potentially hostile social environment, in which the faculty tended to ignore their difficulties. MacCuspie's work underscores the complexity of the integration process and the need for structured intervention on the part of educators to build socially inclusive environments.

## Self-Concept and Self-Esteem

Self-esteem and a positive self-concept are key elements in the development of social skills, which are discussed in detail in Chapter 5. The studies briefly described here focus specifically on self-concept and self-esteem in adolescents with visual impairments.

Grønmo and Augestad (2000) found that competence in physical activities and overall fitness seemed to promote a positive self-concept. Cardinali and D'Allura (2001) investigated the relationship between parenting styles of mothers of children with visual impairments and subsequent self-esteem of their children as they became young adults. They looked at three parenting styles: permissive, authoritative, and authoritarian. (See Chapter 5 for a discussion of parenting styles.) Overall, the results indicated that parenting style does have an impact on children's self-esteem, and the strongest positive relationship is attributable to the mothers' reported authoritative parenting. However, the study evidenced such mixed results regarding the impact of parenting styles on the self-esteem of children with visual impairments that it is important to bear in mind the results of the extensive studies of adolescent socialization and parenting style undertaken during the 1990s (Darling & Steinberg, 1993; Steinberg, 2002; Steinberg & Morris, 2001), even though they were undertaken with adolescents without disabilities. These studies replicated Baumrind's (1971) seminal studies of parental influence that indicated that children whose parents were authoritative (firm but warm in their parenting style) showed a greater degree of psychosocial maturity and better adolescent adjustment.

Huurre (2000) and her colleagues (Huurre & Aro, 1997; Huurre, Komulainen, & Aro, 1999) compared the social support and self-esteem of sighted and visually impaired adolescents. According to Huurre (2000), social support is provided by three sources, with the primary source of social support being family and close friends. Other friends, relatives, workmates, and neighbors provide secondary social support; while professionals and authority figures provide tertiary social support. The findings reported by Huurre and her colleagues indicated that although there were no statistically significant differences in the self-esteem of these two groups of adolescents, the self-esteem of young women with visual impairments tended to be lower than the self-esteem of their fully sighted counterparts. The visually impaired young women also had significantly fewer relationships with friends and less perceived support from friends than the fully sighted youths. For both young men and women with visual impairments, relationships with friends contributed significantly to positive self-esteem.

Predictors of high self-esteem in this study included having many friends, fitting in easily with other young people, and ease in making friends. As in the MacCuspie (1996) study, however, these researchers noted that placing adolescents with visual impairments in the same classrooms with students who are not visually impaired does not necessarily lead to interactions between the youths; nor does it automatically foster positive self-esteem among students with visual impairments.

What the theories and studies presented in this chapter indicate is the evolutionary process from dependence to independence, and beyond to interdependence, that seems to culminate in adolescence. Children grow up in a fairly predictable fashion to become young adults who want to establish themselves as entities apart from, but still connected to, their families. The following section discusses this evolutionary process with implications for adolescents who have visual impairments.

## THE EVOLUTION FROM DEPENDENCE TO INTERDEPENDENCE

Although adolescents may act in ways that appear selfish and egocentric, their outward appearance of bravado often masks feelings of insecurity. While these acting-out behaviors may be irksome, they are an important part of building confidence (Fenwick & Smith, 1996). By acting as if they are in control and comfortable with themselves, teens can influence the people around them to think of them in a similar way. Ideally, they will receive positive feedback from their peers and families when they are behaving well (in a socially acceptable manner) and that will help build their self-esteem. They need to know when they look good and when they are performing well. In addition, they need to hear that the people in their lives care about them even when they misbehave and that correcting unacceptable behaviors is indicative of caring and concern. If they don't receive such feedback, their insecurities may multiply, and the response is often to act out more and more outrageously.

A lack of underlying self-confidence is often compounded for youngsters with visual disabilities because their efforts to act out and behave in rebellious ways are often thwarted by their inability to observe this kind of behavior in other teenagers and to see who is around to notice their behavior. This inability to effectively mimic the style of a particular peer group makes it more difficult for teenagers with visual disabilities to fit into social groups or cliques.

Teen involvement with peer groups is an important developmental process that sets the stage for future separation from parents and families. Emotional issues surrounding dependence, independence, and interdependence are often at the crux of many adolescents' seemingly rebellious and self-centered behavior. Early on in adolescence, there is an almost constant struggle between the desire to stay safely within the dependent structure of the family and the desire to experiment with self-rule. As adolescents mature, they move toward mutually beneficial, interdependent relationships. Peer-group involvement is perhaps most intense in the junior high school years, before interest in members of the opposite sex begins to encourage the partnering that is more common in the high school years (Fenwick & Smith, 1996; Steinberg & Morris, 2001).

Often parents, teachers, and other well-meaning adults in the lives of many visually impaired students tend to shelter or overprotect them, which results in a tendency for these teenagers to be socially immature. In addition, Western society tends to support the notion that people with disabilities remain "children" for life. Behavior is contextual; people act in ways that reflect the expectations or perceived expectations of those around them (Chase, 2001). If youngsters with visual impairments are not asked to assume routine chores or asked to be independent, the message they receive is that others do not expect much of them, that they can do little or nothing for themselves, and that they are unable or unworthy (Wolffe, 1999). Overprotecting also impedes the social and emotional development of young people with visual impairments.

## DEPENDENCE, INDEPENDENCE, INTERDEPENDENCE

As previously indicated, separation from parents or primary caregivers is a critical issue in the social development of the lives of adolescents, including those with visual impairments. This is typically manifested by teenagers' rebellious attitudes and behaviors. Teenage rebellion against the strictures of their parents' home and rules is as natural as the sun rising in the east; it is part of the natural evolution from dependence to independence that typically occurs in adolescence during the transition from childhood to adulthood. Generally, it is only in adulthood that people come to appreciate the beauty of interdependence in relationships.

## DEPENDENCE

Children from birth through early adolescence are, of necessity, dependent upon their parents or other primary adult caregivers. A dependent is a person who needs ongoing support from others in order to function (Wolffe, 1998). Dependence is both a social and emotional state and may include reliance on others for all or only some activities necessary for daily living. Some activities in which children and adolescents are generally dependent on a parent or caregiver include provision and management of shelter; acquiring nourishment and nutritional guidance; grooming and personal care; health care; time and money management; advocacy and communication with authority figures; problem solving and decision making; travel, play and leisure arrangements; and formal education and informal learning. The critical element or issue is that dependence involves more than one person being in control or in a decision-making role in an individual's life.

Young children are dependent upon their parents and other caregivers for sustenance, guidance, protection, and most other life functions. As children grow and mature, they are expected to assume more and more responsibility for themselves and become less and less dependent upon the adults in their lives. In the United States, parents are legally responsible for their children until they are 18 years of age, unless arrangements have been made to extend their protection and support through limited or unlimited guardianship. Although some individuals with severe multiple disabilities will require assistance throughout their lives, it is unusual for individuals to require assistance in all areas of functioning; total dependence on others for life is rare.

The norm is for individuals to gain some independence over time as they mature, regardless of their disabling conditions.

For youngsters who are blind or visually impaired, dependence on others may be prolonged due to the nature of their disabilities. They learn to rely on others for assistance with activities in which vision is an asset; for example, reading menus, price tags, handwritten notes from teachers or friends, and so forth; getting to and from places easily by car; moving easily and comfortably in an unknown environment; and choosing clothes or gifts that will appeal to the sighted individuals in their lives. In addition, they learn to depend on others for help in tasks that are more quickly or more efficiently accomplished by sighted individuals, such as making a bed, mowing a lawn, tidying the house or apartment, washing the dog, weeding the garden, and so forth. Unless visually impaired youngsters are encouraged to do such chores or activities for themselves and are taught alternative techniques to do them effectively, they may become very comfortable relying on others. This is a serious risk to the independence of youngsters with visual impairments that is perpetuated when people continue to do tasks for these youngsters instead of giving them the opportunity to try various activities for themselves.

## INDEPENDENCE

Independence means that an individual is solely responsible for certain activities of daily living and decision making. An independent person typically can live alone, care for him- or herself, get to and from school or work without assistance, and generally manage his or her own personal, social, vocational, and avocational affairs. With independence comes responsibility for oneself and one's possessions or surroundings. Typically, children gain independence over time. In their early years, children are taught first to take care of themselves and second to take care of their possessions. Independence is an important social and emotional milestone. Many young people go to great lengths to attempt to demonstrate their independence, but to gain independence, children have to be given responsibilities and taught how to handle them. They have to be allowed to try out their newfound skills and be allowed to either succeed or fail in attempting to perform them. If they succeed, they need to receive praise and encouragement to continue to apply what they have learned. If they fail, they need to receive support and encouragement to try alternative techniques that will help them successfully accomplish the task. In some activities—personal hygiene, for example—independence is expected of anyone who is physically capable of performing the specific task. However, in other activities—raising and training a pet, for example—independence is negotiable; a person may share the responsibility with a sibling or a parent, or perform all the activities associated with this responsibility alone.

When children and youths with visual impairments learn to manage aspects of their lives independently, the challenge frequently becomes convincing those around them to let them practice the technique. For example, when a youngster learns how to sweep or mop a floor, he or she needs to be allowed to perform the task even if it takes a bit longer or it is less than perfectly executed. It is through practice that the child achieves better results, and it is by doing such things independently that the youngster acquires self-confidence and the resultant feelings of self-worth. The other big challenge to achieving independence is learning how to thwart well-intentioned strangers who assume visually impaired people need help with everything. Visually impaired youths must find an internal comfort level that enables them to thank an individual for offering unneeded help and simultaneously stymie the person's efforts by being assertive without being rude or offensive.

## INTERDEPENDENCE

Interdependence is a higher order social-emotional state in which an individual does some things without assistance and some things with assistance. Inherent in the concept of interdependence is the notion of reciprocity—exchanges between people of energies, efforts, and assistance. In interdependence, there is a sharing among individuals of what each does best. In interdependent relationships people rely on one another and encourage that reliance. Interdependence is also about sharing responsibilities and working together to make life more enjoyable and comfortable for all. Interpersonal relationships typically achieve interdependence when the parties respect one another and pool their talents to make a better life for themselves and their families or extended families. Social units such as communities or tribes of people are interdependent; they each rely on all the members to maintain the social unit.

Interdependence is integral to social integration and therefore a critical life goal for students with disabilities (Wolffe, 1998). Students with visual impairments need to be exposed to the concept of interdependence and encouraged to work toward establishing relationships with others whose talents and interests complement their own. They need to learn that interdependence does not mean abdicating responsibility for taking care of oneself; rather, people who are interdependent take care of themselves and help those they care about to do the things that they can do best. Interdependence is about the sharing of talents and skills so that all participants in the relationship are more comfortable and everyone can benefit.

## CONCLUSION

The theories and research on the psychosocial development of adolescents presented in this chapter illuminate the impact that visual impairment may have on teenagers and how it can affect their progress in developing the social skills needed for successful interdependence in our society. Chapter 12 will examine the implications of this theoretical foundation for teaching social skills and provides specific strategies and suggestions for working with students in this age group.

## REFERENCES

Anderson, E. M., & Clarke, L. (1982). *Disability in adolescence.* London: Methuen & Co.

Bandura, A. (1977). *Social learning theory.* Englewood Cliffs, NJ: Prentice-Hall.

Bandura, A. (1979). *Principles of behavior modification.* New York: Holt, Rinehart, & Winston.

Bandura, A. (1986). *Social foundations of thought and action: A social cognitive theory.* Englewood Cliffs, NJ: Prentice Hall.

Bandura, A. (1989). Social cognitive theory. *Annals of Child Development, 6,* 1–60.

Baumrind, D. (1971). Current patterns of parental authority. *Developmental Psychology Monographs, 4*(1, Pt. 2), 1–103.

Beaty, L. A. (1991). The effects of visual impairments on adolescents' self-concept. *Journal of Visual Impairment & Blindness, 85*(3), 129–130.

Beaty, L. A. (1994). Psychological factors and academic success of visually impaired college students. *RE:view, 26,* 131–139.

Bee, H. (1997). *The developing child* (8th ed.). New York: Addison-Wesley.

Cairns, R. B. (1986). A contemporary perspective on social development. In P. S. Stain, M. J. Guralnick, & H. M. Walker (Eds.), *Children's social behavior: Development, assessment, and modification.* Orlando, FL: Academic Press.

Camarena, P. M., Sarigiani, P. A., & Petersen, A. C. (1990). Gender-specific pathways to intimacy in early adolescence. *Journal of Youth and Adolescence, 19*(1), 19–32.

Cardinali, G., & D'Allura, T. (2001). Parenting styles and self-esteem: A study of young adults with visual impairments. *Journal of Visual Impairment & Blindness, 95*, 261–271.

Chase, J. B. (1986). Psychoeducational assessment of visually-impaired learners. In P. J. Lazarus & S. S. Stirchart (Eds.), *Psychoeducational evaluation of children & adolescents with low-incidence handicaps* (pp. 41–74). Orlando, FL: Grune & Stratton.

Chase, J. B. (2001). Technology and the use of tools: Psychological and social factors. In B. Silverstone, M. A. Lang, B. P. Rosenthal, & E. E. Faye (Eds.), *The Lighthouse handbook on vision impairment and vision rehabilitation.* New York: Oxford University Press.

Corn, A. L., & Rosenblum, L. P. (2000) *Finding wheels.* Austin, TX: PRO-ED.

Corn, A., & Sacks, S. Z. (1994). The impact of nondriving on adults with visual impairments. *Journal of Visual Impairment & Blindness, 88*(1), 53–68.

Cowen, E. L., Underberg, R. P., Verrillo, R. T., & Benham, F. G. (1961). *Adjustment to visual disability in adolescence.* New York: American Foundation for the Blind.

Damon, W. (Ed.). (1983). *Social and personality development.* New York: W. W. Norton.

Darling, N., & Steinberg, L. (1993). Parenting style as context: An integrative model. *Psychological Bulletin, 3*, 487–496.

Dasberg, L. (1983). A historical and transcultural view of adolescence. In W. Everaerd, C. B. Hindley, A. Bot, & J. J. van der Werff ten Bosch (Eds.), *Development in adolescence: Psychological, social and biological aspects* (pp. 1–15). Boston: Martinus Nilhoff Publishers.

Deitz, S. J., & Ferrell, K. A. (1994). Project PRISM: A national collaborative study on the early development of children with visual impairments. *Journal of Visual Impairment & Blindness, 88*, 470–472.

Duck, S. (1988). *Relating to others.* Milton Keynes: Open University Press.

Duck, S. (1991). *Friends, for life: The psychology of personal relationships.* Hertfordshire, UK: Harvester Wheatsheaf.

Dworetzky, J. P. (1981). *Introduction to child development.* St. Paul, MN: West Publishing Co.

Eaglestein, A. S. (1975). The social acceptance of blind high school students in an integrated setting. *New Outlook for the Blind, 69*, 447–451.

Elkind, D. (1984). *All grown up and no place to go: Teenagers in crisis.* Reading, MA: Addison-Wesley.

Erikson, E. H. (1963). *Childhood and society* (2nd ed.). New York: Norton.

Erikson, E. H. (1980). *Identity and the life cycle.* New York: Norton. (Original work published 1959.)

Erin, J. N., & Wolffe, K. E. (1999). *Transition issues related to students with visual disabilities.* Austin, TX: PRO-ED.

Fenwick, E., & Smith, T. (1996). *Adolescence: The survival guide for parents and teenagers*. London: Dorling Kindersley Limited.

Ferrell, K. A. (1986). Infancy and early childhood. In G. T. Scholl (Ed.), *Foundations of education for blind and visually handicapped children and youth* (pp. 119–135). New York: American Foundation for the Blind.

Ferrell, K. A. (1996, October). PRISM update. Paper presented at American Printing House for the Blind annual meeting, Louisville, KY.

Ferrell, K. A. (1996). Your child's development. In M. C. Holbrook (Ed.), *Children with visual impairments: A parents' guide* (pp. 73–96). Bethesda, MD: Woodbine House.

Ferrell, K. A. (2000). Growth and development of young children. In M. C. Holbrook & A. J. Koenig (Eds.), *Foundations of education: Vol. 1: History and theory of teaching children and youths with visual impairments* (2nd ed.; pp. 111–134). New York: AFB Press.

Fraiberg, S. (1977). *Insights from the blind*. New York: Basic Books.

Frame, M. J. (2000). The relationship between visual impairment and gestures. *Journal of Visual Impairment & Blindness, 94*, 155–171.

Freeman, R. D. (1987). Psychosocial interventions with visually impaired adolescents and adults. In B. Heller, L. Flohr, & L. S. Zegans (Eds.), *Psychosocial interventions with sensorially disabled persons* (pp. 153–166). Orlando, FL: Grune & Stratton.

Freeman, R. D., Goetz, E., Richards, D. P., & Groenveld, M. (1991). Defiers of negative prediction: A 14-year follow-up of legally blind children. *Journal of Visual Impairment & Blindness, 85*(9), 365–370.

Freud, S. (1905). The basic writings of Sigmund Freud (A. A. Brill, Trans.) New York: Random House.

Gesell, A. (1928). *Infancy and human growth*. New York: Macmillan.

Gesell, A. (1946). *Developmental diagnosis*. New York: P. Hoeber Publishing.

Gesell, A. (1956). *Youth: Years ten to sixteen*. New York: Harper & Row.

Gesell, A., & Thompson, H. (1929). Learning and growth in identical infant twins: An experimental study of individual differences by the method of co-twin control. *Genetic Psychology Monographs, 6*, 1–124.

Gesell, A., & Thompson, H. (1941). Twins T and C from infancy to adolescence: A biogenetic study of individual differences by the method of co-twin control. *Genetic Psychology Monographs, 24*, 3–121.

Goetz, L., & O'Farrell, N. (2000). Connections: Facilitating social supports for students with deaf-blindness in general education classrooms. *Journal of Visual Impairment & Blindness, 93*, 704–715.

Gold, M. (2002). The effects of the physical features associated with albinism on the self-esteem of African American youths, *Journal of Visual Impairment & Blindness, 96*, 133–142.

Grønmo, S. J., & Augestad, L. B. (2000). Physical activity, self-concept, and global self-worth of blind youths in Norway and France. *Journal of Visual Impairment & Blindness, 94*, 522–527.

Hartup, W. W. (1981). *Symmetries and asymmetries in children's relationships.* ERIC Document No. ED208986.

Hartup, W. W. (1992). *Having friends, making friends, and keeping friends: Relationships as educational contexsts.* ERIC Document No. ED345854.

Hartup, W. W. (1996). Cooperation, close relationships, and cognitive development. In W. M. Bukowski, A. G. Newcomb, & W. W. Hartup (Eds.), *The company they keep: Friendship in childhood and adolescence.* Cambridge, UK: Cambridge University Press.

Head, D. (1979). A comparison of self-concept scores for visually impaired adolescents in several class settings. *Education of the Visually Handicapped, 10,* 51–55.

Hodges, J. S., & Keller, M. J. (1999). Visually impaired students' perceptions of their social integration in college. *Journal of Visual Impairment & Blindness, 93,* 153–165.

Huurre, T. (2000). *Psychosocial development and social support among adolescents with visual impairments.* Finland: Tampere University of Public Health.

Huurre, T., & Aro, H. (2000). The psychosocial well-being of Finnish adolescents with visual impairments versus those with chronic conditions and those with no disabilities. *Journal of Visual Impairment & Blindness, 94,* 625–637.

Huurre, T. M., Komulainen, E. J., & Aro, H. M. (1999). Social support and self-esteem among adolescents with visual impairments. *Journal of Visual Impairment & Blindness, 93*(1), 26–37.

Jan, J. E., Freeman, R. D., & Scott, E. P. (1977). *Visual impairment in children and adolescents.* New York: Grune & Stratton.

Kaufman, A. (2000). Clothing-selection habits of teenage girls who are sighted and blind. *Journal of Visual Impairment & Blindness, 94,* 527–531.

Kef, S. (1997). The personal networks and social supports of blind and visually impaired adolescents. *Journal of Visual Impairment & Blindness, 91*(3), 236–244.

Kef, S. (1999). *Outlook on relations: Personal networks and psychosocial characteristics of visually impaired adolescents.* Amsterdam: Thelathesis.

Kim, Y. (2003). The effects of assertiveness training on enhancing the social skills of adolescents with visual impairments. *Journal of Visual Impairment & Blindness, 97,* 285–297.

Kroksmark, U., & Nordell, K. (2001). Adolescence: The age of opportunities and obstacles for students with low vision in Sweden. *Journal of Visual Impairment & Blindness, 95,* 213–225.

Lorenz, K. Z. (1958). The evolution of behavior. *Scientific American, 199,* 67–78.

Lorenz, K. (1965). *Evolution and modification of behavior.* Chicago: University of Chicago Press.

Lowenfeld, B. (1971). *Our blind children: Growing and learning with them* (3rd ed.). Springfield, IL: Charles C Thomas.

MacCuspie, P. A. (1996). Promoting acceptance of children with disabilities: From tolerance to inclusion. Halifax, Nova Scotia, Canada: Atlantic Provinces Special Education Authority.

Pavlov, I. P. (1927). *Conditioned reflexes.* London: Oxford University Press.

Peterson, G. W., & Leigh, G. K. (1990). The family and social competence in adolescence. In T. P. Gullotta, G. R. Adams, & R. Montemayor (Eds.), *Developing social competency in adolescence* (pp. 97–138). Newbury Park, CA: Sage Productions.

Piaget, J. (1932). *The moral judgement of the child.* New York: Macmillan.

Piaget, J. (1952). *The origins of intelligence in children.* New York: International Universities Press.

Piaget, J. (1977). *The development of thought: Equilibration of cognitive structures.* New York: Viking Press.

Rosenblum, L. P. (1997). Adolescents with visual impairments who have best friends: A pilot study. *Journal of Visual Impairment & Blindness, 91*(3), 224–235.

Rosenblum, L. P. (1998). Best friends of adolescents with visual impairments: A descriptive study. *Journal of Visual Impairment & Blindness, 92*(9), 593–608.

Roy, A.W.N., Dimigen, G., & Taylor, M. (1998). The relationship between social networks and the employment of visually impaired college graduates. *Journal of Visual Impairment & Blindness, 92,* 423–432.

Sacks, S. Z., & Wolffe, K. E. (1998). Lifestyles of adolescents with visual impairments: An ethnographic analysis. *Journal of Visual Impairment & Blindness, 92*(1), 7–17.

Sacks, S. Z., Wolffe, K. E., & Tierney, D. (1998). Lifestyles of students with visual impairments: Preliminary studies of social networks. *Exceptional Children, 64*(4), 463–478.

Salkind, N. J. (1985). *Theories of human development* (2nd ed.). New York: John Wiley & Sons.

Scholl, G. T. (1975). The psychosocial effects of blindness: Implications for program planning in sex education. In *Sex education for the visually handicapped in schools and agencies: Selected papers* (pp. 20–28). New York: American Foundation for the Blind.

Sharkey, W. F., Asamoto, P., Tokunaga, C., Haraguchi, G., & McFaddon-Robar, T. (2000). Hand gestures of visually impaired and sighed interactants. *Journal of Visual Impairment & Blindness, 94,* 549–563.

Sharma, S., Sigagoos, J., & Carroll, A. (2000). Social skills assessment of Indian children with visual impairments. *Journal of Visual Impairment & Blindness, 94,* 172–176.

Skinner, B. F. (1938). *The behavior of organisms: An experimental analysis.* New York: Appleton-Century-Crofts.

Skinner, B. F. (1957). *Verbal behavior.* New York: Appleton-Century-Crofts.

Skinner, B. F. (1976). *Walden two.* New York: Macmillan.

Steinberg, L. (2002). *Adolescence* (6th ed.). Boston: McGraw-Hill.

Steinberg, L., & Morris, A. S. (2001). Adolescent development. *Annual Review of Psychology, 52,* 83–110.

Tanner, J. M. (1962). Growth at adolescence (2nd ed.). Oxford: Blackwell.

Tuttle, D., & Tuttle, N. (1996). Self-esteem and adjusting with blindness (2nd ed.). Springfield, IL: Charles C. Thomas.

Van Hasselt, V. B. (1983). Social acceptance of the blind. *Clinical Psychology Review, 3,* 87–102.

Weiner, I. (1970). *Psychological disturbance in adolescence.* New York: John Wiley.

Wolf, A. E. (1991). *Get out of my life but first could you drive me and Cheryl to the mall?* New York: Noonday Press.

Wolffe, K. E. (1998). Transition planning and employment outcomes for students who have visual impairments with other disabilities. In S. Z. Sacks and R. Silberman (Eds.), *Educating students who have visual impairments with other disabilities.* Baltimore: Paul H. Brookes.

Wolffe, K. E. (Ed.). (1999). *Skills for success: A career education handbook for children and adolescents with visual impairments.* New York: AFB Press.

Wolffe, K. E. (2000). Growth and in middle childhood and adolescence. In M. C. Holbrook, & A. J. Koenig (Eds.), *Foundations of Education, Vol. 1: History and theory of teaching children and youths with visual impairments* (2nd ed.; pp. 135–160). New York: American Foundation for the Blind.

Wolffe, K. E., & Sacks, S. Z. (1995). Social network pilot project: Final report. (Department of Education grant H023A30108). Unpublished manuscript.

Wolffe, K., & Sacks, S. Z. (1997). The social network pilot project: A quantitative comparison of the lifestyles of blind, low vision, and sighted young adults. *Journal of Visual Impairment & Blindness, 91*(3), 245–257.

# The Elements of Social Success

How does one define social success? There are many aspects to the concept of a socially successful human being, and from an individual's perspective, some of those aspects may be more important than others. Most people would agree, however, that strong self-esteem, with its accompanying dimensions of identity and self-worth, is a cornerstone of social success. Healthy and vital friendships with others are also commonly seen as indicators of social competence.

The chapters in Part 3 explore the components of social skillfulness, along with ways in which these components can be supported and enhanced through peer interaction and integration within schools and the community. This section serves as a bridge between the personal and theoretical perspectives presented earlier and the practice of effective social skill interventions.

For students with visual impairments to succeed socially, they need to develop strong identities as individuals with visual impairments. In Chapter 5, Lewis and Wolffe focus on ways in which families and professionals can enhance self-esteem among children and youths who are blind or visually impaired. When students feel good about themselves, they are willing to reach out to others.

Friendship is an essential aspect of positive social relationships. Chapter 6 examines the important elements of friendship and describes how friendships influence the social development of students with visual impairments. Drawing on her own research, Rosenblum provides numerous strategies that families and professionals can use to foster and promote friendships among students who are blind or visually impaired and their sighted and visually impaired age-mates. These strategies are particularly important since the majority of students with visual impairments are included in the general education classroom and need to interact effectively in other community contexts such as leisure and work settings.

Another important influence on the social success of students who are blind or visually impaired is the support of peers and role models to enhance socialization in school, home, and community environments. In Chapter 7, Sacks describes the elements of peer-mediated and peer-support networks, strategies that have been used effectively with students who are blind or visually impaired. She also describes strategies for effectively using role models and mentors to enhance the social competence of visually impaired students and promote interdependence.

Chapter 8 draws on the information provided in the previous chapters to examine ways in which students with visual impairments can be successfully integrated into the social milieu of the general education classroom. MacCuspie describes the influence of the peer culture as a driving force for models of inclusion and provides a model that focuses on collaboration and partnerships among families, teachers, administrators, and support personnel. Examples of strategies to promote social inclusion in the classroom and in the community are included. In Chapter 9, Sacks and Barclay provide a comprehensive overview of social skills assessments for children and youths with visual impairments. They describe numerous social skills assessment techniques and discuss how professionals and families can work together in the assessment process. This chapter includes a variety of sample interviews, observation forms, and samples of specific social skills assessments for students who are blind or visually impaired.

These five chapters set the stage for a comprehensive examination of social skills interventions across age and ability groups. Nurturing self-esteem, developing positive social relationship, enhancing socialization with peers and role models, and finding ways to promote social skills for students with visual impairments in inclusive school and community settings, combined with effective assessment of an individual student's needs, are the elements upon which interventions are based. The scope of this section allows the reader to draw on theory and research and apply them to practice.

# CHAPTER 5

# Promoting and Nurturing Self-Esteem

## Sandra Lewis and Karen E. Wolffe

How people feel about themselves influences their engagement in social relationships with others, while at the same time, the social relationships in which people engage affect how they feel about themselves. When people study the development of social skills, they must investigate the role that self-esteem—one's satisfaction with one's self—plays in that development. In this chapter, the factors that typically influence the development of self-esteem will be described. The threats to the development of a healthy self-esteem in children who have visual impairments will also be discussed. Finally, some ideas for encouraging a positive sense of self in children with visual impairments will be presented.

Sacks & Silberman (2000) describe a three-level schema through which children develop social skills. At the highest level, students achieve cognitive social understanding through the ability to interpret social situations, the awareness of the social needs of others, and the purposeful application of strategies to enhance social competence. Immediately prior to this level, students achieve interactive social skills through their awareness of other people's needs coupled with the use of strategies that facilitate positive interactions. Social awareness and self-identity are at the base of this model.

In fact, the development of a self-identity, or one's set of beliefs about oneself, is one of the primary tasks required of children as they grow from infancy to adulthood. Children are not born with the understanding that they are distinct beings. A rudimentary sense of self-awareness first emerges between 12 months and 2 years of age (Feldman, 2001). It is also during this period that young children first demonstrate early skills of empathy, reflecting a growing social awareness.

Self-identity, or self-concept, and the quality of social interactions are intimately linked throughout infancy, early and middle childhood, and adolescence. The development of autonomy and initiative in toddlers tends to result in children who feel safe and independent, who are self-assured and competent—two of the characteristics of children who take social initiatives and who are popular with their preschool peers. Similarly, adolescents who are well liked by others and who have close friends possess high self-esteem (Papalia & Olds, 1992). These adolescents are more involved in extracurricular school activities and have more close friends than their less popular peers (Franzoi, Davis, & Vasquez-Suson, 1994).

To understand how teachers of children with visual impairments can facilitate the acquisition of social skills in their students, teachers must understand the principles of the development of self-esteem, including the factors that influence this development and the barriers that are created when a child has a visual impairment. This chapter discusses these principles along with some strategies for overcoming the barriers faced by children with visual impairments.

## SELF-CONCEPT AND SELF-ESTEEM

Our ideas about who we are—what we look like, how we think, what we consider to be our strengths as well as our weaknesses—make up our *self-concept*. Included in this broad notion of "who I am," or self-concept, is information about both the subjective self (the child's recognition that he or she is a separate entity from parents and others of the same race or ethnic grouping) and the objective self (the child's understanding that he or she is also an entity with shared properties such as gender, race, and so forth). Self-concept begins to emerge between 9–12 months of age, when a child typically grasps the concept of object permanence and recognizes that he or she has some permanence and exists outside of the environment. Self-concept continues to evolve over the course of early childhood, adolescence, and into early adulthood for individuals in Western, industrialized countries. In less industrialized countries the patterns of development, including acquisition of a fully developed self-concept or self-identity, may occur differently because of lifestyle demands and other cultural influences (Bee, 1997).

One's self-concept generally does not involve a value judgment; it is simply a description of one's perception of one's self or one's abilities. For example, two girls may perceive themselves as curly-haired, and therefore, have the same self-concept. Their degree of satisfaction with their hair—their feelings about this characteristic—includes a value judgment and reflects different levels of *self-esteem.*

Self-esteem is defined as a sense of how favorably one's abilities or characteristics compare to those of others based on both internal and external evaluation and input. In other words, input about one's prowess or worth from others, as well as self-evaluation of one's abilities, establish an individual's level of self-esteem. At age 7, the self-esteem of most children is based on a global, undifferentiated perspective, usually based on competence and social acceptance. Children of this age tend to believe that these two dimensions are independent and unrelated. That is, children believe they are either relatively competent or relatively incompetent, and also believe that they are either socially accepted or not. From the age of 7 through the middle childhood years, children come to realize that they can have strengths and weaknesses in a variety of areas, and both their self-concept and self-esteem become differentiated (Feldman, 2001; Lefrancois, 1995). Over time, adolescents use these varying perceptions of themselves (for example, rating themselves as relatively competent, important, and successful) to create a global sense of their own worth. Developmental psychologists often refer to this process as *global* self-evaluation and believe that in normally developing children this process continues through early adulthood. It is the overall evaluation of one's worth that defines one's self-esteem (Bee, 1997).

## FACTORS INFLUENCING SELF-ESTEEM

Harter (2001) frames the concept of self-esteem by stating that a child's self-esteem is based first upon an internal assessment of the degree of discrepancy between what the child would like to be and what the child thinks he or she is. This internal assessment is not the same for every child; rather it is dependent upon the value that a child and the culture in which he or she lives place on particular skills. For example, some children value aesthetic skills (such as singing, dancing, or drawing) while other children value athletic skills (such as jumping, running, or swimming). When there is only a slight discrepancy between what the child desires and what the child can achieve, the child's self-esteem is typically high. Similarly, when the discrepancy is great (that is, there is a significant difference between what the child wants to be able to do and what the child *can* do) the child's self-esteem is typically low (Harter, 2001). Children over the age of 7 tend to make these self-assessments in the following five areas: scholastic competence, athletic competence, social acceptance, behavioral conduct, and physical appearance. Over time, the emphasis placed on the value of these different areas shifts.

Harter also identifies the child's perception of the overall level of support received from significant others, especially parents and classmates, as a critical factor in a child's level of self-esteem. When children feel that the important people in their lives like them and feel that they are doing well, they have higher levels of self-esteem. Harter has found that teachers and close friends are also sources of support, though less so than parents and classmates.

The two components of self-esteem, overall support from others and the discrepancy between the way people perceive themselves and the way they would like to be, evolve from birth and are influenced by many factors, including the level of attachment developed with caretakers, the style of parenting one experiences, types of praise and criticism received, the level of initiative one is allowed to develop, the achievement of social competence, and the development of a sense of industriousness and self-efficacy. These factors are described in the following sections as they apply to typically developing children and then are reexamined in the content of how they can be influenced by a visual impairment.

## ATTACHMENT

A secure level of attachment that an infant forms with his or her caregivers is one of the first factors in the development of positive self-esteem. Secure attachments form when the primary adults in a child's life are responsive to the child and provide extensive physical contact (Trawick-Smith, 2000). Children who establish a secure attachment with caregivers believe that they can trust those caregivers to meet their needs. They typically find the world safe and predictable and are more likely to feel efficacious. Secure infants are more likely to develop into preschoolers who have positive views of themselves, are more friendly, and experience greater competence (Sroufe, 1985). Children who do not form a secure attachment during the early years tend to have difficulty forming social relationships later in life (Trawick-Smith, 2000) and either tend toward overdependence, timidity, and whininess (Erickson, Sroufe, & Egeland, 1985; Turner, 1993) or toward more aggressive, impulsive, and less cooperative behavior than securely attached children (Sroufe, Fox, & Pancake, 1983).

## PATTERNS OF PARENTING

Parents maintain their influence over a child's sense of self-esteem, even as classmates increase their influence as the child ages. Parenting style is a critical factor related to this influence. Coopersmith (1967) found that boys with high self-esteem were parented by mothers and fathers who also had high self-esteem. These parents created families with warm, supportive personal relationships and with less conflict among individual family members. Their parenting was characterized by consistency in the application of rules, democratic decision making, encouragement of independence, and reinforcement for desirable behaviors. They were perceived as strict, less permissive, and more demanding of their children. This parenting pattern is similar to the authoritative parenting style described by Baumrind (1971) in which parents are relatively strict and set clear and consistent limits; however, they are loving and emotionally supportive of their children. Children of authoritative parents generally are friendly, cooperative, well-liked, and motivated to achieve (Feldman, 2001). In contrast, permissive parents set few or no limits or control on their children's behavior and provide inconsistent feedback to them. Authoritarian parents set rigid limits on their children's behavior and expect unquestioning obedience; they tend to be rigid and cold emotionally. Uninvolved parents are detached and simply view their role as providers of food, clothing, and shelter; they are typically indifferent to their children. These parenting patterns sometimes are associated with less desirable social outcomes.

## POSITIVE AND NEGATIVE COMMENTS

Verbal abuse and negative statements from parents have also been found to negatively influence self-esteem (Blake & Slate, 1993). Interestingly, positive statements have more weight than negative ones.

Burnett (1996), in an investigation of the relationship between children's self-reported perceptions of statements made by significant others in their lives and their self-esteem, found that higher self-esteem was more highly related to positive statements. Burnett suggests that hearing positive statements seems to have a greater influence over a child's self-esteem than hearing negative comments.

This finding does not mean that children should never hear negative comments or be criticized. Children learn when they make mistakes and are assisted in understanding their mistakes by loving, accepting adults. Adults who provide children with moral and social guidance must inform them of ways to improve their behavior. Negative comments are damaging when they far exceed the positive comments the child hears and when they are used to describe the child, not the child's behavior.

## AUTONOMY AND INITIATIVE

Developing autonomy and initiative are key elements in the development of self-esteem, as reflected in Erikson's (1959/1980) theory of social development (see Chapters 3 and 4). The first three of his stages of social development cover the common challenges of children as they mature from birth to about their 6th birthday. The first of these challenges relates to establishing enough trust in the world to be able to explore it. The second stage is defined by the child's challenge to establish autonomy—a feeling of control over one's behavior; this challenge occurs when the child is roughly between 18 months to 2 or 3 years old. Parents often refer to the "terrible 2s" to describe this phase of the child's life because children tend to be defiant as they experiment with their newfound sense of self and their ability to explore their world. Erikson believed that children who do not establish autonomy develop a sense of shame and doubt about themselves. For children between the ages of 3 and 6, Erikson identified the primary challenges as developing the initiative to act on the world and achieving increasing independence from parents.

Interestingly, while Erikson's second stage of emotional development focuses on children's understanding of themselves as unlike others in their world, children in Erikson's third stage attempt to prove who they are by trying to be like their parents. This is the period in which pretend play emerges, as children "try on" new roles for themselves. Children of this age use their improved motor and language skills to explore their physical and social environments. Their increasing autonomy from and identification with their parents facilitates the development of initiative and responsibility.

Children develop initiative when they are encouraged by their caretakers to explore the world, allowed to act independently in it, and are praised for their attempts. Young children between the ages of 3 and 6 years are much more interested in the process of creating or doing something than in the final outcome of their activities. They view the creative or independent act as defining themselves and believe they are successful when their attempts are recognized by others. Successful children of this age have a positive self-concept, take risks, and view their abilities optimistically. In fact, when assessing their competence, preschoolers tend to believe that they can accomplish difficult tasks, even when they have not succeeded in these tasks previously (Stipeck, Recchia, & McClintic, 1992). Preschoolers who are punished for their efforts or who are often criticized develop a negative sense of self, may develop a belief in themselves as "bad," and tend to reduce or eliminate their efforts (Trawick-Smith, 2000). Similar reactions occur in children who are not encouraged to be independent or who are overprotected. It is theorized that children feel guilt if they don't try to assert independence and choose the path of least resistance by electing to remain in the protective environment created by their parents. This guilt can influence the social and emotional development of these children throughout life (Feldman, 2001).

## SOCIAL INITIATIVE AND COMPETENCE

Social initiation is also important for preschoolers as they define themselves. Children who take social initiatives tend to be more self-assured, less dependent, and more liked by their peers. Being liked by peers is one of the two interrelated aspects of social competence, the other being possessing the skills to interact effectively as social beings. Popular children demonstrate the following social behaviors: they are socially active, highly directive, linguistically effective, diplomatic, skilled in group entry, and competent in interpreting social situations (Trawick-Smith, 2000). They also display a positive affect, are skilled in conflict resolution, and are more likely to compromise when disagreements arise. They are accomplished at "reading" social settings (Dodge & Price, 1994) and seem to be aware of which social skills strategies are most successful with different peers in varying situations.

Researchers evaluating the social competence of preschoolers have identified two other groups of children based on their social competence: those who are rejected and those who are neglected. Children in these groups are either actively avoided or ignored by their peers. Rejected children tend to be whiny, have a negative affect, be unpredictably aggressive, unskilled at interpreting social situations and the feelings of peers, and generally antisocial. Many are isolated and prefer to play alone (Asher & Dodge, 1985). Isolation from peers is also a characteristic of children who are neglected; this group also tends to be anxiously shy. Typically, these youngsters are unskilled at entering play groups, in capturing the attention of their peers, and in play leadership. These children are socially inept and frequently respond inappropriately to the initiations of others. Both neglected and rejected children are at risk for developing low self-esteem, as they don't get the opportunities necessary to improve the social interaction skills that will increase their acceptance by peers.

Newcomb, Bukowski, & Pattee (1993) reviewed several studies that had investigated the popularity of children in middle childhood. These studies found a correlation between popularity and social competence. Unpopular children lack the social competence necessary to initiate and sustain relationships and exhibit poor social skills in general. Children who are highly regarded by others tend to have high levels of social competence; they are also reported to have higher levels of self-esteem. This relationship between high self-esteem and social competence continues through adolescence (Franzoi, Davis, & Vasquez-Suson, 1994; Lefrancois, 1995).

It should be noted that having even one friend can protect a child from the negative effects of being not liked, whether the child is rejected or neglected (Hartup & Moore, 1990). A single friendship may be reassuring to the child, whose self-worth is reaffirmed by having a close relationship to a peer (Trawick-Smith, 2000).

## INDUSTRIOUSNESS AND EFFICACY

Erikson (1959/1980) defined the primary crisis for children in middle childhood as resolving the conflict between industry (or competence) and inferiority. Mastering the skills valued by society is critical for the development of a positive sense of self. Youngsters between the ages of 7 and 12 are industrious—busy developing competence academically, socially, and in other domains. While in earlier years they were satisfied with initiating new tasks, at this stage they want to master and complete those activities. Industriousness in childhood has been found to be more closely related to success in adulthood than either intelligence or family background (Vaillant & Vaillant, 1981).

In addition, children in middle childhood increasingly turn to their peers for affirmation of their success, though the influence of adults is still strong. Peers provide the comparison against which children can determine their own strengths and weaknesses. They help children to see themselves as others do and to modify undesirable traits or behaviors. Through the peer group a child establishes his or her own values and belief systems separate from those that have been emphasized by parents. Peer groups also provide emotional support to manage any conflicts between the child's values and those of the parents.

During the years from ages 7 to 12, children begin to shift from thinking of themselves in physical terms to defining themselves based on internal, psychological characteristics (Feldman, 2001; Papalia & Olds, 1992). Most children enter this period with a positive overall sense of self—they view themselves as generally successful and well-liked (Harter, 1990). However, some youngsters of this age have already developed the sense that they are not valued.

Children with low self-esteem often become trapped in a cycle of thinking and behavior that further damages their sense of self. When presented with a challenging task, the child who already has experienced frequent failure may expect to do poorly. Low expectations often lead to increased anxiety, which can affect performance, and decreased effort, as the child's previous experiences have convinced him or her that such effort is not effective. The high level of anxiety and the low level of effort combine to fulfill the child's expectation of failure, the child's sense of failure is confirmed, and low self-esteem is reinforced (Feldman, 2001).

Low expectations, or a low sense of *self-efficacy*, can be very damaging. Self-efficacy is the term used to describe the learned expectation that one is more or less capable at a particular task or when faced with a challenging situation (Bandura, 1986, 1993). A high sense of self-efficacy promotes motivation, persistence, and calculated risk-taking, whereas a low sense of self-efficacy results in timidity and, in extreme cases, what has been termed learned helplessness. Children with low self-efficacy choose not to attempt or persist at an activity rather than to fail, since they have learned that there is little correlation between their efforts and success at a task.

A continuing theme throughout childhood is the child's desire to be in control. This struggle is evident from the first time a toddler says "No!" to a parent or caretaker. Ideally, childhood is a period during which children are gradually allowed to make decisions about their own lives, to manage the consequences of those decisions, and to make judgments about their competence in a variety of domains. Children who are not provided adequate guidance as they establish control over themselves or who are inhibited from acquiring such control frequently lack a positive sense of self-efficacy, which has an impact on their overall evaluation of themselves.

## IDENTITY DEVELOPMENT IN ADOLESCENCE

During adolescence the capacity to view oneself abstractly emerges. That is, the self-concept becomes more differentiated as individuals are better able to see various aspects of themselves—both positive and negative—at the same time. Adolescents are also more capable of understanding the perspective of others, and they can see how their own self-perception differs from the perceptions that others hold about them. As adolescents' self-concept becomes more clearly defined, however, their self-esteem can become threatened, since awareness of weaknesses is more acute. Self-esteem also becomes more differentiated as teenagers come to like and dislike certain aspects of themselves. The task of adolescence for the individual is to generate an identity from these sometimes conflicting opinions of the self.

Teens are said to experience an "identity crisis" as they seek to commit to goals, values, and beliefs in order to establish a self-definition. The resolution of this crisis is influenced by all their past experiences that have created the differentiated self-concept, their relationship with their families, their increasing sexuality and desire for intimacy, and the values and beliefs of their chosen peer group. When adolescents have experienced challenges in areas that are meaningful to them, received constructive feedback, and achieved genuine successes based on their efforts, they are more likely to establish an identity that is based on their personal perceptions. They are ready to establish plans for their future and act on those plans based on their unique set of strengths and weaknesses. On the other hand, teens who have remained dependent, who have a poor sense of self-efficacy, and who frequently experience failure are more likely to rely on the opinions of peers and family to identify who they are. Since their identity is not self-defined, some of these individuals adopt socially unacceptable roles and struggle to forge meaningful personal relationships (Feldman, 2001). Still others may not even experience an identity crisis; rather, they accept the decisions made by others about their lives.

The creation of a distinct identity requires that adolescents increase their autonomy and personal control over their lives. It is not unusual for teens to experience conflict with their parents as they move toward greater independence. While they choose to be different from their parents, their need to belong is so strong that most adolescents are part of some identifiable group (Feldman, 2001). Group membership and relationships are important avenues for sharing common experiences and discussing the physical and emotional changes of adolescence. Peers provide the basis for social comparison, a process teenagers use to learn about themselves and others as they compare and evaluate their abilities and opinions.

## ACCURACY OF SELF-CONCEPT

People use the term self-esteem to indicate the degree to which individuals perceive themselves to be competent, important, and successful—and to be worthy of high regard by others. It should be noted that a healthy sense of self-esteem is based on an accurate self-concept (Klein, 2000). There has been much written lately on the problems of children and adults who have high levels of self-esteem that are based on inaccurate perceptions of their abilities. It has been found, for example, that high self-esteem is often associated with individuals who are violent and aggressive (Baumeister, Smart, & Boden, 1996). Individuals who have an inflated sense of importance, one that is not based on an accurate self-appraisal, may become aggressive when challenged in order to prove their superiority both to themselves and others. People who have received false praise or unconditional, uncritical acceptance that is not reflective of their accomplishments often feel so good about themselves that they believe that they are entitled to whatever they want without applying any effort. To avoid this situation, it is important that children be helped to become satisfied with themselves and also be helped to acknowledge weaknesses and discover positive strategies for dealing with them.

High self-esteem based on an accurate self-appraisal is a desirable characteristic, as it is related to ease in making friends, having more friends, being more creative, being less sensitive to criticism, and exhibiting less self-consciousness. It is associated with happiness and high motivation, social adjustment, and feelings of general well-being. Individuals who feel good about themselves are prepared to manage the challenges of adulthood and can contribute within the home, work, and community environments.

## SELF-ESTEEM AND BLINDNESS

Tuttle and Tuttle (1996b) have undertaken one of the most comprehensive examinations of self-esteem and adjustment to blindness to date. In their work, the authors investigated the impact of blindness on the development of self-esteem in children and adults with visual impairments and discussed guidelines for nurturing high self-esteem.

The authors noted that because blindness has an inherent negative impact on achieving independence (before an individual acquires compensatory skills such as navigating in the environment using a long cane or other mobility tools, learning to read and write with braille or through the use of optical devices, and so forth), it may inhibit the development of positive self-esteem. In other words, to the extent that congenitally or adventitiously blinded individuals may lack or lose independence, their self-esteem is affected. Tuttle and Tuttle believed that lower levels of self-esteem can be positively enhanced by the acquisition of skills or competencies that reduce the impact of the visual impairment on one's daily functioning.

However, in addition to the impact of these personal-skill development issues or internal factors, Tuttle and Tuttle (1996b) reinforced the notion that self-esteem and self-confidence are also strongly influenced by the opinions of others. Two overriding issues must be considered when discussing the influence of others on the development of self-esteem and building self-confidence in children and youths with visual impairments: the typical absence in their lives of positive social role models and the stereotypic attitudes of the general population, including their families, friends, and acquaintances. The authors noted that most blind and severely visually impaired children rarely have the opportunity to be with adults who have similar conditions and have achieved social success in their lives; therefore, the children have a limited basis for comparison of their behaviors to those of positive adult figures. In addition, these children must deal on a daily basis with the misconceptions or prejudices of the general population. Tuttle and Tuttle (1996b, pp. 42–44) identify a number of stereotypic attitudes in the general public that may inhibit the acquisition of a positive self-concept and self-esteem, including the notions that blind people are:

- inferior, subhuman, helpless, and useless
- pitiable, miserable, and wretched
- to be feared, avoided, and rejected, especially in intimate relationships
- emotionally and sexually maladjusted
- so unfortunate that they would "...rather be dead than blind"
- paying for previous sin, immoral, and evil
- to be restricted due to impaired understanding, and other generalized incapacities

- unemployable
- unapproachable with comfort or ease
- living in constant darkness or blackness
- to be tolerated, indulged, or excused
- superhuman, or supernaturally endowed or compensated
- reminders of vulnerability to disabilities in general, and blindness specifically

It is important for teachers, counselors, parents, or others caring for and working with children and adolescents with visual impairments to be aware of and to counter the stereotypic attitudes of the people in contact with visually impaired youngsters, such as general education personnel, members of the local community, relatives or extended family members, and so forth. Children and youths with visual impairments need to be prepared for the negative attitudes they may encounter; they need help in learning how to "bounce back" when others put them down or treat them with pity, sympathy, awe, or other misplaced feelings. Youngsters will be able to recover their equilibrium when they are aware that significant adults in their lives (for example, parents, family, and extended family) love them unconditionally and accept them as they are without hesitation or contingencies. In addition, a concerted effort is needed to bring these children into contact with adults who are blind or visually impaired and can serve as positive role models.

## CRITICAL ISSUES AND CHALLENGES IN DEVELOPING SELF-ESTEEM

The challenges to developing positive self-esteem in youngsters with visual impairments that were described at the beginning of this chapter are explored in this section, along with strategies for engendering a positive, realistic level of self-esteem. Activities that can be used to promote both self-confidence and high levels of self-esteem are also provided.

### ATTACHMENT

As described earlier in this chapter, secure attachment, which is key to the development of positive self-esteem, results when the primary adults in an infant's life are responsive to the child and provide extensive physical contact. For some children with visual impairments, particularly premature or ill infants who spend long periods in neonatal intensive care units, secure attachment is at risk. The parents and caregivers of these babies, respond first to the child's physical and health demands rather than to the child's emotional needs. Sick infants may experience a larger number of caregivers, may not receive the same level of soothing physical contact, and may find that their world seems more hostile compared to infants who are healthy.

Even otherwise healthy infants who are blind or who have low vision may experience difficulty establishing a secure attachment with their primary caretakers. Parents may have difficulty reading the cues that their infants use to communicate their needs and their responses to parental initiations. For example, without the ability to utilize eye contact and smiles effectively, the blind infant may respond positively to the parent's voice by becoming very still to listen carefully; an unprepared parent might interpret such behavior as rejection and reduce contact with the child. Similarly, misinterpretation can occur when the child startles and stiffens in response to being unexpectedly roused from the crib, picked up, and held extended from the parent. Parents, observing their infant's negative reaction, may believe they are not competent and choose to leave the baby in the crib more often.

There are other reasons that parents may not be emotionally available to their visually impaired infants. Parents who are particularly distressed or depressed over their child's diagnosis of severe visual impairment may be distracted by their own emotional needs at this difficult time and therefore may attend to their infant's needs in disorganized ways. They may not be aware of their baby's cues or may not always be able to respond.

Early interventionists can help parents and other caretakers to provide a climate in which the infant with visual impairment is loved, feels safe, and is successful in eliciting a positive response from the adult. These experiences help infants to recognize that they have some control of their environment—a precursor to establishing autonomy and initiative.

Parents and other primary caretakers of children with visual impairment benefit from early intervention services provided by individuals who are knowledgeable about the impact of visual impairment on early childhood development. Knowledgeable early interventionists can assist parents to recognize the cues that infants with visual impairments use to communicate their likes or dislikes of a particular activity. Early interventionists can help parents to develop strategies for communicating with their child so that the child learns to anticipate what will happen next. In addition, they can encourage parents to provide frequent physical contact with their infants with visual impairments, which is a key component to the secure attachment of any child.

Chen (1999, pp. 43–46) suggests that early interventionists help parents to:

- identify and interpret the infant's cues
- identify when the infant is active or alert and ready for interaction
- respond contingently to the infant's behaviors
- identify the infant's preferences for stimulation
- provide contingent sensory stimulation
- create individualized games that both the caretaker and infant enjoy
- use favorite activities
- decrease hand-over-hand guidance
- provide opportunities to make choices

As parents feel more competent in their interactions with their child, they are more likely to meet their child's needs, thereby creating an environment in which the infant feels powerful enough to begin to explore his or her world. Early interventionists can assist parents and other caretakers in preparing for the explorative activities of the toddler by helping them to learn more about the impact of visual impairment on learning and the importance of creating a world of high expectations for their child.

## Patterns of Parenting

As noted earlier, children growing up in families in which parents use an authoritative parenting style tend to have higher self-esteem than children whose parents are authoritarian, permissive, or uninvolved. Authoritative parents use a warm, supportive style, encourage their children to explore and be independent, establish appropriate expectations, set consistent limits, and are relatively strict and firm when disciplining their children. Their children feel safe and secure, and are more likely to be independent, happier, and social than children raised in families who use other parenting styles.

Given the many hazards in the environments in which young children spend time, it is not surprising that parents of children with visual impairments often are preoccupied with ensuring their child's physical safety (Tuttle & Tuttle, 1996a). As a result, they may limit their child's explorations of the environment in their efforts to prevent the child from becoming injured. Although it is important that children with visual impairments be protected from serious dangers, it is not always beneficial to protect them from all mishaps. To do so leaves these children with the impression that the important adults in their lives do not believe in their abilities to manage on their own (and if these all-knowing adults think the world is too dangerous for them to explore, they feel, then it must be true). These youngsters, like everyone else, have the capacity to learn from encountering new and challenging situations, from being hurt and living through the pain, and from achieving independent successes—all vital to the establishment of one's self-esteem.

Children with visual impairments often are raised in homes where there are few expectations that they will contribute and achieve. Families frequently find it easier to do things for visually impaired children rather than to teach them how to help themselves. On occasion, adults feel such sympathy about the child's visual impairment that they believe it is kinder to "help" the child than require the youngster to learn to manage the typical demands of childhood. Without meaning to, these parents may easily fall into a permissive parenting style, which is characterized by requiring little of children and is associated with raising children who are dependent, moody, and lacking in social skills. As with children who are not allowed or encouraged to explore, these youngsters may interpret the low expectations as lack of confidence in their abilities—a lack of confidence that they, too, may adopt.

Parents of children with visual impairments also may experience conflict in the area of discipline (Langley, 1996). A belief that the world is too cruel a place for the child who cannot see well sometimes creates a tendency to be more tolerant of unacceptable behavior. However, blindness cannot be accepted as an excuse for misbehaving. When it is, children are led to believe that they are being singled out because they are different and that the established standards of behavior do not apply to them. These children then may arrive at the conclusion that their differences are due to inferiority.

Parents need to understand the negative effects of overprotectiveness and permissiveness and they need support as they struggle to overcome their natural inclinations to assure their child's safety and happiness. Coordinating opportunities for parents to meet the experienced parents of older, successful children with visual impairments may be beneficial.

In their review of the literature on parenting, Shonkoff and Phillips (2000) noted that while research has demonstrated that parenting style can be changed, it is difficult to do so. Parents of children with visual impairments of all ages often need and want additional guidance on how to raise their children. Professionals working with families need to help them to encourage their child's independent explorations of increasingly larger environments, ensuring that the child is free from major hazards (such as unexpected stairways), but still demanding enough to challenge the child to learn. Orientation and mobility specialists can teach children how to orient themselves in their environments and to use natural cues (such as the slope of the driveway as it approaches the street) or added cues (for example, an area rug at the top of a stairway) to negotiate safely in the environment.

In addition, professionals and families can brainstorm to identify established routines and frequently occurring activities in which the child can increasingly participate. Many parents do not purposefully exclude their children from self-help and other household tasks, but they believe that their visually impaired child, like children with vision, will ask to help (Lewis, Slay, & Pace, 1999). Often, all parents need is a gentle reminder of the importance of getting their child involved, or a simple demonstration of how to involve their child, to change their attitudes and behaviors.

Finally, professionals can discuss with parents and other caretakers that all children, including children who are blind or who have low vision, need limits and expect that the caring adults in their lives will firmly prevent them from overstepping those limits. While parents may feel like it is "unfair" that their child has a visual impairment, and that it is much more difficult for a visually impaired child to learn the rules, children who are blind or who have low vision must learn early on that these same rules apply to them. Differing behavior standards are inappropriate and detrimental to the child's healthy long-term emotional development.

If children with visual impairments misbehave, it is incumbent upon their caregivers and instructional staff to analyze the misbehavior and determine whether it is the result of visual information that they are missing or misinterpreting. If so, instruction needs to address the missing information and an alternative technique needs to be taught that compensates for the missed visual cue or misinterpretation. For example, if a child with visual impairment takes a cookie that another child had placed between them on the snack table, it is first necessary to determine if the child actually thought the cookie was his to take or if he knew that it belonged to his peer. If the act was intentional, the child should experience the consequences any classmate would receive for such behavior. If not, then the teachers need to develop appropriate strategies to deal with the situation, such as establishing a rule that everyone only eats the cookies on the napkin immediately in front of them or placing a mat or tray in front of the child with visual impairment to define his eating area. When a child is simply misbehaving (there is no missing visual information responsible for the behavior), the caregiver or teacher may choose to ignore the behavior (if it does not endanger the child or others) or redirect the behavior. In essence, the child with the visual impairment needs to experience the same consequences that any other child of the same age and abilities would experience.

## POSITIVE AND NEGATIVE COMMENTS

As already indicated, children's self-concept is influenced by both self-appraisal and support from others. Support and acceptance is demonstrated in many ways, including the language that children hear others use to describe them or to provide them with feedback and guidance.

### Strangers' Comments

Parents of children with visual impairments frequently describe situations in which people in their community comment about their child's visual impairment. These curious and unthinking strangers frequently ask questions (such as, "What's wrong with your child?") or express pity by suggesting that the child is such a burden or the parent is a "saint" for dealing with the child. Some parents report that strangers spontaneously give them money for "that poor blind baby." Although directed at parents and caretakers, children with visual impairments hear these comments and their underlying messages that the child is different, inferior, and burdensome. Adults can use these situations to affirm the child's worth by having several replies rehearsed and ready to use, such as the following:

- "What's wrong with her? You would not believe what a great kid this is! She does..."

- "He's not a burden at all! You should see how well he folded the towels yesterday."

- "Parenting is such a challenging job. I think all parents are saints, don't you?"

Children who hear their parents respond to strangers' comments in ways that reflect love and admiration for them and that share their accomplishments are more likely to internalize these positive comments instead of the strangers' negative ones. In addition, hearing these models enables them to use the same kind of strategy if similar situations occur when parents are not around.

## Talking about Visual Impairment at Home

A family's level of comfort in speaking to their child about his or her disability is affected by their cultural values and their own emotional readiness to "move on" with life. It is important for parents to share information about their child's visual condition with the child starting when the child is very young. This information is best provided matter-of-factly and in the course of daily conversation, much as a parent would talk about the child's blond hair, long legs, or slender fingers. The goal is to have the child realize that visual impairment is just one of his or her many characteristics. For example, if a conversation is focused on something that is difficult for the child to accomplish because of the visual impairment, then adults should remind the child of what he or she has in common with all children—that everyone finds some tasks easier or harder than others do. In addition, these times provide excellent opportunities to remind the child with a visual impairment of what he or she can do. As indicated earlier, such positive statements, based on real accomplishments, can have a positive impact on a child's self-esteem.

## Realistic Feedback

Youngsters who are visually impaired need both positive and realistic verbal feedback from others; they need to be told what attributes and talents they have that are well developed (for their ages) and comparable to or better than those of their sighted and visually impaired peers. They do not need, nor will they benefit from, false praise or congratulations for doing things that their peers do routinely. Unfortunately, many visually impaired children are praised for doing ordinary, mundane tasks such as brushing their teeth or hanging up a coat—activities that are taken for granted with fully sighted children the same age—because many adults who are not acquainted with any individuals with visual impairments seem to think that such skills are exemplary for children without sight. At home, at school, and in the community, adults who care for visually impaired children must be on guard for those who would give these children false praise and help the children recognize what skills are ordinary and what skills are extraordinary. All children have certain things that they do well or better than others, however, and these are the talents and attributes that youngsters with visual impairments need to have pointed out to them as acceptable or exemplary so that they can develop positive self-esteem.

## Feedback during Instruction

Youngsters with visual impairments do not always have the capacity to regulate their behavior or get important information by unobtrusively watching others. The child with typical vision can see how the grade on his spelling test compares with his classmates' scores by glancing at their papers. Watching their peers, children can see that everyone gets paint on their hands when in the art center. Observation of others during class, while riding the school bus, or on the playground reveals what clothes peers are wearing and how they are being worn. Children with visual impairments, on the other hand, often need to be provided with specific information and verbal guidance as they attempt to develop skills. However, adults working with children with visual impairments must be sensitive when providing verbal feedback to these students. For the child, verbal feedback and guidance provided by others can sometimes seem more like criticism or disapproval. Consider the following situation:

> Sarah's kindergarten class is celebrating the November birthdays.
> A parent has brought in cupcakes covered with lots of chocolate frosting
> and has passed one out to every child in the class. The teacher walks by
> Sarah, who has low vision, and whispers that she has chocolate on her
> mouth. Sarah picks up her napkin to wipe her face and, in doing so,
> spills crumbs on the table. Seeing that she hasn't wiped her mouth
> completely, the teacher quietly tells Sarah that she has to wipe again
> ("No, you smeared the chocolate—wipe higher," and adds, "You've
> made a mess on the table. You'll have to clean it up." More directions
> follow as Sarah is talked through the process of getting the crumbs
> off the table: "Go get the sponge wet again. You haven't got it
> clean yet."

What Sarah didn't see was that some of her classmates also had chocolate on their faces and were wiping the crumbs from their desks. Because the teacher was trying to handle each case individually and privately, Sarah didn't notice or hear the directions given to her peers. Not knowing that others were having similar problems, Sarah was left feeling different and inadequate, feelings that were only reinforced by the many verbal prompts provided to her when wiping her mouth and the table.

There are no easy solutions to this problem that children with visual impairments must be provided verbal directions and explicit feedback in order to acquire skills—information that can be provided much less intrusively to their sighted peers. Adults working with these youngsters need to remind themselves frequently of the potential that their students will misconstrue directions and feedback as negative comments and criticism. When possible, neutral language can be used: "Oh, goodness, the chocolate smeared!" might feel less negative than "You smeared the chocolate." Another approach is to provide feedback by indicating that the situation is unusual in some way: "That old chocolate is really being stubborn today—it doesn't want to come off the table. Looks like you're going to have to use all of your energy to get it clean." Some children may feel less attacked if, instead of using direct instructions, adults make suggestions such as: "What works for me sometimes is . . ." or "Another one of my students had the same problem and what he/she tried is . . . " In the case of the chocolate cupcakes, it might have been better for Sarah if the teacher had made a statement about the cupcakes to the entire class, such as: "You all look like you could use a bath now!"

Of course, children need to hear positive comments, too. "Ah, you're getting it! It's almost gone!" is more effective than, "No, there still is some chocolate there." Children need to be praised often, both for their efforts and their ultimate achievements, not for simple tasks that they have already mastered or that peers do routinely. Praise should be specific to the situation and to the part of the task that the child performed well, for example: "I can tell you're trying really hard," "Oh, look! You've pulled the covers up without many wrinkles," or "Your studying is paying off. You scored second highest on the math test." Because children with visual impairments cannot always easily compare their efforts and achievements to those of others, use of specific praise is even more critical for them than it is for their sighted peers.

Frequently, teachers and other adults need to provide children with corrective feedback in order to improve the child's performance that the child may interpret as negative. When feasible and educationally appropriate, delaying corrective feedback may prove beneficial, by putting some distance between the learner's effort and the adult's critical comments. This strategy is often used in educational settings, for example, when students take a test on Friday and are given the results on Monday. The time lapse allows students to disengage themselves from the effort expended and the sometimes disappointing outcome. Delaying is especially appropriate for children with visual impairments, who often work one-on-one with adults and are at risk of feeling as though they "never do anything right" because their teachers offer immediate feedback for every error as it is made. Adults working with children with visual impairments need to try to avoid correcting children too frequently since it can lead to overdependence on feedback, perfectionism, and an unwillingness to take risks.

## Accessible Feedback

Tangible evidence of pride in a child's work (such as posting drawings on the family refrigerator), may not be as meaningful to a child who is blind as to a sighted child unless it is made clear to the child that the work is in evidence to sighted friends and family members. When possible, tactile indicators of satisfaction with work accomplished are important. For example, stickers with raised-line smiley faces and brailled messages such as "wow!" "good!" "great!" or "cool!" (such as the Feel 'n Peel Stickers produced by the American Printing House for the Blind) can provide the visually impaired child with positive feedback, and commercially available stickers in simple shapes, such as stars and hearts, that are puffed or raised, provide more tactile feedback than ordinary stickers. Parents and teachers can also make their own praise notes with braille or large-print labelers or on index cards with braille or large-print messages.

Children in school get feedback from their teachers in a variety of ways. One popular strategy is to post children's work on bulletin boards for other students to use as models. This information often is inaccessible to the child with a visual impairment. Students with low vision can be encouraged to use their monocular or another appropriate strategy to examine the work of their peers. For children who are blind, this information can be made accessible by having an adult describe what makes the work worthy of placement on the board or, if the material is primarily text, transcribing it into braille for the child to examine. During these types of interactions, the focus is not directly on what the visually impaired child produced, but rather on how others are performing.

## Sharing Accomplishments

Sharing a child's accomplishments with others is a form of indirect praise that can also be effective in helping children with visual impairment realize their strengths. After the mastery of a difficult or challenging task, teachers can encourage the child to call a parent or caregiver about the accomplishment. Teachers can brag about a student by sharing the child's success with other adults in the child's presence at the school. Similarly, parents can discuss their child's accomplishments and repeat realistic praise that they've heard about their child at the dinner table, or with grandparents and caring friends over the phone. Hearing these comments and sharing genuine successes with others helps children to realize the expectations others have for them; it also helps children define themselves and experience pride—all important components in the development of positive self-esteem.

## Autonomy and Initiative

As described earlier, the desire to keep children safe and the inability of visually impaired children to observe the activities of peers and adults compounds the difficulties in the primary developmental tasks of preschoolers—first to establish autonomy from parents and then to re-create themselves to be like the adults in their lives. Adults are able to maintain control over children with visual impairments far longer than is possible with sighted children, in large part because sighted children use their vision to know about the possibilities for autonomy. In seeing that older children and adults hold their own spoons, toddlers often push away their parent's hand and demand to feed themselves. Similarly, the sighted preschooler sees a parent using a hammer and recognizes that the toy hammer is used for the same purpose; if the child doesn't have the exact toy, he or she can find a suitable substitute. Vision facilitates imitation, which is a primary factor in the initiations of young children.

Two of the challenges facing adults working with young children with visual impairment are to convince their students of the possibilities for independent action and to introduce them to the behaviors of adults. With gentle guidance and perseverance on the part of adults, most young children with visual impairments can be taught to independently manage the demands of early childhood, including those related to dressing, bathing, feeding, and personal hygiene. Adults promote children's autonomy further when they give children choices and honor their selections: "Do you want Chex or Life for breakfast today?" "Are you going to wear the shirt with the Power Rangers on it or the plain white one?"

Children with vision observe their parents' involvement in everyday tasks and, wanting to be like those adults, imitate their behaviors. They push play shopping carts around the living room, vacuum the rug with plastic carpet sweepers, and help outside to dig in the garden. When these initiations are recognized by others, the child's self-perception is enhanced. This kind of play is promoted by vision. The child who has never pushed a shopping cart through a grocery store has still observed it and thus knows how to accomplish the task.

The experience of a visually impaired child with shopping cart, however, may be limited to riding in the cart, starting and stopping and occasionally hearing something fall as it is placed in the cart. Even if parents describe what they are doing ("I'm putting the butter in the basket"), a visually impaired child is likely to have an incomplete understanding of the task. The reality of learning for children with significant visual impairments is that they must experience the real activity to know about it. The foundation necessary for children to imagine themselves in the roles of the adults in their lives and to engage in meaningful pretend play can be established only after an activity is experienced often enough to be understood.

Adults must provide young children who are visually impaired with a variety of experiences and help them to understand the overall purposes and individual parts of these experiences before they will be able to imagine themselves in the controlling role. Children with visual impairments need to vacuum with real vacuum cleaners—they need to feel the dirty carpet before and after the vacuum moves over it, feel the air being sucked into the machine, and store the device when finished. These children need to help push the cart around the grocery store, select items from the shelves, put them in the basket, place them on the conveyer belt, help the parent find the money to pay for them before leaving the store, and help put them in their proper places at home in order to understand the grocery-shopping experience. There are thousands of similar experiences that children with vision understand and can imitate because they can see but that must be shown to youngsters who are blind or who have low vision.

Visually impaired children who have been shown how and encouraged to make toast or to get their own drink from the refrigerator are more likely to initiate these activities—and even more creative ones—on their own. Similarly, the child at preschool who has been taught to travel independently in the classroom, who can get his or her own mat before naptime, and can safely negotiate the monkey bars is more likely to feel confident enough to explore the outer edges of the physical environment, to take risks, and learn from the consequences of his or her independently conceived actions.

The direct involvement of young children with visual impairments in a variety of activities and experiences contributes to their becoming more competent in the cognitive, social, and motor skills that lead to success. Children who are engaged in many activities have something to talk about with adults and peers, know enough about their world to be able to understand the stories that they hear or read, and, are familiar with the ways of controlling one's own body. Their growing competence affects how they feel about themselves and how others perceive them.

## SOCIAL INITIATIVE AND COMPETENCE

Children under the age of 7 judge themselves and their peers based on their perception of their own competence and social acceptance. Reviewing the characteristics of popular, rejected, and socially neglected children can show what skills are valued by peers, and therefore, which skills need to be emphasized in interventions. As mentioned earlier, Asher and Dodge (1985) reported that preschoolers who are rejected by others are whiny, have a negative attitude (affect), are unpredictably aggressive, and have difficulties interpreting social situations, while popular children are diplomatic, competent in group entry, and skilled at negotiating compromises. Because so much of the interpretation of social situations is based on visual input, young children with visual impairments are at risk for being rejected or neglected by their peers. Thus, social skills instruction needs to provide visually impaired children with opportunities to develop their skills in these areas and to prevent or diminish those characteristics other children view as negative.

### Involvement with Same-Aged Peers

The need to continue to hone skills related to social initiative and competence persists throughout childhood. As children enter middle childhood and adolescence, involvement with both sighted and visually impaired peers becomes an increasingly important component in the development of healthy levels of self-esteem. Peer groups (social, religious, athletic, and others) and interpersonal relationships (friends and, later, dating relationships) provide the opportunities for youths to learn about who they are and how they compare to others outside of their immediate families. Children and youths with visual impairments need to be engaged in activities that include other children and youths at school, in the community, and in their homes. As early as possible in their lives, they need to help organize and participate in outings with their schoolmates and friends, whether the outings are to libraries, movie theaters, parks, shopping malls, or other destinations.

Part of "fitting in" with the other children or youths at school and in the community is an understanding of what to wear, what to say, and what behaviors are socially acceptable both within and outside a peer group. To be appropriately dressed and groomed (as discussed in more detail in Chapters 4 and 12), a child or youth with a visual impairment may need to solicit input from several sources of information such as friends or trusted family members to help him or her understand what fashions are considered trendy or popular for his age group.

## Exposure to Other Children with Visual Impairment

In addition to being with and working with children without impairments, it is important for children with visual impairments to have exposure to other children who are visually impaired. Very few students with visual impairments attend specialized schools for the blind (Valdes, Williamson, & Wagner, 1990). Most attend local public schools where they are the only visually impaired child in their classes, and there might be one or two others in the entire school. In fact, the incidence of vision impairment is one of the lowest among disabilities in the school-aged population (Kirchner, 1999; Kirchner & Diament, 1999a, Kirchner & Diament, 1999b, Mason & Davidson, 2000). Therefore, the likelihood of children with visual impairments casually encountering others with similar disabling conditions is remote.

Caregivers of such children must reach out to find other children with similar disabilities so that these children do not grow up thinking they are the only ones with limited sight or related attributes. Attending summer camps or specialized schools can afford opportunities for interaction with peers who are visually impaired. Many of the special schools for students who are blind or have low vision offer short-term placements that emphasize instruction in disability-specific curricular areas such as orientation and mobility, assistive technology, activities of daily living, and so forth. In addition to the opportunity to learn valuable skills, these programs also afford youngsters the chance to meet others with similar disabilities, a great advantage for a child who has always been compared only to siblings and same-aged peers without disabilities. In this environment, visually impaired children have a chance to evaluate themselves in comparison with others who see (or don't see) like they do. It also affords them the chance to learn how other students with visual disabilities have adjusted to the demands of a sighted world and how they accommodate to the demands of such a world.

## INDUSTRIOUSNESS AND EFFICACY

## Competence in the Home and Community

The development of competence, or in Erikson's (1959/1980) terminology, "industry," is the main challenge of middle adolescence. Youngsters in this age range typically are busy proving to themselves and others that they can master the skills needed in adulthood. Chores at home—helping with activities of daily living such as laundry, meal preparation, housecleaning, and so forth—provide opportunities for children to learn domestic tasks that they will continue to use throughout their lives and also contribute to the well-being of their families. Tasks undertaken in the neighborhood or community—helping an elderly neighbor with yard work or housework, taking care of a friend's pet while he or she is on vacation, helping out at a garage sale, or the like—help children to recognize that they have skills that are useful outside of the home and that they are appreciated in the larger community. Churches, synagogues, community recreation centers, nursing homes, senior centers, and hospitals are always looking for volunteers, and youngsters can often find tasks that need doing in such facilities. Youngsters might also volunteer for community service in conjunction with scouting organizations or become active in school extracurricular groups such as band, clubs, or athletic departments. Such active participation and involvement promotes positive self-esteem.

Opportunities to contribute at home and in the community are both important in the development of children with visual impairments. By giving of themselves to others through volunteerism and helping family members or acquaintances, children with visual impairments learn that they are capable human beings with gifts to give others. For much of recorded history, people with disabilities have been perceived as needy, capable only of receiving assistance, and dependent on charity. Today's children with disabilities need to reach out and give so they can help dispel this myth.

## Competence through the Expanded Core Curriculum

The development of alternative techniques and strategies for independently accomplishing everyday activities is critical to the overall competence of youngsters with visual impairments. These techniques (using braille or optical devices for reading and writing, learning to get around in the community with appropriate orientation and mobility skills, accessing computer software programs with assistive technology, and so forth) and strategies (being driven by friends and family members or using public transportation alternatives to driving, for example) allow children to demonstrate competence and to engage in age-appropriate activities with their peers; they are the substance by which children develop a healthy self-concept and, ultimately, develop positive self-esteem.

In the field of blindness, teachers and related service personnel are focusing on the expanded core curriculum (Hatlen, 1996; Huebner, Merk-Adam, Stryker, & Wolffe, 2004) as a guide for the alternative techniques or competencies that are required for children and youths with visual impairments to make a successful transition out of school and into adulthood. The traditional core curriculum—English, physical education, mathematics, science, history, and so forth—is not ignored, but is supplemented with the expanded core curriculum specific to the needs of students with visual impairments. The expanded core curriculum includes the following eight areas of learning:

*Compensatory academic skills, including communication modes.* Students with visual impairments need the skills or supportive services necessary to receive through auditory or tactile means all the information that is presented visually to a class of sighted students or captured by sighted students through visual observation. Compensatory or functional academic skills include use of braille or low vision devices to read and write; organizational skills; use of alternative communication systems (such as sign language for students with the additional disability of hearing impairment or calendar systems for students with cognitive impairments in addition to their visual impairment), using recorded materials; and effective listening skills, among others. Instruction that promotes concept development and spatial awareness through learning experiences also falls into this area.

*Social interaction skills.* As discussed throughout this book, social interaction skills often need be taught to children with visual impairments because they are unable to casually observe how people interact and socialize with one another. Students therefore need to be taught when and how to smile, frown, nod, wink, shrug, and the many other nuances of nonverbal communication skills. Social interaction skills include all the ways we interact with other people: family, friends, acquaintances, teachers, supervisors, and so forth. In many instances, ongoing enjoyment of other people results from shared or similar interests, experiences, and attitudes or opinions. It also helps to have an understanding of the way positive, two-way communication works: good communicators do not interrupt, they always show interest, and they give others their full attention. Most sighted individuals who are socially successful learn the elements of positive social interaction by visually observing others, imitating the behaviors they have observed, and noting how others respond to their efforts to communicate. How do blind and visually impaired students learn these skills? Typically, they evolve over time with good instruction and support, and, in the best of all worlds, their parents and family members collaborate with teachers and other service providers in the teaching of appropriate, positive social interaction skills.

*Recreation and leisure skills.* We know from research with blind and visually impaired adults (Kirchner, McBroom, Nelson, & Graves, 1992) that students with visual impairments are at risk for living a life without exercise, engaged in predominately passive activities (listening to the radio, watching television, communicating via e-mail, and so forth), without experiencing the pleasures of roller skating, dancing, hiking, bicycling, swimming, or other similar activities. This limitation occurs in part because students are not taught about the choices available in the community for recreation and are not generally encouraged to try such activities or shown how to play. In fact, well-intentioned teachers, friends, and family members often tell students with visual impairments that they can't take part in such activities because they might be hurt or injure someone else. How do blind and visually impaired children make informed decisions about recreational activities? They have to be active—to try the activities and experiment with the different options available.

*Use of assistive technology.* As part of the curriculum, students with visual impairments need instruction in the use and maintenance of assistive technology as a complement to their use of mainstream computer hardware and software programs. Assistive technology enables students who are blind or visually impaired to access and store information from libraries and other sources around the world via the Internet. In addition, students with visual impairments can use assistive technology for notetaking, studying for tests, research, and a variety of other academic uses as well as for independent living.

*Orientation and mobility.* Orientation and mobility (O&M) training offers alternatives to using sight for safe and independent travel. O&M teaches children and youths how to orient themselves to the environment and, when appropriate, how to use the long cane to travel. Students learn to use optical devices while traveling, such as telescopes or monoculars, to maximize any remaining vision that they may have. O&M instruction needs to be initiated soon after birth and needs to continue throughout school. It is important to note that O&M instruction needs to take place in the specific environments that children visit: home, school, community facilities.

*Independent living skills.* Independent living skills include all the chores that people perform, according to their abilities, that enable them to manage their homes and personal lives. These chores include grooming, eating and preparing meals, taking care of the household (both inside and outdoors), managing money and time, and any other activities related to sustaining life and providing a clean, safe living environment. These skills usually must be taught to children with visual impairments and should be included as part of their educational program so that when they leave school, they will be capable of living on their own.

*Career education.* Career education for students with visual impairments needs to begin as early as possible. It is important to include self-awareness and career-exploration activities, instruction in job-seeking and job-keeping skills, and opportunities for gaining work experience.

*Visual efficiency skills.* Children with impaired but functional vision need to be taught skills to make the most effective use of the limited sensory information they can receive. Instruction in these visual efficiency skills includes the use of optical devices such as magnifiers (videomagnifiers or closed-circuit television systems, as well as handheld and stand magnifiers), bioptic aids, telescopes, magnification software, and so forth. Many children can benefit from a carefully planned, systematic program of vision utilization that increases the effectiveness with which they interpret the visual information that they can receive.

*Self-determination.* Skills of self-determination relate to the ability to advocate for oneself and to be the primary decision maker in one's life. Students who are self-determined know themselves and their needs well. They have the skills to recognize their needs for assistance in completing a task, to identify suggestions for making appropriate accommodations to the task, and to assertively request those accommodations from responsible others. These students have developed negotiation skills that respect themselves and others. They use these skills to advocate for themselves in school and community environments and for planning their future. Self-determination skills evolve with knowledge, confidence, and practice. Teachers of students with visual impairments infuse instruction of these skills in children of all ages, at first modeling their use, then gradually increasing the responsibility of their students in this area.

By working on the skills included in the expanded core curriculum, teachers and parents can encourage children to engage in age-appropriate activities with their peers and to feel competent in doing so. Feeling competent and performing well reinforce a healthy self-concept and high levels of self-esteem. A listing of curricular materials that can be used to teach the eight areas of the expanded core curriculum can be found on the Web site of the Texas School for the Blind and Visually Impaired under Resources for the Expanded Core (www.tsbvi.edu/recc).

# DEVELOPMENT OF SELF-ESTEEM IN ADOLESCENCE

One of the challenges of adolescence is discovering the answer to the question, "Who am I?" Teens answer this question by evaluating their own competence, their social relationships, their sense of self-efficacy, and the perceptions that they believe others hold of them. If a teen lacks the experiences and opportunities that lead to self-knowledge in these areas, then finding an answer to the question, "Who am I?" is more difficult.

As has been discussed throughout this chapter, children and youths with visual impairments may experience many barriers in the process of developing a positive sense of self. Their attachment to caretakers, the parenting style adopted by their families, the degree to which they are allowed and encouraged to take initiative, their social competence, their sense of self-efficacy, and their competence in meeting typical life demands are all affected by circumstances related to not seeing well. Tuttle and Tuttle (2000) describe the tendency of some adolescents with visual impairments to be more immature, egocentric, self-conscious, socially isolated, and dependent as a result of failing to achieve the developmental milestones of early and middle childhood. It is not surprising, then, that some adolescents with visual impairments enter this period without a firm foundation on which to determine their identity.

Even for those youths with visual impairments who enter adolescence with competence and social skills comparable to their peers with vision, there exist challenges to the maintenance of a healthy self-esteem. At this age, conformity to the standards set by the reference group of peers (those peers adolescents want to be like) is important, and differences, such as in appearance or methods of accomplishing tasks, are not easily tolerated and accepted by peers. Visual impairment magnifies these differences, making conformity all the more difficult for the teen who is blind or who has low vision. Attempts by visually impaired teens to establish independence from their parents are often frustrated by family members whose fear about the youths' safety drive them to establish inordinate authority over the youths' life. In addition, teens who want to rebel by, for example, wearing their clothes differently, using makeup, or smoking, may be inhibited because of the difficulty of hiding their actions from parents and other adults (Wolffe, 2000). Similarly, in group situations, having a visual impairment often makes it difficult to monitor and emulate the behaviors of others. (See Chapters 4 and 12 for additional discussion of these issues.)

To the extent that blindness and low vision creates situations of dependence, an adolescent's self-esteem is at risk. Tuttle & Tuttle (2000) observed that "anyone on the dependent-receiving end of a relationship is often deemed less valued and less acceptable" (p. 169). As adolescents with visual impairments confront the undeniability of their own dependence in critical areas, such as transportation, their sense of adequacy and worth is threatened. They may respond to these feelings with aggression, hostility, passiveness, or withdrawal. Resolution is achieved only as a teen's self-concept is strengthened through realizing his or her competence or, sometimes, through the use of adaptive behaviors. As one's overall self-worth is strengthened, assistance, when needed, can be accepted more graciously.

The use of adaptive behaviors and alternative skills are frequently central to the establishment of the identity of adolescents who are visually impaired, particularly those individuals with low vision. In an attempt to hide their difference, teens with low vision often are reported to reject the use of the strategies and tools that increase the effectiveness with which they function. Canes, monoculars, and magnifiers are put away as the youths attempt to "pass" as a sighted person. Tuttle and Tuttle (1996b) note that the motivation to pass is rooted in negative beliefs about the capabilities of people with visual disabilities and in personal shame. Attempting to pass as fully sighted adds stress to one's life, as the possibility of exposure is very real. The achievement of self-acceptance—a prerequisite for positive self-esteem—is not possible when one purposefully deceives relevant others about oneself.

## EXPOSURE TO ADULTS WITH VISUAL DISABILITIES

It is advantageous to expose youngsters of all ages with visual impairments to adults who are blind or have low vision. This practice is particularly effective with adolescents. By interacting with adults who are visually impaired, young people can experience for themselves that having a visual problem need not inhibit their ability to grow up successfully—to have families of their own, to work and play in the community, to contribute to the larger society, and generally to be full participants in adult living. Although there are more visually impaired adults than children, there are usually few such adults in any one community. Therefore, people who work with visually impaired children who have additional disabilities may need to help put these youngsters in touch with adults with similar disabilities. The two major consumer groups whose members include people with visual impairments and their families, the American Council of the Blind and the National Federation of the Blind (see the Resources section at the end of this book for contact information) each have members who are willing to mentor young people with similar disabilities. In addition, the American Foundation for the Blind (see Resources section) maintains a database known as CareerConnect of successfully employed adults who are blind or who have low vision and who are willing to mentor young people by sharing information about their career paths and jobs. Public and private rehabilitation agencies in some communities can help visually impaired youngsters to meet adults with similar disabilities.

## ACTIVITIES TO ENCOURAGE HIGH LEVELS OF SELF-ESTEEM

Self-esteem evolves over time. Its beginnings are in infancy as children are loved and made to feel safe, and it is strengthened in early childhood when children are parented firmly with consistent boundaries, encouraged to explore, provided with constructive feedback, and allowed to become increasingly independent. In middle childhood the development of competence and strong social relationships outside the family reinforces a child's sense of self-worth. Eventually, an identity emerges that is based on the adolescent's response to all his or her positive and negative experiences. However, for children and youths with visual impairments, there are many barriers to the formation of healthy, positive self-esteem.

Tuttle and Tuttle (2000), in discussing the emphasis that is placed on academic performance, stress that "developing and maintaining the integrity of the whole child and nurturing healthy self-esteem should be the highest priorities. When all else is said and done, the most crucial and vital contributors to a full, rich, and satisfying life are broader and more basic than completing one academic grade after another" (p. 169). They suggest that adults should create an environment in which children can develop the skills and attitudes necessary for a positive self-image. Within that environment, students should be given opportunities to accept themselves, be socially connected, make informed choices, be genuinely productive, and relax and have fun.

Self-esteem, then, is not static. It can be altered through activities and experiences that are designed to change an individual's competence, social interactions, or way of thinking about the self. The ideas presented throughout this chapter have focused largely on helping families influence the self-esteem of children with visual impairments as they grow and develop. Although teachers may have only a limited impact on their students' family life, they have much more control over their instructional activities. Preschoolers who are not being provided opportunities to explore or take initiative at home need to be provided those opportunities at school. Teachers can share with their young students the wonder of a chrysalis, the excitement of finding a bird's nest, and the pleasure in learning what is on the principal's desk. They can provide simple cooking experiences that involve pouring, spreading, scooping, mixing, and washing. Youngsters can be taught to take pride in being able to sharpen pencils, count out snacks, and take the attendance list to the office. Through these kinds of experiences, young children with visual impairments can participate in their world and begin to establish an understanding of their capabilities.

In middle childhood, children with visual impairments, particularly those who have a low sense of self-efficacy, need frequent, carefully designed opportunities to practice tasks until mastery is achieved and to demonstrate their competence to others. Teachers can play an important role in the development of these skills in two ways. First, they can create lessons that focus on the skills included in the expanded core curriculum, skills that lead to greater competence and increased confidence. Perhaps more important, a teacher's belief in a child's ability to master difficult tasks can be infectious; a teacher's confidence in a child's abilities, often turns the child's attitude from negative to positive and boosts his or her determination to succeed.

Young people with visual impairments, like other children, develop self-esteem by helping others in their families, at school, and in the community. Young people need to complete chores and help out around the house and can benefit from opportunities to help their siblings or neighboring children with craft projects, school assignments, surprises for their parents, and neighborhood efforts, from lemonade stands to snow shoveling.

Mangold (1980) recommends that children with visual impairments keep lists of the skills that they have mastered. An itemization of "I can" activities documents progress and strengthens the child's awareness of his or her positive characteristics. Mangold (1980) suggests that children find it easier to accept their disability when they can refer with pride to a list of their accomplishments.

Shared reading of biographies about people who are disabled is another strategy that can be successful with students who are learning to accept their differences and to identify their rightful place in the world. The achievements of others can inspire students with visual impairments to persist toward their goals, can offer information about how others solved common problems, and can provide insights through which students can better understand themselves and others.

Other key components in the development of self-esteem are related to positive social experiences with same-age peers, including peers with visual impairments. For some children with visual impairments, the social and recreational activities offered by school or civic and religious groups provide these opportunities. Identifying an area of interest and developing enthusiasm around it can often lead to successful interpersonal relationships as youths meet with others who have similar interests. The range of possibilities is as long as the list of groups that are found at school (the Chess Club, Key Club, Spanish Club, or Future Farmers of America, to name a few) or within the community (these might include stamp collecting, Baroque music enthusiasts, mystery novel reading, or ballroom dancing). Adolescents and youths who develop an interest in sports can usually find companions who share their passion. When children with visual impairments engage in games or competition with their peers, they learn to work with children their own age and they feel connected to peer groups. Competitions in which children can perform well help them to develop both confidence and self-esteem.

Often, the identification of interests requires considerable exploration and involves many dead ends as students try a variety of new sports or hobbies until they discover one they enjoy. The advantage of joining groups or clubs is that the shared interest in the activity often acts as a bridge, creating a connection with nondisabled peers. Instead of focusing on how the visually impaired individual is different, the emphasis is on what the group members have in common.

Finding paid employment is another strategy through which students with visual impairments can further develop an appreciation for their likes and dislikes and their strengths and weaknesses. Work provides an opportunity to meet others and to utilize one's social skills in a different kind of environment, while at the same time building skills. Transition programs provide opportunities to experiment with different types of work and are often designed to facilitate realization of students' self-identity. In one unique transition program, introduced by the Texas Commission for the Blind in 1992, counselors identify visually impaired high school students who have demonstrated evidence of leadership. Students participate in positive, confidence-building experiences that hone their leadership skills (Kay, 1997). Of course, just being identified as having leadership qualities would boost the self-concept of most teens.

Another powerful way to test children's mettle and encourage the development of self-confidence can be provided by participation in ropes courses or challenge courses. These courses are available in many communities and consist of a series of physical challenges, such as scaling a tower, swinging out over an expanse of water on a rope swing, zipping along a line between two high towers using a metal hook and canvas harness, or similar efforts. Some of the challenges are completed alone; others are only achievable through group efforts. The beauty of such courses is that they encourage youths to push themselves to engage in activities that they would not normally experience; successful completion of such activities builds self-confidence.

Participation in day or overnight camps is another activity in which the shared experience of meeting new challenges can focus children on their commonalities. Whether students participate in camping adventures with Boy Scouts, Girl Scouts, Indian Princesses, Campfire Girls, or other religious or secular groups, these outings are an important part of growing up and developing self-confidence and self-esteem. There are also camps that offer programming specifically for children with visual impairments, and these opportunities can provide positive venues for increasing competence and creating relationships with others. Parents need to carefully choose the camp to which they send their child, taking into consideration their child's current skills, the skills of their child's peers, the availability of adapted equipment, and the level of support provided by counselors (not too little, not too much). The ideal camp will offer appropriate challenges and supportive peers and counselors. Participation in camp experiences with both children who are disabled and those who are not offers the best of both worlds to campers with visual impairments.

Other enjoyable activities include orienteering and braille rallies, activities that combine the skills of participants who are visually impaired with those of participants with vision. Introduced in 1972 by the Braille Institute in Los Angeles, California, and replicated throughout the United States, braille rallies set up a prescribed motor course in which young, visually impaired braille readers are paired with sighted drivers to negotiate the course. The visually impaired youngster functions as navigator and must read the course directions, which are written in braille, to the driver, who negotiates the car through the course. The drivers, who have no advance information or familiarity with the course, are typically volunteers and have not met the navigators prior to the event. The team of driver and navigator must confirm their arrival at each checkpoint, where they receive the next set of directions. The winning team is the first to arrive at the end point, without having exceeded the posted speed limit.

Orienteering, an activity enjoyed by both visually impaired and sighted individuals, has many variations. Orienteering may include solo racing events in which athletes maneuver through complex courses, guided only by a map and under strict time constraints; outdoor adventure activities in which participants use a map to locate a series of control flags and then mark their competition cards with a punch or stamp to prove that they found the location; and an untimed, noncompetitive outdoor activity in which participants use a map to find their way from location to location, typically scenic ones (see Northern Ireland Orienteering Club, 2003). Tactile maps and brailled instructions enable visually impaired youngsters to actively participate in orienteering activities.

## CONCLUSION

A sense of personal adequacy is a universal basic need upon which an individual's mental health and personal adjustment depend (Tuttle & Tuttle, 1996). Personal adequacy, or self-esteem, evolves from infancy through adolescence and early adulthood. It is shaped by life experiences and is responsive to situational demands. Other factors, for individuals growing up with visual impairments, include the impact of their visual impairment on attachments, initiatives, explorations, competencies, and social interactions. Children with visual impairments can develop positive self-concepts when they are provided with love and acceptance, opportunities to explore, high expectations, and meaningful shared experiences with others, including both blind and sighted peers.

For those youngsters whose self-concept has been negatively influenced by the barriers to healthy self-esteem presented by blindness or low vision, teachers and other adults can present planned opportunities to learn skills and master social situations. These opportunities must be valued by the child, be attainable through persistence and true effort, and be challenging enough to conflict with the child's current self-concept.

The long-term goal of nurturing self-esteem in children is for individuals to accept and like themselves, connect socially, make informed choices about their lives, be genuinely productive, and relax and have fun. Professionals who work with children with visual impairment and their families cannot afford to ignore this critical area of development.

# REFERENCES

Asher, S. R., & Dodge, K. A. (1985). Identifying children who are rejected by their peers. *Developmental Psychology, 22,* 444–449.

Bandura, A. (1986). *Social foundations of thought and action.* Englewood Cliffs, NJ: Prentice-Hall.

Bandura, A. (1993). Perceived self-efficacy in cognitive development and functioning. *Educational Psychologist, 28,* 117–148.

Baumeister, R. F., Smart, L., & Boden, J. M. (1996). Relation of threatened egotism to violence and aggression: The dark side of high self-esteem. *Psychological Review, 103,* 5–33.

Baumrind, D. (1971). Current patterns of parental authority. *Developmental Psychology Monographs, 4*(1, Part 2).

Bee, H. (1997). *The developing child* (8th ed.). New York: Addison-Wesley.

Blake, P. C., & Slate, J. R. (1993). A preliminary investigation into the relationship between adolescent self-esteem and parental verbal interaction. *The School Counselor, 41,* 81–85.

Burnett, P. C. (1996). An investigation of the social learning and symbolic interaction models for the development of self-concepts and self-esteem. *Journal of Family Studies, 2,* 57–64.

Chen, D. (1999). Interactions between infants and caregivers. In D. Chen (Ed.), *Essential elements in early intervention: Visual impairment and multiple disabilities* (pp. 22–54). New York: AFB Press.

Coopersmith, S. (1967). *The antecedents of self-esteem.* San Francisco: W. H. Freeman.

Dodge, K. A., & Price, J. M. (1994). On the relation between social information processing and socially competent behavior in early school-aged children. *Child Development, 65,* 1385–1398.

Erickson, M. F., Sroufe, L. A., & Egeland, B. (1985). The relation between quality of attachment and behavior problems in preschool in a high-risk sample. In I. Bretherton & E. Waters (Eds.), *Growing points for attachment theory and research* (pp. 147–166). *Monographs of the Society for Research in Child Development, 50* (Serial No. 209).

Erikson, E. H. (1980). *Identity and the life cycle*. New York: Norton. (Original work published in 1959.)

Feldman, R. S. (2001). *Child development* (2nd ed.). Upper Saddle River, NJ: Prentice-Hall.

Franzoi, S. L., Davis, M. H., & Vasquez-Suson, K. A. (1994). Two social worlds: Social correlates and stability of adolescent status groups. *Journal of Personality and Social Psychology, 67*, 462–473.

Harter, S. (1990). Processes underlying adolescent self-concept formation. In R. Montemayor, G. R. Adams, & T. P. Gullotta (Eds.), *Advances in adolescent development, Vol. 2: From childhood to adolescence: A transitional period?* Newbury Park, CA: Sage.

Harter, S. (2001). *Construction of the self: A developmental perspective*. New York: Guilford.

Hartup, W. W., & Moore, S. G. (1990). Early peer relations: Developmental significance and prognostic implications. *Early Childhood Research Quarterly, 5*, 1–17.

Hatlen, P. (1996). The core curriculum for blind and visually impaired students, including those with additional disabilities. *RE:view, 28*, 25–32.

Huebner, K. M., Merk-Adam, B., Stryker, D., & Wolffe, K. (2004). *The national agenda for the education of children and youths with visual impairments, including those with multiple disabilities* (rev. ed.). New York: AFB Press.

Kay, J. L. (1997). Implementing a student leadership committee. *Journal of Visual Impairment & Blindness, 91*, 296–300.

Kirchner, C. (1999). Prevalence estimates for visual impairment: Cutting through the data jungle. *Journal of Visual Impairment & Blindness, 93*, 253–259.

Kirchner, C., & Diament, S. (1999a). Estimates of the number of visually impaired students, their teachers, and orientation and mobility specialists: Part 1. *Journal of Visual Impairment & Blindness, 93*, 600–606.

Kirchner, C., & Diament, S. (1999b). Estimates of the number of visually impaired students, their teachers, and orientation and mobility specialists: Part 2. *Journal of Visual Impairment & Blindness, 93*, 738–744.

Kirchner, C., McBroom, L. W., Nelson, K. A., & Graves, W. H. (1992). *Lifestyles of employed legally blind people: A study of expenditures and time use*. Mississippi State, MS: Mississippi State University Rehabilitation and Training Center on Blindness and Low Vision.

Klein, H. A. (2000). Self-esteem and beyond. *Childhood Education, 76*(4), 240–241.

Langley, B. (1996). Daily life. In M. C. Holbrook (Ed.), *Children with visual impairments: A parents guide* (pp. 97–127). Bethesda, MD: Woodbine House.

Lefrancois, G. R. (1995). *Of children: An introduction to child development* (8th ed.). Belmont, CA: Wadsworth Publishing Company.

Lewis, S., Slay, S., & Pace, E. (1999). *Preschool attainment through typical every day routines: Curriculum guide*. Tallahassee: Florida State University, Department of Special Education.

Macoby, E., & Martin, J. (1983). Socialization in the context of the family: Parent-child interaction. In E. M. Hetherington (Ed.), *Handbook of Child Psychology, Vol IV: Socialization, Personality, and Social Development* (4th ed.; pp. 1–101). New York: Wiley.

Mangold, S. S. (1980). Nurturing high self-esteem in visually handicapped children. In S. S. Mangold (Ed.), *A teacher's guide to the special educational needs of blind and visually handicapped children* (pp. 94–101). New York: American Foundation for the Blind.

Mason, C., & Davidson, R. (2000). *National plan for training personnel to serve children with blindness and low vision.* Reston, VA: Council for Exceptional Children.

New Comb, A. F., Bukowski, W. M., & Pattee, L. (1993). Children's peer relations: A meta-analytic review of popular, rejected, neglected, controversial, and average sociometric status. *Psychological Bulletin, 113,* 99–128.

Northern Ireland Orienteering Club. (2003). *What is orienteering?* Retrieved August 2, 2003, from www.niorienteering.org.uk/what.html.

Papalia, D. E., & Olds, S. W. (1992). *Human development* (5th ed.). New York: McGraw-Hill, Inc.

Sacks, S. Z., & Silberman, R. K. (2000). Social skills. In A. J. Koenig & M. C. Holbrook (Eds.), *Foundations of education, Vol. 2: Instructional strategies for teaching children and youths with visual impairments* (2nd ed., pp. 616–652). New York: AFB Press.

Shonkoff, J. P., & Phillips, D. A. (Eds.). (2000). *From neurons to neighborhoods: The science of early childhood development.* Washington, DC: National Academy Press.

Sroufe, L. A. (1985). Attachment classification from the perspective of infant-caregiver relationships and infant temperament. *Child Development, 56,* 1–14.

Sroufe, L. A., Fox, N., & Pancake, V. R. (1983). Attachment and dependency in developmental perspective. *Child Development, 54,* 1615–1627.

Stipeck, D., Recchia, S., & McClintic, S. (1992). Self evaluations in young children. *Monographs of the Society for Research in Child Development, 57*(1, Serial No 226).

Trawick-Smith, J. (2000). *Early childhood development: A multicultural perspective* (2nd ed.). Upper Saddle River, NJ: Merrill-Prentice Hall.

Turner, P. J. (1993). Attachment to mother and behavior with adults in preschool. *British Journal of Developmental Psychology, 11,* 75–89.

Tuttle, D., & Tuttle, N. (1996a). Nurturing your child's self-esteem. In M. C. Holbrook (Ed.), *Children with visual impairments: A parents guide* (pp. 159–174). Bethesda, MD: Woodbine House.

Tuttle, D., & Tuttle, N. (1996b). *Self-esteem and adjusting with blindness: The process of responding to life's demands* (2nd ed.). Springfield, IL: Charles C. Thomas.

Tuttle, D. W., & Tuttle, N. R. (2000). Psychosocial needs of children and youths. In M. C. Holbrook & A. J. Koenig (Eds.), *Foundations of education,*

*Vol. 1: History and theory of teaching children and youths with visual impairments* (2nd ed., pp. 161–172). New York: AFB Press.

Vaillant, G. E., & Vaillant, C. O. (1981). Natural history of male psychological health: 10. Work as a predictor of positive mental health. *The American Journal of Psychiatry, 138,* 1433–1440.

Valdes, K. A., Williamson, C. L., & Wagner, M. M. (1990). *The national longitudinal transition study of special education students. Statistical almanac, Vol. 6: Youth categorized as visually impaired.* Menlo Park, CA: SRI International.

Wolffe, K. E. (2000). Career education. In A. J. Koenig & M. C. Holbrook (Eds.), *Foundations of education, Vol. 2: Instructional strategies for teaching children and youths with visual impairments* (2nd ed.; pp. 679–719). New York: AFB Press.

# CHAPTER 6

# Developing Friendships and Positive Social Relationships

## L. Penny Rosenblum

---

*"If you're friends because you like their personality and what's inside and you look beneath the skin, then I think that's what makes a friend."—10th grade sighted student who is the best friend of a blind 10th grader (Rosenblum, 1997a, p. 245)*

---

Friendships are a cornerstone of our lives, as we are social beings. Making a friend, being a friend, and relying on a friend for caring and companionship contribute to the quality of one's life. When a child has a visual impairment, it may be challenging to make and maintain friendships. Through intervention, a child can learn the essential skills necessary to develop and nurture friendships with peers. This chapter describes the importance of friendships and other social relationships in children's lives and provides guidance to those supporting children with visual impairments in their development and maintenance of friendships and other social relationships, should these not occur naturally.

Friendship is a construct that does not lend itself to a single definition. Friendships are characterized as nonkinship selective relationships shared by two individuals (Cotterell, 1996); however, there is often a distinction made between the term "best friend" and "close friend." A best friend for an adolescent is a relationship with a high level of intimacy, trust, loyalty, and sharing of mutual interests (Cottrell, 1996; Rosenblum, 1997a); a close friendship can be thought of as an acquaintance within a peer group with whom one shares mutual interests (Rosenblum, 1997a). These peer groups are often referred to as cliques (Cottrell, 1996). There is an extensive body of literature that examines the friendship patterns of typically developing children (Rosenblum, 1997a), and a brief synopsis of this literature is provided in the following sections that includes information relevant to children and adolescents with visual impairments.

## ELEMENTS OF FRIENDSHIP

What makes someone a "friend" varies from one person to another. Although the presence of a visual impairment may affect an individual's ability to interpret social interactions intrinsic to a friendship, friendships are critical to everyone. Thus, it is important for children with visual impairments to develop and maintain friendships so that they can reap the satisfaction, support, and enjoyment that come from being a friend and having a friend. To be successful within friendships, children and youths with visual impairments must learn the basic skills of how to be intimate (emotionally, intellectually, or physically) within a friendship and how to be a loyal and trustworthy friend. The different levels at which individuals relate to others—as acquaintances, friends, or intimates—are considered in greater detail in Chapter 12.

Friendships are important relationships in the lives of both children and adults. By the time a typical child is 3 years of age, he or she is beginning to have friendships with age-mates. During the preschool and early elementary school years, friendships are based on "someone to play with" and are not intimate, meaning they are not about sharing feelings, hopes, dreams, and so forth. In the late elementary years and into adolescence, the focus of friendships turns more to intimacy, and issues such as trust, loyalty, and respect become critical. For adolescents, "friendships do not just happen; they have to be made—made to start, made to work, made to develop, kept in good working order, and preserved from going sour. To do all this we need to be active and we need to be skillful" (Duck, 1983, p. 9). The skills involved in developing a friendship are numerous; for instance, being able to read the nonverbal cues of others, knowing how to reciprocate, being able to maintain conversations, understanding the feelings and needs of a friend and acting in accordance with them, and so forth. (Sidebar 6.1

## Sidebar 6.1

### TIPS FOR DEVELOPING FRIENDSHIP-BUILDING SKILLS

Making friends can take some thought and effort, but there are skills for making and keeping friends that can be learned, such as the following:

#### Reading the Nonverbal Cues of Others

- Listen carefully to the tone of others' voices. Does the speaker sound cheerful, anxious, sad, or angry?
- Ask if you have understood the other person correctly based on what you hear in his or her voice.
- Listen for extraneous movement, such as a finger or foot tapping, which may indicate that the person is nervous or anxious.
- Notice when you take another's arm (for guidance) or shake hands how the person feels—relaxed, tense, uncomfortable, or comfortable.
- Ask for input about a speaker's body language or facial expression if there is someone you trust who is in close proximity.
- Preface comments that you make in response to another's communication with phrases like, "It sounds like you mean," or "I think I understand you to be saying," or "Do I understand your meaning? I think I hear you expressing (fill in a feeling like happiness, sadness, fear, anger)."

#### Knowing How to Reciprocate

- When others ask you questions, respond with details—not just monosyllabic answers.
- If someone gives you something (a gift, time, a ride) recognize that you must respond in kind—with a gift, your time, money toward gas,

*(continued on next page)*

Sidebar 6.1 *(continued)*

or the like—even if the person says that it is not expected. At a minimum, you must thank others for their gifts and understand that if
you want them to continue giving you things, you must give them
something in return.

- When someone is struggling (with packages, perhaps, or with a hard
assignment or a relationship), it is important to listen to the person's
concerns and offer any assistance that you can provide—for instance,
help carry the packages, assist on the assignment, or share how you
have dealt with a similar relationship problem.

- Follow a greeting by asking how the other person is doing; respond
positively (great, wonderful, fine) when asked how you are doing, and
thank the person who's made the inquiry.

- Remember friends' birthdays and note the religious and secular holidays
that they typically celebrate.

**Maintaining Conversations**

- Be prepared to initiate social interactions by greeting others and then
asking others to identify themselves (if they forget to do so) and to tell
a little bit about themselves. Be prepared to also tell a little about
yourself (where you are from, what you like doing, some basic details
about your family—how many children or pets there are, and so
forth).

- Identify mutual concerns and areas of interest.

- Ask questions about the other person's interests, family, friends, school
or civic activities, extracurricular pursuits, and what the person does
(vocational or volunteer types of activities).

- Remember the names of people's family members, pets, and other
friends—ask how they are doing.

- Remember where people have been or what they have done that is
unusual or adventuresome, and ask about those incidents.

- Listen to what people say to you and respond to them accordingly—
do not change the topic of discussion (to you, to some insignificant
detail, or to another topic altogether).

- Ask what plans others have for the future. Share what plans you have
for the future, unless by so sharing you will make the other person
uncomfortable. For instance, if a friend tells you that she is not going

to be able to attend the big ball game because she can't afford it, it would not be nice to say that you plan to go.

- Remember that to sustain a conversation, you must stay focused on the conversation and the person trying to communicate with you. You can't also do other things, such as play games, talk on the phone, shuffle papers, watch television, or look out the window (even if you can't see, you must look toward the speaker).

**Understanding the Feelings and Needs of a Friend**

- Pay attention to what others say and respond with caring comments.
- Remember what people tell you about what their plans are and act accordingly. For example, if your friend tells you that he is planning to study on Sunday for a big test, and you call to see if your friend would like to do something fun with you on Saturday, acknowledge that you have remembered his plan for Sunday. If a friend shares his worries about a confrontation with his parents over an imposed curfew that he feels is unfair, you may want to ask him if he's thought about their concerns and how he might address them. You may want to share how you spoke with your parents about your own curfew issues. Sometimes, you may want to simply be there for a friend—be a "good ear," someone with whom he or she can discuss feelings.
- Remember stories that your friends share with you and refer back to those stories when appropriate with comments like, "I remember when you told me about that adventure you went on with ___ and how much you liked it" or "Remember when we went to ___ and how much fun it was?"
- When someone sounds sad or unhappy, ask if there is anything you can do to help. Let the person know that you are concerned that he or she sounds unhappy.
- Don't be afraid to ask others how they are feeling and share with them how you feel. Friends share insights about their feelings with one another.

KAREN WOLFFE

offers some suggestions for students on how to develop friendship-building skills.)

During the elementary and early adolescent years, friendships are predominately with peers of the same gender (Clark & Ayers, 1991; McCoy, 1992; Ritz, 1992; Sharabany, Gershoni, & Hofman,

1981). It has been reported that up to 90 percent of friendships in childhood are with same-sex peers (Clark & Ayers, 1991; Jones, 1985). Cross-sex friendships are rare. From an early age children are taught, often subtly, that girls play with girls, and boys play with boys. Girls are expected to be emotional, intimate, and close while boys are expected to be rational, strong, and active (Shechtman, 1994). Girls generally expect more of their friends than do boys (Claes, 1992). Also, girls mature at an earlier age than do boys and, on the whole, are believed to be better at discussing emotions (Kon, 1981). Different levels of maturity and different expectations, coupled with what is deemed socially acceptable, teach children from an early age that same-sex friendships are more acceptable than cross-sex friendships. Rosenblum (1997a) found that for 40 adolescents with visual impairments, 33 of the friendships were with a peer of the same gender. Three of the relationships that crossed gender lines were characterized as dating relationships.

Adolescents are generally within one year of the age of their best friend (Jones, 1985). Rosenblum (1997a) found that, on average, the 40 adolescents with visual impairment in her study were within 3 months of their best friends' age, and over two-thirds were within 15 months. Claes (1992) found that the number of best friends for sighted children ranged from 1 to 4, with males having fewer best friends than females, whereas the number of close friends for sighted adolescents in another study ranged from 3 to 30 (Urberg, Degirmencioglu, Tolson, & Halliday-Scher, 1995). Kef (1997) found that males who were visually impaired had fewer friends (an average of 4.7) compared to females who were visually impaired (an average of 5.7). The visually impaired adolescents in Kef's sample had fewer friends than a comparison group of sighted adolescents. (Kef did not distinguish between best friends and close friendships.) Rosenblum's findings (1997a) were similar, with the 20 males in her study reporting slightly fewer best friends (an average of 2.05) than the 20 females (2.45).

The intricacies of friendship change over time (Claes, 1992; Jones, 1985; Ritz, 1992; Sharabany et al., 1981). As children grow older they know more about their best friends' likes, feelings, and thoughts, which is a reflection of the emergence of more intimate friendships during adolescence (Sharabany et al., 1981). There are a variety of benefits to be derived from participating in a friendship including opportunities to communicate, social support, a sense of belonging and acceptance, reassurance about one's worth and value, love, and an opportunity to help others (Duck, 1983). As Hartup (1993) put it:

Good developmental outcomes depend on having friends and keeping them. Friendships furnish the individual with socialization opportunities not easily obtained elsewhere (including experiences in intimacy and conflict management), and these relationships are important in emotion regulation, in self-understanding, and in formation and functioning of subsequent relationships (including romantic relationships). [p. 11]

The structure of friendships changes with age and time. Their breadth and depth and the amount of interaction involved—in short, the level of intimacy—increases (Sharabany et al., 1981). The level of interaction depends on the type of friendship—best, close, or casual—in which the friends are engaged. Sharabany and her colleagues (1981) reported that the level of intimacy within the friendship is higher for a best friend than for a close friend. Serafica and Blyth (1985) stated, "Young adolescents conceptualize friendship as a relationship where there is mutual intimacy and mutual support. Such a view of friendship leads them to value understanding, empathy, loyalty, and trustworthiness as the defining attributes of a friend" (p. 270).

Children with visual impairments may lack the skills to easily develop successful friendships (Hoben & Linstrom, 1980; MacCuspie, 1990, 1996; Warren, 1994). They may not read nonverbal signals correctly or know how to initiate interaction. They may not fully understand the need to reciprocate and may not develop age-appropriate interests and hobbies that are often the cornerstone of a friendship. Thus, it becomes important early on in children's lives for families and professionals to ensure that children have practice in developing these skills and have opportunities to meet potential friends. There is a tremendous amount for children with visual impairments to gain from being with other children of the same age.

## LAYING THE FOUNDATION FOR SUCCESSFUL RELATIONSHIPS

Friendships are one of many relationships in people's lives. In addition to friendships, individuals have relationships with their families—parents, siblings, and extended family members. These family relationships are the building blocks for nonfamilial relationships outside the home. Children may also have relationships with other important adults in their lives—teachers, neighbors, coaches, group leaders, religious leaders, and so forth. They have relationships with other children, too, although these relationships may not be friendships. For example, they have classmates at school, teammates, children in the neighborhood with whom they socialize, and children they see at religious services or school. Some of these relationships may be superficial; however, all a person's relationships have an impact on the individual.

The individuals in one's life who are significant (friends, family members) are considered as part of one's personal network, which serves as a source of social support. Kef (1997) examined the personal networks of 316 individuals with visual impairments between the ages of 14 and 23 in the Netherlands. She found that the personal networks of her subjects ranged in size from 8 to 13 individuals, compared to 15 to 20 individuals in the personal networks of sighted individuals as reported in Kef's review of the literature. The many relationships in an individual's personal network have different reasons and serve a multitude of purposes. Someone of the same gender and approximately the same age may be considered a friend—someone to whom the individual turns to seek emotional support. The individual may look to a teacher or coworker for practical support, in helping to get work accomplished.

One's ability to be successful in the development and maintenance of friendship and other social relationships hinges on many factors, including family, community, and professional support as well as opportunities to engage in interactions with others. A well-rounded individual who has opportunities to interact with others and who receives positive feedback from others is more likely to succeed in all aspects of social interaction.

## FAMILY INVOLVEMENT IN FRIENDSHIP BUILDING

The role of the family in the social development of children with visual impairments was discussed in Chapter 2. Families are the first socializing agent in children's lives. From the day a child is born, the child looks to his or her parents to nourish, protect, and nurture. Children with visual impairments, like all children, enter the world unable to meet their own basic needs for food, clothing, and shelter. Babies who are born into families that are able to meet these needs quickly learn that a cry summons someone to change them, feed them, hold them, dress them, and so forth. Babies who are born into families that are unable to consistently meet these basic needs will not learn to trust their caregivers (Feldman, 1998).

When a child is born with a visual impairment, or any disability, the family often goes through a grieving process for the loss of the "normal" baby they had expected (Herring, 1996; Tuttle & Tuttle, 1996, 2004). This process is often equated to the experience with a death of a loved one. Emotions experienced in the grieving process may include anger, guilt, fear, resentment, and denial (Herring, 1996). The grief families experience at having a child who is "not normal" is likely to recur when transitions occur in the life of the child. Events such as the first day of kindergarten or reaching the age at which teenager's ordinarily would obtain a learner's driving permit can trigger feelings of anger, guilt, fear, resentment, and denial for family members (Herring, 1996).

The attitudes family members have toward a child's visual impairment are likely to influence how the child comes to view his or her own visual impairment (Tuttle & Tuttle, 1996, 2004). Depending on the cause of the visual impairment and the family's prior experience with visual impairment, they may view the child as a child first who happens to be visually impaired; or they may view him or her as a visually impaired child, with the visual impairment front and center. Placing too much emphasis on the visual impairment and not enough emphasis on the child as an individual can potentially have a negative impact on the child. The visual impairment may affect relationships within the family, including the parents' marital relationship, sibling relationships, and allocation of time by parents (Bolinger & Bolinger, 1996). Furthermore, it may also influence how the family views the child's social abilities and needs. Some children with visual impairment may not feel included within the family. Gail, an eleventh grader who is blind, describes her experience: "Our family doesn't do a lot together, or at least they do and I kind of do something separately: They go camping. They go bike riding and hiking, go up the back into the woods, and stuff like that" (Rosenblum, 1997a, p. 225).

If a child such as Gail is not included within the activities of her family, then she is missing out on important opportunities to build social skills, such as the use of nonverbal behaviors and learning to communicate about the world outside the home. Although parents need to take time for themselves, for their marriage, and for each of their children, it is important that the child with the visual impairment be included when family activities such as camping trips, visits to relatives, or movie nights are planned.

Although children with visual impairments need to be included in their family's activities, as they move into adolescence, an age at which sighted teens begin to spend more time with friends than family, they too need to spend less time with family and more time with friends. Including the child with visual impairment within the typical activities of the family lays the groundwork for later independence and ultimately helps to promote the development of age-appropriate friendships. The following strategies indicate how families can support the social development of their children.

## STRATEGIES FOR SOCIAL SUCCESS
# Suggestions for Families

- Try to help your child eliminate or reduce mannerisms (such as head shaking, hand flapping, rocking) that make your child look different from others. Not only do these behaviors discourage others from relating to the child socially, but when children engage in them, they are not engaging in other appropriate activities. The teacher of students with visual impairments and other specialists can help the family to develop specific strategies to decrease mannerisms for individual students.

- Engage in conversations with your child—not just a question-and-answer session. Model for your child how to engage another person in appropriate conversation by using a combination of asking questions and sharing your experiences. Remember that the more experiences a visually impaired child has, the more he or she will have to share during conversation with others.

- Teach your child nonverbal behaviors that are age appropriate. Other children will respond to a visually impaired child's use of such nonverbal behaviors as nodding, using hand gestures (such as the "thumbs up" sign), smiling, or frowning. Sharing with your child when you use these types of nonverbal cues and when you observe others using them is important. Physically guide the child to make appropriate gestures, provide positive reinforcement when he or she makes an appropriate facial expression, and provide your child with verbal cues to use these nonverbal behaviors when interacting with you, as appropriate.

- Provide your child with gentle but realistic feedback on all aspects of life. Let the child know when a conversation he or she had with someone worked—or did not. For example, if the child was simply asking a series of questions rather than truly conversing, you could role play with the child to experiment with how the conversation could have evolved using different techniques, such as self-revelation or information sharing. Give your child feedback about his or her appearance, use of nonverbal behaviors, travel skills, and so forth; take into consideration how your child's skills compare to the skills of same-aged peers. When a child is blind or has severe low vision, family members often need to help the child "observe" others.

◆ Promote independent travel. For young children this may mean using a modified human guide technique (letting the child hold the wrist of the guide rather than the elbow); for older children it could include using a cane or using residual vision to travel under supervision. Children who are always taken places may not learn how to move about in the environment to seek out age-mates in social situations (Rosenblum & Corn, 2003).

◆ Encourage your child to wear socially appropriate clothing for his or her age. While families should not feel compelled to spend an excessive amount of money on trendy clothing or hair styles, they do need to be aware of their child's appearance and how it compares to that of same-age peers. Children who are blind or who have severe low vision may not be aware of how personal appearance influences others. Discussion of these considerations needs to take place as children help select their clothes, hairstyle, accessories, and so forth in the younger years and take increasing responsibility for these choices as they grow older.

## INVOLVEMENT OF SIGNIFICANT OTHERS

Children with visual impairments are more often than not assumed to be in need of help. A peer at school may be assigned to walk with the visually impaired student; another peer may be requested to read information from the board to the child; a sibling may be asked to watch a brother or sister who does not see well. The adults in these instances, though well-meaning, convey the message to both the child with the visual impairment and the helpers that the child is less capable or needs to be helped. Although this may be accurate, adults need to be careful to balance situations in which the child needs assistance with situations in which the child can assist others. They will be of considerable help to the child with a visual impairment if they teach the skills needed so that he or she can also be the helper. For example, children with visual impairments can be taught to play board games (adapted board games are available from companies listed in the Resources section) and encouraged to help others learn them at a house party, at a scouting or similar meeting, during recess, or other such times.

When adults provide intervention related to social skills, they need to find that a delicate balance between providing too much information and direction and not providing enough. For example, young children in preschool or early elementary school have playtime or recess on a daily basis. This time is typically not adult focused, and the children are free to choose their playmates and their activities within the play space. When a child is blind or has significantly restricted visual abilities, he or she may not be able to determine where the materials are or where the child is that he or she wants to play with. By the time the child makes these determinations, the materials may have been taken or the other child may have moved somewhere else. Helpful adults may overstretch their roles by jumping in by making assumptions about the child's wishes and taking the child where he or she seems to want to go or making other children give up toys that they have taken so the child who is visually impaired can play with them. Adults acting as intermediaries in this manner may be interfering with the natural development of children's relationships. Conversely, the adult who does nothing is not providing enough input for the child to learn strategies needed to succeed socially in such an environment. The following suggestions can help adults enhance the likelihood of achieving social success for children who are blind or visually impaired without overdoing their assistance.

## STRATEGIES FOR SOCIAL SUCCESS

# Suggestions for Teachers and Other Adults

- ◆ Be certain that the child is well oriented to the play area and can easily find important landmarks (swings, seesaw, monkey bars, merry-go-round, water fountain, and so forth) both when the area is deserted and when the area is in use.

- ◆ Set limits on the amount of time that any one child or group of children may play with any of the toys or playground equipment.

- ◆ Encourage the visually impaired child to partner with another child before heading off to the play area; in this way, the sighted child can assist with finding a desired site or toy.

- ◆ Set the stage for social success so that play time is not always unstructured by establishing days of the week during which play time is devoted to specific activities such as table games or group activities like jump rope, Red Rover, Simon Says, Hot Potato, dodgeball, or the like.

Although children and youths with visual impairments may be physically included in a general education class, they may not be socially included (Hatlen, 2004). The concept of inclusion was intended to cover all aspects of the school environment, from the classroom to the cafeteria to the playground. Some children may realize that they are not included within the "popular kids" circles at their school and not be bothered by this (Rosenblum, 2000). Others may not fully recognize that they are not part of the complete peer culture in their school (MacCuspie, 1990). Professionals in the field of visual impairment and families have a responsibility to monitor how a child fits in socially with peers in the classroom and school, and to ensure that the child has the skills to develop friendships and positive social relationships. Sidebar 6.2 presents some observational techniques adults can use to determine if children are developing friendships and other age-appropriate peer relationships.

## Sidebar 6.2

### HOW DO YOU KNOW IF A CHILD HAS FRIENDS?

Adults need to be keen observers to get a realistic picture of the social network of a child who is visually impaired. Real friends are not students assigned by the teacher to work with the child or students the child attempts to talk to when they don't seek him or her out as well. Make several observations and look for patterns. If the same children are interacting with the target child, then there is a strong possibility that the relationship extends beyond simply being classmates. Here are some things to watch for:

- When children are allowed to pick where they sit and with whom, does the visually impaired child have one or a small group of individuals he or she seeks out? Is the child sought out by these same individuals?
- During recess or other nonstructured activities is the visually impaired child alone or with others?

*(continued on next page)*

Sidebar 6.2 *(continued)*

- Does the visually impaired child exchange belongings with others (for example, sharing CDs or exchanging books)? Is this a two-way interaction?

- Does the visually impaired child make plans with others to spend time together outside of school? Do others make plans with the child?

- Does the visually impaired child have a hobby or interest that is age appropriate and that is shared with others? Do others share hobbies or interests with the child?

- Does the visually impaired child express empathy for others and appear to be sensitive to their feelings? Are others sensitive to the child, without being patronizing or taking on a parental role?

- Do others defend the visually impaired child if he or she is teased? Does the visually impaired child stick up for others who are teased?

## RELATIONSHIPS OF CHILDREN WITH VISUAL IMPAIRMENTS

Having a visual impairment affects all relationships in the lives of children and youths, and these relationships, in turn, affect the development of friendships. This section discusses the variety of relationships, starting with the family. This is followed with community relationships, because children ultimately move outside of their homes and have opportunities to interact with others. The discussion then moves on to role models in the lives of children and youths with visual impairments, school relationships, and friendships. Although these five types of relationships are addressed separately, it is important to recognize that there is often overlap and that individuals in a child's life often perform in multiple roles. For example, a sibling who is a family member may also be a role model. In addition, while acknowledging the influence of visual impairment on relationships, they are also affected by many other characteristics of the child, such as personality, temperament, and family values.

As an adult with low vision, the author of this chapter has often considered how her own visual impairment affects the various relationships in her personal and professional life. It is impossible to sort out which of the many characteristics that define oneself result from a visual impairment. For young people who are visually impaired, having a visual impairment is a part of who they are and thus its influence on relationships must be recognized.

## FAMILY RELATIONSHIPS

All families have unique interaction styles and provide varying levels of both support and stress among the family members. The amount of time family members spend together and the activities they share as a family vary, and their acceptance of individual characteristics and behaviors of family members may change regularly. For example, a father may not care for the music his teenage son is listening to, a daughter may resent the extra time her mother is spending helping a sister with her schoolwork, or a brother may feel overprotective of a younger sister who is teased at school because of her weight. A year from now, however, the son's taste in music may change; the sister may change schools and no longer be teased. Children at times may perceive that their families are accepting of their visual impairment. Irene, an eighth grader with low vision, reported her family's reaction to her visual impairment was that, "They just take it in stride. It's just a log in the middle of a road that you have to go around" (Rosenblum, 2000, p. 438). Yet, Irene also found that there were times when her family was less accepting of her visual impairment, or perhaps did not know how much assistance she did or did not require in a specific situation:

> Even my Grandma and Grandpa [with whom I've lived for nine years] treat me like I'm younger.... They'll ask me if they can cut my food [even though] I'm capable of doing that.... My Grandma, for instance, when we're talking somewhere [for example, a store] and she'll say "OK, this looks like this," and she'll hold it way up to my face, and I can feel the fabric coming [and it embarrasses me]. [p. 438]

Families need to communicate regularly about a child's visual impairment so that the child has an opportunity to vent frustration, ask questions, and give and receive clarification about the impact of the disability.

Many children with visual impairments have siblings. Their siblings may be fearful that they too will become visually impaired. In situations in which there is a hereditary component to the visual impairment, this is a possibility. When children are older, some of these families may choose to undergo genetic counseling so that all of the family members can clearly understand the genetic risks. Siblings need information and assurance about the ways in which their visually impaired brother or sister is both like and different from themselves. There will be times when siblings overprotect a brother or sister with a visual impairment, or are embarrassed by the visual impairment, or choose to ignore the visually impaired sibling altogether. Siblings need to have their feelings validated and their concerns addressed; they need to get information about the impairment when they seek it from parents or from the visually impaired sibling. Siblings may benefit from participating in workshops specifically designed for children who have a brother or sister with a disability. Such opportunities offer them information and reassurance that they are not the only one with a brother or sister with a disability. Well-informed siblings will be in a better position to interact with and promote the social development of their visually impaired brother or sister (Bolinger & Bolinger, 1996).

Parents are the primary means of support in the lives of their children and for visually impaired children they are also the first line of defense. Chang and Schaller (2000) found that in a group of 12 adolescents with visual impairments, ages 14 to 20, parents were important sources of three types of support: emotional support, which included having a safe place, being included, and having one's emotions acknowledged; informational support, which included obtaining information about one's visual impairment, relationships with friends, and personal interests; and tangible aid, which included providing resources for personal interests, for career goals, and for obtaining services for the visual impairment such as placement in public school. Parents need to have a full understanding of their child's visual impairment in order to provide the appropriate amount of information needed by the child and to play the varying roles required of parents. Chang and Schaller (2000) suggested that many parents may need support in order to be responsive to the needs of their visually impaired child. It is inevitable that the child with a visual impairment will experience some challenges, from being the object of teasing to learning effective alternative strategies to travel as a nondriver. The family's response to these challenges and the values they instill in the child influence how the child copes.

Parents and other family members may experience discomfort when the child with a visual impairment is teased by age-mates, whether at school or in the neighborhood or community at large. Rosenblum (2000) found that many adolescents with visual impairments reported incidents of teasing during their childhood. Children who have a strong sense of self and feel accepted by their own families are in a better position to ignore such taunts.

As the child who is visually impaired reaches the age at which a driver's permit can be obtained, both the parents and the child may experience increased levels of stress, especially if the topic has not been discussed openly and the child has not been prepared to accept his or her status as a nondriver. Adolescents with visual impairment who recognize that they are not going to be able to drive give great consideration to its ramifications. For example, Katie, a tenth grader who is blind, lamented, "I wish I could go for driver's ed this fall. I can't do that because what's the point. I want to be able to drive.... Then I could get to places on my own easier" (Rosenblum, 1997a, p. 231). Together families can explore options for nondrivers and begin to plan for the future when the young person leaves home. Important resources can include tools such as *Finding Wheels: A Curriculum for Non-Drivers with Visual Impairments for Gaining Control of Transportation Needs* (Corn & Rosenblum, 2000). Ultimately the adolescent's ability to develop effective strategies to meet transportation challenges will be more easily developed if the individual has good social skills. Being an effective nondriver will provide the adolescent with opportunities to travel and meet other potential friends.

The following suggestions may offer parents assistance in providing support to their child who is visually impaired.

## STRATEGIES FOR SOCIAL SUCCESS
# Offering Parental Support

- Love your child unconditionally and tell the child that he or she is loved, but always expect appropriate social behaviors. Calling a child to task for misbehaving communicates that the behavior is unacceptable, not that the child is unloved.

- Model social amenities for your child—for instance, saying "please," "thank you," and "you're welcome" as appropriate; using greetings consistently when you encounter people in the environment; and holding the door or waiting for someone to enter before you do. When other people do not follow these social rules, point out the error to your child and explain the impact that the person's rude behavior has on others.

- Encourage your child to invite other children to your home and be prepared to take your child to classmates' birthday parties, sleepovers, or other child-related activities.

♦ Encourage your child's active participation in community-based recreation and leisure activities.

♦ Provide opportunities for your child to develop hobbies or interests, such as playing a musical instrument, demonstrating computer expertise, performing gymnastics, engaging in sports such as swimming or wrestling, learning martial arts, and so forth. These activities also serve as age-appropriate topics for discussion that are of interest to peers.

## COMMUNITY RELATIONSHIPS

Once a child enters school, he or she has increased interactions with individuals outside the home, including classmates, teachers, school personnel and therapists, employees and patrons of businesses, other community workers, and people who attend the same religious or secular groups that the family does. The attitudes of these people influence how the child begins to view him- or herself. Although the vast majority of people the child meets in the community will be positive toward the child and the child's visual impairment, there may also be occasions when this is not the case. Visual impairment is frequently viewed negatively in our society (Wagner-Lampl & Oliver, 1994). Terms such as "blind," "visually handicapped," and "visually disabled" are more often perceived as negative than positive (Rosenblum & Erin, 1998). Individuals who have negative attitudes toward people with disabilities may treat a child with visual impairments in a negative fashion.

Even if there is an occasional negative experience, however, community interaction benefits the child in many ways. The more experiences the child has in the community the more comfortable the child will be in going to new places and interacting with unfamiliar people. Beginning when the child is quite young, parents and other family members can take him or her along as they accomplish everyday tasks such as banking, grocery shopping, and getting the car washed. These outings are opportunities for children to become familiar with neighborhood businesses and community members. In addition, social interactions will occur naturally, affording the child the opportunity to practice age-appropriate social behaviors and receive feedback from family members about these interactions. Involvement in the community also provides opportunities for the child to learn about the many jobs and careers available and many of the tasks and skills these entail—an important consideration for later social and vocational growth (Wolffe, 1998).

As the child matures, participation in community activities such as scouting, youth groups, and after-school clubs can provide opportunities to interact with a variety of individuals of a similar age outside the classroom. Learning new skills and taking part in group activities can foster the development of the child's self-esteem (Tuttle & Tuttle, 1996). When helping the child select such activities, it is important to consider the child's chance of success at the activity. For example, a child with low vision who has difficulty visually tracking objects may not find a competitive soccer team to be the best choice for a sporting group; rather joining a bowling league or archery club may lead to a better social outcome for the child.

Many of the adults in charge of these venues may lack experience with visually impaired individuals. It may be necessary for parents or professionals to provide in-service training to both adults and the child's peers to foster understanding about the child's visual impairment and any adaptations that may be necessary for the child to participate fully. Involving the child in providing this type of information can be a valuable way to assist the child in learning to explain his or her visual impairment to others and talking in front of groups. As the mother of an 8-year-old with low vision commented: "Maureen is getting teased in her new after-school program. I told her we needed to pull out our vision simulators [homemade glasses to simulate the daughter's vision loss], braille books, and cane and go and do an in-service for her new group. . . . I find we have to do this from time to time when she goes to a new place" (V. Hayden, personal communication, October 16, 2001).

Older elementary-school-age children and adolescents can benefit from interactions with adults in the neighborhood. When children do such tasks as yard work, pet sitting, or snow shoveling, whether volunteered or paid, they interact with adults while experiencing the realities of the world of work (Wolffe, 1998). These experiences give them an advantage when they seek to enter the work force. In addition, these experiences widen their social circles and provide a venue to increase their age-appropriate, social interaction skills. Some ways of involving visually impaired students in the community include the following.

## STRATEGIES FOR SOCIAL SUCCESS
# Encouraging Community Involvement

◆ Offer to provide in-service training to adults in the community with whom the visually impaired child interacts (such as Little League coaches, scout leaders, religious school teachers, music teachers, martial arts instructors, dance teachers, gymnastics coaches, and the like). Whenever possible, conduct these in-service training sessions with the student in attendance and as an active participant.

♦ Encourage and support visually impaired students who volunteer at local businesses or community organizations. Provide job coaching for these students, if necessary, and access to assistive technology.

♦ Support local businesses that provide on-the-job training and employment to students and adults with disabilities. Let the owners or managers of these businesses know of your support and acknowledge their efforts.

♦ Encourage local newspapers and television stations to run stories about successfully employed blind and visually impaired adults in the community and about community-based activities in which visually impaired individuals participate; for example, volunteer efforts such as food drives or litter pick-up campaigns.

## ROLE MODELS

Children all have people they look up to. Some are people in their lives such as grandparents, older siblings, or teachers; others may be role models or public figures such as sports heroes, royalty, political leaders, historical figures, or actors. Though all children need a variety of role models in their lives, children with visual impairments can benefit from having the chance to meet other individuals older than themselves who are visually impaired. Such opportunities are generally limited, in large part because of the current educational model in which 90 percent of children with visual impairments attend public schools (Corn, Bina, & DePriest, 1995). The visually impaired child is often the only one in the school who is blind or who has low vision. Although it is important for all children to have a variety of role models, it is particularly important for children who are blind or visually impaired to meet other visually impaired individuals; providing such opportunities early on in the child's life is also a consideration.

Hodges and Keller (1999) noted that high school students who are visually impaired often benefit from meeting successful college-aged students with visual impairments. The younger students are able to learn from their older counterparts and determine what strategies work both academically and socially in a college environment. The same is true for school-age children; they benefit from meeting older students with visual impairments who can share their successes, struggles, and strategies (Sacks & Silberman, 2000).

Parents and professionals may need to think creatively in order to assist the young person with a visual impairment in meeting others who may serve as role models. Involvement in summer camps or weekend recreational groups for children with visual impairments is one such avenue. Mary, an eighth grader with adventitious low vision, remembers fondly her attendance at a summer camp for visually impaired children the previous summer: "I really fit in because everybody was visually impaired, so you complained that you couldn't see something, it was not a big deal. Nobody cared and they were like, 'Oh, I can't see that either.'" (Rosenblum, 1997a, p. 234).

Participation in organizations such as Ski for Light or the U.S. Association for Blind Athletes can bring people with visual impairments of varying ages together to engage in a common athletic interest with the side benefit of forming friendships and mentoring relationships. Consumer organizations for people with visual impairments and organizations that focus on a specific eye disease (see the Resource section for a listing of such organizations) often hold meetings, workshops, or conferences where individuals may gather. Even if the event is designed for adults, there may be child care or alternative activities available for children during the course of the event. Thus, while the adult family members are gaining new knowledge, the children have an opportunity to interact and learn from each other.

As a public school student who was the only visually impaired student in her school from kindergarten through high school, the author of this chapter looked forward every year to the two weeks of summer camp for children with visual impairments. In this special environment, visually impaired children are free from explaining to others about their visual impairment and from feeling self-conscious. Everyone else had trouble seeing and naturally understood the challenges that my school peers and family did not. In addition, it was often of value to talk to older campers to learn what was ahead (such as the transition from junior high to high school and ways of coping when friends get their driver's licenses).

Families and professionals can work together to plan opportunities and devise strategies that will allow children with visual impairments to meet others who are visually impaired, such as the following (also see Chapter 7 for additional discussion of role models).

STRATEGIES FOR SOCIAL SUCCESS
# Providing Role Models

- ◆ Teachers of students with visual impairments and O&M specialists can plan field trips or activities for several students on their caseloads who attend different schools to come together for joint activities.

- ◆ Summer camps, weekend recreation programs, and vocational programs specifically for students with visual impairments can provide excellent opportunities for students to meet others who are visually impaired.

- ◆ Adults in the community who are visually impaired can be invited to school to make presentations or participate on presentation panels at workshops or conferences that students attend, or students can interview them (for example, about their transportation arrangements or adaptations on the job) as a class research project. Encourage students to ask older students and adults with visual impairments how they handled difficult or challenging social situations.

- ◆ Students can visit the job sites of adults with visual impairments and "shadow" them. This type of activity provides the student with both vocational information and the opportunity to socialize with an adult who is visually impaired.

- ◆ Students can use the Internet (closely monitored by parents or professionals) to communicate via e-mail with others who have visual impairments around the country and around the world. The American Foundation for the Blind CareerConnect Web site offers opportunities to connect with successfully employed adults with visual impairments (see the Resources section for more details) and students can also join electronic mailing lists where topics related to visual impairment are discussed, including use of technology, braille, career opportunities and challenges, as well as other topics of interest related to specific etiologies.

- ◆ Pen pal relationships can be established with another individual who is visually impaired Professionals or parents attending conferences can seek out others who may know a student that would like a pen pal and the two can be introduced.

- ◆ Families can be encouraged to join consumer organizations such as the American Council of the Blind, National Association of Parents of Children with Visual Impairments, or National Federation of the Blind or its division, the National Organization of Parents of Blind Children (for specific information see the Resource section).

## SCHOOL RELATIONSHIPS

School is the key place that children meet their potential friends. In a sample of 40 adolescents with visual impairments, Rosenblum (1997a) found that 70 percent of the relationships described as best friends were developed at school with classmates. This figure is similar to findings among adolescents who do not have visual impairments (Claes, 1992; Urberg et al., 1995). Thus, ensuring that children are fully included in all aspects of their school life, regardless of the placement, is critical.

At school, children have opportunities to interact with classmates, teachers, and other children. The attitudes of these individuals will influence how the child views his or her visual impairment. As Sacks (1996) noted,

> Many children with low vision perceive themselves as sighted but with limited visual abilities, and their teachers and parents often promote the idea that they are just children who have poor vision. Yet many of their visual behaviors, such as experiencing the rapid eye movements that characterize nystagmus, viewing materials close up, not making eye contact, and wearing thick eyeglasses, cause them to be labeled as different. As a result, many find it difficult to identify with any peer group or to feel comfortable about themselves. [p. 34]

The concern that Sacks raises is an important one. Although in this case Sacks referred to children with low vision, children who are blind will have similar experiences since they may be traveling with a cane, using braille for reading and writing activities, and using assistive technology, all things that make them obviously different from their sighted peers. Indeed, children with visual impairments often have lower self-concepts than their sighted peers. In their study of Spanish children with low vision and their sighted classmates, Lopez-Justicia, Pichardo, Amezcua, and Fernandez (2001) found that children as young as 7 years of age who had low vision had lower self-concepts than their sighted age-mates. These authors stressed the importance of promoting acceptance of individual differences by teachers and peers and the need for intervention to assist visually impaired children in developing positive feelings about themselves.

A child who is included in a general education classroom based on educational placement is not automatically included in the social milieu of the classroom (Hatlen, 2004; Hoben & Linstrom, 1980; MacCuspie, 1990). In a study of five elementary-school-age students with visual impairments in inclusive classrooms, MacCuspie (1990) found that although the children were academically included they were not socially included in many of the aspects of the school experience. The children in this study were found to have a neutral social status, neither disliked nor popular with peers. The five children were often not aware of the subtle social culture of the classroom.

For visually impaired students, the school experience can provide the foundation for building relationships with peers and adults. However, teachers need information about visual impairment and the adaptations and equipment that enables students to succeed not only academically, but in all aspects of the school experience. Parents and teachers need to take an active role in helping the child who is visually impaired to develop age-appropriate skills, such as talking about topics of interest to peers, playing games that peers play, or sharing materials during a group project (Sacks & Silberman, 2000). Following are some strategies that parents and professionals can use to promote social interactions and foster friendships.

## STRATEGIES FOR SOCIAL SUCCESS

# Supporting Friendships

- Encourage and support the student's involvement in cooperative learning opportunities (see Chapter 8).
- Encourage participation in a variety of after-school activities that enhance self-esteem and confidence such as dance or music lessons; band or choir, creative dramatics; sports such as downhill or cross-country skiing; and volunteering in the community.
- Encourage participation in clubs and organizations (such as debate, foreign language, farming or animal husbandry, chess, or the like) in which the student can take on a leadership role while interacting with peers.
- Help the student to develop a series of icebreakers that may be used to gain entry into groups, such as asking about a popular television show or video game, bringing a snack to share with the group, or commenting positively on others' clothes, jewelry, or personal appearance.

◆ Encourage the student to compliment others when interacting with peers.

◆ Encourage the student to help and support others by helping friends with tasks they cannot complete and taking responsibility for jobs around school.

## PROMOTING FRIENDSHIPS AND PEER RELATIONSHIPS

Promoting academic success for school-aged children and young adults with visual impairments is typically the focus of the school experience. The recognition of parents and educators of the need to include skill areas other than academics, such as social skills, for students with visual impairments was the impetus behind the expanded core curriculum (Hatlen, 1996; Hatlen & Curry, 1987; Huebuer, Merk-Adam, Stryker, & Wolffe, 2004). Professionals and families may need to use a variety of strategies to assist the child or adolescent with a visual impairment in the development of relationships. The development of friendships and peer relationships can be encouraged through providing realistic feedback, teaching initiating and reciprocating skills, aiding children in developing age-appropriate hobbies and interests, and promoting independent travel. Each of these topics is discussed in the following sections.

### REALISTIC FEEDBACK

Adults need to provide realistic information to children and young adults with visual impairments (Tuttle & Tuttle, 1996, 2004; Wolffe, 1998). Information about both positive observations (for example, that the child appropriately engaged in turn taking, offered to assist a peer, or looked in the direction of the speaker) and areas in need of improvement (for example, that the child barged into a group or engaged in rocking during an interaction) should be shared with the child in a constructive manner (Sacks & Silberman, 2000). An eighth grader who is blind recalled realistic feedback he received from his father that changed the way he interacted with peers. He commented, "He said if you ever want to make friends you've got to quit pushing them away like you are. He basically told me that if he wasn't my dad he wouldn't want to hang out with me the way I was acting" (Rosenblum, 1997a, p. 200).

The possibility exists that a child's social shortcomings will be overlooked by general educators, peers, and family members because they assume that such behavior is characteristic of visually impaired individuals. This is not acceptable. Information about mannerisms, dress, makeup, voice quality, nonverbal behaviors, and so forth must be provided to the child with a visual impairment in a positive manner (Bolinger & Bolinger, 1996). When necessary, instruction—for example, by role playing how to invite a peer over to play, showing an adolescent girl how to apply makeup, or developing a behavior modification plan to decrease mannerisms—must be addressed by the entire educational team if the child is ultimately going to have high self-esteem and positive interactions with others (Tuttle & Tuttle, 1996).

## TEACHING INITIATION AND RECIPROCATION

Often it is the individual with a visual impairment who must initiate an interaction in order to set the ball in motion toward the development of a friendship (Hodges & Keller, 1999; Rosenblum, 1997a). The need for the individual who is visually impaired to first initiate an interaction may stem from a lack of knowledge on the part of the sighted individual about how best to approach a person who is blind or has low vision. Nancy, a 13-year-old eighth grader who is sighted became best friends with Mary, a 14-year-old eighth grader with low vision, but she was initially apprehensive when Mary first started coming into her classroom. Nancy recalls:

> There was her [Mary] and a couple of other kids that were special ed kids that came into our class. All the kids [typical peers] were different about it at first, but then they got used to it and no one was really big about it or anything. . . . I was worried if I had to act different around her or treat her differently. After awhile it just seemed to disappear in a way. [We] talked to each other normally. [Rosenblum, 1997a, p. 236]

MacCuspie (1996) pointed out that children with visual impairments in an inclusive classroom are often helped by peers but rarely have the opportunity to be in the role of the one providing the help. Children with visual impairments need to be taught about the importance of reciprocation within a relationship. Reciprocation can be thought of as an exchange of ideas, information, affection, support, or objects. In order to reciprocate one must be able to recognize what it is a friend needs or wants (for instance, someone to listen, someone to provide orientation to a new school, or someone to spend time with). (For additional examples, see Sidebar 6.1.) Children must also have the necessary skills to enable them to reciprocate. For example, Chuck and Douglas have reciprocation within their friendship. In talking about school, Douglas notes about Chuck: "He helps me if I don't understand something. He'll explain it to me. Sometimes I can explain something better to him then he can, or you know, the other way around." Chuck says that Douglas "helps me get different places, like finding better ways to go places, shortcuts" (Rosenblum, 1997a, p. 221).

In teaching about reciprocation, it may be helpful to have children list areas in which they feel competent and skills that they can share with others. The list may include things such as listening when someone has a problem, helping someone with homework, or teaching someone a skill, such as playing a musical instrument, dancing, or using a computer program. Visually impaired children may also want to consider ways to thank someone who assists them. For example, they could bring a special snack to share at lunchtime, loan a favorite toy or music CD, invite the person to swim in the family pool after school, or ask a parent to drive friends to the mall or on an outing.

## DEVELOPING AGE-APPROPRIATE INTERESTS

Barclay (1999) recognized that the elementary-school-age children with visual impairments in her resource room often socialized with each other on the playground; they didn't seek out their sighted peers. Since the yo-yo was popular among students at that time, she provided yo-yos and instruction in how to use them to her students with visual impairments. The availability of yo-yos in her classroom enticed the sighted students to spend time with the visually impaired students, and this in turn got her students out onto the playground with their sighted age-mates.

Adults may need to spend time, as Barclay did, introducing popular games and activities to children with visual impairments and providing them with instruction in the skills involved in playing them (Sacks & Silberman, 2000; Wolffe & Sacks, 2000). Rosenblum (1997a) found that common interests were often the catalyst in starting friendships between sighted and visually impaired students in her study. For example, Chuck reports about the start of his friendship with Douglas in the seventh grade:

> Douglas just always kept coming up to me and trying to talk to me, and I'd always try to push him away. And finally, one day I just kind of decided I'd listen to what he had to say. We had the same interests, like working on cars and carpentry and all that

stuff. So we started talking about that, and then we got to be closer and closer friends, and ever since then he's been my best friend. [p. 219]

Regardless of age, the recognition that two individuals share a common interest can become the cornerstone on which a friendship is built (Hodges & Keller, 1999; Rosenblum, 1997a, 2000). Hodges and Keller (1999) recommended that adolescents with visual impairments join clubs in order to learn hobbies. Participation in after-school activities with others often leads to the development of friendships.

## INDEPENDENT TRAVEL

The importance of orientation (knowing where one is in space) and mobility (knowing how to move safely and efficiently in space) is well documented (Griffin-Shirley, Trusty, & Rickard, 2000). The need for travel independence is significant from a social perspective, as well. Children with visual impairments must be able to get to the local hangouts if they are to have opportunities to meet others, get to know others, and ultimately develop friendships. In the school environment socializing often does not occur in the classroom where adults are in control; rather it occurs in the cafeteria, playground, and hallways. Therefore, the individual with a visual impairment must be able to travel independently within these environments to have sufficient opportunities to meet peers. Chuck, the seventh grader mentioned earlier, shared how the presence of his instructional assistant hampered his ability to interact with peers in class and as he traveled from class to class:

> Well it's, it kind of gets annoying even for me too, you know, because you can't really open up [with other kids], you know, because she's an adult, a teacher and everything, [you] can't act like you normally do. If kids want to hang out I just tell them I've got lunch or something. [Rosenblum, 1997b]

As they move into the later elementary-school years and beyond, children with visual impairments socialize outside of school hours in the neighborhood and community. Having the orientation and mobility (O&M) skills to travel to the same places that peers do increases the probability of making friends. An O&M assessment can yield information about what travel skills a visually impaired child has and what skills he or she needs to develop. When designing the goals and objectives for O&M instruction, consideration should be given by all team members to teaching the child routes and travel techniques that will maximize his or her ability to travel to the places where social opportunities occur.

Recognizing that the majority of adolescents with visual impairments will not drive and helping these adolescents and young adults to prepare for meeting their transportation needs is critical (Corn & Rosenblum, 2000; Erin & Wolffe, 1999; Sacks & Silberman, 2000; Wolffe, 2004). Six visually impaired college students interviewed by Hodges and Keller (1999) said that their inability to drive was a barrier to developing relationships on the college campus. Adolescents and young adults need to be innovative in meeting their transportation needs. Finding ways to maximize independence in travel will ultimately provide them with more opportunities to meet potential friends. Suggestions to help inform nondriving students about options for getting around in the community are provided in Chapters 4 and 12.

## CONCLUSION

Success in social relationships, including friendship, comes easily to some and not so easily to others, for students with visual impairments as for everyone else. But, because children with visual impairments may not recognize the inherent subtleties of social relationships or may find it challenging to engage others in social interactions, it is important for professionals and family members to support the development of friendships and other social relationships by assuring that children receive realistic feedback about their interactions with others, the social signals they are sending, and the way in which they are being perceived. Children with visual impairments need to learn to reciprocate, not always be the one receiving, in ways as simple as listening to another or sharing an activity, as well as an exchange of tangible goods such as toys, DVDs, books, or clothing.

In order to make friends, young people with disabilities have to share common interests with age-mates. Professionals and families can facilitate the acquisition of interests and hobbies and help them develop independent travel skills.

The development of friendships and positive social relationships is essential for success in adulthood. Parents and professionals who work with children with visual impairments who are not naturally developing friendships and other social relationships need to make sure that these students receive guidance and, when necessary, instruction. Often, it is the professional in the field of visual impairment who is called on to lead these efforts. As a team, professionals, families, and children with visual impairments, can develop action plans that include specific strategies and improve the likelihood of success in forming friendships and other positive social relationships.

# REFERENCES

Barclay, L. (1999). Yo-yo magic or a teacher of the visually impaired learns another lesson in social skills. *RE:view, 31*(3), 126–128.

Bolinger, R., & Bolinger, C. (1996). Family life. In M. C. Holbrook (Ed.), *Children with visual impairments: A parents' guide* (pp. 129–157). Bethesda, MD: Woodbine House.

Chang, S. C., & Schaller, J. (2000). Perspectives of adolescents with visual impairments on social support from their parents. *Journal of Visual Impairment and Blindness, 94*(2), 69–84.

Claes, M. E. (1992). Friendship and personal adjustment during adolescence. *Journal of Adolescence, 15,* 39–55.

Clark, M. L., & Ayers, M. (1991). Friendship similarity during early adolescence: Gender and racial patterns. *The Journal of Psychology, 126*(4), 393–405.

Corn, A. L., Bina, M. J., & DePriest, L. B. (1995). *The parent perspective on schools for students who are blind and visually impaired: A national study.* Alexandria, VA: Association for Education and Rehabilitation of the Blind and Visually Impaired.

Corn, A. L., & Rosenblum, L. P. (2000). *Finding wheels: A curriculum for nondrivers with visual impairments for gaining control of transportation needs.* Austin, TX: Pro-Ed.

Cotterell, J. (1996). *Social networks and social influences in adolescence.* New York: Routledge.

Duck, S. (1983). *Friends, for life: The psychology of close relationships.* Brighton, England: Harvester Press.

Erin, J. N., & Wolffe, K. E. (1999). *Transition issues related to students with visual disabilities.* Austin, TX: PRO-ED.

Feldman, R. S. (1998). *Child development.* Upper Saddle River, NJ: Prentice Hall.

Griffin-Shirley, N., Trusty, S., & Rickard, R. (2000). Orientation and mobility. In A. J. Koenig & M. C. Holbrook (Eds.), *Foundations of education, Vol. 2: Instructional strategies for teaching children and youth with visual impairments* (2nd ed.; pp. 529–568). New York: AFB Press.

Hartup, W. W. (1993). Adolescents and their friends. In B. Laursen (Ed.), *Close friendships in adolescence* (pp. 3–22). San Francisco: Jossey-Bass Publishers.

Hatlen, P. (1996). The core curriculum for blind and visually impaired students, including those with additional disabilities. *RE:view, 28*(1), 25–32.

Hatlen, P. (2004). Is social isolation a predictable outcome of inclusive education? *Journal of Visual Impairment & Blindness, 98*(11), 676–677.

Hatlen, P. H., & Curry, S. A. (1987). In support of specialized programs for blind and visually impaired children: The impact of vision loss on learning. *Journal of Visual Impairment and Blindness, 81*(1), 7–13.

Herring, J. (1996). Adjusting to your child's visual impairment. In M. C. Holbrook (Ed.), *Children with visual impairments: A parents' guide* (pp. 49–72). Bethesda, MD: Woodbine House.

Hoben, M., & Linstrom, V. (1980). Evidence of isolation in the mainstream. *Journal of Visual Impairment and Blindness, 74*(8), 289–292.

Hodges, J. S., & Keller, M. J. (1999). Visually impaired students' perceptions of their social integration in college. *Journal of Visual Impairment and Blindness, 93*(3), 153–165.

Huebuer, K. M., Merk-Adam, B., Stryker, D., & Wolffe, K. (2004). *The National Agenda for the education of children and youths with visual impairments, including those with multiple disabilities* (rev. ed.) New York: AFB Press.

Jones, G. P. (1985). The development of intimate friendship in childhood and adolescence (Doctoral dissertation, University of Southern California, 1985).

Kef, S. (1997). The personal networks and social supports of blind and visually impaired adolescents. *Journal of Visual Impairment and Blindness, 91*(3), 236–244.

Kon, I. S. (1981). Adolescent friendship: Some unanswered questions for future research. In S. Duck & R. Gilmour (Eds.), *Personal relationships 2: Developing personal relationships* (pp. 187–204). New York: Academic Press.

Lopez-Justicia, M. D., Pichardo, M. C., Amezcua, J. A., & Fernandez, E. (2001). The self-concepts of Spanish children and adolescents with low vision and their sighted peers. *Journal of Visual Impairment and Blindness, 95*(3), 150–160.

MacCuspie, P. A. (1990). The social acceptance and interaction of integrated visually impaired children (Doctoral dissertation, Dalhousie University, Halifax, Nova Scotia, Canada, 1992).

MacCuspie, P. A. (1992). The social acceptance and interaction of visually impaired children in integrated settings. In S. Z. Sacks, L. S. Kekelis, & R. J. Gaylord-Ross (Eds.), *The development of social skills by blind and visually impaired students* (pp. 83–102). New York: American Foundation for the Blind.

MacCuspie, P. A. (1996). *Promoting acceptance of children with disabilities: From tolerance to inclusion.* Halifax, Nova Scotia, Canada: Atlantic Provinces Special Education Authority.

McCoy, J. K. (1992). The importance of individual and family characteristics in predicting adolescent friendship quality (Doctoral dissertation, University of Georgia, 1992). (UMI No. 9316369)

Ritz, S. (1992). Intimate friendship and social competency through early adolescence (Doctoral dissertation, Virginia Commonwealth University, 1992). (UMI No. 9310463)

Rosenblum, L. P. (1997a). Friendship dyads of adolescents with visual impairment. *Dissertation Abstracts International*, 58 (04A), 1247. (UMI No. AAG 97229535)

Rosenblum, L. P. (1997b). [Friendship dyads of adolescents with visual impairment.] Unpublished data.

Rosenblum, L. P. (2000). Perceptions of the impact of a visual impairment on the lives of adolescents. *Journal of Visual Impairment and Blindness, 94*(7), 434–445.

Rosenblum, L. P., & Corn, A. L. (2003). Families promoting travel skills for their children with visual impairments. *RE:view, 34*(4), 175–180.

Rosenblum, L. P., & Erin, J. N. (1998). Perceptions of terms used to describe individuals with visual impairment. *RE:view, 30*(1), 15–26.

Sacks, S. Z. (1996). Psychological and social implications of low vision. In A. L. Corn & A. J. Koenig (Eds.), *Foundations of low vision: Clinical and functional perspectives* (pp. 26–42). New York: AFB Press.

Sacks, S. Z., & Silberman, R. K. (2000). Social skills. In A. J. Koenig & M. C. Holbrook (Eds.), *Foundations of education: Instructional strategies for teaching children and youth with visual impairments: Vol. II* (pp. 616–652). New York: AFB Press.

Serafica, F. C., & Blyth, D. A. (1985). Continuities and changes in the study of friendship and peer groups during early adolescence. *Journal of Early Adolescence, 5*(3), 267–283.

Sharabany, R., Gershoni, R., & Hofman, J. E. (1981). Girlfriend, boyfriend: Age and sex differences in intimate friendship. *Developmental Psychology, 17*(6), 800–808.

Shechtman, Z. (1994). The effect of group psychotherapy on close same-gender friendships among boys and girls. *Sex Roles, 30*(11/12), 829–834.

Tuttle, D. W., & Tuttle, N. R. (1996). Nurturing your child's self-esteem. In M. C. Holbrook (Ed.), *Children with visual impairments: A parents' guide* (pp. 159–174). Bethesda, MD: Woodbine House.

Tuttle, D. W., & Tuttle, N. R. (2004). *Self-esteem and adjusting with blindness: The process of responding to life's demands* (3rd ed.). Springfield, IL: Charles C. Thomas.

Urberg, K. A., Degirmencioglu, M., Tolson, J. M., & Halliday-Scher, K. (1995). The structure of adolescent peer networks. *Developmental Psychology, 31*(4), 540–547.

Wagner-Lampl, A., & Oliver, G. W. (1994). Folklore of blindness. *Journal of Visual Impairment and Blindness, 88*(3), 267–276.

Warren, D. W. (1994). *Blindness and children: An individual differences approach.* New York: Cambridge University Press.

Wolffe, K. (1998). *Skills for success: A career education handbook for children and adolescents with visual impairment.* New York: AFB Press.

Wolffe, K. (2004). Transitioning young adults from school to public transportation. *EnVision: A publication for parents and educators of children with impaired vision, 8*, 7–9.

Wolffe, K. E., & Sacks, S. Z. (Eds.). (2000). *Focused on: Social skills.* New York: AFB Press.

# CHAPTER 7

# The Importance of Peers and Role Models

Sharon Z. Sacks

Visual information plays an integral role in developing and refining social skills. Kekelis (1992) aptly states, "Eye gaze regulates turn taking, gaze and gestures establish topics of conversation, smiles and gaze acknowledge and invite responses from partners, and contextual information enables children to monitor and respond to the interests of peers" (p. 13). Whereas sighted children learn and master these skills through imitation and experiences with one another, children with visual impairments require consistent and ongoing support from family members, teachers, and peers to gain equal access to social experiences in school and community settings.

Although the majority of students with visual impairments have been educated alongside their sighted age-mates for over a half-century, there is continued concern that the social experiences of many students who are blind or visually impaired is less than adequate. Several studies have clearly demonstrated that without appropriate social skills interventions students are at risk for social isolation and may not have opportunities to engage successfully with peers and adults (Bishop, 1986; Hatlen & Curry, 1987; Hoben & Lindstrom, 1980; Kef, 1997; Kekelis & Sacks, 1992, Sacks & Gaylord-Ross, 1989, Sacks, Wolffe, & Tierney, 1998; and Wolffe & Sacks, 1997). In order for students with visual impairments to develop positive social relationships with peers they must have opportunities to learn from, and engage with, competent sighted as well as blind or visually impaired peers.

The social networks of students who are blind or visually impaired are influenced by the complexity of the socialization process. At a most basic level, the acquisition of social skills for students with visual impairments is highly dependent on early experiences that nurture and encourage reciprocal interactions, turn taking, use of gestures and eye gaze, and positive initiations. However, interactions with sighted and competent visually impaired peers can offer unique opportunities for children with visual impairments to develop and maintain a repertoire of behaviors and skills that ultimately will allow them to gain entry into groups, develop play and interactive skills, initiate and maintain age-appropriate conversation topics, and exhibit skills to promote self-advocacy and self-determination.

Previous chapters focus on developmental issues and theoretical constructs as they relate to the acquisition of social skills for students with visual impairments. The chapters on self-esteem and friendship discuss the importance and influence of peers as partners in the socialization process for students with visual impairments, and how peers combined with family support can promote prosocial behavior and truly inclusive experiences for these students in a variety of social environments. This chapter offers interventions and strategies that can be provided by peers and role models. Many of the interventions are based on research studies, which are therefore described in some detail so that practitioners and family members can replicate these valuable strategies. A series of activities is also offered to assist teachers and other professionals in designing peer-directed interventions that enhance socialization for students who are blind or visually impaired.

## PEER-DIRECTED INTERVENTIONS

Peers provide a natural way for students with visual impairments to learn social skills. Peer-directed interventions are usually facilitated by classmates or others the same age as the student with a visual impairment. Peers chosen for this intervention are usually sighted students who demonstrate a solid repertoire of social skills and are socially competent. Under the direction of a teacher or another adult, the selected peers receive instruction on how to target selected social skills for training for the visually impaired student. The peers may also initiate a specific social skills intervention. Technically, peers may not have the expertise or knowledge in specific teaching strategies, but the power of peer support and feedback motivates students who are blind or visually impaired to learn and maintain a variety of skills within several different environments.

## INITIAL STUDIES

Few studies have examined the impact of peers as teachers of social skills for students who are blind or visually impaired. Early studies examined the play behavior and levels of social interaction between young children who were blind or visually impaired and their sighted age-mates. Erwin (1994) and Skellenger, Rosenblum, & Jager (1997) found that most young, visually impaired children in their studies were engaged in solitary play rather than interactive play with peers. Kekelis & Sacks (1992) and Kekelis (1992) in their ethnographic studies learned that young children with visual impairments direct their social interactions more toward adults than peers. However, various studies have documented marked increases in social competence among students with visual impairments as a result of using peer interventions (D'Allura, 2000; Peavey & Leff, 2002; Sacks & Gaylord-Ross, 1989, 1992; Sisson, Van Hasselt, Hersen, & Strain, 1985).

Initial studies of peer-directed interventions were based on the constructs of social learning theory. Researchers believed that nondisabled peers could be trained to initiate and to model appropriate social behavior for students with disabilities. For example, Gaylord-Ross, Haring, Breen, & Pitts-Conway (1984) used social initiators (radios, handheld video games, and chewing gum) to stimulate social interactions between students with autism and their nondisabled peers in a leisure environment (brunch time) on a comprehensive high school campus. Using scripts developed by the special education teacher to assist students with initiating conversations, engaging in conversation, and elaborating conversations, the nondisabled peers modeled appropriate use of the initiators and prompted students through each script in the classroom and in natural environments such as at breaktime in the school's quad, or during lunch in the cafeteria.

Sisson, Van Hasselt, Hersen, and Strain (1985) initiated a peer-mediated social skills training intervention with elementary-school-aged students (9–11 year-olds) with visual impairments and multiple disabilities who attended a specialized school for students with visual impairments. Nondisabled peers from a local elementary school were recruited to assist their age-mates in acquiring appropriate play and social interaction skills. Each nondisabled peer was provided with instruction from the students' classroom teacher and one of the lead researchers. The instruction provided the sighted peers with strategies to promote effective play and expanded interactions with their blind counterparts. Results indicated that all the students with visual impairments demonstrated substantial increases in appropriate play and in the number and quality of social interactions during the training. Moderate increases in play and interactive activities were observed during nontraining sessions and on three-month follow-up observations across settings and with other students.

More recently, D'Allura (2002) initiated a social skills intervention with peers that included reverse mainstreaming (sighted students work with and engage in social and academic experiences in the special education class for students with visual impairments) and cooperative learning strategies (students work in small groups of four as a team, each having specific duties; see Chapter 8 for more detail). In D'Allura's study of the acquisition of social skills by a group of preschool students with visual impairments, one group of students who were blind or visually impaired was assigned to a special day class for students with visual impairments. The other students with visual impairments were placed in an integrated preschool class that included four students with visual impairments and four students who were sighted. At the beginning of the study, all the students with visual impairment directed their social interactions and play requests toward adults. When the cooperative learning strategies were introduced in the integrated visually impaired classroom, however, spontaneous social interactions with peers increased dramatically and were maintained relatively well over time. The preschoolers in the self-contained classroom made few changes in their social behavior. They continued to direct their social attention toward the adults rather than the other students with visual impairments.

Peavey and Leff (2002) wanted to enhance the social competence of five visually impaired high school students who attended local high school programs. Each of the five students was placed in a group with six to ten sighted classmates who had volunteered for this special program. Prior to the initiation of group activities, each student with a visual impairment was assessed for his or her level of social competence by using the Social Skills Assessment Tool for Students with

Visual Impairments (SSAT-VI) (McCallum & Sacks, 1994; Sacks & Wolffe, 2000). To determine the sighted peers' level of social acceptance of each student with a visual impairment, they were asked to complete a confidential written assessment of preference for friends. Each sighted peer was asked to select one person in the group to be with if only one choice were allowed and to provide a reason for his or her choice. Then they were asked to choose their next favorite person, until they had selected every member in the group, whether visually impaired or sighted. This assessment was repeated after the group intervention took place to determine whether there were shifts in social acceptance.

During the group activities the students engaged in trust-building and problem-solving activities. These ice-breaking activities allowed the students to develop a relaxed, caring environment in which social issues could be discussed and shared among all of the participants. The following are some examples of the activities:

- A member would fall because he or she trusted that the group would catch him or her....
- One group member was asked to sit in the center of the gathering and listen as the other group members said what they liked about him or her....
- The students each had $500 to spend on what they valued, from a list with the following choices: health, beauty, adventure, love, and knowledge. After they chose how to spend their money, they explained to the group why they had made their choices.
- In small groups the students were asked to design a world on the basis of unique "what ifs." For example, "What would the world be like if all people looked exactly alike?" (Peavey & Leff, 2002, p. 809)

As the students gained trust and respect for one another, the sighted students began to feel comfortable asking questions about the students' visual impairments and their level of functioning. In turn, the students with visual impairments asked for feedback and suggestions for how to be more successfully included in social groups and activities. Because both groups of students felt comfortable expressing their feelings and ideas, social acceptance of the students with visual impairments improved and the level of social competence increased for the majority of the visually impaired students who were included in the group process.

# TEACHER-DIRECTED VS. PEER-MEDIATED INTERVENTIONS

The studies cited in the previous section demonstrated that interventions by peers could be successful in enhancing the social skills of visually impaired students, but how effective would such strategies be compared to teacher-directed interventions? In their seminal research, Sacks & Gaylord-Ross (1989, 1992) examined the viability of teacher-directed versus peer-mediated social skills interventions for elementary-aged students who were blind or visually impaired. They hypothesized that while adult trainers may have more experience and success at targeting and training specific social skills, peer interventions would have stronger and more lasting effects on the abilities of students with visual impairments to interact effectively with sighted age-mates over time and in a variety of settings.

Using a multiple baseline design across behaviors Kazdin (1982) and Sacks and Gaylord-Ross compared the frequency and duration of eye contact, frequency of appropriate body posture, frequency of positive social initiations, frequency of joining in group activities, and frequency of sharing in group activities. Fifteen students who were blind or visually impaired were randomly assigned to one of three treatment groups: teacher-directed, peer-mediated, or control.

## TEACHER-DIRECTED

The five students who received the teacher-directed approach were provided with 12 instructional sessions. Each session provided the student with structured social skills training based on strict behavioral constructs. These included introduction and definition of the targeted behavior, modeling of the appropriate social behavior, practicing the targeted behavior by using typical role-play scenarios, providing physical and verbal feedback, engaging in an additional role-playing scenario, and reviewing the targeted behavior and activities undertaken during the training session. At the end of each session, the student was given homework to practice the targeted social behavior in the natural environment.

Sidebar 7.1 provides an example of a structured social skills intervention using teacher and student role play in a typical situation in which a student with a visual impairment wants to join a group. The teacher provides verbal feedback and physical modeling to assist the student in understanding the concept. After the role playing is

## Sidebar 7.1

**STRUCTURED SOCIAL SKILLS TRAINING: JOINING A GROUP**

The following dialogue is an example of a structured social skills training intervention in which a teacher and student role play a common social situation:

**Teacher:** Good morning, Jenny. Today we are going to talk about joining groups of friends on the playground. I've noticed that sometimes you have a hard time knowing when to join in. Can you tell me the kinds of activities kids play or do at recess?

**Jenny:** Well, sometimes the girls just talk to each other. Sometimes they play jump rope, wall ball, or tether ball.

**Teacher:** Those are great activities. Do you know how to play these games? Do we need to spend some time working on learning how to play these games?

**Jenny:** I know how to play jump rope and wall ball, but I need to learn how to play tether ball.

**Teacher:** Okay, I will work with you on that, but first let's talk about the steps in joining a group. First, you have to find the group. You may need to ask for assistance to find a specific group of friends. Then, you sort of hang out. Remember, we talked about body space and listening for a lull in the conversation. When there is a pause, you face the group of students [physically demonstrate facing the group], casually provide a greeting, and ask, "What's happening," or "What's going on?" Wait for a response from a peer. If there is no response, try the process again with a peer's voice that is familiar to you. Then, if the activity is something you want to do, ask if you can join in. You might need to be a bit assertive. Do you remember what that word means?

**Jenny:** Yes, assertive means that I just don't jump in or get too pushy. I use words like, "I'd really like to play the game. I know I can do it."

**Teacher:** That's great. Now tell me the steps you would use for joining a group. [Have the student retell the steps, filling in where needed.] You did a good job describing the steps, but you

*(continued on next page)*

Sidebar 7.1 *(continued)*

forgot about facing the students using eye contact. Remember, that's an important way to get your friends' attention. Remember, it's important to keep an imaginary fence, a 12- to 18-inch space between you and your friends. Let's practice that.

[Jenny stands and turns her head toward her teacher, looking at her and makes sure she is a reasonable distance from the teacher.]

**Teacher:**  Yes, that is very good. You've got the idea. Now, I'm going to give you a typical situation you might encounter with your friends on the playground. I'll be your friend Jane, and you'll be yourself. Here's the situation: It's snack recess, and a group of girls from your class are standing around. They are sharing their snacks with each other and talking about a movie they saw over the weekend. What do you do?

**Jenny:**  I walk up to the group with my snack [a bag of chips]. I listen for a few seconds and wait for a break in the conversation. Then, I turn to Jane and Alison and ask if they want chips. If they want chips, I give them some and get involved in the conversation. If not, I wait my turn to try to get involved in the conversation.

**Teacher:**  Good, you've got the idea. Now let's role play.

completed, the teacher requests that the student practice the newly learned skills by joining groups during recess time. At the end of the session, the teacher reviews the steps for joining a group.

When adults are providing the contexts for social skills training, it is important for them to use scenarios that are typical of the student's school and play experiences. The role-play scenarios depicted in Sidebar 7.2 illustrate situations that may be encountered by students with visual impairments in school or community environments. These scenarios may be modified to meet the age and ability level of each student. (Additional examples of role-play scenarios can be found in Chapter 9.)

## PEER-MEDIATED

Another five students with visual impairments received the peer-mediated intervention from nondisabled peers from their classes who were recruited to participate as social skills trainers. Each sighted peer

## Sidebar 7.2

**EXAMPLES OF ROLE-PLAY SCENARIOS**

The following examples of situations that are typical of classroom behaviors are listed to stimulate discussion and problem-solving sessions between visually impaired students and their teachers.

**Preschool and Kindergarten**

- You are sitting on the carpet getting ready for story time. You are seated in front, but your friends push you out of your place. What do you do? How do you tell the teacher?
- You are on the playground, and one of your classmates tells you that you can't go on the slide because you are blind. What do you say to your classmate?
- You cannot open your milk carton at snack. Your classmate grabs your milk from you. What do you do?

**First to Third Grade**

- You are in line to play jump rope on the playground at recess. A few kids whom you don't know push in front of you in line. What do you say to these students?
- At lunch in the cafeteria, a student who is new to the school starts calling you names like "blindy" and "stupid." This new student wants you to move, but you are sitting with your best friend and don't want to move away. What do you say to the new student?
- The kids in your class are always touching your braillewriter and asking if they can play with it. What do you tell them?

**Fourth to Sixth Grade**

- You are at home, and you want to play video games with your brother. Your brother tells you that you cannot play because you are blind and can't see the screen. What do you tell your brother?
- Your class is having an overnight camping trip. Your parents and your classroom teachers are a bit nervous about you going on the trip. How do you let them know that you will be able to handle the trip?

*(continued on next page)*

Sidebar 7.2 *(continued)*

- You are on the playground at recess waiting in line to play wall ball. One of the kids from your class tells you that you can't play. What do you tell this student?

### Seventh to Ninth Grade

- A number of your classmates are trying out for the middle school basketball team. You feel that you have enough sight to participate. How do you convince the coach that you should be given the opportunity to try out for the team?

- You are at a school dance, and the lighting is quite weak and glaring. You want to find a couple of your friends so you can hang out. What do you do to find your friends?

- Your math teacher put all of his examples of mathematical equations on the overhead projector. It is really difficult to follow the information he is providing to the students. How would you handle this situation?

- You have just bought your lunch in the cafeteria. You notice that a group of students whom you like are sitting together. How do you ask them if you can join the group and eat lunch together?

### Tenth Grade to Young Adult

- You really like one of the girls in your English class. She has started many conversations with you. You want to ask her to the Homecoming Dance. How do you ask her to the dance? How do you let her know that you can't drive her to the dance?

- You are an excellent singer, and you have participated in the beginning drama class. You want to try out for the spring musical. The director tells you that this is not possible. What do you do? How do you convince the director that you can participate in the show?

- You want to earn some extra money after school. You decide to apply for a job at the local coffee bar. After successfully completing the application, the owner schedules an interview. How will you let the owner know that you can do the job? What social amenities will you use to convince the owner of your abilities?

received training prior to each session with their visually impaired peer. The training for sighted peers included information to promote understanding about the student's visual impairment and strategies and techniques for initiating and modeling the targeted social behaviors. The sighted peers were reminded that their relationship with the student who was blind or visually impaired was to be equal and that when activities were selected during the peer training, they were to be mutually determined. Sidebar 7.3 provides examples of the training for sighted peers.

Initially, each sighted peer was given information about the etiology of the student's eye condition, the visual impairment itself, and how the student functioned in school and in the community. The sighted peer also learned about equipment and devices that the visually impaired student used throughout the day. Prior to each training session, the researcher met with each sighted student to review the target behavior for intervention, provide examples of training strategies, and role play typical situations that might be encountered during the peer training sessions.

The peer-mediated intervention consisted of a total of 12 40-minute sessions, offered three times per week over a period of four weeks. The training took place in the resource room for students with visual impairments and on the playground when it was not in use. The intervention sessions took place at times during the school day that were convenient for both students, and did not interfere with their academic routines. When the sighted peer entered the resource classroom, the training session began. The teacher of students with visual impairments prompted the students involved in the training sessions by asking, "What are you going to do together today?" If no activity was mutually agreed on within a five-minute period, the teacher would provide a list of activities and require the students to make a choice. Table 7.1 provides examples of the types of activities undertaken for each targeted behavior, the training strategies used by the sighted peers, and the responses of the students with visual impairments.

## CONTROL

Students in the control group received neither the peer-mediated nor the teacher-directed social skills training interventions. However, each student in the control group was paired with a student from one of the intervention groups so that the dates and frequency of observations were nearly identical. For example, if a student from the control

## Sidebar 7.3

**IN-SERVICE TRAINING PROTOCOLS FOR USE WITH
SIGHTED PEER TRAINERS**

### Introduction to the Visually Impaired Student and a Description of His or Her Visual Impairment

*Procedure*

Name and describe the specific visual disability. Use simulation of the visual impairment to help the peers understand the adaptations and limitations incurred by the visually impaired student. Discuss the ways in which visually impaired students can adapt and participate in activities in school and community during each session. Follow the sequence of training for the peer-mediated approach and randomly select a targeted behavior for training. Answer questions and clarify any preconceived notions about how visually impaired individuals perform tasks.

*Outcomes*

The peer trainers will develop a heightened awareness and sensitivity to the students' abilities and limitations and more realistic expectations of them.

### Direction of Gaze (Eye Contact) and Body Posture

*Procedure*

Name and define the behavior being targeted for training. Discuss the importance of using appropriate eye contact and body posture in social situations. Have the sighted peers identify the elements of acceptable eye contact and body posture. Ask the students to interpret the meaning of specific behaviors being modeled by the investigator; for example, talk to students while not looking at them or keep your head down while engaged in a conversation. Ask the students how they would change these behaviors. If the students do not respond, provide specific prompting procedures, such as verbal cues ("Look up") or physical prompts (a tap on the shoulder). Provide role-play scenarios in which the sighted peers must employ corrective feedback or praise. Encourage the peers to praise their visually impaired counterparts, but also to give honest feedback. Use role plays that reflect the experiences of peers. Have the sighted peers practice praise and corrective responses through the role-play scenes until the desired responses are used with 80 percent proficiency.

*Outcomes*

The visually impaired students will improve their ability to initiate and to maintain appropriate gazes and postures in a variety of social contexts. The incidence of mannerisms (such as rocking and head or hand waving) will be reduced to enhance acceptable body posture.

**Positive Social Initiations**

*Procedure*

Name and define the behavior being targeted for training. Discuss with the sighted peers the way they greet friends, the topics they discuss, and the games and activities they particularly like to play. Have the sighted students role play a typical social interaction or greeting. Ask the students to analyze the good and bad parts of the interaction. Emphasize that interactions or initiations have a beginning, a middle, and an end. Ask the sighted peers to think about what part of an initiation may be particularly difficult for a visually impaired student. If the sighted students have difficulty responding, you may prompt some thoughts (for example, "If you cannot see another person standing nearby, how would you know the person's identity or that there is a peer close by?") Encourage solutions, such as providing verbal feedback or using auditory cues or sensation cues (changes in temperature or shadows). Engage in role plays with the sighted peers in which you assume the role of the visually impaired student and include a variety of situations in which the visually impaired student does not initiate a conversation, is overly verbal, or is overly aggressive and uses hostile phrases to engage in social interactions. Provide verbal feedback (praise or prompts) for each response by the sighted peer. Model specific responses or initiators to specific situations. For example, if the visually impaired student is overly verbal (talks about the same topic or self), have the sighted peer use phrases, such as, "You always talk about that. How about changing the subject?" or "Gee! I really like you, but I can't get a word in. You're always talking." Encourage the sighted student to train the visually impaired student to use complimenting statements about others (such as "good shot" or "that's great"). Have the sighted peer practice phrases and statements that will prompt the visually impaired student to use initiators (for example, "Hi, how ya doin'? I like what you're wearing today"), icebreakers (such as, "Wanna have lunch together? Hey, did you watch Cosby last night?"), or engaging statements (for instance, "You were great in class today. I have that

*(continued on next page)*

Sidebar 7.3 *(continued)*

Transformer"). Practice role plays until prompts and feedback responses are used with 80 percent proficiency.

*Outcomes*

The visually impaired students will demonstrate increased positive initiations with peers, expanded conversations, and greater use of complimenting statements.

**Joining In Group Activities**

*Procedure*

Name and define the behavior being trained. Have the sighted students describe how they join a group on the playground at recess, in the cafeteria at lunch, or in the classroom during a free-time activity. Explain or reinforce how the effect of limited vision or no vision may influence joining a group. Blindfold or use vision simulators on the sighted students. Have the sighted students practice joining a group and engaging in play while under simulation. Have the sighted peers provide impressions and discuss ways to facilitate joining. If the sighted students do not provide solutions, offer several suggestions (such as meeting a friend at a designated spot and having the visually impaired student practice asking for assistance to find a friend or a particular game on the playground). Have the sighted students practice phrases that will help the visually impaired students gain entry to groups in a positive manner (for example, "Gee, can I play?" or "How about playing _____?"). Use role plays and actual practice in natural settings until phrases and prompts are used with 80 percent proficiency.

*Outcomes*

The visually impaired students will enter group activities in an independent manner. If assistance is needed, they will use statements that generate positive responses from peers.

**Sharing in Group Activities**

*Procedure*

Name and define the behavior being trained. Ask the sighted peers to describe both positive and negative sharing techniques. Help them understand that students without sight or with limited vision may need help with turn taking, in game playing, or with interrupting in actual conversations. Teach the sighted students phrases or statements to help the visually impaired students become aware of turn-taking techniques (for instance, "Hey, _____, just wait a minute," or "Wait for your turn," or "You're interrupting me, wait a minute, okay?"). Have the sighted students teach the visually impaired students statements that will facilitate sharing and turn taking (such as, "It's just a game," or "You don't always have to win," or "Don't get so upset, it's only a game."). Provide role-play situations in which the sighted students can practice corrective responses and honest feedback with 80 percent proficiency.

*Outcomes*

The visually impaired students will increase their ability to share in a variety of group situations using turn-taking techniques and asserting their rights in a positive manner.

---

Adapted with permission from S. Z. Sacks and R. J. Gaylord-Ross, "Peer Mediated and Teacher-Directed Social Skills Training for Blind and Visually Impaired Students," in S. Z. Sacks, L. S. Kekelis, and R. J. Gaylord-Ross, Eds., *The Development of Social Skills by Blind and Visually Impaired Students: Exploratory Studies and Strategies* (New York: American Foundation for the Blind, 1992), pp. 122–124.

group was paired with a student in the teacher-directed group, and the latter was absent from school for two days, data would not be collected on the control-group student until the other student returned to school.

As predicted in the original research hypothesis, visually impaired students in both the teacher-directed and the peer-mediated groups demonstrated increases in all the targeted social behaviors. However, the students in the teacher-directed intervention showed greater increases in acquisition of social behaviors than did the peer-mediated group during the training phase of the study. When data from observation in a non-training setting and later follow-up observational data were compared statistically and graphically, students with visual impairments in the peer-mediated intervention showed greater increases and stability in performance of the targeted behaviors over time than the teacher-directed participants. These findings substantiate the importance of peer-directed approaches in acquiring and maintaining positive social behaviors for students with visual impairments.

**TABLE 7.1**  Peer-Mediated Training Activities, Interactions, and Responses

| Behavior | Activities | Input from Sighted Peers | Responses of Visually Impaired Students |
|---|---|---|---|
| Direction of gaze and body posture | Board games (checkers, Simon, Sorry, Connect Four, Monopoly, Fish, 21, Othello), computer games, outdoor games, using play equipment, hand-clapping games, finger plays | Phrases used: "Hey! Sit up!" "_____, when you talk to me, how about looking at me?" "_____, [pause]." "_____, you look really neat." "_____, please stop that." | Verbal responses: "Okay, I forgot." "Thanks for reminding me." "Ya, I'll stop." "Ya, I know I do." Nonverbal responses: sits or stands with appropriate posture and longer gaze |
| Positive initiations | Drawing on blackboard; playing with dolls, dollhouse, Transformers, or action figures; sharing a snack or toy; talking about school | "Gee, you did a good job." "What do you want to play? You decide." "Hi! What's new?" "What did you watch on TV last night? So what's happening?" "It would sure be great if you could come over after school." "Hey, did you hear about _____? He likes _____." | "Ya, thanks, it's a _____." "How about dolls or a game?" "Hi, how ya doin?" "Hey, did you see *Friends* last night?" "I'd like to, but I have to ask my mom, and figure a way home." "No, what happened? He's cute." |
| Joining in group activities | Playing on play equipment (dramatic play), kickball, wall ball, basketball, tag, jump rope | "Okay, _____, let's meet and then we can play _____." "Wanta play kickball?" [peer runs off] "Okay, _____, it's your turn." | "I'll meet you at the drinking fountain." "Ya, wait for me." "Thanks, but where do I stand?" |

*(continued)*

**TABLE 7.1**  *(continued)*

| Behavior | Activities | Input from Sighted Peers | Responses of Visually Impaired Students |
|---|---|---|---|
| Joining in activities and sharing in group activities | Dramatic play with action figures, waiting in line for food in the cafeteria, eating lunch on the grass (small group), hanging out on a bench (conversing), walking around the play area, indoor activities (cooking projects, computer games, puzzles, hangman, board games, art projects) | "Just wait _____, I'll go after you, all right? It's _____ turn." "First you'll have a turn, and then me." | "Okay, I'll wait." "That sounds great." |

*Source:* Adapted with permission from S. Z. Sacks, L. S. Kekelis, & R. J. Gaylord-Ross, "Peer-Mediated and Teacher-Directed Social-Skills Training," in S. Z. Sacks, L. S. Kekelis, & R. J. Gaylord-Ross (Eds.), *The Development of Social Skills by Blind and Visually Impaired Students: Exploratory Studies and Strategies* (New York: American Foundation for the Blind, 1992), pp. 125–126.

## PEER-SUPPORT NETWORKS

Another peer-directed strategy that has been widely used in general education classrooms with students who exhibit a range of disabilities, including visual impairment is the peer-support network (Denti, 1992). In this intervention, three nondisabled peers are assigned explicit roles in assisting the student with a disability. For example, one student may be assigned to support the student with a visual impairment in setting up and keeping track of his or her equipment and special devices. Another student may support the student by sitting next to him or her in the classroom and reading information from the whiteboard or overhead projector, cueing the student to raise his or her hand, and alerting the student to nonverbal actions or activities taking place in the classroom. The third peer-support student might assist the student with a visual impairment with activities at recess by including him or her in games and activities on the playground and at lunch by inviting the student to join his or her group of friends.

Sighted peers who volunteer for the peer-support network are interviewed by the classroom teacher and teacher of students with visual impairments. Once selected, they receive training about the student's visual impairment, strategies to facilitate inclusion of the student with visual impairment into the peer group, and effective methods to reinforce appropriate social behavior. The teachers emphasize to the peer-support students that they are to be friends, not teachers, when interacting with their visually impaired age-mates.

## GUIDELINES TO SUPPORT SOCIAL COMPETENCE WITH SIGHTED PEERS*

Many of the interventions described earlier are based on research studies that have demonstrated an increase in social competence for students with visual impairments. However, additional factors may influence a student's ability to socialize with peers in an effective manner. For example, exposure to a wide variety of hands-on, real-life experiences promotes independent decision making, risk-taking behavior, and enhanced self-esteem. By providing visually impaired students with these kinds of experiences at an early age and throughout their school years, their ability to play and to communicate effectively with peers can be enhanced.

A number of additional factors can also have a significant influence on students' level of social competence, including

- classroom placement
- selection of activities and materials
- support in the general education classroom
- support from the teacher of students with visual impairments
- appropriate use of paraeducators
- support from the family

The following sections examine each of these factors in turn and offer some observations and key points about how each situation can best be structured to promote the social confidence of students who are visually impaired. Specific suggestions and strategies are offered for

---

*Many of the strategies listed in this section are adapted from S. Z. Sacks and L. S. Kekelis, "Guidelines for Mainstreaming Blind and Visually Impaired Children," in S. Z. Sacks, L. S. Kekelis, and R. J. Gaylord-Ross (Eds.), *The Development of Social Skills by Blind and Visually Impaired Students* (New York: American Foundation for the Blind, 1992), pp. 133–149.

each situation and are directed to professionals and family members to help them in providing genuine and positive social experiences for their students with sighted peers.

## CLASSROOM PLACEMENT

The classroom teacher's philosophy and style of instruction affects the academic and social gains made by visually impaired students, particularly those students who rely on the input of others to acquire skills that are generally learned through observation and modeling. It is critical that the classroom environment in which a student with a visual impairment is placed promotes the social well-being of all students and encourages altruistic behavior among classmates.

## STRATEGIES FOR SOCIAL SUCCESS

# Classroom Placement

## Suggestions for General Education Teachers

◆ Provide a general education experience that is structured and organized, so that the student with a visual impairment knows what to expect.

◆ Create seating arrangements that enhance social experiences for the student with a visual impairment. For example, including the student with a visual impairment in a cooperative learning group of four to six students may assist him or her in gaining entry into peer groups.

◆ Change seating assignments regularly so that the student who is blind or visually impaired has an opportunity to meet a wide variety of classmates.

◆ Provide opportunities for the student with a visual impairment to choose partners for group or play activities. Encourage and promote opportunities for sighted classmates to ask questions about the student's visual impairment and provide opportunities for the sighted students to experience typical school activities with a simulated visual impairment.

## Suggestions for Teachers of Students with Visual Impairments

◆ Attempt to find placements in classrooms in which affective education— opportunities to enhance self-concept and social skills—is emphasized for all students.

- At the primary level, select classroom environments in which academic performance and social competence are equally important.

- Create opportunities in the general education classroom or in the special day classroom in which the educational team can facilitate discussions of the physical, social, or emotional differences between sighted students and students with visual impairments in a relaxed, free-flowing manner.

- Help both students with visual impairments and their sighted classmates become sensitive to the strengths and limitations of all students through discussion, curricular activities, or lessons on literature, language arts, and social studies in which the subject is incorporated.

## Suggestions for Parents

- Observe potential classrooms or schools in which your visually impaired child may be placed to determine if affective or character education (respecting and caring about each student as an individual) is a priority.

- Work closely with the teacher of students with visual impairments to ensure that your son or daughter has an opportunity to become familiar with the school and classroom environment in order to optimize social experiences with peers.

- Try to become involved in school activities, including volunteering in your child's classroom or meeting other parents whose children may show interest in your child.

- Have clear expectations for your child's academic and social performance in school, at home, and in the community. To ensure consistency, communicate regularly with the general education teacher and the teacher of students with visual impairments.

## SELECTION OF ACTIVITIES AND MATERIALS

Materials and activities for use in the general education classroom should support and enhance socialization between students who are sighted and students who are visually impaired. It is important to consider how the materials and activities contribute to ensuring positive social interactions rather than isolation. Select materials and activities that utilize a multisensory approach and allow the student with a visual impairment to be included with sighted peers without direct adult support. In addition, confining activities on the playground or in the classroom to a specific area helps the student who is visually impaired to have easy and independent access to each environment.

# Classroom Activities and Materials

## Suggestions for General Education Teachers

◆ In primary classrooms, use toys with many different pieces, such as Lincoln Logs, blocks, Legos, and puzzles, to allow students with visual impairment to work with their sighted classmates on an equal footing. These toys allow young children with visual impairments to engage in group activities. These toys also promote pretend and imaginary play between students. It is helpful if these activities take place in a confined space on the floor or on a tabletop.

◆ Encourage visually impaired students to participate in art activities in the classroom by organizing and describing the materials and the finished product—for example, the color of paints, selection and texture of paper for cutting and pasting, and description of shapes and forms for clay and sculpting activities.

◆ Create art activities that involve a group of students, such as painted murals, papier-mâché, or wood or metal sculpture.

◆ Design activities within the classroom that promote creative thinking and imaginative play through creative dramatics. For example, have students pretend they are an animal or a cartoon character and have the other students guess what they are portraying. Students with visual impairments may need to team up with another student who describes the action or activity.

◆ Encourage instruction in and use of board games for sighted students as well as students with visual impairments. The general education teacher will need to monitor and organize these activities so that the students understand the rules of the game and also ensure that the student with a visual impairment is free to ask for assistance from peers without being teased or taunted.

◆ Create opportunities for visually impaired students to share their equipment and devices with the sighted students in the class and allow them opportunities to use an adapted computer, braillewriter, or closed-circuit television or video magnifier.

◆ Encourage visually impaired students to share their expertise in specific activities with the class. For example, have the student who is blind or visually impaired demonstrate the use of a braille notetaker.

◆ Encourage students with visual impairments to be advocates for themselves. Create activities in which they have to make decisions and choices that will have an impact on the outcome of the activity for all of the students—for example, have students design and build a structure or sculpture in a group and have the student who is visually impaired take the lead in making decisions about the construction of the sculpture or structure; or have students work on a topical group project for social studies or health and have the student who is blind share his knowledge of history, and lead the group to a topic of interest.

◆ In primary classrooms, establish designated areas for specific activities such as playing house, building with blocks, and listening and reading centers. Allow the child with a visual impairment to become familiar with the materials and toys in each of these areas of the classroom.

◆ Demonstrate the use and function of toys and materials that are available in free-play situations, for example, toy pots and pans in play kitchens or toy cars in a pretend garage or speedway.

◆ At recess provide toys and materials that will bring sighted peers to the student who is blind or visually impaired. For example, bring an activity table to the sidelines of the playground and encourage the visually impaired student to bring out water toys, Legos, action figures, or toys trucks or cars.

◆ During physical education or other nonacademic activities, teach games that will allow all students, including the student with a visual impairment, to participate actively, such as twosquare or foursquare, tether ball, jump rope, wall ball, and dodgeball.

◆ Encourage games that promote group cooperation and facilitation. (See Sidebar 7.4 for examples.)

## Suggestions for Parents and Teachers of Students with Visual Impairments

◆ Spend instructional time to introduce students who are blind or visually impaired to age-appropriate toys, games, and activities.

◆ Foster opportunities for the student with a visual impairment to have hands-on experiences with toys, games, and activities in the home, school, and community so that there is transference from what is

## Sidebar 7.4

**GAMES THAT STUDENTS WITH VISUAL IMPAIRMENTS CAN PLAY WITH THEIR SIGHTED PEERS**

### "Rattlers," or the Predator-Prey Game

For this game, everyone forms a circle around two players, who are blindfolded. One of the two acts as the predator, and the other acts as the prey. Each one holds a can that has been filled with beans, pebbles, or similar items that make sounds (they can either sound the same or be filled with different objects so as to distinguish the predator from the prey). The outside circle of players are told that their job is to define the boundaries for the two blindfolded players. That is, they must make sure that neither the predator nor the prey wanders outside the circle. The game begins when the predator shakes his or her can. The prey must respond by shaking his or her can. The predator tries to catch the prey, and the prey tries to avoid being caught. The shaking of the cans continues until the predator catches the prey.

### "The Blob"

This game requires total cooperation by the players. Initially, the children are paired up—a sighted child with a visually impaired child, or a sighted child with another sighted child who is blindfolded to simulate visual impairment. The boundaries are set and are shown to the players. One child or one group of players is declared "it." When those who are "it" tag a child, that child or group must attach themselves to the original "it" by holding on to each others' hands. Thus, the blob grows. Now, instead of one or two being "it," anywhere from two to four are "it." The blob continues to grow with each addition. In one version, the blob can split itself, but each blob has to contain a minimum of three players.

The game can become wild and confusing. Trying to keep track of the blobs, trying not to get whipped around when a blob gets too big, and trying to keep track of the boundaries are just some of the challenges. Although the pairs work together, the blobs provide opportunities to develop teamwork, cooperation, and communication and listening skills (Are they going too fast or too slow? In what direction are you going?).

Since the sighted child must learn to describe to the visually impaired child the necessary information, he or she learns what information is

*(continued on next page)*

Sidebar 7.4 *(continued)*

needed and what is extraneous. The children also learn to pay attention to one another's needs and abilities and to trust each other. The visually impaired child must trust his or her partner, and the partner, in turn, must learn how to foster that trust and to communicate his or her trust. Finally, all the children experience what it is like to run around freely.

**"Ooh-Ahh" or "Pass the Squeeze"**

The children stand in a circle, all holding hands, and the teacher chooses one child to squeeze the hand of the player to his or her right. From then on, the squeeze is passed around the circle. The object of the game is to get the squeeze to travel as quickly as possible. The game can be adapted by (1) changing the direction in which the squeeze travels, (2) initiating simultaneous squeezes going in both directions, and (3) changing the game to the Ooh-Ahh game. In the Ooh-Ahh game, the right hand is Ooh and the left hand is Ahh. Depending on which way the squeeze is passed, the children will shout Ooh or Ahh as they squeeze the next player's hand.

Although this game is more passive than the others, it can become confusing when the players have to shout Ooh and Ahh. It is a good game for working on listening skills, cooperation, the use of right and left, following directions, and for breaking down barriers that come with holding hands with members of the opposite sex.

**Parachute Games**

A great deal can be done with just one parachute. In fact, many ideas come from the students themselves. The parachute can be used in the following ways:

1. By holding its edges, the children lift the parachute up and down and see how high they can make it go, how quickly they can bring it to the ground, and how large a bubble they can make with the captured air.
2. The children run around in a circle while holding onto the edges of the parachute.
3. Each child is assigned a number, and the numbers are called out at random, either singly or in groups. When a student hears his or her number called, he or she tries to run under the parachute while the others continue to raise and lower it as quickly as they can. The parachute offers children a chance to create their own games and accompanying rules.

**"The Lap Sit"**

For this game, participating players stand in a circle, shoulder to shoulder. They are instructed to turn to their right and take one step into the center of the circle. Counting to three, they all gently sit down on the lap of the person behind them. The aim is to all sit down at the same time and form a circle. If they do so and all are "comfortably" seated, then they can give back or shoulder rubs to the person in front of them. The game can be changed so the players take more than one step or alternate which foot to start with, or lift their right feet and arms and then lift their left feet and arms as they walk into the center.

Adapted with permission from J. Macks, "The Creative Games Project," in S. Z. Sacks, R. J. Gaylord-Ross, & L. S. Kekelis (Eds.), *The Development of Social Skills by Blind and Visually Impaired Students: Exploratory Studies and Strategies* (New York: American Foundation for the Blind, 1992), pp. 173–176.

heard or explained (for example, in commercials on television) to the actual participation (for example, manipulation of the toys or game pieces).

♦ Provide community experiences or activities that enhance or expand communication skills. For example, trips to the grocery store, going to the movies to see a popular film, or attending a baseball game promote opportunities for children to share new experiences and ideas.

♦ Facilitate fantasy play, through problem-solving activities, role play, or group play, in a comfortable setting, such as in the home or the resource room for students with visual impairments.

♦ Orient the student with a visual impairment to toys, games, and activities available in the general education classroom prior to the beginning of each school year.

♦ Reorient the student who is blind or visually impaired whenever new toys, games, or activities are available or the layout of the classroom changes.

♦ Provide structured games or activities on the playground or in the community that facilitate social interaction between the student with a visual impairment and sighted peers. For example, teach students with visual impairments hand-clapping games like "Say, Say O Playmate."

◆ Find toys, games, and activities that will entice sighted peers to engage in play with the child who is visually impaired (for example, adaptive computer games).

◆ Work with the student who is blind or visually impaired, through role plays and modeling, to exhibit age-appropriate conversation skills and play behavior.

◆ Encourage the development of a skill or activity (such as use of the computer or notetaking device or singing a solo at the school talent show) that will enhance the student's social status and level of competence among sighted peers.

◆ Teach the student to use icebreakers to gain entry into group activities. For example, "Hi, I'm really good at playing wall ball. Can I join in? What's the score?"

◆ Encourage students with visual impairments to invite sighted peers to share prized possessions, such as a favorite toy, computer game, or memento.

◆ Encourage and model complimenting behaviors toward other peers in play encounters.

## SUPPORT IN THE GENERAL EDUCATION CLASSROOM

In addition to academic criteria, social skills need to be considered when evaluating students with visual impairments for inclusion in general education classes. The involvement of the teacher of students with visual impairments in the general education classroom and with the general education teacher facilitates the socialization of students who are blind and visually impaired.

## STRATEGIES FOR SOCIAL SUCCESS

# Classroom Practice

### Suggestions for General Education Teachers

◆ Create a classroom environment that is organized and consistent so that the student who is blind or visually impaired has access to both peers and materials in the classroom.

◆ Provide opportunities for the student with a visual impairment to select a peer as a partner for a classroom project or an outdoor activity.

◆ Assist the student with a visual impairment in assuming and orchestrating the responsibility for selecting a peer to participate in a buddy system in the classroom, during recess or break times, and at lunchtime.

◆ Provide opportunities in the general education classroom or in the resource classroom for the student who is blind or visually impaired to invite a friend or small group of friends to work on a project, play a board game, or master an adaptive computer game.

◆ Design activities that promote cooperation between the student who is visually impaired and students who are sighted.

◆ When an aide or educational specialist (a teacher of visually impaired students, speech and language pathologist, or orientation and mobility specialist) works with the visually impaired student in the general education classroom, develop lessons and activities that include sighted classmates.

◆ Create activities in the general education classroom that do not isolate the student with a visual impairment.

## Suggestions for Teachers of Students with Visual Impairments

◆ Foster an atmosphere for communication with the general education teacher in which questions can be answered and concerns can be discussed.

◆ Provide opportunities for the general education teacher to cooperate in the design and implementation of instruction and activities for the student.

◆ Observe and participate in general education classroom activities on an ongoing basis to determine if the student with a visual impairment is participating with his or her peers.

◆ Work closely with the general education teacher to ensure that the student who is visually impaired interacts more consistently with peers than with adults, such as classroom assistants and parent volunteers.

◆ Develop education sessions for classmates of the student with a visual impairment in which he or she can discuss his or her visual impairment and demonstrate equipment and devices. Answer questions together with the student.

◆ Coordinate with the general education teacher to provide opportunities for the student with a visual impairment to act as his or her own advocate, ask for assistance from peers, or interact in a social situation that may be new or uncomfortable to handle (for example, playing a board game in which the playing pieces are difficult to see).

## SUPPORT FROM THE TEACHER OF STUDENTS WITH VISUAL IMPAIRMENTS

The role of the teacher of students with visual impairments is unique. It requires the inclusion of the expanded core curriculum in the services that are provided to students. The teacher of visually impaired students must promote and facilitate social experiences for students across all grade and ability levels.

## STRATEGIES FOR SOCIAL SUCCESS

# Support from the Teacher of Students with Visual Impairments

- ◆ Incorporate social skills instruction into lessons and activities.
- ◆ Encourage appropriate social behavior; for example, require the student to keep his or her head up and to maintain appropriate body posture.
- ◆ Find time to discuss activities, games, or social activities, such as movies that are popular with sighted age-mates.
- ◆ Provide opportunities for students to practice newly learned social skills with their sighted peers within the resource room or during times when the teacher for students with visual impairments is engaged in individual instruction.
- ◆ Work with the general education teacher to design games that allow full participation for students with visual impairments. (See Sidebar 7.4 for specific examples.)
- ◆ Adapt games and activities so the student who is blind or visually impaired can participate in them with his or her classmates. For example, provide a beeper ball so that the student who is blind can play catch or dodgeball with his classmates.
- ◆ Practice games or activities that are popular with sighted peers, such as hand-clapping games or use of play equipment.

◆ With the assistance of the general education teacher, identify class-mates that the visually impaired student prefers.

◆ Encourage the student to express positive feelings toward sighted classmates.

◆ Encourage visually impaired students to select peers as partners for games or projects, rather than directing their attention toward adults.

◆ Encourage the student to help his or her sighted peers and to show empathy toward other students.

◆ Facilitate discussion about friendship so that the visually impaired student may become more sensitive about the development of positive peer relationships. For example, discuss the importance of reciprocation in developing a solid friendship (see Chapter 6).

◆ Encourage the student to compliment others.

◆ Teach and encourage the student to communicate his or her visual needs to classmates and adults in a simple, straightforward manner.

◆ Help students learn how to communicate effectively about their visual impairment to others.

◆ Give sighted students clear information about the visual status of the student who is blind or visually impaired.

◆ Help the sighted students find alternative ways of implementing a visual activity. Allow the students to develop their own solutions.

## APPROPRIATE USE OF PARAEDUCATORS

Paraeducators have a professional role that is distinct from that of either a teacher or parent in the school environment and from the role of a friend or relative. Paraeducators are an integral part of the educational team, but they must follow the instructional direction of the teacher for students with visual impairments in initiating and implementing social skills interventions. The role of the paraeducator is to assist the student who is blind or visually impaired and the general education teacher in the delivery of instruction and development of materials; and they may also help students with campus mobility. It is important for paraeducators not to hover over students, speak for them, or make decisions regarding selection of play activities or peers to interact with in the classroom or on the playground. Direct instruction in social skills is facilitated and initiated by the teacher of students with visual impairments. The educational team, including the paraeducator, determines how to reinforce the student's appropriate social behavior.

## STRATEGIES FOR SOCIAL SUCCESS

# Role of Paraeducators

- ◆ It is essential to have open and frequent communication among the teacher of students with visual impairments, the general education teacher, and the paraeducator to ensure that the feedback about the social competence provided to the visually impaired student is consistent.

- ◆ It is important to nurture interdependence with peers and independent decision making by the student who is blind or visually impaired throughout the school day.

- ◆ When assisting the student who is visually impaired, it is important to become a part of the classroom or other school environments such as the playground, the cafeteria, the library, or the computer laboratory, so that the focus of support is not always directed toward the student who is blind or visually impaired.

- ◆ Include sighted students in the delivery of instruction and assist sighted students along with the student with a visual impairment in completing classroom activities to avoid isolation of the visually impaired student and increase interaction with his or her peers.

- ◆ When assisting the student who is blind or visually impaired in nonclassroom environments such as the playground, the cafeteria, or the library, encourage assistance from peers rather than adults.

- ◆ Try to ensure that the visually impaired student focuses his or her attention and interest toward peers rather than adults during nonstructured activities, such as recess, lunch, or free time in the classroom; redirect the student toward activities that involve peers whenever possible.

- ◆ Direct students with visual impairments who tend to engage in conversations with adults to talk to peers. Model appropriate social initiations, greetings, and conversation topics.

- ◆ In less structured environments, such as lunch, recess, or free time, be aware of the physical proximity to the visually impaired student; hovering over the student discourages social contact with peers.

- ◆ During classroom instruction, classroom rules should be applied equally to students who are blind or visually impaired and for their sighted age-mates. For example, if the student with a visual impairment does not raise his or her hand and wait to be called upon to speak, the student should be reprimanded for not following classroom rules.

## SUPPORT FROM THE FAMILY

Parents and other family members need to foster and promote the acquisition and use of appropriate social behavior within the home and in community environments. It is important for parents to provide a range of experiential activities that enhance learning and development and to promote interdependence through nurturing a sense of responsibility in their child, having clear expectations, and facilitating decision-making activities.

## STRATEGIES FOR SOCIAL SUCCESS
# Support from the Family

◆ Include the child with visual impairments in family activities and chores.

◆ Give the child who is blind or visually impaired specific tasks to complete on a regular basis, such as setting the table, clearing dishes from the table, throwing dirty laundry in the clothes hamper.

◆ Provide consistent feedback about the child's social behavior. Physically model and verbalize what is appropriate social behavior, and reinforce the social behavior when it is exhibited or observed.

◆ Introduce the student who is blind or visually impaired to a variety of activities within the community, such as swim lessons, dance lessons, park activities, and team sports.

◆ Allow the child with a visual impairment to experiment with risk-taking behavior that promotes exploration and independent mobility within the home environment and around the neighborhood, such as rough-and-tumble play or riding a bike without training wheels.

◆ Make the home a social place in which children who are sighted want to play and interact with the child who is blind or visually impaired.

◆ Become involved in playgroups and other organized groups for parents and children (such as scouting, or church or synagogue youth groups) that foster friendships for both parents and children.

◆ Encourage the child with a visual impairment to invite peers to birthday parties, sleepovers, or family events.

◆ Encourage older students who are blind or visually impaired to travel independently to stores, recreational activities, and school, along with their friends.

◆ Encourage the visually impaired student to volunteer for jobs in the neighborhood or community, such as feeding and walking pets, taking in a neighbor's mail, or collecting canned goods for the needy or homeless during the holiday season.

◆ Help extended family members, including grandparents, siblings, and other relatives, understand the child's strengths and abilities by allowing them to observe him or her carrying out newly learned skills or tasks around the house.

◆ Encourage and promote self-advocacy on the part of the child who is blind or visually impaired by modeling assertive behavior and providing opportunities to practice and use these skills.

◆ Become an active member of the student's school and extracurricular activity environments by volunteering for committees and by attending programs and activities in which the student may participate.

## SOCIAL EXPERIENCES WITH PEERS WHO ARE BLIND OR VISUALLY IMPAIRED

Although it is important for students who are blind or visually impaired to establish strong social relationships with sighted age-mates, it is just as important for these youngsters to have experiences with peers who are blind or visually impaired. Often, a student who is visually impaired is the only such student in his or her local school or region, making it critical to provide opportunities for students with visual impairments to meet and interact with one another. Students not only need to meet others with similar eye conditions and share strategies for functioning in school and in the community, they also need the chance to relax and be themselves without any concern about preconceived judgments about their capabilities or skills. These experiences allow students with visual impairments to network and to develop lifelong friendships. The following suggestions may assist both teachers and families of students with visual impairments in facilitating such experiences.

# Facilitating Social Experiences among Students with Visual Impairments

◆ Encourage students to participate in after-school and weekend programs sponsored by agencies or organizations for persons who are blind or visually impaired.

◆ Encourage students to attend summer camps and other outdoor adventures, such as skiing, kayaking, biking, and wall climbing, with other students who are blind or visually impaired.

◆ Encourage participation in goal ball or beeper baseball teams.

◆ Arrange for students with visual impairments within a geographic region to come together for instruction in daily living skills, recreational activities, or field trips.

◆ Encourage students with visual impairments to participate in summer enrichment programs, such as computer camps, braille camps, or transition programs sponsored by specialized schools for the blind and visually impaired or agencies for the blind.

◆ Develop a penpal network among visually impaired students who have similar interests. Teach students to use the Internet and e-mail as a way to enhance social communication.

# THE IMPORTANCE OF ROLE MODELS AND MENTORS

While peers play an integral role in the socialization process for students who are blind or visually impaired, role models and mentors are equally important. Traditionally, adults with visual impairments have helped teens and young adults learn more about employment and specific job tasks. However, role models can also be used effectively to model appropriate social skills.

For young children who are blind or visually impaired, role models can also be older students who can assist the teacher of students who are visually impaired by sharing with the younger students effective strategies for making and keeping friends, teaching games and activities that are popular among sighted children, and modeling ways to inform others about the student's visual impairment. Pairing role models with students who have similar visual impairments allows the younger students to interact with an older, successful-appearing student who shares similar attributes. The development of this relationship affords the younger student who is blind or visually impaired the opportunity to ask questions about how the role model functions in various environments, handles teasing, and gains more independence at home, as well as ways to be more assertive and a more effective self-advocate.

According to Chen and Dote-Kwan (1999), elementary and high school students with visual impairments who can articulate their preferences, abilities, interests, responsibilities, and experiences with jobs they have accomplished are able to assist younger students in developing a strong sense of self and enhancing students' social abilities. In the preschool environment, role models can share their experiences by demonstrating devices and specialized equipment. For example, an elementary-aged student may share with the preschool class a story he or she has composed in braille by reading the story to the children, demonstrating the use of the braille writer, and allowing the students in the class to practice "reading" the braille characters. Similarly, a high school student may bring in his or her dog guide and discuss travel experiences with the children.

Older students can also be role models for elementary-school students with visual impairments, providing the opportunity for the mentor and the mentee to develop a strong, ongoing relationship in which both students benefit. The younger student can learn by observing the older student engage in independent travel, participate in extracurricular activities at school and in the community, and effectively use adaptive technology to obtain and complete class assignments and projects. The older student benefits by reaching out to help support the needs of others, which, in turn, helps the younger student become socially competent and capable.

Family members and teachers of students with visual impairments can encourage a variety of role-model experiences for their students. The following activities and suggestions for enhancing relationships with role models can be used to help students who are blind or visually impaired develop effective strategies for becoming socially competent.

# Providing Role Models and Mentors

- Provide opportunities for younger students with visual impairments to meet older, socially competent students with visual impairments.

- Invite older students with visual impairments to share information about their interests and responsibilities with younger students.

- Encourage role models to talk about their visual impairments with younger students.

- Encourage the older students to share their equipment and devices with younger students so that the younger students can learn about their function and use.

- Facilitate opportunities for younger students to shadow an older student with a visual impairment at his or her high school or college.

- Encourage students to attend a meeting or conference of the National Federation of the Blind or the American Council of the Blind, where they can meet and observe many potential role models.

- Encourage adult role models to meet and talk with the parents of students with visual impairments so they can share their early experiences and answer questions about their social experiences.

- Encourage role models to demonstrate and discuss how they travel with a long cane, dog guide, or sighted assistance.

- Have role models discuss the importance of interacting with other students with visual impairments and provide resources for attending camps and weekend programs for the blind and visually impaired.

As students who are blind or visually impaired move into adolescence and young adulthood, role models and mentors can play an increasingly significant role in the acquisition of social skills. Role models can provide valuable information about dating, social communication in large groups, nonverbal cues and gestures, appropriate dress and grooming for school and for work, as well as information about employment, work behaviors, and specific job duties. Role models and mentors can also offer feedback to the teen or young adult with a visual impairment about social behavior in a range of contexts. The following suggestions for students regarding their relationships with role models or mentors (from Wolffe, 1999, pp. 799–800) focus on establishing relationships with mentors in work-related situations, but they are applicable for developing and maintaining social relationships as well.

- Prepare for meeting prospective mentors by thinking and writing about the kinds of things you will want to share about yourself as well as what you want to find out from them.

- When meeting a prospective mentor for the first time, plan to spend 15–20 minutes in discussion. If you like the person, and it seems to be mutual, you may want to make a follow-up appointment.

- Prepare for communication with your prospective role model by writing a series of questions about working, accomplishing daily living tasks, or developing relationships with others. Some questions might include: How do you travel to work? What training did you receive to do your job? What do you do for fun after work?

- Follow-up your visits with thank you notes. If a relationship develops, you may ask to arrange to job shadow or spend time with the role model.

- If you accompany your role model to work, it is critical that you know and understand the social rules of the workplace. The role model may want to prepare you about the use of specific behaviors prior to the work-site visit.

- During the job shadowing experience, if you are invited to lunch or are included in a coffee break, it is important to reciprocate by offering to treat the role model.

## CONCLUSION

One of the main goals of social skills instruction for students with visual impairments is to develop skills that promote positive interactions with peers. Without opportunities to engage with both sighted and visually impaired age-mates, students face isolation and limited inclusion into society and the world beyond home and school.

When students who are blind or visually impaired interact effectively with peers, their success in inclusive classrooms and other settings will result in positive outcomes. Successful interactions can be fostered through the collaboration of teachers of students with visual impairments and general education teachers to ensure that the experiences of students who are blind and visually impaired in general education settings are meaningful and appropriate. The essential elements for students' social and academic success include evaluating the classroom placement for students, examining the classroom organization and structure, and developing strategies for including students who are blind or visually impaired in the milieu of the general education classroom. Classroom teachers, teachers of students with visual impairment, paraeducators, educational specialists, and family members all need to work in tandem to create social experiences that promote use of appropriate social behavior, sharing of toys and materials, development of reciprocal relationships, and nurturing of friendships.

In addition to social interactions with sighted age-mates, it is also important to develop strong relationships with others who are blind or visually impaired. Relationships with competent role models and mentors who are blind or visually impaired enhance the social experiences for these students and allow for the sharing of ideas and strategies. Peers who are blind or visually impaired share a level of understanding and camaraderie that enhances and supports the development of close, positive relationships.

This chapter has provided a solid foundation for initiating strategies that foster positive peer relationships. The following chapter expands on the importance of peer interactions and relationships and examines the culture and nature of inclusive education for students with visual impairments as it relates to the development of social competence among students who are blind or visually impaired.

# REFERENCES

Bishop, V. E. (1986). Identifying the components of successful mainstreaming. *Journal of Visual Impairment & Blindness, 80*, 939–946.

Chen, D., & Dote-Kwan, J. (1999). Promoting opportunities to work. In K. E. Wolffe (Ed.), *Skills for success* (pp. 129–135). New York: AFB Press.

D'Allura, T. (2002). Enhancing the social interaction skills of preschoolers with visual impairments. *Journal of Visual Impairment & Blindness, 96*, 574–586.

Denti, L. (1992). Peer support networks: Including students with severe to mild disabilities in regular education classrooms. In S. Z. Sacks, M. Hirsch, D. Tierney-Russell, & R. J. Gaylord-Ross (Eds.), *The status of social skills training in special education and rehabilitation: Present and future trends*. San Francisco: San Francisco State University.

Erwin, E. J. (1994). Social competence in young children with visual impairments. *Infants & Young Children, 6,* 26–33.

Gaylord-Ross, R. J., Haring, T. G., Breen, C. G., & Pitts-Conway, V. (1984). The training and generalization of social interaction skills with autistic youth. *Journal of Applied Behavior Analysis, 17,* 229–247.

Hatlen, P. H., & Curry, S. A. (1987). In support of specialized programs for blind and visually impaired children: The impact of vision loss on learning. *Journal of Visual Impairment & Blindness, 81,* 7–13.

Hoben, M., & Lindstrom, V. (1980). Evidence of isolation in the mainstream. *Journal of Visual Impairment & Blindness, 74,* 280–292.

Kazdin, A. E. (1982). *Single-case research design: Methods for clinical and applied settings.* Baltimore: University Park Press.

Kef, S. (1997). The personal networks and social supports of blind and visually impaired adolescents. *Journal of Visual Impairment & Blindness, 96,* 23–27.

Kekelis, L. S. (1992). Peer interactions in childhood: The impact of visual impairment. In S. Z. Sacks, R. J. Gaylord-Ross, & L. S. Kekelis (Eds.), *The development of social skills by blind and visually impaired students: Exploratory studies and strategies* (pp. 13–35). New York: American Foundation for the Blind.

Kekelis, L. S., & Sacks, S. Z. (1992). The effects of visual impairment on children's social interactions in regular education programs. In S. Z. Sacks, R. J. Gaylord-Ross, & L. S. Kekelis (Eds.), *The development of social skills by blind and visually impaired students: Exploratory studies and strategies* (pp. 59–82). New York: American Foundation for the Blind.

Macks, J. (1992). The creative games project. In S. Z. Sacks, R. J. Gaylord-Ross, & L. S. Kekelis (Eds.), *The development of social skills by blind and visually impaired students: Exploratory studies and strategies* (pp. 171–179). New York: American Foundation for the Blind.

McCallum, B. J., & Sacks, S. Z. (Eds.). (1994). *Santa Clara County social skills curriculum for children with visual impairments.* Santa Clara, CA: SCORE Regionalization Project.

Peavey, K. O., & Leff, D. (2002). Social acceptance of adolescent mainstreamed students with visual impairments. *Journal of Visual Impairment & Blindness, 96,* 808–811.

Sacks, S. Z., & Gaylord-Ross, R. J. (1989). Peer-mediated and teacher-directed social skills training for visually impaired students. *Behavior Therapy, 20,* 619–638.

Sacks, S. Z., & Gaylord-Ross, R. J. (1992). Peer-mediated and teacher-directed social skills training for blind and visually impaired students. In S. Z. Sacks, R. J. Gaylord-Ross, & L. S. Kekelis (Eds.), *The development of social skills by blind and visually impaired students: Exploratory studies and strategies* (pp. 103–127). New York: American Foundation for the Blind.

Sacks, S. Z., & Kekelis, L. S. (1992). Guidelines for mainstreaming blind and visually impaired students. In S. Z. Sacks, R. J. Gaylord-Ross, & L. S. Kekelis (Eds.), *The development of social skills by blind and visually impaired students: Exploratory studies and strategies* (pp. 133–150). New York: American Foundation for the Blind.

Sacks, S. Z., Wolffe, K. E., & Tierney, D. (1998). Lifestyles of students with visual impairments: Preliminary studies of social networks. *Exceptional Children, 64,* 463–478.

Sisson, L. A., Van Hasselt, V. B., Hersen, M, & Strain, P. (1985). Increasing social behavior in multihandicapped children through peer interactions. *Behavior Modification, 9,* 293–321.

Skellenger, A. C., Rosenblum, B.L.P., & Jager, B. K. (1997). Behaviors of preschoolers with visual impairments in indoor play settings. *Journal of Visual Impairment & Blindness, 91,* 519–530.

Wolffe, K. E. (1999). Using role models in career exploration for students with visual impairments. *Journal of Visual Impairment & Blindness, 93*(12), 798–800.

Wolffe, K. E., & Sacks, S. Z. (1997). The social network pilot project: A quantitative comparison of the lifestyles of blind, low vision, and sighted young adults. *Journal of Visual Impairment & Blindness, 91,* 245–256.

# CHAPTER 8

# Social Skills in School and Community

## P. Ann MacCuspie

During the last few decades we have made tremendous strides as a society toward the inclusion of individuals with disabilities. Students with severe visual impairments, who had few opportunities for academic success in the regular classrooms of the 1960s, now routinely realize their academic potential in the public school setting. Students who rely on braille as their primary reading medium are commonly enrolled in the regular classroom for the majority of their instructional time. Previously limited, opportunities for educational programming for children with multiple disabilities in addition to blindness have been dramatically expanded with the provision of supports that allow these children to attend public schools with their age-appropriate peers. In the United States, approximately 85 percent of students who are blind or visually impaired are educated in public schools (American Printing House for the Blind, 2003). In Canada, with only one residential school for the blind, the percentage is even higher. Both segregated and inclusive learning environments face challenges in addressing all the goals and objectives of society's education system. Those goals relevant to peer acceptance and social interaction must be recognized as critical to the development of children who are visually impaired. Therefore, inclusion of students with visual impairments in the public school setting must address both social and academic goals.

It is essential that children and youths with visual impairments become an integral part of our schools and communities in order to develop the social abilities they need to participate fully in the life of our society. Skills that enhance meaningful participation in all aspects of society must be developed during the school years as children develop socially and intellectually. Academic achievement, good interpersonal communication skills, and acceptance by peers are highly correlated with future success in adulthood (Walz & Bleuer, 1992). Yet, parents and teachers of students with visual impairments routinely report concerns that these students are not actively involved in social activities with their peers in the integrated setting. Research exploring the friendships and social interaction of children and youths with visual impairments supports the legitimacy of these concerns (Crocker & Orr, 1996; Huurre & Aro, 2000; MacCuspie, 1966; Rosenblum, 2000; Wolffe & Sacks, 1997). As research on the social acceptance of students with visual impairments accumulates, it has become evident that social inclusion is not a natural consequence of enrollment in the regular classroom. However, inclusive settings offer fertile ground for promoting the development of social skills; these settings need to be exploited for that purpose.

To ensure the social interaction and acceptance of students with visual impairments, specific programming and instruction needs to be committed to this goal. Parents and teachers must devise specific strategies, implement programs, and routinely evaluate their progress. Creating a social environment that values the positive acceptance of differences and supports the cognitive, physical, and social development of all students is a prerequisite for inclusion (MacCuspie, 1996; McLeskey & Waldron, 2000). Learning and using appropriate social skills have been identified as critical needs for students with visual impairments as they take their place in inclusive educational settings (Hatlen & Curry, 1987; Sacks, Kekelis, & Gaylord-Ross, 1992). The other side of the coin is that these settings need to be used to promote and support the practice of such skills. Although instruction to ensure the acquisition of social skills must be a compulsory part of educational programming for these students, the greatest challenge for both educators and parents is to fully understand and address the complexities inherent in social inclusion while attending to the practical implications of this process in the day-to-day lives of school children.

# THE CONCEPT OF INCLUSIVE EDUCATION

Inherent in the concept of inclusion is the belief that children with disabilities will benefit from living and learning in the same environments with their peers who do not have disabilities, from participating in the same types of daily routines and experiences, from upbringing with the same family supports and activities, and from exposure to similar community rituals and events. It is believed that inclusion can provide greater social and academic benefits to children and youths both with and without disabilities than did previous educational approaches. The concept of inclusion is, by its very nature, a complex and multidimensional one. It is also an evolving one. When looked at from the sociological perspective of North American culture, it could be said that schools are a testing ground for society's endeavors to integrate and sometimes assimilate people of various ethnic, religious, and cultural backgrounds (Nixon, 1994). There exists in the education system today many variations of the concept of inclusion (McLeskey & Waldron, 2000). This is not necessarily an unfavorable situation, as it can be viewed as part of an evolving process. Early studies that explored the integration of students with visual impairments often found difficulties associated with both the frequency and the nature of their social interactions (Bishop, 1986; Hoben & Lindstom, 1980). Educators' initial response to these research findings was to provide programming designed to change the behaviors of the student with the visual impairment. More recent research examining the social inclusion of these children from preschool through adolescence (Crocker & Orr, 1996, MacCuspie, 1996, Wolffe & Sacks, 1997) contends that enhancing social inclusion requires changes from all participants in the school environment—teachers, parents, and students. It is of paramount importance to focus intervention on creating a social environment that promotes social acceptance and in turn can contribute to the development of visually impaired students as social beings. The recent research literature on inclusion and inclusive practices does, in fact, describe a movement toward learning environments that promote the creation of a school community that recognizes the individual needs of all students and celebrates diversity (McLeskey & Waldron, 2000). Although inclusive schools are not identical throughout the country or sometimes even within the same school district, there are a number of assumptions about inclusive schools that underlie the adoption of the practice of inclusion and can be used as guides for the creation of successful inclusive settings (Bauer & Shea, 1999). Some of these are as follows:

- Inclusive schools create and promote an inclusive learning environment that enables all students to participate and learn.
- Student diversity in any given class is to be valued.
- Inclusive classrooms can meet most of the unique educational, curricular, and learning needs of all students within the general education system.
- Inclusive schools create a caring community such that its participants initiate actions to ensure all students are included.
- Inclusive schools provide every student with the support services and special curricular instruction needed to accommodate unique needs (such as speech and language therapy, orientation and mobility training, or reading and writing braille), and in most cases, this is provided within the context of the regular classroom.
- Students with disabilities attend their neighborhood schools.
- School-based planning and program implementation by school teams address the needs of any student who requires accommodations to ensure meaningful participation in both social and learning activities.
- Students with disabilities are enrolled in age-appropriate classrooms with a natural proportion of students with disabilities attending any school and classroom.
- The use of team teaching, collaboration, and cooperative education practices are the norm in inclusive schools.
- Peer support and friendships among students are promoted in inclusive schools.

The practice of inclusion cannot be viewed as an add-on program to a school. The philosophies and practices inherent to inclusion require serious consideration as school staff work toward achieving an inclusive school. In their publication, *Inclusive Schools in Action: Making Differences Ordinary*, McLeskey and Waldron (2000) suggest that stakeholders must be committed to the belief that the "goal of an inclusive school is to prepare and support teachers to better meet the needs of all students" (p. 121). They recommend the creation of a core inclusion planning team consisting of highly respected teachers and other stakeholders who oversee the implementation, monitoring, and evaluation of the process of inclusion. The creation of a school culture that enhances the inclusion of students with disabilities must be a major focus of the work of the school team.

## The Culture of School Children

This author's research (MacCupsie, 1996) examining the social interaction and acceptance of students with visual impairments identified a number of basic assumptions inherent to student culture that have a significant influence on the process of inclusion for these students. This research also pointed to the critical importance of the classroom as the focus for intervention to enhance social inclusion.

On first examination, student culture may appear as a hostile environment in which children seem cruel and intolerant. In fact, children are known for their gregarious nature, enjoyment of play, and sense of fairness. Yet, each individual child is a developing social being. The socialization process initiated in the preschool environment is extended throughout the school years at an increasingly sophisticated level as the child grows to adulthood. As with other developmental areas (physical, emotional, and intellectual), there is a broad range of social ability and performance levels within the population at any given age. What seldom varies in the social context of children is the role of the group in the socialization process. Harris (1998) presented a group socialization theory in which she contended that the group consisting of individuals who are the same age and sex is the most significant socializing agent for school-age children. She noted, "Socialization is the process of adapting one's behavior to that of the other members of one's social category" (pp. 357). Just as MacCuspie (1996) discovered the existence of firmly established friendship cliques or groups (such as "best friends," "okay friends," or "not friends") within the classrooms in her study, Harris (1998) maintained that:

> In the peer groups of childhood and adolescence, kids take on the behaviors and attitudes of their peers and contrast themselves with the members of other groups—groups that differ in sex or race or social class or in their propensities and interests. The differences between these groups widen because the members of each group like their own group best and are at pains to distinguish themselves from the others. [pp. 359]

The existence of groups or cliques among children, especially adolescents, is not a new concept to either educators or parents. What is startling in today's society is the power of a child's peer group to have a long-term effect on personality development and the intensity with which a child struggles to fit in or be part of a group. Indeed, being accepted as a member of an identified group is probably one of the top priorities of childhood.

Yet, much of the research examining the social acceptance of students with visual impairments in integrated settings has suggested that these students experience tolerance rather than acceptance by their peers (MacCuspie, 1991; Rosenblum, 2000; Wolfe & Sacks, 1997). Tolerance is characterized by the indifference to or ignoring of one's presence, whereas acceptance refers to a relationship between a child and his or her peer group in which there is active and spontaneous interaction. Acceptance is reflected in the perception of group members that another child is an appropriate playmate or classmate, who should be routinely included in classroom, playground, and after-school activities. An accepted child is infrequently discouraged from participating in the day-to-day activities characteristic of his or her age group. The goal of social inclusion is to create an environment in our schools and communities that reflects acceptance of all members, even those who may be perceived to be different.

Social inclusion is an achievable goal. As the concept of inclusion has gained broad acceptance throughout North America, much has been written about the benefits of inclusion and factors that appear to be prerequisites for its success (MacCuspie, 1996; McLeskey & Waldron, 2000; Vaughn & Schumm, 2000). The factors commonly associated with successful and responsible inclusion are positive acceptance of difference, presence of a collaborative school team, a problem-solving perspective, and a supportive administrator.

## POSITIVE ACCEPTANCE OF DIFFERENCE

The positive acceptance of difference is a complex concept intrinsically linked with what is valued in our culture. When a student with a visual impairment is enrolled in a classroom in the neighborhood school, there may be a number of differences that immediately distinguish this child from others in the class. The student may have different learning materials from his or her peers, special equipment not used by other students, unfamiliar physical characteristics, or behaviors perceived as unusual. Furthermore, this student may require assistance to travel outside the classroom, special teachers who visit on a regular basis, or even an adult assistant assigned to be with him or her for most of the day. Although some of these signs of difference may be eliminated or minimized through thoughtful planning, others are inevitable. While we cannot change the differentness imposed by visual impairment, we can change how these differences are valued and accommodated within the learning environment. Open discussion of what is valued in schools sets the stage for consideration of how best to promote the positive acceptance of differences among children. This is a concept that must be nurtured. More than any other, the positive acceptance of difference is a prerequisite for the social acceptance of students with visual impairments. Furthermore, it is a concept that is strongly supported as a characteristic of inclusive education.

## PRESENCE OF A COLLABORATIVE SCHOOL TEAM

Schools create collaborative educational teams to oversee the planning, implementation, and evaluation of programs for students with disabilities. For students with visual impairments, team membership usually includes the principal or designee, classroom teachers, teacher of students with visual impairments, and parents or caregivers of the student. Other team participants might include resource personnel such as resource room teachers, specialist teachers (such as physical education or music teachers), the guidance counselor, and the school psychologist, the student who is visually impaired and his or her classmates; teacher assistants, and even teachers who may be involved with the student in future years. The ultimate goal of the team is to ensure social and academic inclusion for the student who is visually impaired and to help the child develop the skills necessary to participate in an inclusive setting.

Each team participant brings a different perspective and, in many cases, different expertise, skills, and understanding to the team. Since regular classroom teachers have been designated as having the major academic responsibility for students who are integrated in the regular classroom, it is important for these teachers to participate fully in designing programs and in implementating plans. Parents know their child intimately and can work to ensure that programming plans address their priority concerns for the academic, social, and emotional development of their child. The teacher of students with visual impairments has an in-depth understanding of the implications of vision loss for learning and can help to ensure that teaching strategies and materials are appropriate for the particular student. In the final analysis, what is critical is a collaborative approach in which the contribution of each team participant is equally valued and the focus of the group is on enhancing both the social and the academic development of the student.

## A Problem-Solving Perspective

Social acceptance is a multifaceted phenomenon. There are conceivably hundreds of aspects of a given situation that influence the quantity and quality of social interactions that students with visual impairments experience. Although there are some teaching strategies and learning environments that are commonly believed to enhance or detract from social acceptance, many variables are unique to specific students and particular situations. Therefore, educators and parents need to develop a problem-solving perspective as they analyze and assess intervention in a given situation. Identical questions posed in two different schools might generate very different responses. Approaches developed by school team members who are aware of their unique circumstances and those of their students will be the most successful. A problem-solving model focuses on the components of the problem, rather than on the behavior or characteristics of the student (Bauer & Shea, 1999). Interventions derived from a problem-solving perspective focus on how to support the learner in the given situation. The dilemmas that may arise in relation to the integration of students with visual impairments (for example, use of equipment that isolates the student but provides independence) are complex ones. However, a problem-solving approach can generate appropriate and workable solutions to most problems that arise.

## A Supportive Administrator

"Inclusion begins with influential voices," according to McLeskey and Waldron (2000, p. 137). Administrators who work to create inclusive schools recruit support for their venture. Guided by a principal who routinely espouses the importance of social inclusion, school staff will be encouraged to attend to social acceptance in their classrooms. Supportive administrators also ensure the availability of necessary resources. Working as a member of a school team, employing a problem-solving perspective, attending meetings, and observing students are time-consuming activities. The best of teachers' intentions can be sabotaged if plans are not devised to accommodate the additional demands made upon the time available to teachers to complete many of the tasks involved. This is particularly true in the initial stages of program development. Administrators must consider the most effective ways to employ team members, options for accessing assistance for the teacher, and specific plans to ensure teachers have the support they need to develop an inclusive classroom environment.

## SOCIAL INCLUSION: THE GOAL OF SOCIAL SKILLS INSTRUCTION

Learning is a social activity. Successful social interaction necessitates the use of effective social interaction skills. Mastery of social skills may be the single most influential determinant of future success and happiness. However, the provision of social skills instruction in a way that enhances social acceptance is a challenging task, one that requires perseverance, diplomacy, commitment to the goal, well-developed interpersonal communication skills, and an outstanding ability to persuade. Addressing the social competence and social skills of students with visual impairments is easily set aside while tackling needs that are perceived to be more urgent (the upcoming math exam or the braille lesson). In many schools, social skills are not routinely evaluated or well documented on report cards. Also, the day-to-day application of social skills is not easily assessed, unlike other compensatory skills, such as mastery of braille reading or the use of adaptive technology. Yet, without an appropriate level of social competence, the likelihood that a student will be able to effectively use many of the lessons taught in school is significantly reduced. Teachers and parents of students with visual impairments are in a unique position to advocate for social skills instruction as part of all school programs. Furthermore, they can play a significant role in the implementation and evaluation of the programs and the instruction provided to enhance social inclusion. The benefits of social skills instruction to the child are enormous. In short, to survive in today's society students need many skills in addition to those that have been traditionally taught in our schools. Never before has the compulsory inclusion of social skills instruction in every child's individualized education program (IEP) been more warranted than it is today.

Teaching social skills is a complex undertaking that involves many factors: the attitude of the classroom teacher, the personality of the child who is blind or visually impaired, the social environment of the classroom, the nature of peers and parent expectations, to name a few. Although the mastery of effective social skills is only one piece of the puzzle leading to social inclusion, it is an essential one. The development of social skills is critical for children's social development and social adjustment in the classroom (Nezer, Nezer, & Siperstein, 1985). Social development, like cognitive and motor development, occurs over time as children gain experience with their social environment and have opportunities to practice and refine social skills in various situations and circumstances. Social cognition, the ability to relate to those in one's environment, is influenced by variables such as intelligence, personality, experience, and culture. The development of both social cognition and social skills occurs through interaction with others, beginning with the parent-child relationship during the preschool years and advancing to peer relationships, such as friendship, during the school years. Children use their relationships to family, friends, classmates, and others to explore and experiment with a variety of social behaviors. They gradually learn which behaviors meet their needs, and, it is hoped, to respect the integrity of others.

Social development is an integral part of childhood learning. During the elementary school years, popularity is largely determined by how a child behaves toward his or her peers. Observation of children who are sought out by others indicates that these children are gregarious, not critical, and display an interest in their peers. Such behaviors are inextricably linked with the mastery of social skills, such as initiating interaction with others, recognizing the feelings of others, expressing an interest in others, negotiating, and sharing. These are skills that can be taught and practiced during routine classroom instruction.

It is particularly important for children and youths with visual impairments to receive specific intervention to learn social skills. Incidental learning of social skills by one who is blind or one who has limited vision is problematic because of the reduced access to visual information (for example, the nonverbal communication necessary to show interest in what a peer is saying). Yet addressing social skills is critical, for many reasons, including the following:

- The long-term effects associated with peer rejection, which can result from a lack of social skills, can be devastating (including dropping out of school, drug and alcohol abuse, destructive and self-destructive behavior). Skills that enhance one's personal safety and ability to be a self-advocate (including assertiveness and maintaining body posture that discourages victimization) are essential if students are to be successful in achieving independence and taking an active role in an inclusive society.

- The frequency of social interaction largely depends on the degree to which a student has mastered appropriate social skills.

- The influence of peer interactions on self-esteem is critical since self-esteem (one's personal judgment of one's worthiness) evolves partly in response to reflections from others.

- Good social skills enhance the development of friendships, within which participants experience companionship, intellectual stimulation, social comparison, and affection.

- Positive relationships with both peers and adults are correlated with a child's level of social competence or mastery of social skills. As children begin to spend more time interacting with peers than with adults, acceptance by the peer group becomes increasingly important and requires the addition and cultivation of new social skills and concepts.

- Mastery of social skills takes practice.

- There are lifelong benefits for the child who is socially competent. A student's capacity to learn in a group situation (such as the social environment of the classroom) cannot be separated from the social competence required to interact effectively within this environment.

- When students practice appropriate social skills in the classroom, teachers reap long-term benefits of easier classroom management and a more effective learning environment.

- Parenting a child who interacts positively with family, friends, and those in the community is a positive and rewarding experience.

- Schools are where children gather and routinely interact and therefore provide a social environment conducive to learning and practicing social skills.

This is not an exhaustive list of reasons to teach social skills to those with visual impairments in our public schools; there may be numerous other context-specific reasons. Perhaps the question should not be why teach social skills, but rather why would one not?

## CHALLENGES TO TEACHING SOCIAL SKILLS IN THE INCLUSIVE SETTING

Despite the critical importance of incorporating social skills instruction within the daily school and home routines, a number of factors can serve as impediments to this goal. These factors are usually not conspicuous disagreements with the importance of teaching social skills, but rather, relate to the nature of the school environment and underlying beliefs held by educators and parents.

The additional time demands of teaching the expanded core curriculum for students with visual impairments (as described in the next section) concurrently with the regular curriculum in the inclusive school setting create tremendous challenges and pressures on educators and students alike. Educators struggle with the challenge of how to fit it all in. Working to create a truly inclusive social environment in schools, identifying the priority and timeliness of social skills instruction, and developing lesson plans to incorporate social skills instruction in an integrated fashion also requires much time and energy on the part of parents and educators.

While some schools are making commendable progress in restructuring the focus of education to meet the needs of the whole child, a significant number of schools across North America continue to respond to the public pressure to focus their efforts primarily on academic instruction. This is particularly evident at the upper grade levels.

Social learning and development of the skills of effective social interaction appear to happen naturally for most children without disabilities who have daily opportunities to interact with age-mates in group settings. The expectations of both parents and teachers that social learning happens naturally can interfere with planning that is focused on promoting social inclusion. They may believe that social development will happen naturally in the inclusive setting or that social skills instruction is not a legitimate area of education. They may hold lower expectations for the development of social competence for students with visual impairments than for their peers who are sighted. In addition, formalized intervention to change social behaviors that are a direct consequence of the reduction or absence of vision (for example, teaching the child who is blind to face the person to whom he or she is speaking) may contradict an essential assumption of inclusion: the positive acceptance of difference. It raises questions about the efficacy of having children who are blind learn social behaviors that are meaningful to those who are sighted but irrelevant to those who are blind.

Parents and educators need an opportunity to openly discuss their feelings and beliefs associated with social acceptance of students with disabilities as a prerequisite to participation in providing social skills instruction. Moreover, the process of observing and assessing a student's social performance may create a perception that the student's behaviors are being overanalyzed and criticized. The amount of expertise and time required to plan, implement, and evaluate educational programs for students with visual impairments in the inclusive setting may contribute to a sense that the student is being "viewed under a microscope."

Because the mastery of social skills requires practice and ongoing shaping and refinement throughout the school years, educators and parents must make long-term commitments to the process. The nature of social skills instruction also requires that participants develop trusting relationships. A risk-free learning environment is essential if educators, parents, the student who is visually impaired, and peers are to address the sometimes sensitive issues associated with learning social skills.

## GETTING STARTED

Developing social competence is much more complicated than learning a specific social skill and then applying it. The process of social interaction is complex and fraught with exceptions and accommodations necessitated by a given social context. For example, different social skills are required to initiate a conversation with a stranger in each of the following scenarios: being seated next to a passenger in an airplane, entering a cocktail party, and attending a wake. While all three scenarios require some common responses (for example, some form of self-identification), how does one determine which situations would warrant a formal introduction (such as giving both first and last names) or which would require eye contact with the speaker? Factors such as age, gender, and number and nature of participants would also affect one's interaction in each situation. Family and cultural expectations, familiarity with participants, and social context are but a few of the multiplicity of factors that can come into play in any given social exchange. Acquiring social competence across a broad range of social settings requires much knowledge, experience, and practice.

Both parents and teachers need to take advantage of unanticipated "teachable moments" relevant to social skills instruction that arise during an activity. For example, receiving and responding to an invitation to a birthday party could involve numerous skills: How did you feel when you read the invitation (identifying feelings)? How should you respond to the invitation (social knowledge)? What might the child giving the birthday party be thinking about (perspective-taking)? What do you need to do before the party (problem solving)? These types of spontaneous events provide excellent opportunities to introduce, practice, and reinforce social skills. Such lessons are often the most interesting and applicable to the child's learning and need to be emphasized throughout childhood.

Assessment of social skills first involves an information-gathering process that may include a wide range of activities. Checklists of social skills and factors specific to the social context may be helpful in isolating specific skill strengths and needs, particularly in an environment with a high level of interaction such as the classroom. Role-play tests, problem-solving scenarios, interviews, use of sociometric measures, and analysis of videotaped observations are examples of instruments that may be helpful in the assessment process. The involvement of the members of the student's educational team is essential to planning for and completing the assessment. Once the assessment information is collected and analyzed, the team is ready to begin planning for intervention.

# SOCIAL SKILLS AS A COMPONENT OF THE EXPANDED CORE CURRICULUM

The expanded core curriculum that designates the disability-specific skills and knowledge that students with visual impairments need to accommodate or address the implications of their vision loss. Hatlen (1996) established the language used to describe the unique skills (including braille reading and writing, use of adaptive technology, orientation and mobility, and visual efficiency training) that are essential to educational programming for children and youths with visual impairments. The expanded core curriculum must be taught in addition to the regular curriculum presented to all students, such as science, mathematics, and reading. Social interaction skills are included as one of the eight categories in the expanded core curriculum (see Chapter 5).

Because of the limitations a visual impairment imposes on incidental learning and practice of social interaction skills, formal intervention is essential to ensure the acquisition of social skills. Instruction relevant to social interaction focuses on the knowledge and skills that assist people who are visually impaired in having access to visual information or performing a task without visual input. Goals and objectives for this instruction must be included in the IEP for every student who is visually impaired.

Instruction in areas of the expanded core curriculum requires specific planning, implementation, and follow-up. Koenig & Holbrook (2000) outline eight points to consider when planning specialized instruction in the expanded core curriculum. Along with some examples of applications relevant to social skills instruction, they include the following:

- Specify measurable long-term goals. A goal for a third-grade student might be to locate friends on the playground and initiate appropriate actions to join their play activity.

- Identify short-term objectives necessary to reach the long-term goal. The third-grade student would need to know how to ask for directions in locating friends, move to the specified area of the playground, and know what social strategies to use to join the group.

- Analyze skills or tasks. Teachers and parents need to determine the specific step-by-step skills the student will need to complete a task. For example: What information does the student need to know about the layout of the playground? What information do the student's peers need to encourage and promote the student's initiatives?

- Use an appropriate instructional approach. The teacher of students with visual impairments could videotape a student joining a group on the playground and discuss the tape with the student who is visually impaired. The classroom teacher might role play the scenario in the classroom.

- Use appropriate instructional strategies. The teacher of students with visual impairments could coach the student on the playground by providing prompts and feedback during the first few attempts to join a group.

- Use appropriate instructional materials. The teachers might create a list of steps to follow when joining a group or asking for directions, or prepare audiotapes to demonstrate tones of voice that convey disinterest, interest, or enthusiasm for joining a group.

- Increase the student's proficiency in completing tasks. The third-grade student might be required to practice the skills at least once a day, and teachers would observe the process weekly to provide feedback and assist the student in refining the skills.

- Evaluate the effectiveness of instruction. Parents and other teachers could be asked to observe the student's attempts to join groups in other settings to identify what seems to be working and what detracts from success, and the student could be questioned about his or her perceptions of what is happening as he or she attempts to join the group.

The social context in which students with visual impairments learn and practice social interaction skills warrants specific consideration in the instructional planning process. In an inclusive setting, social skills that enhance the student's interaction with sighted peers may be different from those needed at home with siblings or in activities involving other students with visual impairments. When students with visual impairments participate in group social skills instruction with peers who are sighted, some adaptations may be required. The method used to teach the skill might need adapting; for example, rather than viewing a visual demonstration, the child would be physically guided through the action or provided with verbal directions about how to move his or her body. Other adaptations may be related to the specific information required; for example, to learn about body language, a child who is blind might first need to learn about the existence of certain gestures; next, to acquire information about when the gestures are used and learn how to make the gestures; and, finally, to practice the gestures until their presentation is natural in appearance. Written materials can be provided in braille, in large print, or on audiotape, or can be read with the use of a low-vision device.

It is more difficult to adapt visual information that requires interpretation, such as social skills activities associated with interpreting facial expressions or those that require the student to interpret social scenarios from pictures. Although tactile diagrams or models such as puppets or dolls may be useful in demonstrating some concepts, others may require unique solutions. Parents are usually an excellent resource and may be readily available to demonstrate and provide a hands-on model—for example, by allowing the child to feel their face when smiling or frowning. However, verbal explanation and prompts may frequently be the most effective and readily available adaptation for visual materials when teaching social skills.

## INDIVIDUALIZED GOALS FOR ALL STUDENTS

In an inclusive setting, the entire class usually has group social goals that are integrated into their activities—for example, giving positive feedback to group members. In addition, social goals are specifically identified for each student in the class. For the student who is visually impaired, these goals are identified by the child's educational team and are recorded in the child's IEP.

Because of the greater difficulty and the number of skills to be learned by students with visual impairments, educational team members need to give serious consideration to setting priorities for specific skills to be taught. The timeliness of skills in relation to the student's current peer-group activities and the prerequisites required for positive interaction within these group activities are important. For example, learning an appropriate way to join a group activity on the playground increases the likelihood that a student will be invited to be part of that group in the immediate future. It is also important to identify skills that do not warrant mastery by the student. For example, nonverbal communication entails a multitude of gestures and expressions. Although students who are visually impaired may learn about a sampling of them, it is unrealistic to expect students to learn and incorporate a vast number of them into their communication style.

## STRATEGIES FOR INSTRUCTION

Many social skills curricula have been developed during the past decade. Some have been created specifically for students with disabilities, while others are designed for classroom instruction with all students. Strategies for instruction for most curricula typically include such activities as modeling, coaching, peer training (training a peer how to provide immediate feedback to the child for appropriate social responses), role playing, interviews with students, problem-solving scenarios, videotaping, and so forth. For students with visual impairments, the majority of these strategies are effective if the appropriate adaptations are made in advance. For example, the student could receive a verbal description of some nonverbal information that might be exchanged in a role play or social scenario. When imitation of a skill is required, the student will need some physical guidance or verbal prompts to access the information, but it is of utmost importance that peers and adults respect the student's integrity and right to personal space and privacy. A student must be asked for permission before physically guiding him or her through an action. Teachers and parents need to be aware of any sense of embarrassment or sensitivities a student may have—even if they seem unwarranted—in relation to learning or practicing social skills in a public forum. Discussion of some skills may need to be done privately with the student prior to presentation of the skill to the classroom group.

It is also important to examine specific strategies for instruction in relation to the age and grade level of the students. Appropriate activities and instructional strategies, and the sensitivities of students, are very different in eighth grade than they are in second grade. Finally, the individual or group providing social skills instruction needs to be identified and noted in the lesson plan. Parents, classroom teachers, teacher of students with visual impairments, and peers all bring advantages and disadvantages to the task that must be identified and considered in relation to both the specific student who is visually impaired and the social environment of the classroom.

# TEACHING SOCIAL SKILLS IN THE INCLUSIVE SETTING

Research examining the teaching of social skills to students with disabilities has frequently reported difficulties associated with the long-term maintenance of learned skills (Erin, Dignan, & Brown, 1991; Gresham, Sugai, & Horner, 2001). Skills mastered during the treatment phase of the research may fade or may not be generalized to environments beyond the research scenario (Jindal, Kato, & Maekawa, 1998). In schools where the philosophy and practice of inclusion has truly been integrated and creating a sense of acceptance by peers and belonging to the classroom group are primary goals, opportunities and support for teaching social skills are mandatory. All participants of a child's educational team are made aware of the particular social skill being taught so that practice and mastery of the skill can be closely monitored and difficulties in maintaining the skill can be addressed as they are noted.

However, even legislation mandating inclusion of students with disabilities throughout most of North America does not necessarily ensure that inclusive education practices have been implemented in all schools or to the extent required (McLeskey & Waldron, 2000). This is precisely why parents and educators need to examine the practices that have supported and promoted social inclusion in schools and become advocates for changes that will ensure their implementation, including instruction in appropriate social interaction skills for children and youths with visual impairments. Armed with this knowledge, they can identify strategies and practices that can be incorporated by their school teams as they plan for social skills instruction. These practices include the creation of a classroom community and the use of peer tutoring, peer coaching, and cooperative working groups.

## CREATING A CLASSROOM COMMUNITY

While inclusive education requires everyone's participation, the focus of instruction for promoting social inclusion and teaching specific social skills is the student's classroom. Research has shown that the majority of social interactions among schoolchildren take place during the school day in the students' own classroom (MacCuspie, 1996). The inclusive learning community is a caring one in which students learn to value all of their classmates and initiate actions to ensure that everyone has an opportunity to participate. Students participate in the establishment of classroom rules and procedures by holding class meetings and are given the responsibility for creating a sense of community for all members of their class. Students are empowered to take leadership roles through student-led conferences focusing on classroom organization or potential problems. Within a classroom community, students discuss such issues as conflict resolution and fair play. In such an environment, all teachers and students become aware of the implications of vision loss on learning and social interaction so they can respond to difficult situations as they arise. The student who is visually impaired, like all students in the classroom, participates in activities designed to teach group social skills (such as responding to a complaint). In addition, the student may be working on an individual skill specifically addressing an issue associated with being visually impaired (for example, turning toward the speaker). Classmates are taught to encourage and acknowledge the successful use of social skills, whether group or individual ones.

## Peer Tutoring

Peer tutoring is generally characterized by two students working together, with one student providing instruction to the other. Both students in the pair may be from the same classroom or each may be in a different class. Peer tutoring requires close monitoring and follow-up by the classroom teacher and the teacher of students with visual impairments. Assigning a popular classmate as a tutor provides an opportunity for two students to become better acquainted and enhances the probability that the student who is visually impaired will perceive the arrangement to be a positive one, as will other peers. For example, since students in the upper grades in a given school are generally viewed as having higher status than those in the lower grades, assigning a sixth-grade student to work with a second grader (cross-age tutoring) would usually be viewed very positively by both the younger student and his or her classmates. When organizing peer tutoring, many variables must be considered: the skill and personality of the tutor, the gender of both the tutor and the student being tutored, the nature of the social skill to be taught, the process for documenting progress, and the working relationship between the two students. Peer tutors require specific training in the process of tutoring, the specifics of the social skill to be taught, and the strategies to use when interacting with an individual who is visually impaired. Studies have shown that the tutor also experiences several benefits from the tutoring experience, for example the development of empathy for others, an increase in self-esteem, and an improvement in problem-solving skills (Bradley & Graves, 1997). It is also critical for students with visual impairments to have opportunities to act in the role of the tutor.

## Peer Coaching

Peer coaching is an approach used when the student has mastered most of the component skills of a social behavior but does not know when to implement them or needs to practice in a structured environment. The coach provides a social scenario and presents the student with an array of questions relevant to successful execution of the various skills. The coach provides verbal prompting and feedback after each response. Peer coaches must have well-developed social competence and a demonstrated ability to provide appropriate verbal feedback and guidance. Typically, peer coaches are older students in the school or very socially capable classmates. The same prerequisites outlined for peer tutors are appropriate for peer coaches.

## Cooperative Learning Groups

In cooperative learning groups, students work together to complete a specific learning assignment. Over two decades ago, Johnson and Johnson (1981) outlined the benefits of cooperative learning groups in building friendships among students with disabilities and their regular classroom peers. Developed into a formal learning structure, cooperative learning is one of the most effective processes available to educators anxious to promote the social inclusion of students with visual impairments and to enhance the mastery and practice of social skills. Accomplishing both of these goals in a natural classroom environment is one of the greatest strengths of cooperative learning. In addition, the process of integrating social skills instruction into the routine activity of the work groups is one that can be used effectively from kindergarten through high school.

Cooperative learning encompasses such practices as cooperation with peers, motivating or encouraging others, shared responsibility for learning goals, understanding group dynamics, and learning essential social skills. There are five basic elements of cooperative learning: positive interdependence, face-to-face interaction, individual accountability, interpersonal and small-group skills, and group processing

(Johnson, Johnson, & Holubec, 1990). These elements are presented and discussed in relation to their potential influence on the social acceptance and interaction of students with a visual impairment in the following sections.

*Positive Interdependence.* Positive interdependence is the first prerequisite for a cooperative group and exists when students believe the group cannot be successful unless each member is also successful. Each group member is responsible for both his or her individual learning as well as that of each of the other members of the group. For students with significant cognitive disabilities, the task is adjusted to ensure meaningful participation and to prevent other group members from perceiving them as lowering the chances for the group's success. Positive interdependence promotes the sharing of ideas, responsibilities, materials, and resources and requires the active participation of each member of the group. The tendencies of capable students to take over and complete most of the work, or for unmotivated students to provide limited input, are eliminated because the group's success is determined by the level of achievement of each member. Thus, each member has a vested interest in the learning of every other student.

Significant opportunities for social integration are inevitable when students with visual impairments participate in groups characterized by positive interdependence. For example, they have the opportunity to help other students, to make meaningful contributions to the work of the group, to be doing and mastering the same task as other group members, and to participate in much social interaction. There are also other positive spin-offs associated with working in a cooperative group. To participate, students who are visually impaired must have access to the information being learned by the group members. This requires that teachers or members of the group attend to their need for access to information and timely explanations of new concepts. Of major significance is the opportunity cooperative learning provides for students with visual impairments to routinely demonstrate their learning strengths and abilities while being actively involved in completing the group assignment. The following is an example of positive interdependence:

> *Hannah is a sixth-grade student who uses braille. In social studies class she is one of a group of five children who have been asked to locate six Canadian cities that are located next to bodies of water. To ensure that Hannah can participate effectively within the group, she has been provided with a tactile map of Canada. The other children use their print atlases. Hannah is the recorder for the group and uses her*

*BrailleNote to list each city and the body of water on which it is located. Because tactile maps tend to be somewhat cumbersome, her group members assist her in locating the cities on her map as they identify them. Hannah enters the information and at the end of the lesson, makes a print copy for her group members and a braille copy for her own use.*

*Face-to-Face Interaction.* The second element of cooperative learning is face-to-face interaction. This component requires that students promote each other's learning through interaction such as explaining information or encouraging the learning of others. Group pressure may be exerted to encourage reluctant participants to increase their contributions. Furthermore, these interactions create a situation in which group members cannot avoid interaction with a given student; in fact each person must make considerable efforts to negotiate positive social interaction if the group is to be successful. In this way, the group members come to know each other as individuals—another positive benefit.

Face-to-face exchange for students with visual impairments is typically less frequent than for their sighted classmates, thereby reducing the opportunity for the visually impaired student to practice and refine social skills. In a cooperative learning group the student who is visually impaired has an opportunity to get to know classmates as well as to obtain a realistic perspective of his or her own strengths and weaknesses. In turn, classmates have an opportunity to overcome their fears or other negative attitudes associated with interacting with someone who is visually impaired. These changes occur spontaneously for both parties as they become more familiar with one another through routine interaction.

Face-to-face interaction provides a tremendous opportunity for the student who is visually impaired to verbalize and clarify conceptual learning in an accepting environment. Classmates quickly become skilled at detecting the types of misconceptions or misunderstandings that often result when vision loss interferes with access to information. With practice and experience, peers become well informed not only about the implications of vision loss for learning, but also of alternative ways to present information that is more useful for a student with a visual impairment.

The following example of face-to-face interaction illustrates the benefits of this component of cooperative learning groups:

*Jordan is a student with low vision who has just started middle school. His new school is large and requires several changes of classes and teachers during the day. Although it is only early in September, Jordan already knows many of his new classmates. He is assigned to cooperative learning groups for math, language arts, and science. Each group consists of different members. During the discussion in the math and science groups, Jordan is able to get clarification on the details of diagrams and charts that he would struggle to access visually. Although he has large-print copies, there are many details, and he can only view one aspect at a time using his handheld magnifier. The teacher has asked the science group to practice the social skill of asking for and clarifying information during their discussion and completion of the assignment. This provides Jordan with improved access to information, an opportunity to interact with his peers, practice with an important social skill, and a chance to demonstrate his excellent memory for details. Jordan's peers have similar opportunities, as well as the chance to learn to be at ease with someone who is visually impaired and to become familiar with situations that pose difficulties for visual access and those that are manageable.*

*Individual Accountability.* Another element of cooperative learning is individual accountability. Because each group member is responsible for learning the assigned material, the teacher may use individual testing, random questioning, and group self-checking to ensure individual accountability. It is difficult for reluctant students to get by on the efforts of others. For students with significant learning difficulties, aspects of the IEP can be incorporated within the group assignment and the student can be tested on these aspects.

It is common for expectations of students with visual impairments in integrated classrooms to be reduced. With individual accountability, however, accommodations are only applied to performance differences that are outlined in a student's IEP. Therefore, the expectations for students with a visual impairment are more apt to be the same as those for other participants in the group. The students themselves coach and evaluate one another as they strive to ensure each participant has mastered the material assigned. This process creates the expectation that the student who is visually impaired will not only learn but will coach others. Because the teacher provides feedback on both the group's achievements and those of individual members, the classmates routinely receive accurate information about the performance of the visually impaired student, so that they have a more realistic idea of his or her capabilities.

The following is an example of individual accountability.

*Natania is a third-grade student who uses braille. In her language arts group, there are four other children working together to master new vocabulary words from a story about space travel. Erin, another student in the group, struggles with reading and has difficulty decoding the new vocabulary. Natania easily learns the new words and then helps Erin to practice reading and spelling the new vocabulary. At the end of the group session, Erin is able to recall eight of the ten words. Natania's teacher notes that Natania has mastered all the words and notes the words Erin will need to practice later in the day. Natania enjoys having an opportunity to assist her classmates, as they are often asked to work with her when braille copies of handouts are not readily available.*

*Interpersonal and Small-Group Skills.* Learning and using interpersonal and small-group skills is the fourth element of cooperative learning. Teachers provide formal instruction in specific social and organizational skills that help students get into their groups and organize their environment, as well as interpersonal communication strategies that promote positive interaction and learning. The emphasis is on two categories of skills—those required to work effectively with people and those that facilitate the completion of the task. People skills include such things as how to listen effectively, disagree in a respectful manner, identify the errors of others without judging them, encourage others to speak, reduce group tension, and express appreciation. Examples of task skills include staying on task, paraphrasing, seeking opinions, delegating, following directions, and checking the understanding of all members of the group. These collaborative skills are, of course, essential to effective group dynamics at any level—home, school, or workplace.

Because the teacher is instructing students in social skills as part of the process of cooperative learning, many of the skills specifically needed by the student who is visually impaired can be addressed naturally in the classroom. Making eye contact when speaking with someone or assessing a person's response to one's idea from facial expressions or the tone of voice are skills that are frequently troublesome for those with a visual impairment. In a classroom incorporating cooperative learning, such skills would be presented and practiced as a routine part of the learning process.

In the group setting, a student with a visual impairment has regular opportunities to get to know and trust classmates, encourage and assist others, and resolve conflict in a constructive manner. Practice of such skills dramatically increases both the likelihood that the student will interact in a meaningful way outside the classroom and the probability that educators will address the need for social skills instruction for the student because participation in the group depends upon effective communication skills. Skills that are most problematic for students with a visual impairment become evident when the group members are asked to assess one another's use of specific skills. An example of using interpersonal and small group skills follows.

*Juan is a natural leader. He likes to take control of a situation and delegate tasks to realize the completion of an assignment. Juan, who has been blind since birth, has a tendency to press his eyes and move his head from side to side as he talks. Each day Juan participates in several cooperative learning groups in which his teachers assign practice in both task-completion skills and social skills. This week the group is focusing on how to delegate and how to seek the opinions of others. Juan needs practice with the latter but is a role model for the former. In addition, he has been asked to abstain from eye pressing and to keep his head still during the group discussions. Juan receives reminders from peers when he forgets and he, in turn, assists other members with individual social skills. Much trust has developed among the group members and they have become comfortable keeping one another on task and using appropriate social skills.*

*Group Processing.* In the group processing element of cooperative learning, group members assess and discuss how well they accomplished the assigned goal and generate strategies to overcome behaviors or actions that detracted from their complete success. This debriefing process is a powerful means for students to analyze and learn from their errors. It also provides an opportunity for students to take pride in their accomplishments and have their performance acknowledged.

For the student who is visually impaired, group processing provides an opportunity to share perspectives on a given situation, increasing awareness of both parties. It also ensures that the student receives feedback about his or her performance. For example: Did mannerisms such as rocking interfere with communication? Did the student direct his or her gaze toward the speaker? Was the student able to encourage and assist other students in learning the material? Were the student's organizational skills, working habits, and pace appropriate? These are the types of interactions that are frequently limited or nonexistent in traditional classrooms where learning is individualistically or competitively structured. The following is an example of group processing:

*Kenzie is a student with low vision who tends to be self-conscious and shy. In her tenth-grade English class, she is one of seven students assigned to a cooperative learning group to analyze the meaning of a group of modern poems. At the end of each session, her group members evaluate their group's effectiveness. In the beginning, Kenzie was too shy to express her opinion because she was afraid she might be wrong or others might judge her based on her response. However, a more confident group member encouraged Kenzie's participation by continually asking her what she thought. When the group discussed their effectiveness, group members commented positively on Kenzie's insight and her increasing participation in the group. This encouragement contributed to Kenzie's growing comfort with participating in a group and offered a risk-free environment in which to try out her ideas on the interpretation of poetry. She improved her ability to understand the perceptions of others and learned how she could fit in and participate as a responsible member of the group.*

## SMALL-GROUP INSTRUCTION

Working with a small group (two to five students) who share a common learning need provides an opportunity for the teacher to focus on the learning styles of the students and the problems they are encountering. The group may consist of students with similar or mixed abilities, organized for various purposes (for example, researching a project or practicing a new skill). Groups can be kept together until the task is completed or can be maintained and given new assignments. The small group is usually a safe environment in which to practice newly emerging social skills before they are incorporated in the larger class setting. The teacher has an opportunity to closely monitor and coach the social interaction of all group members and to provide prompts, instruction, and immediate feedback about performance. Small groups are an ideal size for using common social skills instructional methods such as role playing. The classroom teacher and the teacher of students with visual impairments can share instruction of both the small group and the larger classroom group, thus creating the perception that the "special teacher" is for all the students in the classroom, not just the student with the visual impairment.

## INDIVIDUALIZED TEACHER INSTRUCTION

Although one-to-one student instruction is a demanding goal for classroom teachers, they usually incorporate this practice spontaneously during the school day as a particular student encounters difficulty. When a teacher of students who are visually impaired is available in the class, the classroom teacher may take advantage of this time to address the individual needs of the student who is visually impaired. One-to-one instruction will be required for students who are visually impaired for some social skills, especially for skills that focus on the reduction of inappropriate behaviors (such as eye pressing). These instructional sessions may be held outside the classroom to ensure the child's privacy and protect the child from embarrassment. In most cases, the teacher of students with visual impairments has the appropriate expertise and should be the provider for this type of individual instruction. However, because the teacher of students with visual impairments may only be in the classroom on a periodic basis, the classroom teacher may be in a better position to monitor and assist the visually impaired student with many social skills. The roles of the classroom teacher and the teacher of students with visual impairments need to be flexible to provide the most effective approach to instruction.

## CENTER-BASED INSTRUCTION

Center-based instruction is a method of organizing the classroom to accommodate a broad range of students' abilities, cover an array of curricular content areas, and provide opportunities to learn and practice social skills. Areas of the classroom are set up with activities in a given subject area or on a specific topic—for example, a science station with measurement activities, a center focused on pioneer days, or one on social skills). Center activities are organized to provide a range of difficulty, a variety of options for reporting responses (such as writing, drawing, tape-recording), and opportunities to work independently or in small groups. The procedures students follow to work effectively in centers require learning and practicing many social interaction skills, such as requesting and giving assistance, staying focused on the topic, and responding appropriately to the ideas of others. Because the teacher circulates among the centers and is not always available to assist, students must take responsibility for their own learning and that of group members.

Classes that are organized for center-based instruction provide many opportunities to incorporate the teaching and practice of social skills. First, one of the four to six learning centers can always be focused on activities that require the practice of social skills. For example, there could be a drama center, a public speaking center, a center with activities using characters from a popular television show, or even a center where students are required to role play social scenarios, evaluate their performance, and generate potential solutions. Second, each student in the class can choose or be assigned a social skill to practice during the week. For a child who is visually impaired, the assignment might be to ask for clarification or to face the speaker. Group members can record each time a given social skill is executed successfully and strive to increase the frequency each week.

There are other socially relevant spin-offs to center-based instruction for students who are visually impaired. Centers focus on topics or themes that are of particular interest to the specific age group of the class members. The information and ideas brought to the centers provide students with a wealth of practical knowledge, stimulate new interests, and expose students to topics that are popular for discussion among peers. Finally, center-based instruction provides an opportunity for the teacher of students who are visually impaired to be an active part of the class unit, model instructional strategies that are helpful when working with a student who is visually impaired, and build a collaborative relationship with the classroom teacher.

## USING MULTIPLE INTELLIGENCE THEORY

Gardner (1985) put forth the theory that human intelligence is demonstrated in areas other than those measured on traditional tests of intelligence—that is, linguistic and logical-mathematical domains. Gardner identified six additional areas of intelligence—spatial, musical, bodily-kinesthetic, interpersonal (interpreting and responding to the needs of others), intrapersonal (having detailed and accurate self-knowledge), and naturalistic (differentiating among living things and knowledge of the natural world). Skills that are needed to survive in society are viewed as equally important as those needed to do well in school. Gardner proposed a revamping of the assessment process to identify aptitudes in all eight domains of intelligence so as to design school curricula that would help all students realize their potential. Using a student's identified intelligence in all eight areas when planning instruction was proposed as a more effective and equitable approach to schooling.

Inclusive schools consider both the strengths and needs of students when they are planning for instruction. The importance of the interpersonal and intrapersonal domains as they apply to success beyond the school years is of particular relevance to students with visual impairments. At all school levels, but particularly at the high school level, schools must focus instruction on skills that enhance the students' potential to live successfully in society; that is where they will spend 75 percent of their lives. When parents and educators plan for the instruction of social skills, they can neither underestimate the value of social learning nor ignore the fact that active participation in the community is as important as it is in the school.

## THEMATIC UNIT INSTRUCTION

As the name applies, thematic unit instruction involves teaching all aspects of the curriculum using a common theme or topic. The theme is incorporated within activities in all subject areas and may be used for a week or more, depending on the complexity of the theme. For example, a thematic unit could be developed around the sinking of the *Titanic*. Students could complete reading and writing assignments about the ship (language arts), solve mathematical problems related to volume and mass, and trace the ship's city of origin and follow the route of its perilous journey (geography). An array of concepts could be presented in association with sea travel and navigation, such as the use of a life jacket and how constellations and stars are used as landmarks. All the flexible instructional arrangements previously discussed could be incorporated in the completion of activities focused on a given theme. Thematic unit instruction provides any number of opportunities to incorporate social skills instruction for various age levels. For example, students could role play the process of purchasing tickets (involving make eye contact and using appropriate manners) or determine who should be placed in the lifeboats (using negotiation skills and dealing with issues of morality). An additional benefit of thematic units is in providing a topic for conversation and a shared interest for the student who is visually impaired and his or her peers.

Instructional and curricular practices that support the inclusion of students with disabilities will be effective for all students. Indeed, teachers who have switched to inclusive practices routinely report that the changes implemented to address the needs of a more diverse classroom population improved the learning environment and results for all students (McLeskey & Waldron, 2000). Social skills instruction is considered to be a compulsory component of any inclusive setting. Advocacy by parents and educators to provide instruction in social skills will be helpful in bringing schools on track with this initiative.

The reluctance of some educators to embrace change is usually based on sound logic; they first need to know the implications of the changes and to feel that their competence as a teacher will not be compromised by significant changes in their instructional approaches. Participating on a team, having open discussions of the issues inherent to inclusion, and acquiring specific knowledge and experience with the process will support both educators and parents in this learning opportunity. Inclusion is an evolving and dynamic process, necessitating ongoing evaluation and restructuring.

# STRATEGIES AND SUGGESTIONS FOR PROMOTING SOCIAL INCLUSION

The adults in a student's life—parents, teachers, teacher assistants, principals, leaders of recreation and leisure activities, and so forth—all have an important role in promoting the social inclusion of students with visual impairments. Following are suggestions that can support this goal.

## STRATEGIES FOR SOCIAL SUCCESS

# Promoting Social Inclusion

◆ Discourage the development of a special status associated with being blind or visually impaired. Invariably, as the novelty of the status wears off, students who have been given special recognition or attention because of their visual impairment find themselves isolated from their peers. Rather, accomplishments and successes of students with a visual impairment should be acknowledged in the same way as those of their peers. Adults should take care not to exaggerate their accomplishments or to lower expectations for them. Unwarranted adult attention, such as singling out only the student who is visually impaired for staying in line with the class as they move down the hallway, contributes to the creation of a special status and inevitably detracts from the student's social acceptance.

◆ Attend to the aspects of peer culture that influence the acceptance of group membership. Use observation and discussion with children and youths to become an expert on youth culture and its beliefs and rules. Understand the role friendship plays in the affective development of children and apply this knowledge in planning for social skills instruction and for social inclusion in the home, school, and community.

◆ Prepare well in advance of the visually impaired student's initial exposure to new groups or experiences. For example, substitute teachers need to be advised of the student's programming needs; parents will want to meet with recreational group leaders to discuss their child's social inclusion prior to the first gathering of the group members; the teacher of students with visual impairments can discuss expectations for the student's social acceptance with other educators in the school prior to the first day of school each year; and the principal needs to routinely discuss the social inclusion of all students with the entire school staff.

♦ Raise the concept of the positive acceptance of difference with educators and other adults in the students' lives, and discuss the contradictions and dilemmas it creates in our society. Truly inclusive schools derive their vision from this concept and it will be readily apparent in all aspects of the school: the way instruction is provided, the way student progress is assessed, and the way the school day is organized.

♦ Model open and spontaneous discussion of visual impairment to assist others in appreciating both the differences and similarities of individuals with a visual impairment and the implications for learning and development. Adults legitimize topics that are suitable for exploration or discussion in home and school when they are a part of open, spontaneous, and natural discussion. If visual impairment is not raised as a topic in the home and in the classroom, both students with visual impairments and their sighted classmates may interpret this awkwardness as an indication that visual impairment is bad, immoral, or something about which one should feel ashamed.

♦ Take every opportunity to discuss similarities that students with a visual impairment share with their peers. For example, in the presence of peers, initiate conversations about the student's interests, favorite television shows, or family activities the student enjoys. This provides peers with accurate information about the student who is visually impaired and points out similarities that encourage inclusion.

♦ Orchestrate routine opportunities for visually impaired students to function independently, take risks, and assist others to prevent them from developing an attitude of "learned helplessness." To accommodate the impact of vision loss on their learning and development, children with visual impairments frequently require more assistance in the initial stages of learning a new skill. Often, there may be a tendency for the amount of assistance offered to remain the same despite the increasing competence of the child. Therefore, the child learns to expect help with most activities and may assume that receiving help is a direct consequence of visual impairment.

♦ Help students who are visually impaired to identify and discuss interests that can be shared with peers. For some students, the visual impairment becomes the focus of their lives. If students routinely initiate discussion about their visual impairment, redirect conversation to other topics. Play down the notion that the visual impairment is of primary importance by initiating conversations about students' ideas, hobbies, or talents.

◆ Help students with visual impairments realize that all people make mistakes and have strengths and weaknesses that they must deal with on a daily basis. Adults can verbalize their own mistakes or personal weaknesses that pose difficulties for them when the opportunity presents itself, with such statements as "Darn, I spilled ketchup on my shirt," or "I usually have difficulty finding my car in mall parking lots." Frequently children with a visual impairment come to believe that all their problems—not having a friend, being a poor reader, not winning the race—are a result of their impairment and, hence, may avoid addressing aspects of their personality or behavior that could improve their performance.

## SUGGESTIONS FOR TEACHERS OF STUDENTS WITH VISUAL IMPAIRMENTS

Teachers of students with visual impairments play a crucial role in the social inclusion of their students. Social interaction skills are identified as one of the eight components of the expanded core curriculum to be taught by teachers of students with visual impairments. As an active member on the school team, they provide expertise in the area of visual impairment and direct instruction to the student who is visually impaired. In the general education classroom, they work collaboratively with classroom teachers to assist them in their instruction of the visually impaired student and to demonstrate effective interaction and instructional strategies to use when working with the student.

During the student's preschool years, teachers of students who are visually impaired work in the homes with parents to help them with strategies to use during play and everyday routines with their child. Often, this parent-teacher relationship is maintained throughout the student's school career. In the community, the teacher of students with visual impairments provides consultation and assists those who interact with the student—a scout leader or swimming instructor, for example—to include the student in meaningful participation in activities of interest to the student. For a child who is visually impaired, positive social interaction sets the stage for long-term relationships. Teachers of students with visual impairments have both the expertise and the opportunity to advocate for social skills instruction as a routine part of every student's IEP and social inclusion as a goal for all children. Following are some suggestions to assist in this endeavor.

## STRATEGIES FOR SOCIAL SUCCESS
# Suggestions for Teachers of Students with Visual Impairments

◆ Make observations of the interactions of the visually impaired student a priority. While observing, take note of needed adaptations, social skills, or strategies that would enhance the participation of the student in both classroom and playground situations. Monitor the student's access to information and how much meaningful learning is taking place. The knowledge of the teacher of students who are visually impaired, based on experience with a number of students, is a valuable source of both insight and potential solutions to social inclusion difficulties.

◆ Monitor the child's social development closely. As children grow and develop, so does the complexity and variety of social skills they require to interact effectively in their social environments. Students with visual impairments need routine and ongoing instruction and monitoring of their social skills to ensure that their changing needs are being addressed. Inclusion of social skills goals in the student's IEP helps to ensure that both parents and educators will continue to monitor and evaluate social development in the same manner as they do academic progress.

◆ Provide simulators (goggles with lenses that simulate various eye conditions such as reduced acuity, cataracts, or restrictions of peripheral vision) to represent the student's visual condition when presenting information or awareness activities to others. Focus discussion on how the visual impairment affects the student's access to social information and communication. Assist others in generating possible solutions to problems of access to social interaction information and the required skills so that both the visually impaired student and his or her peers can find ways to accommodate the visual impairment.

◆ Allow classmates to use or try some of the special equipment and materials provided for the student with a visual impairment. This exposure helps to increase awareness of the adaptations used by the visually impaired student and to eliminate the special status associated with them.

◆ Provide an opportunity for the classroom teacher to work individually with the student who is visually impaired while you work with the other students. Inclusive instructional practices such as team teaching, monitoring cooperative learning groups, and assisting in center-based activities provide opportunities to incorporate the instruction and practice of social interaction skills.

◆ Provide classroom teachers and parents with feedback relevant to the inclusion of the visually impaired student and the appropriate teaching methods and materials for this student. Make suggestions and acknowledge the incorporation and use of these ideas.

◆ Identify activities that may entice classmates of the visually impaired student to initiate interaction or to join the student in an activity. Develop a collection of games and learning activities, such as braille or large-print editions of Scrabble or Monopoly or electronic question-and-answer games with speech output, that promote the social and instructional inclusion of students with a visual impairment. Make these available to classroom teachers.

◆ Acknowledge the expertise of parents and educators in their given areas (such as parenting, physical education, or language arts) and request their feedback about appropriate recommendations made to accommodate the student's needs, both academic and social, in a related subject or circumstance.

◆ Emphasize the importance of spending instructional time with the student to teach the social skills required to participate competently in both classroom and extracurricular activities. Be available after work hours to accompany parents to planning sessions with staff in charge of recreational and leisure activities to ensure meaningful inclusion of the student.

◆ Encourage children with visual impairments to search for solutions from an early age to problems of visual access or ways to complete activities that require some adaptations to accommodate their visual impairment. Children who display self-initiative and can advocate for themselves are less likely to become victims of learned helplessness (Corn, 1989). If students develop a problem-solving approach to accessing information, their teachers and peers will also feel more comfortable and capable when accommodating someone with a visual impairment. Practice in generating solutions to accommodate their visual impairment helps children develop a belief that they can participate in most activities and decreases the likelihood that they routinely perceive activities as too difficult or impossible and avoid them.

## SUGGESTIONS FOR PARENTS

Parents of children with visual impairments are the foremost advocates for social inclusion for their children because they observe firsthand on a daily basis the joys and sorrows of childhood relationships. Parents are also the primary source of social support for children and youths who are visually impaired (Chang & Schaller, 2000). Parents have so much to gain when their child experiences meaningful inclusion and so much to lose when peer acceptance is not forthcoming. Professionals who take full advantage of the expertise of parents in planning and implementing social inclusion will appreciate the benefits of a productive relationship (Alper, Schloss, & Schloss, 1996). Parents know their children's likes and dislikes, strengths and weaknesses, and things that motivate and discourage the child. Realizing social inclusion of a child who is visually impaired without the assistance and support of parents is an onerous challenge. Therefore, parents are an essential and primary participant in their child's school program planning team. As an active member of the school team, parents provide expertise and guidance in relation to their child and take on the responsibility of teaching and supporting the practice of social skills in the home and community. A collaborative relationship between home and school ensures success. Following are some suggestions to assist parents in promoting the social inclusion of their child.

# STRATEGIES FOR SOCIAL SUCCESS

# Suggestions for Parents

◆ Insist on taking an active role in the planning and implementation of the child's school program. Monitor both academic progress and social acceptance and interaction. Ask specific questions about how social skills are being incorporated in daily activities and about the individual and group instruction being provided. These important questions are relevant throughout the child's school years, even in high school. Ensure that IEPs have appropriate social goals that reflect the student's needs and interests. Provide educators with an outline of the expanded core curriculum for students with visual impairments (Hatlen, 1996) and identify social interaction skills as a compulsory area of instruction.

◆ Develop a support network with other parents of children with visual impairments. Parent groups are valuable sources of both moral support and creative solutions to difficulties that may arise. Each year in a child's development brings new issues and challenges. Make use of the expertise of other parents who have older children who are visually impaired. They have valuable experience to share. Act as a mentor for parents who have newly diagnosed children.

◆ Expose your child to an array of community activities, such as swimming, skating, karate, aerobics, drama, dance, Sunday school, scouting, music programs, and library story time. Groups that provide one-to-one or small-group instruction are easier for a student who is visually impaired. However, your child's interests and those of the child's friends and peers are important considerations in choosing activities.

◆ Stay abreast of the language, music, television programs, dress, and fashions of the peer culture in your child's school and neighborhood. Observe both school activities and extracurricular activities to become familiar with the interests of other children. Discuss these with your child, and introduce toys, games, and other activities that are popular. Give the child a head start; if skipping rope is a popular activity in the first grade, start working with your child on that skill before he or she enters first grade.

◆ Plan activities that encourage your child's interaction with classmates, such as inviting them home to play or allowing the child to take popular games to school. Organize a monthly parent-child activity group—for example, doing arts and crafts—with two or three other parents and their children. This social group provides another opportunity for you to observe your child's interaction and for the child to practice social skills and to have fun.

◆ Encourage your child to volunteer or to assist in some aspect of a community activity. Community recreation groups always need individuals to assist with instructional support. Neighborhood children can benefit from being tutored with their school work, assistance with music practice, or practice reading. Senior citizens often appreciate a visit and may welcome help with chores such as picking up groceries or walking the dog. Helping others provides opportunities to practice social interaction skills and generates feelings of value and high self-esteem.

◆ Initiate discussions with your child about relationships and friendships. Encourage the child's interest in others, for example, by complimenting the performance of others and seeking their opinions. Discuss social skills routinely as part of the family's interaction and review appropriate behaviors before attending activities outside the home. Role play conversations to practice such skills.

◆ Discuss your feelings and perspectives about routine events in your life. Provide the child with information about how people may feel or respond in given situations, such as helping a friend or being left out of an activity, so your child can develop an appreciation of the similarities and differences among people in general. Information about emotions is often expressed nonverbally through facial expressions and gestures that are not readily accessible to those with visual impairments.

◆ Use a checklist and set goals to master age-appropriate independent living skills (such as dressing, eating, and household chores) and social interaction skills (for example, good manners or initiating conversations). Help your child to develop organization strategies that enhance efficiency and time management. In school, a student who is well-organized and who can locate the learning materials needed for a lesson is perceived as competent.

◆ Discourage stereotypical mannerisms from an early age. Provide the child with candid feedback about how such mannerisms are viewed by others. Use encouragement and positive feedback to help the child monitor his or her own mannerisms and discuss the issues with teachers to make sure that they reinforce similar practices during school hours. Work collaboratively with the teacher of students who are visually impaired to identify appropriate intervention and follow-up.

◆ Limit the number of solitary and sedentary activities (such as watching television or listening to music). Talking on the telephone, ham radio activities, and Internet discussion groups provide opportunities to interact, and recreational pursuits that promote physical fitness are not only essential to good health but also frequently provide opportunities for social interaction. When children are exposed to a variety of activities, they develop a broad knowledge base, potential interests, and topics for conversations with peers.

## SUGGESTIONS FOR CLASSROOM TEACHERS

Classroom teachers are in the best position to observe the social interaction of students with visual impairments and therefore play an essential role in both teaching social skills and promoting the meaningful social inclusion of all students in the class. Positive social interaction with one's peers is highly correlated with academic progress and success after school graduation (Walz & Bleuer, 1992). The interdependence of most adult work environments demands that students master the skills of teamwork and effective interpersonal communication skills as a prerequisite to success in their adult life. Employers routinely cite an inability to get along with peers as the main reason for dismissing an employee. When classroom teachers incorporate the instruction and practice of social interaction skills in their learning activities, all students benefit, particularly those who are struggling to be accepted by and involved with their peers.

## STRATEGIES FOR SOCIAL SUCCESS

# Suggestions for Classroom Teachers

◆ Encourage the principal and other teachers in the school to consider their role and responsibility in ensuring that all students have the social skills essential to function effectively in society. Inclusive schools make the positive interaction and social development of all students a top priority.

◆ Plan objectives in advance so they are accessible when needed. Do not be afraid to acknowledge that a particular activity is inappropriate for an individual with a visual impairment, but describe it as inappropriate rather than something this student cannot do. Classroom teachers are role models for inclusion, both academic and social, of students with visual impairments. When inclusion is demonstrated through actions to be important and valued, those involved will recognize it as such.

◆ Provide a variety of activities to help the students in the classroom become better acquainted during the first week of school. Plan to create a cohesive class group. Provide the student who is visually impaired with a list in his or her preferred reading medium (braille or print) of the names of classmates. Younger students can use a tape recording of the voices of each classmate to assist in identification of classmates. Develop the habit of calling on students by name rather than gestures such as pointing.

◆ Alternate group seating arrangements and group membership for various activities to ensure that all students have an opportunity to become well acquainted with one another, including the student who is visually impaired. Provide opportunities for students with a visual impairment to choose a partner for academic or leisure activities. However, as a matter of practice, occasionally preassign students to groups or partnerships to limit the likelihood of the same children routinely being chosen last. Identify classmates who are receptive to working and playing with the student who is visually impaired and those whom this student finds appealing; then orchestrate opportunities for these mutually accepting parties to work and play together. Refrain from routinely assigning the same students to interact with the visually impaired student.

◆ Teach students how to work effectively in groups prior to assigning them to this learning environment (see Sidebar 8.1 for some suggestions). Monitor and adjust group arrangements to enhance the performance and behaviors of specific students.

◆ Provide a variety of games and learning activities that entice other children to participate with the student with a visual impairment. Consider the type of interaction encouraged by different activities. For example, individual activities such as coloring involve less interaction than imaginary play or activities requiring cooperation. Develop a resource file of cooperative games and learning activities that enhance social interaction and active participation of all students.

◆ When preparing lesson plans, consider those program adaptations that are the least isolating for students with visual impairments. Analyze the dilemmas associated with developing independence and the use of special equipment or techniques. Flexible guidelines to accommodate such dilemmas need to be established. For example, having a student travel with a sighted guide to the cafeteria increases the probability that the student will eat with classmates. Opportunities for independent travel can be found easily during other parts of the school day.

◆ Encourage students with a visual impairment to participate in activities that increase their exposure to peers such as working in the cafeteria or on the school newspaper or taking part in other extracurricular activities.

◆ Promote the maintenance of class friendship groups when student placements are being considered for the following school year. A student who appears to be isolated from the group needs to be placed with peers who appear to be most receptive to this student.

◆ Become familiar with programs that are designed specifically to promote social interaction and the development of relationships

## Sidebar 8.1

### SUGGESTIONS TO HELP TEACH STUDENTS TO WORK IN GROUPS

Learning to work effectively in groups requires mastery of new skills. Schools offer unique opportunities for practice in an environment in which group participants can discover the benefits of working as a group and the power of cooperation. Following are some suggestions for teaching students to work effectively in groups.

**Laying the Groundwork**

- Discuss the concept of teamwork. Use examples such as sports teams, large corporations, completion of work in beehives or anthills, or the roles of various family members to demonstrate how important teamwork is in our world.

- Have the children experiment with the effectiveness of groups by assigning a task to both groups of students and to students working independently (for example, "In five minutes, list as many words as you can that have *qu* in them," or "List ways you would solve" a given problem). Discuss why the groups outperformed the students who were working independently.

- Emphasize the importance of the specific role of every group member, how each member has a responsibility to complete the task of the group and a right to take pride in the group's success. "There is no *I* in *team*."

- Set up specific roles for the group participants based on the group's assignment. Most groups need to have a recorder, a reporter, a timekeeper, someone assigned to keep the group on task, someone to motivate the participants or to encourage responses from everyone in the group, and so forth. Discuss these roles and responsibilities with students. Post the assigned roles on the classroom wall. (Students who are visually impaired will need to have their own copies in braille or print.)

- Teach students the basic skills required for effective group participation—turn taking, effective listening, valuing all perspectives, brainstorming techniques, decision-making skills, encouraging participation from each group member, voicing disagreement, and analyzing and evaluating the success of the group—before assigning formal group work. Post guidelines for each of these skills on the wall.

*(continued on next page)*

Sidebar 8.1 *(continued)*

**Getting Started**

- Provide daily practice in group participation skills, noting the developing skill level of each student. In the beginning, keep group numbers small (three to five students). Assist students who require additional instruction and practice.

- Organize the groups so that all participants are likely to be able to cooperate with one another, especially in the beginning. Arrange groups of mixed gender, abilities, and personalities and separate children who are close friends and those who do not get along well.

- Begin formal group work with an activity that is nonthreatening to individual students and is enjoyable; for example, identify five things you could do to increase the possibility of being rescued if you were marooned on a secluded island.

- Assign groups a specific social skill to practice during their group work for a given day (face the speaker, ask for clarification when confused, give a compliment, participate actively in the conversation, use good manners) in addition to the main task of the group,

- Take the time to discuss how each group performed to identify both what made the group work well and what detracted from the work and success of the group.

**Ongoing Group Work**

- Provide students with longer and more complex tasks as students demonstrate greater ability to work effectively in groups.

- Use groups for long-term project work as well as for activities in daily instruction. Change group members regularly for the latter.

- Experiment with groups of different sizes and with various types of assignments.

- Provide lots of support and positive feedback to group members for successful group accomplishments.

between students with disabilities and their peers, such as Circle of Friends or Special Friends Clubs (Bradley & Graves, 1997). These types of intervention programs strive to form a network of social support for a student with a disability and are well known to guidance counselors and other resource personnel in schools. Although these programs are not appropriate for all students, they are often effective for children who have behavioral or cognitive challenges in addition to a visual impairment. The programs recruit students who are well-liked by their peers and are actively involved in the school community to participate in activities with students with disabilities on a regular basis. Many helpful suggestions and strategies used in these programs can be readily adapted for use with students with visual impairments.

◆ Inform classmates of the types of activities in which their visually impaired classmate is involved when they receive disability-specific instruction outside the classroom. Accurate information relevant to the special instructional needs of the student with a visual impairment increases the knowledge and understanding of classmates.

◆ Organize the classroom and the storage of equipment and materials to enhance the mobility, independence, and efficiency of the student with a visual impairment. A competent student functioning independently is more acceptable as a member of the group.

## CONCLUSION

For students with visual impairments who have experienced inclusion as it is intended to be implemented—that is, in programs organized to address both their unique academic and social needs—participation in their home community has usually been a positive experience. Although these same students cherish time spent with friends who are visually impaired, they are, first and foremost, children and youths. They want to experience their childhood years with their families and in an inclusive setting—sometimes even when it doesn't feel or appear very inclusive. Therefore, parents and educators need to work collaboratively so they can help to change attitudes and expectations to create a learning environment that not only promotes but celebrates the positive acceptance of difference.

Social inclusion of students with disabilities in their neighborhood schools is an evolving process. As educators and parents compile their practical experience with the findings of research, greater insight and knowledge is becoming available—information that can assist in program and instructional planning. There is good reason to be optimistic about the social inclusion of children and youths with visual impairments if educators and parents understand that the meaningful inclusion of these students cannot be left to chance but must be carefully planned and closely monitored. In the last decade much research has been directed toward exploring the social interaction and the friendships of students with visual impairments in the public school setting. Curricula concentrating on teaching social skills to these students are now readily available. Parents and educators are aware of the critical importance of formalized intervention to enhance social inclusion and the prominent place social skills instruction has been given in the expanded core curriculum for children and youths with visual impairments. They understand the concept that, "You learn to talk by talking. You learn to read by reading. You learn to write by writing. You learn to include by including" (Bunch, 1999, p. 9). Most important, children learn to interact with peers by interacting with peers.

As classroom instruction becomes more student-centered and teachers at all levels adopt instructional and curricular practices that are not only conducive to inclusion but require the incorporation of social skills instruction, more students will experience real inclusion. Although there is still a great need for more research to understand the effects of blindness and visual impairment on social development and the complexities of inclusion, there is now a solid foundation of knowledge to guide day-to-day programming to promote the positive acceptance of difference in our homes, schools, and communities.

# REFERENCES

Alper, S., Schloss, P. J., & Schloss, C. N. (1996). Families of children with disabilities in elementary and middle school: Advocacy models and strategies. *Exceptional Children, 62*(3), 261–270.

American Printing House for the Blind Federal Quota Census. (2003). Louisville, KY. Available: www.aph.org/fedquotpgm/dist03.html.

Bauer, A. M., & Shea, T. M. (1999). *Inclusion 101: How to teach all learners.* Baltimore: Paul H. Brookes.

Bishop, V. E. (1986). Identifying the components of success in mainstreaming. *Journal of Visual Impairment & Blindness, 80,* 939–946.

Bradley, D. F., & Graves, D. K. (1997). Student support networks. In D. Bradley, M. King-Sears, & D. Tessier-Switlick (Eds.), *Teaching students in inclusive settings: From theory to practice* (pp. 384–403). Needham Heights, MA: Allyn & Bacon.

Bunch, G. (1999). *Inclusion how to: Essential classroom strategies.* Toronto, Ontario, Canada: Inclusion Press.

Chang, S. C-H, & Schaller, J. (2000). Perspectives of adolescents with visual impairments on social support from their parents. *Journal of Visual Impairment & Blindness, 94*(2), 69–84.

Circle of Inclusion. [www.circleofinclusion.org]. September 12, 2001.

Corn, A. L. (1989). Employing critical thinking strategies within a curriculum of critical things to think about for blind and visually impaired students. *Journal of Vision Rehabilitation, 3*(4), 17–36.

Corn, A. L., Bina, M. J., & DePriest, L. B. (1995). *The parent perspective on schools for students who are blind and visually impaired: A national study.* Alexandria, VA: Association for Education and Rehabilitation of the Blind and Visually Impaired.

Crocker, A. D., & Orr, R. R. (1996). Social behaviors of children with visual impairments enrolled in preschool programs. *Exceptional Children, 62*(5), 451–462.

Erin, J. N., Dignan, K., & Brown, P. A. (1991). Are social skills teachable? A review of the literature. *Journal of Visual Impairment & Blindness, 85*(2), 58–61.

Gardner, H. (1985). *Frames of mind.* New York: Basic Books.

Gresham, F. M., Sugai, G., & Horner, R. H. (2001). Interpreting outcomes of social skills training for students with high-incidence disabilities. *Exceptional Children, 67*(3), 331–344.

Harris, J. R. (1998). *The nurture assumption.* New York: Touchstone.

Hatlen, P. (1996). *Core curriculum for blind and visually impaired students, including those with additional impairments.* Austin: Texas School for the Blind and Visually Impaired. Available: www.tsbvi.edu/agenda/corecurric.htm.

Hatlen, P. H., & Curry, S. A. (1987). In support of specialized programs for blind and visually impaired children: The impact of vision loss on learning. *Journal of Visual Impairment & Blindness, 81*(1), 7–13.

Hoben, M., & Lindstom, V. (1980). Evidence of isolation in the mainstream. *Journal of Visual Impairment & Blindness, 74,* 289–292.

Huurre, T., & Aro, H. (2000). The psychosocial well-being of Finnish adolescents with visual impairments versus those with chronic conditions and those with no disabilities. *Journal of Visual Impairment & Blindness, 94*(10), 625–637.

Jindal, D., Kato, M., & Maekawa, H. (1998). Using self-evaluation procedures to maintain social skills in a child who is blind. *Journal of Visual Impairment & Blindness, 92*(5), 363–366.

Johnson, D. W., Johnson, R. T., & Holubec, E. J. (1990). *Circles of learning: Cooperation in the classroom.* Edina, MN: Interaction Book.

Johnson, R. T., & Johnson, D. W. (1981). Building friendships between handicapped and non-handicapped children: Effects of cooperative and individualistic instruction. *American Educational Research Journal, 18,* 415–423.

Koenig, A. J., & Holbrook, M. Cay (2000). Planning Instruction in Unique Skills. In A. J. Koenig & M. C. Holbrook (Eds.), *Foundations of Education, Vol. 2: Instructional Strategies for Teaching Children and Youths with Visual Impairments* (2nd ed.). (pp. 196–222). New York: AFB Press.

Kregs, C. S. (2000). Beyond blindfolds: Creating an inclusive classroom through collaboration. *RE:view, 31*(4), 180–186.

MacCuspie, P. A. (1992). The social acceptance and interaction of visually impaired children in integrated settings. In S. Z. Sacks, L. S. Kekelis, & R. J. Gaylord-Ross (Eds.), *The development of social skills by blind and visually impaired students* (pp. 83–102). New York: American Foundation for the Blind.

MacCuspie, P. A. (1996). *Promoting acceptance of children with disabilities: From tolerance to inclusion.* Halifax, Nova Scotia, Canada: Atlantic Provinces Special Education Authority.

McLeskey, J., & Waldron, N. L. (2000). *Inclusive schools in action: Making differences ordinary.* Alexandria, VA: Association for Supervision and Curriculum Development.

Nezer, H., Nezer, B., & Siperstein, G. (1985). *Improving children's social skills: Techniques for teachers.* (Grant # DIE G5583016). Boston: Center for the Study of Social Acceptance, University of Massachusetts.

Nixon, H. L. (1994). Looking sociologically at family coping with visual impairment. *Journal of Visual Impairment & Blindness, 88*(4), 329–337.

Rosenblum, L. P. (2000). Perceptions of the impact of visual impairment on the lives of adolescents. *Journal of Visual Impairment & Blindness, 94*(7), 434–445.

Sacks, S. Z., Kekelis, L. S., & Gaylord-Ross, R. J. (Eds.). (1992). *The development of social skills by blind and visually impaired students.* New York: American Foundation for the Blind.

Vaughn, S., Bos, C. S., & Shay Schumm, J. (2000). *Teaching exceptional, diverse, and at-risk students in the general education classroom* (2nd ed.). Needham Heights, MA: Allyn & Bacon.

Walz, G. R., & Bleuer, J. C. (Eds.). (1992). *Student self-esteem: A vital element of school success.* Ann Arbor, MI: Counseling and Personnel Services.

Wolffe, K., & Sacks, S. Z. (1997). The lifestyles of blind, low vision, and sighted youths: A quantitative comparison. *Journal of Visual Impairment & Blindness, 91*(3), 245–257.

# CHAPTER 9

# Social Skills Assessment

## Sharon Z. Sacks and Lizbeth A. Barclay

The acquisition and maintenance of a repertoire of social skills is the foundation upon which personal relationships are built. Children and adolescents who use social skills effectively are able to gain entry into groups, interact and play successfully with peers, and demonstrate socially competent behavior in a range of settings. Children and adolescents who have learned the social rules of their peer culture and have established strong ties to their families and the community are more likely to exhibit higher levels of self-esteem and social confidence (MacCuspie, 1996). For students with visual impairments, the process of obtaining and maintaining a requisite set of social skills may be different than it is for sighted age-mates. In order for educators and families to determine the social skills needs of students, it is essential for them to evaluate the children's social competence on an ongoing basis. The following principles, which are elucidated in this chapter, may be used as a guide to this process:

- The assessment of social skills is important in determining effective interventions for students with visual impairments.
- It is critical to determine the environments in which social skills assessment can occur most effectively and who should conduct the assessment.

- Teachers, related services personnel, and parents need to know about effective social skills assessment tools, including observation, for students with visual impairments.

- Supporting adults, including parents, need to be able to identify specialized strategies to assess the social skills of students with visual impairments and additional disabilities.

Social skills assessment provides a baseline for teachers and family members to determine which skills the student can demonstrate and what skills need to be taught in a variety of social environments. Rather than start by examining the instruments and strategies used to assess social skills, the authors have taken a more unconventional, holistic approach. Before assessing social skills, the teacher or specialist needs to evaluate the domains (home, school, and community) in which students encounter social experiences and how the behaviors of others in those environments affect the acquisition of social skills. By observing students who are blind or visually impaired in a variety of environments or domains, teachers can acquire a more realistic view of the student's social performance or aptitude. When social skills assessment is performed in artificial settings (for example, by performing role plays with adult confederates in a classroom setting), responses may not be representative of the student's actual abilities.

## RATIONALE FOR ONGOING SOCIAL SKILLS ASSESSMENT

According to Hill & Blasch (1980), of all developmental processes, socialization is most dependent on visual learning. It is incumbent on teachers and families to understand how a child's development may differ from the norm when social skills assessment takes place. (See Chapter 3 for an examination of social development theories in relation to the unique developmental differences exhibited by young children with visual impairments.) Once evaluators conceptualize the differences in social development among students with visual impairments, they can determine those skills that require intervention and support. Also, assessment allows the evaluator to determine which social skills the student performs well, and which skills will need refinement over time.

In addition, consistent social skills assessment for students with visual impairments influences program accountability for teachers of students with visual impairments and administrators. Assessment affords educators and others working with the student (family members, related service personnel, and outside agencies) the opportunity to design program objectives and benchmarks that influence instruction. The information provided by comprehensive social skills assessments allows educators and program evaluators to measure students' growth and programs' effectiveness. Social skills assessment also provides teachers, families, and others who work directly with the student with the information to make well-founded decisions about instruction and the use of effective intervention strategies.

When social skills instruction is based on thorough assessment, structured training and consistent strategies can be employed in varied environments and with numerous individuals. Without ongoing assessment on which to base instruction, those providing instruction may target a specific skill based on personal values or level of comfort in teaching the skill, and it is unlikely that positive behavioral change can occur for students with visual impairments. When those involved in instruction, including the student, are aware of the behaviors targeted for training and strategies are employed across settings (school, home, work, and the community), then the student is ensured of a meaningful program of instruction.

According to Warren (2000), the development of social skills by students with visual impairments is highly dependent on the experiences and expectations established by family members, friends, and professionals. The more diverse the environments in which these students are allowed to explore, the greater are the opportunities for typical socialization experiences. Warren (2000) maintains that comparisons of developmental milestones between children who are visually impaired and those who are sighted may be counterproductive. Rather, social skills assessment, both summative (a one-time assessment that is usually standardized) and ongoing, provides teachers and family members with valuable information that leads to meaningful intervention for these children. Summative assessment results in the documentation of information regarding the level of social competence and the acquisition of critical social behaviors (such as direction of gaze, positive initiations, and turn taking). Continuous assessment requires the teacher of students with visual impairments to keep accurate anecdotal records of skill attainment through structured learning activities (that is, social skills interventions) and unstructured experiences (such as school field trips or family outings).

The question then arises, what social skills need to be assessed for intervention? As noted, the process of assessing a student's level of social competence is based on the individual needs of the student. However, the social skills listed in Sidebar 9.1 are essential for most

## Sidebar 9.1

**BENCHMARKS FOR SOCIAL SKILLS OF STUDENTS WITH VISUAL IMPAIRMENTS**

The following list represents the basic social skills that visually impaired children of various ages need in their repertoire to be on par with their sighted age-mates.

**Infants, Toddlers, and Preschool Students (ages 0–5)**

- Shows awareness and responds to others with appropriate gestures and facial expressions (such as smiles, giggles, and grimaces)
- Establishes eye contact (direction of gaze) when spoken to by others
- Responds positively to interactions by others
- Explores and interacts with the physical and social environment
- Plays alone with toys and objects in an appropriate manner (for example, uses a wooden spoon in a mixing bowl)
- Responds to hand-clapping games and songs like "Patty Cake" or "Itsy, Bitsy Spider"
- Enjoys roughhousing and rough-and-tumble play
- Interacts with other children with parallel play
- Interacts with other children with interactive or pretend play
- Says or signs simple requests with "please" and "thank you"
- Says or signs "hello" to others when engaged in a social exchange
- Holds head up when engaging with others in a social situation
- Uses appropriate body posture and body space in social interactions with peers and adults

**Elementary School Students (ages 5–11)**

- Uses eye contact in all social situations appropriately
- Allows appropriate body space (18 inches) when interacting with others
- Can initiate a simple social greeting and interaction
- Can maintain an appropriate social conversation for at least two to five minutes with a beginning, middle, and end
- Shares belongings, games, and toys with peers appropriately

- Uses social amenities in an appropriate manner (such as "please," "thank you," and "I'm sorry")
- Compliments others
- Can make an appropriate social introduction including using a handshake
- Does not demonstrate inappropriate mannerisms such as eye poking or rocking
- Demonstrates appropriate social behavior in specific environments (such as raising one's hand in class or waiting one's turn in a food line)
- Does not interrupt a conversation
- Demonstrates turn taking in conversations and when playing with peers
- Demonstrates the ability to join a group that is playing or conversing
- Can participate in age-appropriate games and activities (such as hand-clapping games, wall ball, or tether ball and playing on swings and climbing equipment)
- Asks for assistance from peers or adults in an appropriate manner
- Makes choices and decisions without prompting from adults
- Shows responsibility for belongings, school assignments, and actions taken toward other peers or adults
- Dresses age-appropriately
- Is knowledgeable and can talk about video games, movies, television shows, and popular songs with peers
- Shows understanding and caring for others
- Discusses visual impairment with peers and adults; can identify the name of his or her eye condition and explain it in a simple way

### Middle School Students (ages 11–14)
- Demonstrates appropriate eye contact, body stance, and body space for specific social situations
- Uses appropriate facial and hand gestures to express feelings and ideas
- Can carry on socially appropriate conversations for at least ten minutes with peers and adults
- Shows no inappropriate use of mannerisms
- Initiates conversations with peers and adults using appropriate eye contact and body posture

*(continued on next page)*

Sidebar 9.1 *(continued)*

- Participates in conversations without interrupting, and responds appropriately to questions or comments from others
- Has a repertoire of topics that are age-appropriate to talk about with others
- Can take the role of others and understand others' feelings in various social situations
- Selects clothing that is appropriate for a specific social situation
- Is aware of personal hygiene needs, and knows when clothing is dirty or wrinkled
- Attends and participates in social activities with peers (visually impaired and sighted)
- Hangs out with peers, and travels to malls, restaurants, or school activities with peers
- Understands and can explain visual impairment to others
- Uses problem solving to determine how to act in specific social situations
- Takes responsibility for personal actions in social situations

**High School Students (ages 14–18)**
- Can advocate for his or her own needs in a variety of social situations
- Uses assertive social behavior when interacting with peers and adults
- Asks for assistance in an assertive manner
- Evaluates social situations to determine appropriate use of specific social behaviors
- Uses a range of social skills in an appropriate manner for specific situations (for example, flirting, dating, or job interviews)
- Can converse with others on a range of interesting topics without dominating the conversation
- Compliments others and reciprocates when appropriate
- Takes the role of others, and offers assistance when appropriate
- Interacts effectively in large-group situations such as dances, conferences, or school assemblies
- Interprets nonverbal social cues appropriately

- Uses social etiquette in an appropriate way for the social situation
- Uses appropriate social skills during job or college interviews (arriving on time, shaking hands, using eye contact, asking appropriate questions, and so forth)
- Evaluates social behavior in a variety of environments in a realistic and honest manner
- Uses a trusted friend or colleague to provide information about a specific social situation
- Can easily discuss his or her visual impairment, including expressing specific needs or adaptations
- Dresses appropriately for all social situations, and selects clothing independently, with friends, or with a personal shopper

students who are blind or visually impaired and this list provides a basic foundation for assessment.

# DEFINING AND DESCRIBING SOCIAL COMPETENCE

Before initiating assessment procedures for the instruction of social skills for students with visual impairments, it is necessary to have a clear understanding of terms. Societal rules and values generally define socially competent behavior. In Western culture, for example, close face-to-face contact or averting one's gaze would be viewed as socially inappropriate. Likewise, constantly interrupting in a group conversation that involves two or more individuals would be considered rude and inconsiderate. Students who exhibit socially competent behavior demonstrate a repertoire of social skills that assist them in gaining entry into groups, developing friendships, and interacting effectively with adults. Also, students who exhibit socially competent behavior tend to demonstrate a positive self-concept and accurately perceive their strengths and limitations. (See Chapter 5 for a more detailed discussion of the development of self-concept, self-esteem, and self-image.)

*Self-concept* is the foundation on which social skills are developed. How a person feels about himself or herself is central to a positive self-concept. According to Tuttle and Tuttle (1996), two dimensions of personality influence the development of self-concept: the cognitive component, which relates to factual information about oneself (such as height, hair color, and gender), and the affective component, which relates to how one feels about oneself (internal thoughts such as, "I'm too tall" or "I'm too short").

Family members and professionals are pivotal in helping students with visual impairments to nurture and maintain a positive sense of self. When family and friends perceive the student with a visual impairment as capable and self-sufficient, these positive attitudes promote a socialization process that results in the development of a healthy, positive self-concept. This process begins with deliberate attention to providing positive and accurate personal information to children who are visually impaired from a very early age about who they are and how their social behavior affects others and continues with the provision of opportunities to gain skills and self-confidence through life experiences at home, at school, and in the community.

When beginning to assess social skills for students with visual impairments, the acquisition of self-concept is fundamental to later social development. According to Fitts (1967), *self-concept* is the image, the picture, the set of perceptions and feelings the student has about his or her self. The formation of self-concept for children with visual impairments is challenging because they are often dependent on the attitudes and perceptions of others in their environment. Awareness of varied objects both near and far, refinement of motor proficiency, locomotion, hand-ear coordination, bonding between mother and child, stimulation of exploration, and establishment of object and person permanence can be developed over time, but require extra attention and adaptations by caring individuals in the student's life (Tuttle & Tuttle, 1996).

*Self-esteem* focuses on the affective aspects of self-concept. Self-esteem is a part of, and emerges from, an individual's self-concept. Coopersmith (1967) asserts that self-esteem is the evaluative component of a person's self-concept. Self-esteem is the judgment part of a person's self-concept that allows the person to evaluate his or her strengths and limitations, successes, and capabilities. Once again, family members and professionals who have close relationships with students who are visually impaired play an integral role in providing realistic feedback about the youngsters' levels of social competence and ability to interact effectively with others in home, school, community, and work environments.

By contrast, *self-image* is the part of the self-concept that focuses on one's physical abilities and appearance. Children with visual impairments are highly dependent on parents, family members, peers, and teachers to provide needed feedback about how they act or appear to others. Sighted children acquire these skills and nuances through observation and imitation. Students who are blind or visually impaired require direct input from trusted individuals to mediate their world. Social behaviors that reflect self-image, such as body posture and stance, use of facial expressions and gestures, and knowledge of personal space, should be considered an important part of the assessment process.

Also, a student's self-image is affected by his or her understanding and acceptance of visual impairment. During social skills assessment, it is important to determine if the student can explain his or her visual impairment to others and whether he or she exhibits a sense of ease or shame about the nature of the visual impairment.

In contrast to self-concept and its components, *social competence* is the ability to demonstrate a repertoire of behaviors and actions that promote positive social relationships with others and are accepted by the culture or society in which the student with a visual impairment resides. Students who exhibit socially competent behaviors have a positive sense of self. They understand the rules of their social world. They are able to move from one social situation to another and employ a set of skills that enable them to achieve positive social outcomes with peers and adults.

# OBSERVATION IN SOCIAL SKILLS ASSESSMENT

Through thoughtful assessment, team planning, and information sharing, all aspects of a child's social skills can be observed, assessed, and monitored. Careful and consistent collection of assessment information, through the use of specific evaluation instruments and observation, is the key to successful social skills program planning and implementation. A variety of assessment tools and techniques (described later in this chapter) are important; however, observation strategies provide the foundation for assessment of social skills. Once observation strategies are initiated, the teacher of students with visual impairments, other specialists, and families can use an array of assessment tools and techniques to more accurately assess social skills.

Observation is the first step in the social skills assessment process. It is one of the most powerful tools of assessment and provides valuable insights into the lives of students with visual impairments. Observation allows teachers, families, and other professionals to evaluate a student's social performance on an ongoing basis within natural environments. By simply observing the daily routine of students—their actions and interactions—an educator can begin to objectively interpret a student's behavior, observing precedent and antecedent actions, and therefore, more clearly determine what is needed in terms of instruction and remediation. Observation also allows educators to assess their students in a variety of environments over an extended period of time. The keen observer can document valuable information in an anecdotal or narrative format, providing a documented record of the student's social growth over time. Checklists are often used to assist educators in the observation process. They provide a framework for consistent observation and establish specific guidelines for formative (ongoing) evaluation.

When observing students with visual impairments, the following areas may be considered:

- number of social contacts during an observation period
- behaviors that work for a student during a social interaction
- behaviors that create obstacles for a student in the social interaction process
- ability to sustain conversations that are age-appropriate
- diversity of conversation topics that are meaningful and engaging
- turn taking during conversations and social interactions with peers and adults
- length of social interactions
- interest in peers and peer topics
- knowledge of peer culture: games, dress, peer language, and communication style
- awareness of nonverbal communication: gestures, facial expressions, body language
- social balance: is the student regarded as a peer or someone to care of within social contexts?

For observation to be used effectively as an assessment tool, it is important to consider the domains in which social skills are used and maintained. Much can be learned by observing students with visual impairments in their home, school, and community environments. Sample observation protocols for the teacher or counselor to use in these three domains are included in the appendix at the end of this chapter. These observation tools help teachers of students with visual impairments to target specific social behaviors or needs that require instruction.

## HOME ASSESSMENT

Social skills assessment within the home allows the teacher to evaluate how communication affects socialization. A nurturing home environment allows young children to develop a strong sense of self. Communication is the vehicle by which socially competent behaviors are applied and maintained. Usually, a child's highest level of communication takes place in the home. Observations of social interactions with family and friends in various routines provide a clearer picture of the child's attainment of social skills. The home observation protocol (see Appendix 9 at the end of this chapter) will assist teachers of students with visual impairments in the assessment process.

The impact of a child's visual impairment on family dynamics cannot be overlooked. While some family members embrace and nurture the child's social development, other members may require support from professionals to develop a solid social relationship with the child. Because parents are the primary caregivers, they usually provide the greater opportunity for social interactions within the home. The following questions may help to initiate the assessment process:

- How does the caregiver engage the child in social interactions?
- Do the caregiver and child play and engage in recreational activities together?
- Do the parents or other primary caregivers have clear expectations for the student with a visual impairment about performance of daily routines and chores around the house, or do others wait on the student?
- Are communication skills modeled?
- Is the child given choices during daily routines?
- Is the child included in family activities?
- Do the parents and primary caregiver employ consequences for inappropriate social behavior that seem reasonable?
- Are the expectations for social performance the same for the child who is visually impaired as for any sighted sibling?

In addition to observing interactions between parent or caregiver and child, watching a play session between siblings may also provide clues about the level of social competence of a child with a visual impairment. The level of communicative turn taking, play skills, and cooperation can be observed during home visits. When there is an emphasis on play and recreation within the family, and especially between siblings, there is greater potential for building confidence and for social growth. These activities can provide a vehicle for social interactions with others, both during the activity and after, giving the child experiences to refer back to in future conversation. When evaluating the level of social competence with siblings, the following questions should be considered:

- Do sighted siblings treat the sibling with a visual impairment in a natural manner (play, fight, take toys, get into mischief together), or is the sibling with a visual impairment babied or ignored?
- Does the sighted sibling include the sibling with a visual impairment in games and activities or teach him or her to play games and try new activities?

Finally, social skills assessment that occurs in the home allows the evaluator to observe interactions with peers. Children with visual impairments develop the foundation for making friends through parents' support and modeling. When the parents and other primary caregivers encourage and promote interactions, peer relationships emerge. The following questions can help to support the assessment of the peer interaction process in the home:

- Are other children invited to the home to play?
- Are activities structured for young children to encourage turn taking and social interactions?
- Do older children receive accurate feedback regarding appropriate and inappropriate social interactions with peers?
- Do the parents or other primary caregivers provide opportunities for social interactions with both sighted and visually impaired peers?

These questions help teachers to pinpoint what skills need to be acquired by the student who is blind or visually impaired. This method of assessment provides an objective way to learn more about a student's social activities in the home. By visiting the family and discussing these questions with parents and other caregivers, teachers of students with visual impairments and other professionals can work with families to help them to learn and carry out strategies that will improve their child's level of social competence.

## SCHOOL ASSESSMENT

As children begin their journey through school, the development of social skills takes a new and important turn. The school environment is a natural arena for social interaction and, consequently, the next domain for social skills assessment. School provides a natural context for assessment of social behavior, friendship-making skills, and interdependence. The school setting allows teachers and other professionals consistent opportunities to monitor students' social competence and to create interventions that support positive social interactions with peers and adults. The two observation protocols provided in the chapter appendix for the preschool and elementary level, and the middle school and high school level support teachers in making observations geared to students with visual impairments at those levels.

Beginning in preschool, children learn to negotiate the intricacies of social behavior as they come into contact with classmates. The natural contexts of a preschool setting allow children to experiment with toys and games and to learn how to play and work with peers. Preschool also provides a structure for learning the social rules that govern school routines and acceptable social interactions. According to researchers (Kekelis and Sacks, 1992; Skellenger, Hill, & Hill, 1992), classroom structure, student population, teacher facilitation, and family involvement all play a critical role in promoting the acquisition and maintenance of social skills for young children with visual impairments. When observing young children with visual impairments in a preschool setting, the following questions may assist in the assessment process.

- Does the child use language (verbal or gestures) to communicate interactive intent?
- Does the child play alone or with other children? If the child plays with other children, is the activity facilitated by an adult or by other (older) children?
- Does the child show interest in playing with toys?
- Does the child engage in games or group activities?
- Does the child make choices independently or with adult facilitation?

As young children move from preschool to elementary school settings, school behavior, peer relationships, and play are key elements in achieving social competence and developing relationships with peers. The various school environments—the classroom, the playground, the cafeteria, the school library, the bus, and extracurricular events—provide students with many experiences in which to develop a repertoire of social skills. These are also contexts in which assessment and intervention can occur. The classroom, for example, provides information about a child's ability to interact and to participate within large- and small-group instruction. The following questions, rather than an interview, might be used as a basis for observation in elementary classes:

- Does the student participate in class discussion?
- Does the student talk with other students, and if so, does the student do so easily and reciprocally?
- Does the student move about the classroom independently?
- Does the student locate materials without support?
- Does the student willingly share information and materials with other students?
- Can the student make decisions independently?
- Can the student ask for assistance when needed?
- Can the student let students know when assistance is not needed?
- Does the student actively participate in group work or projects?
- How much time throughout the day does the student spend interacting with other students compared to interactions with adults?

The playground is a testing ground for social abilities, and recess offers a critical environment in which to assess social behavior of elementary-aged students with visual impairments. During recess children move about quickly as they engage in social games, rituals, and routines that are uniquely child centered. Often this is a challenging time for a student who is visually impaired unless social skills interventions have carefully prepared the groundwork. The following questions can provide a solid framework for observation and may assist in the assessment process. Sometimes, however, the assessor may want to question the teacher of students with visual impairments or the paraeducator, particularly if specific behaviors or actions are not observed.

- Does the child interact and play easily with peers?
- Does the student participate in games or activities on the play-ground?
- Does the student know how to engage in age-appropriate games and activities at recess?
- Does the student have a repertoire of conversation topics that fa-cilitate social interactions with peers?

During the middle school and high school years, peer relationships take on tremendous importance for all adolescents, including those with visual impairments (Rosenblum, 1998). A student's social skills at this level must be highly developed in order to successfully navigate the complicated social networks exhibited in adolescence. Not only are communication skills critical, but knowledge of the teen culture and its many nuances are essential. Students with visual impairments must be able to grasp and interpret social situations and analyze the effect of their behavior on others. Often adolescents with visual impairments have particular difficulty with this aspect of socialization because it requires interpretation of visual cues and nonverbal behaviors. When evaluating the student's level of involvement in school activities, the following questions need to be considered:

- Does the student have friends?
- Does the student interact with others during class time?
- Does the student interact with others during breaks?
- Does the student interact with others during lunch?
- Does the student respond appropriately to questions from others?
- Do the student's dress and appearance promote social interaction with peers?
- Does the student participate in school clubs, music, or athletic activities?
- Does the student belong to any after-school religious or secular organizations or service clubs?
- Does the student have a job, either volunteer or paid?
- Does the student demonstrate the skills to travel independently to after-school activities, using public transportation if necessary?
- Does the student's family encourage independent travel and in-volvement in school and after-school activities?

- Does the family provide transportation to social activities when public transportation is unavailable?

While interaction and friendships with sighted peers are important, it is also beneficial for a student to have friends who are visually impaired. Consequently, during the assessment of social skills, relationships with other students who are visually impaired need to be explored. The support networks that students with visual impairments build together can have a lasting and important impact throughout adolescence and early adulthood. The following questions need to be considered when carrying out the observation phase of a comprehensive social skills assessment. Often, these behaviors can be observed, but to determine if the behaviors occur on a regular basis, the evaluator may need to interview the teacher of students with visual impairments or the classroom teacher.

- Does the student have a network of friends who are visually impaired?
- Does the student interact with students who are visually impaired on a regular basis?
- Does the student have opportunities to connect with age-mates who have similar visual impairments?
- Does the student have opportunities to meet and interact with a mentor who is visually impaired?
- If the student with a visual impairment does not have friends who are visually impaired, what are the reasons or causes?

## COMMUNITY ASSESSMENT

Social participation within the community is a key component in the social skills assessment process. How a student with a visual impairment negotiates socially within the broader community is a determining factor in a student's ultimate level of independence in life. Success in the world of work and living independently are strongly influenced by social competence (Wolffe, Thomas, & Sacks, 2000).

The community environment provides natural contexts for social skills assessment. Young children can be observed in child care settings. Students in elementary, middle, and high school environments can be assessed on field trips, during recreational activities, and while engaged in clubs or organized groups. Social skills assessment during orientation and mobility lessons that take place in the community also provide numerous opportunities to evaluate a student's ability to communicate easily with strangers and acquaintances, to interact effectively with peers and adults, and to select appropriate social behavior according to a specific situation or social context.

The larger community of work and vocational education experiences provides an excellent backdrop for assessment of social skills. In the work setting, students with visual impairments must initiate more sophisticated levels of social competence. The understanding of appropriate work-related behavior requires maturity, knowledge, and training. The ongoing assessment process affords the teacher varied opportunities to observe communication skills, social interactions with colleagues, interactions with supervisors, levels of assertive behavior, and a range of work-related behaviors (punctuality, following directions, time management, and level of productivity, for example). Ultimately, the community and work settings are where a repertoire of social skills must be combined in a sophisticated manner to achieve successful outcomes. Ongoing assessment in this area is critical and needs to examine the following questions:

- Does the student communicate in an easy and assertive manner with friends, colleagues, and supervisors?

- Does the student interact with coworkers in a socially acceptable manner?

- Does the student understand the social culture of the work environment?

- Is the student's appearance and dress commensurate with that of coworkers or peers in the community?

Observation of the social skills of students with visual impairments in the natural environments of home, school, and the community provides teachers, families, and specialists with an abundance of information that, over time, will enable them to learn about the students' behavior. This assessment information will lead to informed choices about social skills intervention and curriculum for their students. By using the questions that have been discussed, either as an observation tool or an interview tool, teachers can target specific skills or activities to be enhanced through intervention.

# ASSESSMENT TOOLS AND TECHNIQUES

## SOCIAL SKILLS ASSESSMENT CHECKLISTS

Assessment checklists provide a structured way for teachers and others involved in the social skills assessment process to evaluate a student's level of social competence. Checklists can help to streamline the observation process by listing behaviors or skills. For example, instead of asking questions about friendship, a checklist might include behaviors related to friendship such as sharing toys, complimenting others, and demonstrating reciprocal play. Although there are many commercially available social skills checklists, teachers may choose to create a checklist based on the educational setting or environmental contexts of the student. Many of the questions provided in the previous section could be organized into a checklist specific to the age or abilities of the student. For example, a checklist for a preschool student might include very basic behaviors, like interacting with others or waiting for a turn, while a checklist for an adolescent in an academic environment might examine the student's ability to monitor social situations or interpret nonverbal social behavior. The checklist allows the teacher of students with visual impairments, the general education classroom teacher, other specialists, and family members opportunities to observe the presence or absence of specific social behaviors or skills. Other checklists allow the evaluator to rank a student's social performance. For example, the Social Skills Assessment Tool for Children with Visual Impairments (SSAT-VI; McCallum & Sacks, 1994; Wolffe & Sacks, 2000), shown in Figure 9.1, allows the evaluator to observe specific behaviors and rank them on a scale from 1 (= absent) to 6 (= excellent). This evaluation tool was designed so that teachers and other service personnel could collect ongoing social skills assessment data.

Another useful social skills assessment checklist can be found in the Texas School for the Blind *Independent Living* curriculum (Loumiet & Levack, 1991), a sample of which is shown in Figure 9.2. This Social Competence Assessment has scales for Interaction with Family, Peers, and Others; Self-Concept; Recognition and Expression of Emotions; Nonverbal Communication; Values Clarification; Personal and Social Aspects of Sexuality; Physical Aspects of Sexuality; Courteous Behavior; Problem Solving, Decision Making, and Planning; Scholastic Success; and Personal and Civic Responsibility. This checklist allows the evaluator to tie the assessment directly to the student's Individualized Education Program (IEP). The evaluator indicates the IEP school year at the

## Figure 9.1

SOCIAL SKILLS ASSESSMENT TOOL FOR CHILDREN
WITH VISUAL IMPAIRMENTS
(SSAT—VI)

Student: _____ Assessor: _____ Date: _____
Rate each item as: 1 = absent; 2 = poor; 3 = fair; 4 = adequate;
5 = good; 6 = excellent

### Basic Social Behaviors

#### A. Body Language

1.___ Maintain appropriate eye contact.
2.___ Demonstrate appropriate body posture.
3.___ Maintain appropriate personal body space.
4.___ Utilize and respond to gestures and facial expressions.
5.___ Refrain from engaging in socially unacceptable mannerisms.

#### B. Communication Skills

1.___ Positively initiate interactions with others.
2.___ Exhibit age-appropriate interactions and conversations.
3.___ Expand conversations.
4.___ Listen well.
5.___ Take turns and share.
6.___ Compliment.
7.___ Interrupt appropriately.
8.___ Demonstrate empathy and sympathy.
9.___ Respond appropriately to positive and negative feedback from peers
and adults.

#### C. Cooperative Skills

1.___ Demonstrate cooperation and understanding of group dynamics.
2.___ Demonstrate respect for group leader.
3.___ Sustain group involvement.
4.___ Share in group activity.
5.___ Initiate joining a group.
6.___ Lead group activity.

### Interpersonal Relationships

#### A. Interactions

1.___ Interact appropriately with others: ___ adult ___ disabled peer ___
non-disabled peer ___ younger children ___ older children. *Comment
on type and style of interaction:*

*(continued)*

Adapted with permission from B. J. McCAllum & S. Sacks (Eds.), *Santa Clara County Social Skills
Curriculum for Children with Visual Impairments* (Santa Clara, CA: Score Regionalization Project, 1994).

**Figure 9.1** *(continued)*

2.___ Play with others: ___ one ___ small group ___ larger group.
*Comment on quality of play:*

3.___ Demonstrate ability to engage in a variety of play activities.
4.___ Can compromise.
5.___ Show awareness of common activities and interests.
6.___ Encourage the efforts of others.
7.___ Demonstrate gratitude toward others.

B. Sustaining Relationships

1.___ Demonstrate an understanding of differences between family, friends, acquaintances, and strangers.
2.___ Develop friends and be liked by peers.
3.___ Demonstrate appropriate behaviors for attending social events.
4.___ Interact with peers outside of school.
5.___ Understand the needs of others.
6.___ Demonstrate an age-appropriate awareness of human sexuality, including concepts of public vs. private, and societal values and attitudes.
7.___ Demonstrate an age-appropriate awareness of job related concepts, including assuming responsibility and relating to others in work situations.

Cognitive Social Behaviors

A. Self-Identity

1.___ Demonstrate understanding of visual impairment.
2.___ Demonstrate awareness of personal competencies and limitations.
3.___ Demonstrate awareness of possible adaptations.
4.___ Advocate for self in school, home, and community environments.
5.___ Demonstrate assertiveness in appropriate manner.

B. Interpreting Social Situations

1.___ Observe and identify opportunities for social interactions.
2.___ Interpret social cues and generate strategies for interaction.
3.___ Anticipate consequences of strategies and select most desired.

C. Performance of Social Skills

1.___ Initiate and perform appropriate behaviors.
2.___ Generalize social skills to a variety of situations.
3.___ Sustain social competency over time.

D. Self-Evaluation

1.___ Demonstrate ability to evaluate and monitor own social performance realistically.
2.___ Demonstrate ability to adjust own behavior accordingly.

# Figure 9.2

## SOCIAL COMPETENCE ASSESSMENT

*Interaction with Family, Peers, and Others*

| Age (Years) | Skills | IEP School Year | Competence | Generalized Use |
|---|---|---|---|---|
| 0–1 | 1 Respond to an adult's attempt to interact.* | | | |
| | 2 Initiate interactions with an adult.* | | | |
| | 3 Demonstrate the ability to differentiate between familiar people and strangers.* | | | |
| | 4 Respond to the presence of a peer.* | | | |
| | 5 Accept a substitute activity that replaces a socially unacceptable mannerism. | | | |
| 2–3 | 6 Demonstrate understanding of approval and disapproval of adults.* | | | |
| | 7 Address parents or other familiar adults by name.* | | | |
| | 8 Associate particular adults with routine activities.* | | | |
| | 9 Engage in same activity as a peer.* | | | |
| | 10 Comply with simple directions and limits from adults.* | | | |
| | 11 Interact with peers or siblings.* | | | |
| | 12 Address siblings by name.* | | | |
| 4–7 | 13 Interact with blind, low vision, and sighted peers in common situations.* | | | |
| | 14 Identify the person in charge in various situations.* | | | |
| | 15 Identify situations in which an adult should not be obeyed.* | | | |
| | 16 Initiate interactions with peers.* | | | |
| | 17 Share toys or other items with a peer.* | | | |
| | 18 Use a peer as a resource.* | | | |
| | 19 Indicate preferences in playmates.* | | | |
| | 20 Discuss the concept of friendship. | | | |
| | 21 Describe other people. | | | |
| | 22 Take turns.* | | | |
| | 23 Determine when it is not appropriate to share something, and communicate it in an assertive manner.* | | | |
| | 24 Identify the consequences of behaviors in social interactions.* | | | |
| | 25 Name family members, and discuss the relationship to each of them. | | | |
| | 26 Maintain contact with parents, guardians, and family members when separated for a long period of time.* | | | |

*(continued)*

Excerpted with permission from R. Loumiet & N. Levack, *Independent Living: A Curriculum with Adaptations for Students with Visual Impairments, Vol. 1: Social Competence* (Austin: Texas School for the Blind and Visually Impaired, 1992), pp. 210–214.

**Figure 9.2** (continued)

| Age (Years) | Skills | IEP School Year | Compe-tence | Genera-lized Use |
|---|---|---|---|---|
| | 27 Respond to humor, and use it in social situations. | | | |
| | 28 Recognize sarcasm, and respond in an effective manner. | | | |
| | 29 Interact with blind and low vision adults in a variety of situations.* | | | |
| | 30 Initiate, continue, develop, and conclude conversations.* | | | |
| | 31 Discuss the personal likes and dislikes of other people. | | | |
| | 32 Recognize behaviors that can cause social isolation and demonstrate alternative behaviors that promote social integration.* | | | |
| | 33 Demonstrate affection in socially acceptable ways, considering the person, place, and situation. | | | |
| | 34 Demonstrate the ability to resist peer pressure when resistance is necessary or desirable.* | | | |
| 8–11 | 35 Demonstrate skills for resolving conflicts with siblings and peers.* | | | |
| | 36 Deal with personal insults, ostracism, ridicule, or other mistreatment. | | | |
| | 37 Tolerate some unusual or unexpected behaviors from others.* | | | |
| | 38 Seek interactions with blind, low vision, and sighted peers and adults in a variety of situations.* | | | |
| | 39 Interact positively with friends.* | | | |
| | 40 Discuss some problems that might arise with family members or with friends, and suggest strategies that could be used to resolve them.* | | | |
| 12–15 | 41 Identify how different friends can meet different needs. | | | |
| | 42 Demonstrate various aspects of planning and carrying out social activities with friends.* | | | |
| | 43 Use assertive techniques in appropriate social situations.* | | | |
| | 44 Discuss the rights and responsibilities of an individual in a relationship.* | | | |
| | 45 Establish and maintain a variety of friendships. | | | |
| | 46 Work effectively in various groups that have a defined purpose or structure. | | | |
| 16–21 | 47 Discuss the concepts of role model(s) and/or mentor(s) for self. | | | |
| | 48 Discuss the concept of "networking, and demonstrate an understanding of its value. | | | |

**Figure 9.2** *(continued)*

*Self-Concept*

| Age (Years) | Skills | IEP School Year | Competence | Generalized Use |
|---|---|---|---|---|
| 0–1 | 1 Recognize and respond to name. | | | |
| | 2 Demonstrate interest in a mirror image.* | | | |
| | 3 State own first name.* | | | |
| | 4 Demonstrate a strong desire to perform tasks independently.* | | | |
| | 5 Demonstrate awareness that his behavior has an effect on | | | |
| 2–3 | 6 Indicate a preference.* | | | |
| | 7 Demonstrate recognition of own image in a picture or on a videotape, and/or demonstrate recognition of own voice on an audiotape.* | | | |
| | 8 Use personal pronouns *I, you,* and *me.** | | | |
| | 9 Use a variety of methods to get own way.* | | | |
| | 10 Demonstrate an awareness of himself as a separate person. | | | |
| | 11 Show pride in accomplishing tasks.* | | | |
| | 12 State own first name, last name, and age.* | | | |
| 4–7 | 13 Separate own possessions from those of others.* | | | |
| | 14 Name things that she can do now that she was unable to do at an earlier age, and name things that she will learn to do in the future.* | | | |
| | 15 State basic information about self.* | | | |
| | 16 State basic information about family members.* | | | |
| | 17 Indicate awareness of own visual and other physical abilities, and differences between his abilities and those of others.* | | | |
| 8–11 | 18 Discuss personal likes and dislikes.* | | | |
| | 19 Provide basic information as to own ethnic origin, religious preference, and family background.* | | | |
| 12–15 | 20 Evaluate own personality traits, and attempt to modify those that are not functional.* | | | |
| | 21 State own point of view on various specific topics. | | | |
| 16–21 | 22 State own social security number.* | | | |
| | 23 Obtain and use an identification card.* | | | |
| | 24 Show pride in personal achievements. | | | |
| | 25 Express realistic views of own capabilities and limitations.* | | | |
| | 26 Demonstrate confidence in own decisions, values, and beliefs.* | | | |

time of the assessment for each behavior. If the evaluator observes the behavior being used appropriately in at least one environment, then the box labeled "Competence" is checked. If the student uses the behavior effectively in several different environments, then the box labeled "Generalized Use" is checked. The asterisked items indicate skills that are considered essential. This tool, like the SSAT-VI can be used on an on-going basis as a formative assessment measure.

A number of formal social skills assessment checklists and rating scales are available, although they were designed to measure at-risk students' prosocial and antisocial behaviors with peers and teachers (Elksnin & Elksnin, 1995), they were not designed for students with visual impairments. However, they provide useful information about what general education teachers expect from their students in terms of social performance. When evaluating these checklists, it is also important to recognize that these measures have been standardized either for students who have no disabilities or for those who exhibit learning disabilities, behavior disorders, communication disorders, or cognitive disabilities. Accordingly, the results they yield regarding the social status of students with visual impairments need to be scrutinized carefully. Results on some items—for example "compliments others' attributes or accomplishments" (Merrell, 1992)—may be negatively affected by a student's inability to see or obtain information from others (Wolffe & Sacks, 2000).

In spite of their shortcomings, a number of the formal social skills assessment checklists can provide excellent information for the classroom teacher or the teacher of students with visual impairments. Three specific assessments that are widely used within school programs are described here. (For more information and examples of each assessment checklist, see Wolffe & Sacks, 2000, as well as Elksnin & Elksnin, 1995.)

The *School Social Behavior Scales* (SSBS; Merrell, 1992) includes a 32-item social competence scale and a 33-item antisocial behavior scale. Each scale has subtests that evaluate interpersonal skills, self-management skills, academic skills, antisocial-aggressive behavior, and disruptive-demanding behavior. The SSBS has strong reliability and validity. It is used widely with students in K–12 programs and with students who exhibit learning disabilities and behavior disorders.

The *Social Skills Rating System* (SSRS; Gresham & Elliot, 1990) purports to be the most comprehensive social competence assessment tool. The assessment is designed to evaluate a student's level of academic performance, problem behaviors, and social skills. The SSRS has separate scales for preschool, elementary, and secondary students. Ratings are obtained from parents and teachers, and the elementary and secondary scales encourage students to complete a self-evaluation.

Scores for students with learning disabilities, behavior disorders, and mental retardation have been standardized, and validity and reliability are good. Elliot and Gresham (1991) have compiled a manual describing how to use the assessment outcomes from the SSRS to plan interventions and effective training.

The *Walker-McConnell Scale of Social Competence and School Adjustment* (Walker & McConnell, 1995) is widely used in both general and special education programs. There are two versions, one for elementary school students (K–6) and one for use with secondary students (grades 7–12). The elementary version has three subscales: teacher-preferred social behaviors, peer-preferred social behaviors, and overall school adjustment. The secondary subscales include measures of self-control, peer relations, school adjustment, and empathy. The Walker-McConnell Scales have high reliability and good construct validity (Elksnin & Elksnin, 1995).

## INTERVIEWS

The interview is another useful tool in the social skills assessment process for students with visual impairments. By interviewing families and students, the teacher can learn a great deal about how students use and maintain their social skills across varied environments and situations. Through a structured interview with family members, the teacher can determine the family's priorities regarding the importance and need for teaching social skills and then collaborate with the family to determine what skills or strategies need to be taught. The teacher can also use the interview to evaluate the social dynamics within the home. For example, the teacher might observe that the student's parents are shy and retiring, helping the teacher gain understanding of why the student exhibits similar social behavior. The teacher might then consider working directly with the family and the student to help them understand the importance of using assertive behavior when interacting with others. Throughout the interview process, the teacher must be sensitive to the cultural and familial structure already established within the home.

The appendix to this chapter includes sample interview questionnaires for family members, students, and teachers (in the school observation forms). Interview questions for parents or other family members might include the following items:

- How do you view your child's social skills?
- What are some social behaviors that you think your child might need support to acquire or to improve?

- What activities is your child involved in at school, after school, and in the community?
- What does your child do for fun during free time or in structured activities?
- Who are your child's friends, and how did he or she develop those friendships?
- How would you rate your child's social skills, and what would you want to change?
- What do you discuss with your child about his or her visual impairment?
- How does your child feel about being visually impaired?

Interviews of students provide a way for them to share their thoughts about social skills and provide valuable information in a less structured manner than formal rating scales. The interviewer can provide structured questions or open-ended statements to prompt students' responses.

Examples of interview questions for students may include:

- Tell me what you do with friends on the playground. How do you know when friends want to play with you?
- How do you find your friends on the playground?
- What do you do for free time at home? What do you do with your family or your siblings on the weekends or in the evenings when there is no school?
- What do you tell your teachers and your classmates about your visual impairment?
- How do you let teachers and classmates know that you need help, or that they are giving too much assistance?
- What does it mean to be popular? Can you describe a person in your class who is popular?
- What characteristics do you have that make you likable?
- What characteristics do you have that others may dislike or find annoying?
- What do you like to do for fun by yourself, and with others?

By interviewing students and families, the teacher of students with visual impairments can clearly determine what activities can be initiated during social skills instruction to motivate and reinforce the student's acquisition of social skills.

## SITUATION ROLE PLAYS

Role-play scenarios allow the evaluator to assess typical social situations that the student may encounter during the school day or in after-school environments. Role plays serve two purposes: they can determine the student's strengths and weaknesses within specific social situations, and they can provide a means for evaluating the success of specific social skills training. Situation role plays allow the student with a visual impairment to observe how other classmates, who may be more socially competent, handle a specific social situation or utilize a specific social skill. Holding a group discussion or meeting individually with the teacher of students with visual impairments might help the student to learn new strategies to present him- or herself in a positive light.

Because role playing allows the student to take the role of another classmate or person, the student with visual impairments can experiment with other roles and learn more about the perceptions of others. The evaluator can facilitate situations in which the student with a visual impairment assumes the role of a bossy friend or a classmate who has been teasing the student. Allowing students to discuss their feelings when roles are reversed may elicit some positive outcomes. Even though the focus of the situation role play is for assessment purposes, similar strategies can be applied to direct instruction; the teacher can use a situation role play to help students practice turn taking or complimenting skills. (See Chapters 7, 11, and 12 for specific strategies.)

Situation role plays allow the evaluator to target specific skills for assessment. For example, the teacher or specialist may want to determine how often the student who is visually impaired uses appropriate gaze (eye contact) when interacting with peers. Authentic (real-life) scenarios also give evaluators an opportunity to analyze the student's verbal responses to peers to determine, for example, whether the student engages in age-appropriate conversation, responds with lengthy statements, and uses an engaging quality of voice. This form of authentic assessment can be ongoing, providing the instructor with a realistic assessment of the student's progress over time.

Examples of situation role-play scenarios may include the following:

• You are on the playground during lunch recess. One of your classmates comes up to you, takes your hand, and drags you to the climbing structure to play. You want to go to the swing area. What do you do?

- You are in your seventh-grade math class and your teacher uses the overhead projector to show math examples to the class. Your teacher uses phrases like, "First, you do this step, and then you do this step." You do not understand the concepts that are being introduced. How can you let the teacher know what you need to be successful in class? What do you do?

- You use a monocular in class to read the blackboard. Lately, students have been making comments about the monocular during class changes. How will you handle your classmates' comments? How will you deal with the situation?

- After school, you and a friend decide to walk to McDonald's for a snack. You are a student with low vision who does not appear to be visually impaired. When it is your turn, you ask the person behind the counter to read the menu to you. The server appears very confused and annoyed. What can you do to make the situation more successful?

- Instead of waiting your turn in the cafeteria line with the rest of your class, your teacher insists that you go to the head of the line. How do you handle this situation with your teacher and with your peers?

## PROBLEM-SOLVING SCENARIOS

In order to assess higher-order social skills, the student is asked to evaluate a specific situation, determine what social behaviors need to be used, initiate the social encounter, and evaluate the choices and decisions that were made regarding the social experience. Problem-solving scenarios allow the evaluator to determine if the student is able to combine the appropriate use of behaviors given a specific situation. At this level of socialization, the student must be able to interpret or decode a social situation, use effective behaviors and strategies, and objectively and realistically evaluate the outcomes.

Problem-solving scenarios provide a natural vehicle for authentic assessment of social skills. Each scenario should reflect situations in which the student must make choices and decisions regarding the use of a specific behavior or set of behaviors. For some students with visual impairments, this level of social skills assessment may be too complex. Being able to solve problems and analyze various social situations involves experiences with analytical thinking and perspective taking. When students are unable to capture visually the nuances of a specific situation, they may miss the nonverbal cues and gestures that influence how students may interact with one another. For example, a student with a visual impairment may misinterpret a teacher's actions as mean or angry because the student is interpreting only what is heard and cannot visually observe that the teacher is tired. A visually impaired student may interpret overtures by a classmate of the opposite sex as romantic interest, when in reality the classmate is simply being nice to him or her. Because visual cues help to interpret and clarify social situations, the student with a visual impairment may not have a realistic perspective about relationships.

Using problem-solving scenarios for assessment of social skills assists the teacher in determining if the student is able to interpret social situations correctly and apply a range of strategies to effectively handle a given social situation. The following are examples of scenarios that may be used to assess problem-solving abilities in students with visual impairments:

*You are on the playground with a group of peers and one of the kids hides your cane. What do you do?*

- If the student responds, "I would find a teacher or yard duty person to assist me. I would not get upset because the kids would just laugh," or "I would yell at them to give me back my cane," the teacher could help the student to think of a more effective way to handle the situation.

*You are at a school dance and you are standing in a group, but none of the students have introduced themselves to you. You don't recognize their voices, and it is dark so you can't determine anyone's exact identity. What do you do?*

- If the student responds, "I'll just continue talking and pretend like I know the students," the teacher could suggest other options or ask the student for other ideas.

- If the student responds, "I could just walk away and try to find someone familiar," the teacher might want to query the student about how others might respond to that action.

*You are in the lunch line in the cafeteria at school. Two students step in line in front of you. What do you do?*

- If the student responds, "I would push them out of line and tell them they were butting in," the teacher might ask the student, "What do you think will happen if you push those kids?"

- If the student responds, "I would tell my classmates that they are butting in line and need to go to the back of the line," the teacher could ask the student, "How do you think your classmates will feel about your approach?"

## STUDENT SELF-EVALUATION

Another form of social skills assessment is student self-evaluation. This process allows students to rate themselves on a series of criteria. For example, a student could be asked to listen to an audiotape of an interactive sequence between himself and a peer and evaluate his own social performance. Using a rating scale of 1 (low) to 5 (high), the student could evaluate his voice and tone quality, appropriateness of the conversation, and friendliness. Audiotaped social sequences provide an opportunity for students with visual impairments, particularly those who are functionally blind, to listen carefully to their own interactions and to learn to recognize when they sound passive, overly dominant, or appropriately assertive. Audio recordings can objectively assist students in evaluating the quality and content of their conversations with peers and adults. For example, students might want to determine whether their conversations with peers are interesting and focused or if the conversation topic is of interest only to the student who is blind or visually impaired.

Videotaping an actual social situation between two students so that the student who is visually impaired can evaluate his or her social performance is also an effective social skills assessment strategy. Students with low vision can particularly benefit from this form of evaluation. Often when students are engaged in social situations, they fail to recognize their strengths and limitations. By videotaping a social sequence, the student who is visually impaired can assess various components of the activity: the use of eye contact, the number of positive initiations, or the way in which turns are taken throughout the video sequence. Students can rate themselves using a numeric scale or they can provide verbal or written feedback describing their social abilities.

Students can also write or tape an autobiographical sketch, describing their feelings about themselves and others, including their positive attributes and weaknesses, as another form of self-evaluation. Younger children with low vision can draw pictures of themselves, their family, and their friends, and those without vision can use clay or other materials to create a representation of themselves or others. These art forms may well generate discussion between the student and the evaluator.

# INCLUDING THE FAMILY AND SIGNIFICANT OTHERS IN ASSESSMENT

Building partnerships with families is an essential ingredient in the education process for students with visual impairments. Families play a significant role in the assessment process, particularly in the area of social skills assessment. The Individuals with Disabilities Education Act (IDEA) requires that educators and parents work together in the planning and implementation of students' IEPs. Because assessment of social skills should be ongoing, it is important to nurture and develop partnerships with families. The following guidelines can help to ensure that this partnership is maintained during assessment.

- Identify parent concerns and priorities.
- Parent and caregiver input are invaluable both during the preparation period and the actual assessment process. It is important that family concerns and priorities be addressed in the program planning phases of IEP development.
- Parents and caregivers are the primary sources of information concerning the child's typical social behaviors outside of school. It is essential that teachers and specialists incorporate information from families in the assessment process. For example, some students may demonstrate more assertive behavior at home than in school.

Although much information about a student's history (medical, visual, developmental, and educational) can be obtained through school records, the primary and richest source of information about the student is the family. Through careful interview and discussion during the social skills assessment process, educators can learn about a family's values, cultural perspectives, and the student's developmental milestones, which are not always addressed in written information.

The assessment process can be daunting for parents and caregivers. Carefully preparing them by accurately describing the process, including the role of other specialists, can contribute to greater understanding and comfort with the process.

While social skills instruction is viewed as an essential part of the expanded core curriculum for students with visual impairments

(Hatlen, 1996), families may view this curricular area as less important than the general education core curriculum (academics). Consequently, it is often necessary for teachers of students with visual impairments to help to clarify the importance of social skills assessment and instruction for students throughout their educational careers.

## DEVELOPING RELATIONSHIPS WITH FAMILIES

It is important to develop relationships with families that will allay their concerns about in-home observations and encourage them to share information comfortably. This aspect of assessment requires a high level of sensitivity and interpersonal skills on the part of the educator. The process is started by inviting the family members to be the primary source of information and by asking them to suggest a time, activity, or routine in which to observe their child at home. Observation of a routine will provide many potential assessment topics for discussion. By letting parents take the lead in providing information and focusing on their desires and expectations for their child, teachers can make progress in building a working relationship with the family.

The case study presented in Sidebar 9.2 illustrates how families, teachers, and students work together in using social skills assessment to determine appropriate intervention strategies for students with visual impairments. It also demonstrates the use of some of the assessment tools discussed earlier and presented in the appendix to this chapter. Through ongoing evaluation of social skills, families, teachers, and students can target new social skills for intervention.

# DEVELOPING CULTURAL COMPETENCE WHEN BUILDING PARTNERSHIPS

An educator's job requires a high level of cultural competence, particularly when establishing partnerships with families. Cultural competence is defined as "the integration and transformation of knowledge about individuals and groups of people into specific standards, policies, practices, and attitudes used in appropriate cultural settings to increase the quality of services; thereby producing better outcomes" (Minnesota Public Health Association, 1996, p. 2). Being culturally competent means having the capacity to function effectively in multiple cultural contexts. Cultural competence has been shown to improve the accuracy of assessments and to yield more successful results (Minnesota Public

## CASE STUDY OF A SOCIAL SKILLS ASSESSMENT FOR A MIDDLE SCHOOL–AGED STUDENT WITH A VISUAL IMPAIRMENT

Jonathon, a 12-year-old student with albinism and mild cognitive delays, has relatively good use of his vision for reading with a magnifier and viewing distance with a monocular. He is entering the seventh grade at his neighborhood middle school, but his reading and math skills are at the fourth-grade level. He tends to be easily distracted and cannot follow directions consistently. Prior to the beginning of the school year, his teacher of students with visual impairments, Mrs. Marks, set up an appointment to meet with Jonathon and his family. Although Mrs. Marks knows Jonathon from the elementary resource room program, she wanted to discuss Jonathon's transition to middle school. In particular, Mrs. Marks wanted to talk about Jon's social behavior with peers.

At the end of the school year last spring and during summer school, Mrs. Marks observed Jonathon several times in his general education classroom, the resource room class, on the playground during recess, and at lunch in the cafeteria. During her observations she used the Guide for Observation of Social Skills at School, the Social Skills Assessment Tool for Students with Visual Impairments (SSAT-VI), and she interviewed Jonathon's classroom teacher and paraeducator.

When Mrs. Marks met with Jonathon and his parents, Mr. and Mrs. Berg, she began by asking the parents if they had concerns about Jon's transition to middle school. Jonathon's parents were both concerned about their son's level of independence, his ability to be assertive and let teachers know when he needed help, and his willingness to take responsibility for his belongings. Using the Guide for Observation of Social Skills in the Home, Mrs. Marks recognized that Jonathon had been given very few chores around the house. In fact, every time Jonathon wanted to do something independently, his mother would do it for him. Also, after interviewing Jon with the Social Skills Student Interview, Jon mentioned that he spent most of his time at school and at home alone. He also indicated that he would like to have more friends but acknowledged that when he interacted with schoolmates, he physically got too close to them and sometimes touched them to get their attention.

*(continued on next page)*

Sidebar 9.1 *(continued)*

Mrs. Marks realized that she needed to be sensitive to Jonathon's parents' perspectives about independence and responsibility. She began by describing the expectations for seventh-grade students. Mrs. Marks suggested that it was time for Jonathon to take responsibility for his actions and his school work. She also discussed Jonathon's desire to meet and develop friendships with peers. Together, Jonathon, his parents, and his teacher came up with specific social goals for the school year and a plan for carrying them out. They included:

1. Working on the concept of the "imaginary fence" (body space) and using words to express a desire to interact with others

2. Involving Jonathon in one after-school club or group throughout the school year

3. Providing opportunities for Jonathon to take responsibility, like keeping track of his school assignment and materials, or doing two new chores around the house.

The Bergs and Jonathon's teacher of students with visual impairments established a plan for implementing these goals. Mrs. Marks took responsibility for providing specific social skills instruction for Goal 1. She required that the Bergs provide her with feedback and assist in any homework assignments she gave to Jonathon. Mrs. Berg and Jonathon took responsibility for Goal 2. Mr. Berg developed a plan for teaching Jonathon to mow the lawn and water the vegetable garden to satisfy Goal 3. At the end of their conversation, Mrs. Marks mentioned that she would observe Jonathon in six months and interview him to determine whether the goals needed to be modified or changed.

Health Association, 1996). By taking the time to understand each family as a unique entity within their cultural framework and recognizing one's own cultural values, a more sensitive approach to the individual requirements of families can be established with greater success.

It is important to become knowledgeable about aspects of various cultures and be sensitive to how they might influence decision making about assessment and instruction of social skills. At the same time, it is important for educators not to make assumptions based on this knowledge. Whenever possible, it is important to clarify with family members what they see as important for their child and to allow for growth and change in these priorities over time. What may be viewed as a culturally based decision today may change as a parent or caregiver comes to understand the importance of specific assessment and instruction. How professionals are viewed by family members may influence open communication. If, for example, the educator is viewed by the family or caregiver primarily as the expert or the one who has power, changing this perspective requires the professional to be open and willing to include the family in the assessment of the student. Furthermore, it is important for professionals who teach social skills to students with visual impairments to evaluate their own cultural biases honestly and to reflect on how their feelings may affect interactions with families. All families and professionals bring to bear their own frames of reference, based on cultural values and socioeconomic status, when determining what will be assessed or taught. Consequently, how educators present information and invite dialogue is critical. It is important to avoid operating from assumptions that are culturally based, and to make decisions using valid information based on solid assessment and real partnerships.

## ENCOURAGING COLLABORATION AMONG TEACHERS AND SPECIALISTS

Social skills assessment and implementation is the domain of all teachers and specialists who work with students. Often it is the teacher of students with visual impairments who takes the lead in assessing social skills for students with visual impairments. However, it is only through close collaboration with family members, general education teachers, and related services specialists that thorough assessment and program planning can take place.

The classroom teacher can provide day-to-day observational information regarding a student's level of social competence in the classroom, on the playground, and in other school environments. The classroom teacher has the advantage of observing the student with a visual impairment in relation to his or her classmates. The classroom teacher can provide vital information about a student's typical social behavior and offer a balanced perspective for the team. The teacher of students with visual impairments has the flexibility to evaluate the student's level of social skills in many different environments throughout the student's daily routine. During classroom visits, for example, the teacher of students with visual impairments can discretely make observations when not providing direct service. The teacher of students with visual impairments can observe the student's level of social interactions in small-group activities, the level of participation and assertiveness during class discussions, and general classroom behavior (such as sitting in seat, raising a hand to speak, or turn taking). On the playground at recess, and in the cafeteria at lunch, the student's level of participation and involvement in activities can also be observed.

If a student is engaged in O&M instruction, there are additional opportunities for social skills assessment and instruction. In school and in the community, O&M instruction and practice provides a natural means to evaluate the use of appropriate interactive social behaviors, etiquette skills, assertive behaviors, and decision-making skills in familiar and unfamiliar environments.

Many students with visual impairments, particularly those with multiple disabilities, require services from a speech and language specialist. The speech and language specialist can provide valuable information regarding a student's ability to communicate and to use pragmatic skills to engage in social interactions with peers and adults. A speech and language specialist can provide considerable insight into the developmental influences relating to communication and how they affect the socialization process for students with visual impairments.

Collaboration with the school psychologist who has knowledge of the student's cognitive and educational abilities is also essential in the social skills assessment process. The school psychologist can offer information to the team regarding cognitive strengths and weaknesses that may affect the quality of the student's social interaction. The psychologist may also play a role in the assessment of the student's psychosocial adjustment to visual impairment. In some cases, the school psychologist may be aware of behavioral issues (such as depression, compulsive behavior, or anxiety disorders) that affect a student's social skills in various contexts.

The paraeducator or teaching assistant may play a valuable role in the social skills assessment process. In many cases, the paraeducator has the most sustained contact with the student and can offer day-to-day information about social interactions and the obstacles encountered by the student. The paraprofessional is often the member of the team who is most available to collect social skills assessment data. It is essential, however, that the teacher of students with visual impairments guide and carefully supervise the paraeducator and work together with him or her to create appropriate social skills interventions that meet the individual needs of the student.

# CONCLUSION

Social skills assessment for students with visual impairments is the foundation upon which meaningful instruction can be based. A systematic approach to social skills assessment allows the teacher of students with visual impairments, family members, and others involved in the educational team to provide consistent instruction. Ongoing assessment in this area of the expanded core curricular allows those working with students who are visually impaired to observe their growth over time.

The use of observation provides the basis for social skills assessment in numerous environments. The information acquired through observation can assist the teacher of students with visual impairments and other professionals in acquiring baseline information regarding a student's use of social skills and level of social competence on an ongoing basis. Observation allows teachers, family members, and other professionals to examine the strengths and limitations of each student with a visual impairment as an individual, without comparison to sighted age-mates or other students with visual impairments.

Social skills assessment checklists, situation role plays, problem-solving scenarios, interviews, and student self-evaluation, including audio and video analysis, help students, teachers, and family members to determine what specific social behaviors need to be targeted for intervention. These assessment methods enable teachers and others involved in the assessment process to target intervention strategies on three different levels: the awareness level (targeting specific social behaviors for instruction), the interactive level (combining sequences of social behaviors into meaningful actions), and the cognitive behavioral level (utilizing social rules and behaviors to determine specific strategies for socially competent interactions).

Partnerships with families and collaboration with professionals are keys to successful social skills assessment procedures. Working as a team to provide valuable information about social skills assessment and sharing results in an effective manner help to ensure that interventions will be initiated and implemented consistently. Collaborative efforts among those involved in the social skills assessment process and sensitivity to the individual needs of the student and the student's family can produce the strategies and interventions that successfully enhance social competence for students with visual impairments.

# REFERENCES

Coopersmith, S. (1967). *The antecedents of self-esteem.* San Francisco: W. H. Freeman.

Elksnin, L. K., & Elksnin, M. (1995). *Assessment and instruction of social skills* (2nd ed.). San Diego, CA: Singular Publications.

Elliott, S. N., & Gresham, F. M. (1991). *Social skills intervention guide: Practical strategies for social skills training.* Circle Pines, NM: American Guidance Service.

Fitts, W. H. (1967). *The self-concept as a variable in vocational rehabilitation.* Nashville, TN: Mental Health Center.

Gresham, F. M., & Elliott, S. N. (1990). *Social skills rating system.* Circle Pines, NM: American Guidance Service.

Hatlen, P. (1996). The core curriculum for blind and visually impaired students, including those with additional disabilities. *Re:View, 28,* 25–32.

Hill, E. W., & Blasch, B. B. (1980). Concept development. In R. L. Welsh & B. B. Blasch (Eds.), *Foundations of orientation and mobility* (pp. 265–290). New York: American Foundation for the Blind.

Kekelis, L. S., & Sacks, S. Z. (1992). The effects of visual impairment on children's social interactions in regular education programs. In S. Z. Sacks, R. J. Gaylord-Ross, & L. S. Kekelis (Eds.), *The development of social skills by blind and visually impaired students: Exploratory studies and strategies* (pp. 59–82). New York: American Foundation for the Blind.

Loumiet, R., & Levack, N. (1991). *Independent living: A curriculum with adaptations for students with visual impairments.* Austin, TX: Texas School for the Blind and Visually Impaired.

MacCuspie, P. A. (1996). *Promoting acceptance of children with disabilities: From isolation to inclusion.* Halifax, Nova Scotia, Canada: Atlantic Provinces Special Education Authority.

McCallum, B. J., & Sacks, S. Z. (Eds.). (1994). *Santa Clara County social skills curriculum for children with visual impairments.* Santa Clara, CA: SCORE Regionalization Project.

Merrell, K. W. (1992). *School social behavior scales.* Austin, TX: PRO-ED.

Minnesota Public Health Association, Immigrant Health Task Force. (1996, August). *Six steps toward cultural competence: How to meet the heath care needs of immigrants and refugees.* Minneapolis, MN: Refugee Health Program.

Rosenblum, L. P. (1998). Best friends of adolescents with visual impairments: A descriptive study. *Journal of Visual Impairment & Blindness, 92,* 593–608.

Skellenger, A.A.C., Hill, M. M., & Hill, E. (1992). The social functioning of children with visual impairments. In S. L. Odom, S. R. McConnell, & M. A. McEvoy (Eds.), *Social competence in children with disabilities: Issues and strategies for intervention* (pp. 165–188). Baltimore: Paul H. Brookes.

Tuttle, D. W., & Tuttle, N. (1996). *Self-esteem and adjusting with blindness* (2nd ed.). Springfield, IL: Charles C. Thomas.

Walker, H. M., & McConnell, S. (1995). *The Walker-McConnell Scales of Social Competence and School Adjustment.* Belmont, CA: Wadsworth.

Warren, D. H. (2000). Developmental perspectives: Youth. In B. Silverstone, M. A. Lang, B. P. Rosenthal, & E. L. Faye (Eds.), *The lighthouse handbook on visual impairment and vision rehabilitation, Vol. 1,* (pp. 325–338). New York: Oxford University Press.

Wolffe, K. E., & Sacks, S. Z. (2000). *Focused on: Assessment techniques.* New York: AFB Press.

Wolffe, K. E., Thomas, K. L., & Sacks, S. Z. (2000). *Focused on: Social skills for teens and young adults with visual impairments.* New York: AFB Press.

# 9

# Social Skills
# Assessment Forms

# GUIDE FOR OBSERVATION OF SOCIAL SKILLS IN THE HOME

## Parent Interaction

1. How does the parent engage the child in social interactions? Describe:

   _____

   _____

   _____

2. Do the parent and child play and engage in recreational activities together (e.g., board games, sports activities, music, recreational reading, pretend play)? Describe:

   _____

   _____

   _____

3. Do the parents have clear expectations for the student to perform daily routines and chores around the house, or do others wait on the student?

   _____

   _____

4. Are communication skills modeled for the student? If so, give an example:

   _____

   _____

5. Is the child given choices during daily routines, such as dressing and eating?

   _____

6. Is the child included in family activities? _____

7. Do the parents employ consequences for inappropriate social behavior that seem reasonable?

   _____

8. Are the expectations for social performance the same for the child who is visually impaired as for siblings who are sighted?

   _____

## Siblings and Friends

9. Do sighted siblings treat the sibling with a visual impairment in a natural manner (play, fight, take toys, get into mischief together), or is the sibling with a visual impairment babied or ignored?

   _____

10. Does the sighted sibling include the sibling with a visual impairment in games and activities or teach him or her to play games and try new activities?

    _____

11. Are other children invited to the home to play? _____

*(continued)*

GUIDE FOR OBSERVATION OF SOCIAL SKILLS IN THE HOME *(continued)*

12. (For younger children:) Are activities structured to encourage turn taking and social interactions?

_____

13. (For older children:) Is accurate feedback provided regarding appropriate and inappropriate social interactions with peers?

_____

14. Do the parents or caregivers provide opportunities for social interactions with peers who are visually impaired?

_____

_____

_____

# GUIDE FOR OBSERVATION OF SOCIAL SKILLS AT SCHOOL
## PRESCHOOL–ELEMENTARY SCHOOL

### Preschool

1. Does the child use language (verbal or nonverbal) to communicate interactive intent? Describe:

   _____

   _____

2. Does the child play alone or with other children? If with other children, is the activity facilitated by an adult or by other (older) children? Describe:

   _____

   _____

3. Does the child show interest in playing with toys? Describe:

   _____

   _____

4. Does the child engage in games or group activities? Describe:

   _____

   _____

5. Does the child make choices independently? Or with adult facilitation?

   _____

   Additional Concerns:

   _____

   _____

   _____

### Elementary School

*(If appropriate, questions at the preschool level can also be used.)*

1. Does the student participate in class discussion? _____

2. Does the student talk with other students? Easily and reciprocally?

   _____

3. Does the student move about the classroom independently? _____

4. Does the student locate materials without support? _____

5. Does the child willingly share information and materials with other students? _____

6. Can the child make decisions independently? _____

7. Can the student ask for assistance when needed? _____

8. Can the student let students know when assistance is not needed? _____

*(continued)*

## GUIDE FOR OBSERVATION OF SOCIAL SKILLS AT SCHOOL *(continued)*

9. Does the student actively participate in group work or projects? _____

10. How much time over the course of the day does the student spend interacting with other students compared to other interactions with adults?

_____

Additional Concerns:

_____
_____
_____

### During Recess

11. Does the student interact and play easily with peers? _____

12. Does the student participate in games or activities on the playground?

_____

13. Does the student know how to engage in age-appropriate games and activities at recess?

_____

14. Does the student have a repertoire of conversation topics that facilitate social interactions with peers? _____

Additional Concerns:

_____
_____
_____

## GUIDE FOR OBSERVATION OF SOCIAL SKILLS AT SCHOOL
## MIDDLE SCHOOL–HIGH SCHOOL

*(Some questions for the elementary school level may still be appropriate for students at this level.)*

1. Does the student have friends? _____

2. Does the student interact with others during class time? _____

3. Does the student interact with others during breaks? _____

4. Does the student interact with others during lunch? _____

5. Does the student respond appropriately to questions from others? _____

6. Does the student's dress and appearance promote social interactions with peers? _____

7. Does the student participate in school clubs, music, or athletic activities? List: _____

8. Does the student participate in any after-school activities sponsored by a religious organization or service club?
   _____

9. Does the student have a job, either volunteer or paid? _____

10. Does the student demonstrate the skills to travel independently to after-school activities, using public transportation if necessary? _____

11. Does the student's family encourage independent travel and involvement in school and after-school activities? _____

12. Does the family provide transportation to social activities when public transportation is unavailable? _____

### Mentors and Friends Who Are Visually Impaired

13. Does the student have a network of friends who are visually impaired?
    _____

14. Does the student interact with students who are visually impaired on a regular basis? _____

15. Does the student have opportunities to connect with age-mates who have similar visual impairments? _____

16. Does the student have opportunities to meet and interact with a mentor who is visually impaired? _____

17. If the student with a visual impairment does not have friends who are visually impaired, what are the reasons or causes? _____

*(continued)*

## GUIDE FOR OBSERVATION OF SOCIAL SKILLS AT SCHOOL *(continued)*

### In the Community and on the Job

18. Does the student communicate in an easy and assertive manner with friends, colleagues, and supervisors? _____

19. Does the student interact with coworkers in a socially acceptable manner? _____

20. Does the student understand the social culture of the work environment?
_____

21. Is the student's appearance and dress commensurate with that of coworkers or peers in the community?
_____
_____

_____

## SOCIAL SKILLS FAMILY INTERVIEW

1. How do you view your child's social skills?

   _____

   _____

2. What are some social behaviors that you think your child might need support to acquire or to improve?

   _____

   _____

3. What activities is your child involved in at school, after school, and in the community?

   _____

   _____

4. What does your child do for fun during free time or in structured activities?

   _____

   _____

5. Who are your child's friends and how did he or she develop those friendships?

   _____

   _____

6. What do you discuss with your child about his or her visual impairment?

   _____

   _____

7. How does your child feel about being visually impaired?

   _____

   _____

## SOCIAL SKILLS STUDENT INTERVIEW

1. Tell me what you do with friends on the playground. How do you know when friends want to play with you?

   _____

   _____

2. How do you find your friends on the playground?

   _____

   _____

3. What do you do in your free time at home? What do you do with your family or your siblings on the weekends or in the evenings when there is no school?

   _____

   _____

4. What do you tell your teachers and your classmates about your visual impairment?

   _____

   _____

5. How do you let teachers and classmates know that you need help or that they are giving too much assistance?

   _____

   _____

6. What does it mean to be popular? Can you describe a person in your class who is popular?

   _____

   _____

7. What characteristics do you have that make you likable by others?

   _____

   _____

8. What characteristics do you have that others may dislike or find annoying?

   _____

   _____

9. What do you like to do for fun when you are by yourself?

   _____

   _____

10. What do you like to do for fun when you are with others?

    _____

    _____

11. What aspect of social skills would you most like to work on?

    _____

    _____

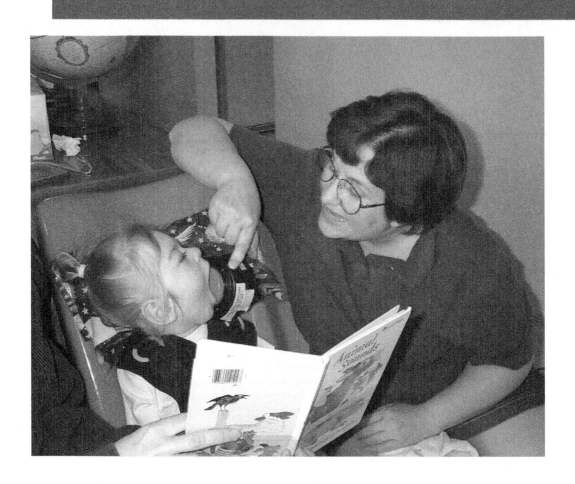

# PART IV

# Intervention
# and Practice

Given the importance of social competence to individual well-being and the need to help visually impaired children learn how to be socially competent, how can social skills be taught? Direct instruction of social skills is essential to the child who is visually impaired and needs to be actively undertaken by both teachers and parents. The chapters in Part 4 offer a compendium of techniques and strategies for helping youngsters of various ages—from young children through elementary and middle school–aged students to adolescents and young adults—including those with additional disabilities, formulate and refine social skills.

This final section provides practical strategies for parents and professionals who are preparing children and youths with visual impairments to succeed in life. In a sense, the preceding sections of this book have been leading up to this culminating collection of techniques for teaching social skills. The emphasis here is on instructional tools that will enhance social skills development, with examples and strategies complementing the body of text. The objective is for parents, caregivers, and professionals to be able to implement a plan of action to remediate or enhance the social skills of the visually impaired children under their care.

Chapter 10 introduces strategies for teaching young children and their families so that family members can provide support for the development of social skills in the home environment. Sacks uses a field study of a preschool child who is blind as a springboard for discussing the factors that affect peer relationships and the importance of supportive family relationships. She also describes the need to establish realistic expectations for appropriate social behavior, encourage early decision-making and risk-taking behavior, and provide consistent feedback to the child about the use of specific social skills.

In Chapter 11, Erin discusses how important it is for students to learn to solve social dilemmas independently, but also explains how professionals and families can support the students' efforts. The strategies offered in this chapter are addressed separately to elementary and middle school students. They include methods for helping youngsters with communication skills, such as assertiveness and how to talk about their vision loss; participating actively in rituals and routines; establishing and maintaining friendships; and a host of other age-appropriate behaviors.

Chapter 12 also deals with age-specific content, focusing on secondary and postsecondary students. Wolffe addresses ways of building relationships, social integration, and self-concept and self-esteem, with an overview of pertinent research and practical suggestions based on the research discussed. She also presents information specific to three themes of particular concern with this age group: understanding how one looks in comparison to others and maintaining an attractive personal appearance; coping with the inability to drive and getting around with the transportation options available to nondrivers; and learning to flirt and date in hope of developing positive, intimate relationships. The strategies presented in this chapter offer specific intervention techniques for this age group.

In the final chapter, the focus is on young people of all ages who have visual impairments and additional disabilities. Wolffe and Silberman present a classification system that looks specifically at the individual student's need for intervention and explain how to determine the appropriate techniques for students based on this system. The authors offer additional information about students' learning styles to help instructional personnel and families maximize students' efforts and make lessons more meaningful. They also discuss social relationships and communication strategies for students with different secondary or tertiary disabilities in various school settings. Specific strategies and instructional techniques are suggested for students who have hearing, physical, or cognitive impairments in addition to visual impairments.

With the presentation of specific techniques to remediate or enhance the social skills of different groups of students, Part 4 completes the process that began with exposure to the personal perspectives shared in Part 1. This journey, from the importance and need for social skills in the lives of young people with visual impairments, to the theoretical underpinnings that support intervention for social skills development, and ending with the strategies that support the interventions, will help parents and professionals apply theory to practice in the development of social skills for their children and students.

# CHAPTER 10

# Teaching Social Skills to Young Children with Visual Impairments

Sharon Z. Sacks

Throughout this book, the authors have shown how vision loss influences all aspects of development, particularly the acquisition of social skills, for children who are blind and visually impaired. As discussed in Chapter 3, factors such as the child's temperament and motivation, family acceptance and support, the presence of additional disabilities, and the quantity and quality of early experiences can influence a child's ability to learn and maintain a repertoire of socially competent behaviors. Building on that foundation, this chapter provides readers with a framework for intervention strategies to use with young children with visual impairments and their families.

Early exposure to peers is particularly important for young children with visual impairments. Often, infants and babies with visual impairments are not provided with opportunities to engage with other children because of their health status, parents' degree of understanding and acceptance of their child's visual impairment, and caregivers' knowledge of how to engage effectively with the child to increase his or her social abilities. Although it is important for educators and others who work closely with young children who are blind or visually impaired to provide social experiences with other young children, both blind and sighted, it is also important to recognize that a child's level of social competence is specific to a given situation; that is, the influence of social setting, activities, materials, and other young children can affect a child's ability to interact effectively with others. The significance of the role of the family in the early social development of children with visual impairments cannot be overemphasized. However, the influence of peer interaction and support is also important. Through peer interaction, children learn to gain entry into groups, attract and direct the attention of others, resolve conflict, and engage in play. Corsaro (1985) describes interaction with family members and with peers when he asserts:

> Within the family, children have relatively little opportunity for negotiation; they must recognize, accept, and adapt to their relationships with parents and siblings. . . . Through interaction with peers, children learn that they can regulate social bonds on the basis of criteria that emerge from their personal needs and social contextual demands. They also learn that their peers will not always accept them immediately; often a child must convince others of his merits as a playmate, and sometimes he must anticipate and accept exclusion. [p. 121]

## LAYING THE GROUNDWORK

Strategies to enhance the socialization process for infants, toddlers, and preschool-age children with visual impairments are especially important because positive experiences with peers lay the groundwork for lasting relationships with others throughout a child's school career and beyond, into adult life. Case studies and descriptions of how young children with visual impairments interact with their classmates are limited. There are few studies that closely document the social interaction of young children who are blind or visually impaired. However, Kekelis (1992a) undertook a field study of a preschool blind child for three reasons: to identify the factors that affect peer relationships; to generate hypotheses for future studies that examine the socialization of students with visual impairments; and to establish a set of guidelines that practitioners can use to promote positive social interaction between children who are blind and sighted children.

The information contained in Kekelis's study has as much value for practitioners today as it did in 1992. Even though the child described in the study is Caucasian and from a middle-class family, the issues related to the acquisition of social skills more than likely would be similar for students from other cultures or ethnic backgrounds. The conclusions that can be drawn from this ethnographic (observational) study support the importance of early social skills interventions. Not only does the case study provide a variety of perspectives regarding Ashley's socialization, it also offers a comprehensive examination of both school and home social experiences of a young child with visual impairment. Throughout the case study, which is reprinted in its entirely in the appendix to this chapter, the following themes are explored, providing insight for teachers and families:

- the influence of classroom environment and physical arrangements within the classroom
- introducing appropriate activities within the classroom that affect socialization and interactions between peers
- training of classroom personnel (regular education teachers and paraprofessionals) to emphasize opportunities to maximize social interactions between students who are visually impaired and their classmates
- providing peers with information about the student who is blind or visually impaired to promote independence and friendships
- the importance of family involvement in the school program.
- providing the student who is blind or visually impaired with strategies and modeling of appropriate language and social behavior

The guidelines supplied at the end of the case study give practical suggestions to assist practitioners in promoting positive interactions between students who are visually impaired and their sighted agemates. The strategies used to engage Ashley in social experiences and the barriers she encountered with peers are particularly noteworthy. It is also important to evaluate how the adults (teachers, classroom assistants, and family members) reacted to Ashley's social behavior in each school environment.

# STRATEGIES TO ENHANCE SOCIALIZATION

Ashley's case study supports the notion that the acquisition of social skills for young children with visual impairments is a multifaceted endeavor involving parents and caregivers, teachers, and peers. Effective strategies that can be used to enhance positive social interactions and peer acceptance are necessary for the successful acquisition and integration of such skills. The following sections address specific interventions that facilitate play and socialization in parent-child interactions, peer interactions, and teacher-directed interventions.

## PARENT-CHILD INTERACTIONS

Parents and caregivers are the first teachers of social skills. Through physical modeling, verbal feedback, tactile cues, and exploration of the environment, family members can facilitate early social interaction. Parents and caregivers must recognize that the way in which young children who are blind or visually impaired develop interactive behaviors may be different from the development of their sighted counterparts. Their ability to develop reciprocal relationships with others may be hampered by their lack of vision. Smiling behavior, for example, may not occur naturally. Parents may need to provide a tactile stimulus (such as rubbing the cheek or gentle tickling) to elicit a smile or laughter.

Consistent verbal cues to indicate changes in the environment or the child's routine can also support parent-child interaction. When young children with visual impairments are able to anticipate change, reciprocal interactions occur with greater success. Parents can pair a verbal and a tactile cue to prepare the child for an unfamiliar or different activity. For example, if taking a walk to the park is a new or unfamiliar activity, the parent may want to inform the child that they are going to the park and suggest that the child feel his or her jacket as an anticipatory cue.

Facilitating interactive play between a young child with a visual impairment and the family or caregiver is a stepping-stone for successful peer interactions. Parents and caregivers need to observe how the child relates to toys and games in the environment and modify the activities according to the child's disposition. For example, if the child reacts negatively to toys that make loud sounds or to soft, cuddly objects by pushing away or clenching fists, then the parent or caregiver may want to present alternative toys or games that elicit positive responses from the child. The following strategies may assist families and caregivers in designing activities that promote socialization and interactive play for young children who are blind or visually impaired.

## STRATEGIES FOR SOCIAL SUCCESS
# Interactive Play

- ◆ Determine activities that are pleasing to the parent or caregiver and that provide interactive responses from the young child. For example, verbal games paired with touch or verbal cues promote social interaction. The parent might recite, "Clap the feet, eat the toes, tickle the tummy, and beep the nose" while performing each action, providing opportunities for reciprocal interactions.

- ◆ Observe the temperament of the young child to determine how activities and play should be initiated. Some children respond to quiet and slow interaction, while other young children enjoy more physical contact and roughhousing.

- ◆ Use sound cues or tactile cues to introduce a new activity. For example, when it is time to change the baby, parents may verbally let the child know it is "time for a diaper change," and pair this verbal cue with the tactile cue of touching the baby with a piece of the diaper. Many young children with visual impairments require additional time to make the transition from one activity to the next, especially when numerous people are interacting with the child.

- ◆ Have parents, caregivers, siblings, and other family members identify themselves when they enter or leave a play situation.

- ◆ Introduce the child to a variety of play activities and environments, such as water play in the bathtub, pretend play with pots and pans in the kitchen, and playing on the swings and slides in the backyard or park.

- ◆ Structure play activities that facilitate exploration. Organize the area so that toys and objects are easily accessible to the child. For example, in the kitchen designate a cabinet that has pots, pans, containers, lids, and utensils that the young child who is blind or visually impaired can explore safely.

- ◆ Organize the play environment so that the young child can become independent in accessing toys and objects. Place similar toys in bins or storage units that allow the child to find them easily.

◆ Provide play activities in natural environments—such as the park, the backyard, and the playground—and promote activities using real objects. For example, if a young child who is blind is pretending to use the telephone, have the child use a real telephone, and model a typical telephone conversation with the child.

◆ Include the child in all family activities (such as meals, outings, and shopping trips), and describe the activities that are taking place. If the child has useful vision, encourage the child to look and visually explore the environment while verbally describing the environment and actions that are taking place. For example, when driving to a familiar destination like the grocery store, point out landmarks (McDonald's or the gas station) and describe the scenery.

◆ Encourage the young child to make independent choices and decisions. Provide positive reinforcement ("Great idea!" or "I like that too!") when such a choice is made.

◆ Encourage the child to respond to social initiations from others through verbal and physical modeling. For example, when a grandparent comes to visit, the parent may want to facilitate positive social communication between the grandparent and the child by verbally framing the situation: "Oh, here's Grandpa. Let's say hello, and give him a hug."

◆ Reinforce and model the use of socially appropriate behavior and manners in environments with peers and adults. For example, when the young child with a visual impairment reaches and shares a toy with another child, verbally praise the child by stating what action was observed, "Oh, I liked the way you shared the truck with Billy. You are a good friend," or "I liked the way you smiled when daddy gave you a cookie. You have nice manners."

## Peer Interactions

Kekelis's case study illustrates the influence of peer interaction on the acquisition of social skills for young children with visual impairments. Play groups and the preschool experience provide opportunities for young children to expand their repertoire of social skills with age-mates beyond the home or child care setting. Through play and developmentally appropriate activities, young children learn the give and take of social interactions. They learn to share toys, take turns, and integrate the unspoken rules of the peer culture. For example, young children who are successful in social situations learn early on that grabbing a toy from another child without asking is unacceptable social behavior. In order for young children with visual impairments to become socially interactive with peers, mediation from adults and greater structure within the play environment may be required.

Toys and materials used to facilitate socialization between blind and sighted young children must be engaging for both groups. Often, real objects (actual utensils, pots and pans, clothing for dress-up, packing boxes, or plastic containers) make excellent toys because they allow children to make play more functional and realistic.

Sometimes young children with visual impairments require mediation, that is, support in the play environment to maximize social interactions with peers. For example, in the case study cited in Appendix 10, one of the children wanted to play on the tires and outdoor play structure with Ashley. Instead of the paraeducator stepping in and showing Ashley what to do, she, along with the classroom teacher, encouraged the peer to show Ashley by modeling a phrase or action: "The tires are here." It is important for the adult who is facilitating social exchanges between children not to become part of the interaction. Those involved in facilitating social interactions between young children with visual impairments and their sighted age-mates must engage the sighted children in describing and mediating the play situation. Providing prompts such as, "Tell Carrie what you're doing with the doll," or "Show Carrie how you wheel the dolly in the stroller," can help to promote more naturalistic interaction. The following strategies may help to encourage positive social interactions between peers.

## STRATEGIES TO PROMOTE SOCIAL SUCCESS

# Peer Interaction

- ◆ Provide sighted children, even preschool-age students, with information about their classmate's visual impairment. Even if the information is rudimentary and simplistic, children are curious and want information about what the student with a visual impairment can see and do in a typical play situation. For example, the teacher of students with visual impairments may tell students the name of the child's visual impairment, or the teacher may say, "Susan can't see as well as you. She can see the sandbox and the swings, but she may not be able to see your face."

- ◆ Provide sighted peers with training to interact most effectively with their visually impaired age-mates. For example, model ways to physically guide the child with a visual impairment through an un-familiar play area. Model appropriate use of language to describe actions within a pretend play situation, for example, "Here come the cars, they're going to crash, bang, boom."

◆ Encourage sighted children to ask questions regarding their peer's visual impairment. Provide honest and useful feedback to promote social interactions.

◆ Encourage young children who are blind or visually impaired to advocate for themselves in social situations. Help the child to prac-tice ways to engage positively with age-mates by using positive social initiators such as, "Want to play with my truck?" or "I go after you."

◆ Encourage play activities that can take place on tables or on the tray of a wheelchair so that the play space is confined and easy to manage (Fazzi, 2002).

◆ Facilitate play on the school playground between young children with visual impairments and their sighted peers by providing toys and materials that promote positive interactions (for example, Matchbox cars, Legos, building blocks, or crayons and other art materials).

◆ Encourage imaginative play that involves a small group of students. Encourage the child with a visual impairment to invite children to play and engage in a game or a free-play activity. Provide props to assist in imaginative play and facilitate social interactions. For ex-ample, designate a dress-up area or a block area where children can create castles and pretend they are kings and queens.

◆ Orient the child with a visual impairment to the environments in which play and social interactions will take place. Demonstrate the use of play equipment, and encourage the child with a visual im-pairment to learn how to use play equipment and toys in multiple environments (Fazzi, 2002).

## TEACHER SUPPORT IN PROMOTING SOCIAL COMPETENCE

In Kekelis's case study, teachers played an integral role in promoting and facilitating positive social experiences for Ashley. They worked with Ashley's family to ensure effective carryover of skills from school to home. When specific social skills interventions are being considered, it is essential that teachers and families work in partnership to determine which skills will be taught. Consistency is critical in teaching social skills, especially to young children with visual impairments, and requires cooperation and collaboration between home and school. When there is a breakdown in communication between teachers and the family, or between the school's teaching staff and the teacher of students with visual impairments, it lessens the likelihood that positive social experiences will emerge. When skills are targeted for intervention, they must be clearly defined and understood by all of the members of the instructional team, doable and easily initiated, and implemented by all those involved in the child's educational program with consistency and a willingness to pursue the intervention to its completion.

The teacher of students with visual impairments plays an especially important role in ensuring that the social skills strategies that are targeted for intervention are carried out in an appropriate manner. The teacher of students with visual impairments can assist the general education preschool teacher in promoting social interactions between the child with visual impairments and his or her classmates by modeling appropriate language to help the child who is blind understand the play activity. For example, if students who are sighted say, "You hit the ball this way," the visually impaired child has no understanding of the process. However, the teacher could model appropriate language by saying, "When you hit the tether ball hard, it will wrap around this pole because it is attached to a long rope." Also, the teacher of students with visual impairments can provide information to the preschool staff regarding the nature and function of the child's visual impairment and offer suggestions about particular toys, games, and activities that will help to include the child who is visually impaired in age-appropriate social activities in the classroom and on the playground.

The following suggestions can help preschool teachers, along with the teacher of students with visual impairments, to facilitate social growth and encourage positive social experiences for the young child who is blind or visually impaired.

## STRATEGIES FOR SOCIAL SUCCESS

# Suggestions for Preschool Teachers

◆ Provide clear and consistent expectations for the child's behavior in the classroom and in other school environments. The same set of rules and expectations must be established for the young child who is visually impaired and for students without disabilities. For example, if a child who is blind is not disciplined for blurting out an answer without raising his or her hand, and a sighted child in the class is reprimanded for a similar action, the visually impaired child quickly learns that there are separate expectations for appropriate social behavior.

◆ Establish a consistent routine for classroom activities so that the child with a visual impairment can anticipate what will come next. This strategy will help the student to become more independent and allow for greater autonomy across activities.

◆ Encourage the child to make choices regarding play activities and social experiences with peers in the classroom. For example, let the child who is blind or visually impaired choose a lunch buddy or a playground buddy instead of assigning a peer to the child.

◆ Create specific activity centers in the classroom to help the student who is blind or visually impaired move independently from one activity to the next with greater independence. Activity centers could include a listening center, a dress-up area, a computer game center, a block-building area, and an area for messy play such as finger painting or modeling clay.

◆ Provide carpet squares or individual seats during group activities such as circle time to help the child who is visually impaired understand the concept of appropriate social distance and personal space.

◆ Encourage the child who is blind or visually impaired to use appropriate social gestures paired with verbal responses. For example, when a preschool child expresses anger toward another child, assist the child in using appropriate words and facial expressions that match the verbal response. Sometimes children who are blind or visually impaired will smile rather than frown if they are angry or unhappy.

◆ Allow extra time to show the young child with a visual impairment any new activities that are introduced in the preschool classroom. Show the child the materials that are used and the steps involved in completing the activity or game. Introduce the language used in the activity to facilitate interaction within the play environment. Sometimes the teacher will have to model the language and the actual play movements. For example, if there are new items in the playhouse (a toy iron or toaster), the teacher might have to demonstrate how these items are used and in what situations. He or she might use language like, "Oh, that iron is hot!" or "Pop, the toast is ready."

◆ Introduce new classroom games and activities to the child with a visual impairment prior to introducing them to the other students.

Allow the child time to learn and practice the activity before participating in the activity with peers.

◆ Encourage the use of real objects when young children are involved in pretend play and encourage sighted children to describe what actions are taking place in the activity. Initially, the teacher may need to model the language that can be used to describe the activity.

◆ Encourage young children who are blind or visually impaired to engage in risk-taking activities, such as riding bicycles and tricycles, climbing on jungle gyms and other play structures, and taking part in ball games, tumbling, and other sports activities.

◆ Ensure that the young child who is blind or visually impaired, just like his or her sighted classmates, is given responsibilities for jobs around the classroom (taking messages to the school office, watering plants, or being a line leader or ball monitor).

◆ Encourage the child to keep a clean and organized work or cubby space.

◆ Provide verbal and physical reinforcement and praise when the young child with a visual impairment shows initiative in engaging in social activities with peers, responsibility for completing classroom jobs and tasks, and appropriate social behaviors to engage with peers and adults. For example, when a young child who is blind establishes eye contact when speaking to a peer or teacher, the teacher of the visually impaired may reinforce the behavior by telling the child, "I liked the way you looked at Susie when playing in the dollhouse."

## CONCLUSION

The foundation for acquiring a repertoire of socially appropriate behaviors and social skills is established in infancy and during the preschool years. As illustrated in Kekelis's (1992) case study of Ashley, young children with visual impairments must be given an array of hands-on experiences to help them to learn and to negotiate their social worlds. It is critical that families and teachers, including the teacher of students with visual impairments and other related service personnel, work in tandem to create positive and meaningful social experiences throughout the early years. Establishing realistic expectations for appropriate social behavior, encouraging early decision-making and risk-taking behavior, and providing consistent feedback about the utilization of specific social skills can support the child who is blind or visually impaired in achieving self-confidence and success in a variety of social environments.

As the young child who is blind or visually impaired enters elementary school, the influence of early social experience will enhance and support the student's transition to a larger school environment. Students who develop a repertoire of play and interactive skills during their early years will be able to engage with peers and develop friendships more easily. The next chapter focuses on students with visual impairments in elementary and middle school programs, and provides examples of strategies and interventions to enhance their social success.

## REFERENCES

Corsaro, W. A. (1985). *Friendship and peer culture in the early years*. Norwood, NJ: Ablex.

Fazzi, D. L. (2002). Social focus. In R. L. Pogrund & D. L. Fazzi (Eds.), *Early focus* (pp. 188–217). New York: AFB Press.

Kekelis, L. S. (1986a). Increasing positive social interactions between a blind child and sighted kindergartners. Unpublished paper. San Francisco: San Francisco State University.

Kekelis, L. S. (1986b). [Pilot study of a blind child's social interactions]. Unpublished raw data.

Kekelis, L. S. (1992a). A field study of a blind preschooler. In S. Z. Sacks, R. J. Gaylord-Ross, & L. S. Kekelis (Eds.), *The development of social skills by blind and visually impaired students: Exploratory studies and strategies* (pp. 39–58). New York: American Foundation for the Blind.

Snow, C. E., & Ferguson, C. A. (1977). *Talking to children*. New York: Cambridge University Press.

## 10

# A Field Study of a Blind Preschooler

## Linda S. Kekelis

This study used an ethnographic approach to examine in detail one blind child's interactions with her classmates. Its goals were (1) to identify factors that affect blind and visually impaired children's interactions with their peers, (2) to generate hypotheses for future studies of blind and visually impaired children, and (3) to develop a set of preliminary guidelines that practitioners can use to promote positive social interactions between sighted children and visually impaired children.

An ethnographic study approach was used to collect and analyze data simultaneously. Although the project was begun with a set of

Source: Reprinted with permission from S. Z. Sacks, R. J. Gaylord-Ross, & L. S. Kekelis, Eds., *The Development of Social Skills by Blind and Visually Impaired Students: Exploratory Studies and Strategies* (New York: American Foundation for the Blind, 1992), pp. 39–58.

general hypotheses, new questions arose during the study and were investigated. With this open-ended study approach, the research issues were not imposed on the data, but emerged from the observations. This technique led to the discovery of issues that are of special importance to visually impaired children and generated hypotheses for future investigations. The study of Ashley was conducted over a four-month period; two to three visits were scheduled with her each week.

## PARTICIPANTS

### ASHLEY

Ashley Addison, who was $3\frac{1}{2}$ years old when the study began, had an active interest in the persons and objects in her surroundings and a creative imagination that she used to entertain herself and engage others in social interactions. During my first visit to her home, Ashley displayed none of the social and linguistic deficits that are common in blind and visually impaired children. She attracted her parents' attention with appropriate formulas such as, "You know what?"; did not ask irrelevant questions or behave inappropriately; and expressed her ideas in creative sentences, rather than in formulaic speech.

Ashley was sighted until age 6 months, when she was physically abused and violently shaken by a babysitter. As the result of the trauma, the retinas of both her eyes detached, leaving her with no useful vision. Her parents received disparate reports on Ashley's condition. Several ophthalmologists told them that her visual functioning would eventually improve, but it did not.

Ashley returned home from the hospital with the competencies of a 2-month-old. Despite this early setback, she quickly reacquired language, cognitive, and motor skills. At 16 months, she was enrolled in a preschool program for blind and visually impaired children. This placement eased Mrs. Addison's anxiety and guilt because she felt confident leaving Ashley in the care of the highly competent staff. The program's instructors reassured Mrs. Addison that Ashley was not developmentally delayed, but was, in fact, advanced for a child with a vision loss.

Throughout this period, the family received educational services and emotional support from a home-based intervention program for blind and visually impaired children and their families. This program helped the Addisons develop realistic expectations for Ashley and gave them reading materials on blindness. The following summer and thereafter, Ashley attended the Sunshine Program, a preschool morning program for sighted children operated by a neighborhood Jewish community center. Although the family was not Jewish, they selected the program because they liked its child-centered curriculum. At age 3, Ashley was also enrolled in the Blind Children's Program (BCP), a preschool morning program for blind and visually impaired children that provided mobility and prebraille instruction. She attended the BCP two days a week and the Sunshine Program three days a week.

Her caregivers described Ashley as strong-willed and, at times, stubborn. These qualities were manifested both positively and negatively. Ashley frequently asserted her independence with the command, "Let me do it by myself!" and often mastered new skills through trial and error. However, she sometimes refused to cooperate in required school activities and defied her caregivers' reasonable requests, just as her sighted classmates did. The expression of these personality traits depended, in part, upon the responses of Ashley's parents, teachers, and peers.

Ashley's humor and imagination also served as both strengths and weaknesses. Playing with sounds, changing people's names, and playing make-believe were her favorite activities. Children and adults sometimes responded to these activities positively, but at other times they responded negatively because the activities prevented meaningful play and conversations.

## THE ADDISONS

The Addisons were an upper-middle-class Caucasian family that valued intelligence, creativity, and independence in children. Mr. Addison was an administrator of a large hospital with a busy work schedule, but he maintained a close relationship with Ashley.

Mrs. Addison was the children's primary caregiver. An articulate and reflective person, she had developed a thorough understanding of Ashley's special needs. She used language and hands-on experiences to expand Ashley's understanding of her environment and encouraged Ashley to be a creative and independent problem solver.

Jake, Ashley's younger brother, was 1 year old when the study began. He had a likable temperament, curiosity, and the ability to entertain himself. Jake was a positive addition to the Addison family and provided Ashley with opportunities to help a less competent partner, to share possessions and the attention of adults, and to develop skills that would help her play with her peers.

# SETTINGS AND ACTIVITIES

To gain as complete an understanding of Ashley's world as possible, I observed her in a variety of settings, including her home, a swimming class, a gymnastics class, a field trip to a library, the Sunshine Program, and the BCP. The majority of observations were made at Ashley's preschool, the Sunshine Program.

## SUNSHINE PROGRAM

Ashley's classmates at the Sunshine Program included 22 children, aged 3 and 4, who came from middle- and upper-class families. Although the program was operated by a Jewish community center, many of the children enrolled were not Jewish. Despite the children's different personalities, temperaments, and social skills, they engaged in a significantly higher rate of interaction with classmates than did Ashley.

The overall sizes of the Sunshine and BCP classrooms were comparable. However, the Sunshine Program had a much larger outdoor play area with two swing sets, a large sandbox, several climbing structures; automobile and truck tires to climb; tables for water play and baking activities; and large, wide-open spaces in which the children ran and rode bicycles. This outdoor play area afforded the sighted students innumerable places to run, hide, and play imaginatively, but it proved to be a restrictive environment for Ashley. Ashley was aware of some of the materials that were available in the yard, but she could not independently move around the grounds because its landmarks were far apart. She could have benefited from mobility instruction in this outdoor area, but mobility lessons were provided only at the BCP. Although the techniques she learned at the BCP were valuable, they would have been more meaningful if Ashley had been taught a path that was important in her day-to-day activities.

In the Sunshine Program, the children were self-directed. They had considerable freedom to select activities and a variety of options from which to choose. The size of the playground, number of classmates, and availability of toys enabled Ashley's classmates to engage in numerous activities. During unstructured playtime, the teachers monitored the children's activities and responded to the children in a nondirective manner. They often set up activities, such as water tables, easels and paints, and clay. This arrangement accommodated the children's individual needs. Some children enjoyed large groups, whereas others liked small groups or to play alone; some enjoyed indoor activities, whereas others preferred gross-motor activities outdoors; and some liked to draw and paint, whereas others preferred building with blocks.

Each day also included a number of routines and structured activities in which the children were expected to participate. At the start of each day, the children gathered in a circle to sing songs, listen to the day's schedule, and share conversations. After outdoor play, they returned to the classroom for snack time. Later, they participated in more free play, art activities, show-and-tell, and story time.

Special activities and materials were offered to the children each day. However, the teachers sometimes described them in a manner that may have been difficult for Ashley to comprehend. Daily agendas were discussed at snack time when the children were absorbed in conversation and eating, were shouted across the outdoor playground while the children were running and yelling, and were announced in songs. Even if the sighted students failed to hear these announcements, they could see the toys and activities. Without visual cues, Ashley may have missed a number of opportunities to participate in activities with her classmates because she did not know they were available.

Overall, the Sunshine Program was not designed for a visually impaired child. Its layout and class size made it difficult for Ashley to be independent and to engage in interactions with her classmates. Recognizing this fact, the program director admitted Ashley under the condition that an aide would be provided to protect Ashley's safety and to keep the teachers' attention from being diverted from the sighted students. A student enrolled in the Department of Special Education of a local college volunteered for the position. The aide primarily served as Ashley's attendant, but she also rotated with the classroom teachers so her service did not set Ashley apart from her classmates. During the field study, the children did not make any comments to suggest they were aware the aide was in their class primarily to assist Ashley. They frequently approached the aide and asked for her assistance and involved her in their activities.

## BCP

At the BCP, Ashley had four classmates—three boys and one girl. Her classmates were between the ages of 3 and 5, and their vision loss ranged from severe visual impairment to total blindness. The two older boys were highly verbal and mobile and engaged in some interactions with Ashley. The younger boy was language delayed and severely emotionally disturbed. The other girl was developmentally delayed and engaged in a great deal of echolalic speech; although her language and social skills were rapidly developing as the result of the program's stimulation, they were not comparable to Ashley's, and the two girls did not often converse or play together. The activities at the BCP were more structured and teacher directed than were those at the Sunshine Program. Teaching occurred both individually and in small groups. The classroom environment was set up for blind and visually impaired children, and the toys, books, and other learning materials were kept in consistent locations. Ashley was expected to travel independently in the classroom and on the playground, although adult supervision was always provided.

The classroom teacher recognized the importance of peer interactions for her students and was adept at encouraging them. Ashley engaged in some positive peer interactions in this program, but she spent a large amount of time playing by herself or engaging in lessons and conversations with the staff. Perhaps if there had been a more competent girl in the class Ashley would have conversed and played more with a peer.

## PARTICIPATION IN TWO PROGRAMS

Neither preschool program could meet all Ashley's needs. Concerned with the lack of appropriate peer models at the BCP, the Addisons looked for an alternative placement. They were encouraged to enroll Ashley in the Sunshine Program by its staff. The Addisons hoped that this program would give Ashley the opportunity to form friendships with sighted children and to learn skills from appropriate role models.

Ashley's participation in the Sunshine Program was helpful to Mrs. Addison, who sometimes doubted Ashley's overall competence. Mrs. Addison saw that the sighted children also had difficulty separating from their mothers, had temper tantrums and crying fits, and sometimes refused to share and cooperate with their peers. These observations helped her to put Ashley's problems into perspective.

Participation in two programs on alternate days appeared to have some drawbacks. At the BCP, in particular, Ashley seemed to be a minor participant in classroom activities. She missed many of its weekly activities and did not share the same background experiences as her classmates. At the Sunshine Program, she was enrolled long after the other children had established relationships with each other.

Despite the shortcomings of the placements, Ashley had positive experiences in both programs, which often complemented each other. With the help of her teachers, she developed a number of skills that were important for her future relationships with peers.

# RESEARCH METHODS

## OBSERVATIONS

### BCP

During the study, I spent several mornings each week at the BCP observing Ashley and conducting an intervention with one of Ashley's classmates (see Kekelis, 1986a). During class time, I observed routines, took notes, and audiotaped Ashley's interactions. I followed Ashley from place to place but attempted to remain as unobtrusive as possible. Often, I sat on the classroom floor in an area adjacent to Ashley and her classmates. My participation in this setting was intentionally limited because there were so many adults in the classroom—the head instructor, two teacher's aides, a speech therapist, and a mobility instructor. Since it was not easy for the head teacher to maintain order given the diversity of personalities, agendas, and comings and goings of adults, it was critical that I did not add to the stimulation in the classroom.

### Sunshine Program

At the Sunshine Program, Ashley was observed one morning each week during the first two months of the study and two mornings a week during the last month. To fit into the Sunshine Program, I adopted a different role than at the BCP. The physical dimensions and size of the classroom allowed for more opportunities to participate in activities. In fact, Ashley's classmates demanded that I do more than observe and record their interactions with Ashley. They asked me questions, requested my permission and assistance in their games, and shared their feelings and ideas with me. Their responsiveness and interest encouraged me to participate in their social world. When several of the children asked why I was taking notes, I told them I was learning about their play—an explanation that seemed to satisfy them. During my visits, I tried not to single out Ashley and, in fact, interacted more with Ashley's classmates than with her. Ashley preferred the company of adults to that of her peers, and I did not want to encourage her to talk or play with me.

### Ashley's Home

Ashley was observed at home on three occasions, and the observations were revealing about her underlying competence and the kinds of expectations her mother had for her. The teachers at the Sunshine

Program used these expectations to develop their goals for Ashley. These visits also yielded information about Ashley's history.

Visits to the Addisons served another important function. Mrs. Addison was interested in Ashley's progress in both school programs, but she had little opportunity to observe Ashley at either site. Ashley went to and from the BCP by school bus. Mrs. Addison drove Ashley to the Sunshine Program and stayed for approximately 10 minutes each school day; she had little opportunity to observe interactions between Ashley and her classmates because Ashley remained by her side while she was there. The observations that were made at both schools were discussed with the Addisons at home.

## INTERVIEWING

Talking about Ashley with her mother and teachers shed light on their behavior and on Ashley's underlying competence and performance. These interviews helped explain the reasons for the discrepancy between Ashley's competence in interactions with adults and her lack of competence in the company of peers. Aside from incidental discussions throughout the project, longer and more formal interviews with Ashley's mother and teachers were scheduled during the final weeks of the project. By this time, the teachers knew me well and understood the kinds of concerns that interested me. During these interviews, a number of helpful insights emerged.

# FACTORS THAT AFFECTED ASHLEY'S SUCCESS

From direct observations and interviews with Ashley's teachers and mother, a number of factors that affected the success of Ashley's interactions were identified. In this chapter, these factors are discussed and guidelines for improving the quantity and quality of blind and visually impaired children's interactions with peers are proposed.

## ASHLEY'S INTERACTIONS WITH PEERS

A number of events were observed in the preschool programs. During the first weeks of observation, Ashley engaged in little conversation and play with other children at either program. Her integration was a particular problem at the Sunshine Program, where she was observed in the presence of children who actively engaged classmates in dyadic and group conversation and play, while she was involved with adults—sometimes the classroom teachers, but most often her aide. On a good day, Ashley participated in only a handful of peer interactions, each lasting a short time.

At the BCP, Ashley's interactions with two of her classmates—the two older boys—were restricted primarily to sound play during snack time. During these interactions, the children attended mainly to each other's language, but only minimally to the events and objects in their surroundings. By playing with sounds, the children could easily monitor and respond to each other's interests.

At the Sunshine Program, Ashley also used sound-play games to interact with classmates. While swinging (her favorite outdoor activity) or waiting her turn at the swings, she often engaged in sound play or fantasy conversations with her classmates. I initially thought that swinging provided few benefits to Ashley, but later discovered that it reduced the impact of her blindness during interactions with classmates, which were the longest while she was swinging. During swinging, the boundaries of the activity were limited, and the children's conversations often focused on previous experiences, rather than on current events Ashley could not see. While Ashley's classmates were on the swings, they continued to monitor other children's activities in the playground and sometimes jumped off the swings to join the others. On those occasions, Ashley was left behind without a word of warning to signal her classmates' departures.

## DEFICITS IN ASHLEY'S SOCIAL SKILLS

At the start of the field study, I looked for the presence of behaviors that are typical of blind and visually impaired children and would impede interactions between Ashley and her classmates, such as shifting from one topic to another, asking repetitive questions, focusing on their own interests, and failing to respond to and imitate other children's language and behavior. It was not until later that I discovered the impact of the absence of certain behaviors on Ashley's relationships with her classmates and teachers.

### Failure to Display Affection

During observations in the classroom, Ashley displayed no affection or attachment to her classmates. This omission first came to light during an interview with Ashley's aide, who said:

> I don't think she has gravitated or warmed up to me in an overly demonstrative way. Sometimes I question, "Shouldn't she be

more attached to me? Shouldn't she be more delighted?" If she had been more attached to me, I would, in turn, perhaps feel a greater commitment. I don't think I have had as strong a commitment as I could have if the child were more receptive to me, if we had clicked more. I don't think she dislikes me, but I don't think there's a strong bond. [Kekelis, 1986b, interview on June 11, 1986]

Following the interview with Ashley's aide, a review of field notes indicated that there was no record of Ashley's showing her preference either verbally or nonverbally for any adult or classmate at her preschools. Ashley did not ask about any of her classmates, request to sit beside anyone during snacks or circle time, or reciprocate the positive feelings demonstrated by her classmates. Ashley's aide reflected:

It's as if she's happy to talk to whoever is there or interact with whoever is there with a few comments or questions. But it's not like she says, "Where's Mary today?" I'm not getting a great many strokes from her, and I think the children would perhaps have been more willing to interact with her if they felt that she at least asked for them. If you don't show them in ways that you're able to show them that you like them, they're not going to be there. [Kekelis, 1986b, interview on June 11, 1986]

In contrast, Ashley's classmates reinforced one another in a number of ways. They smiled and called to their friends at the start of each school day, showed and admired each other's new toys and clothes, and invited each other to birthday parties and overnight parties. Throughout the day, they paid each other compliments and requested and provided assistance to one another.

## Unresponsiveness to Classmates

Given the little reinforcement Ashley gave her classmates, it is surprising that some of them repeatedly approached her. Three classmates at the Sunshine Program (Hannah, Nina, and Hilary) showed considerable interest in her. They initiated conversations with her, saved places in line and at the snack table for her, played next to her, and invited her to their homes. Ashley's aide attributed the success of these relationships to the chemistry between the children, but interest in the relationships appeared to be one-sided, since Ashley displayed no preference for any of them.

Although Ashley and these girls seemed to need help in developing a relationship, finding the right way to assist the girls was not easy, as the following example illustrates. One morning Hannah joined Ashley and her aide as they played with blocks and a dollhouse. Ashley played with dolls and furniture on the shelves where they were stored, while Hannah played on the floor. Hoping that the girls' parallel play might develop into a cooperative venture if they sat side by side, I suggested that Ashley play on the floor. Ashley refused to move. She often played with toys on the shelves, rather than on the floor as her classmates did. Ashley's strategy was adaptive for a blind child in a roomful of sighted classmates. With her toys on shelves and her back to other children, she could play without interruption. When her toys were available to classmates, Ashley was vulnerable; other children might step on them, move them, or take them away. Without vision, it was difficult for her to keep track of her possessions and, if necessary, to retrieve them.

On the last day of school, Hannah announced that she had something she wanted to say to Ashley. At the time, Ashley was looking for a misplaced toy and did not respond to her. With the encouragement of her teacher, Hannah extended an invitation for Ashley to visit her during the summer. Ashley did not acknowledge the invitation; at that moment, her attention was focused on her misplaced toy.

The relationship between Ashley and Nina appeared promising at the start of the year, but it never fully developed. While making challah bread for a Shabbat (Sabbath) celebration, Nina announced that she liked Ashley. Recognizing Nina's interest in Ashley, the classroom teachers often asked Nina to take Ashley's hand and guide her to new activities. The two children also engaged in several play episodes when an adult caregiver was not present. During these interactions with Nina, Ashley was exposed to strategies for resolving conflicts, displaying preferences, and making jokes. Although Ashley's teachers and aide were aware of Nina's interest in Ashley, they did not tell Ashley or encourage her to do or say anything that would have reinforced Nina's interests in her. Before snacks or story time, Nina often told other classmates that she was saving a place for Ashley.

Unfortunately, Ashley was not aware of Nina's intentions and was often guided to a different place by her aide. What was interesting about these unsuccessful attempts was that Nina did not tell Ashley directly that she wanted Ashley to sit by her side.

## Need for Prompts by the Aide

Ashley's aide sometimes tried to sustain interactions between Ashley and Nina, but these attempts were not always successful. One morning, the aide suggested that Ashley and Nina try a different activity, since they had been playing by a row of tires and a climbing structure for awhile. Nina walked to a nearby slide and waited for Ashley. When Ashley did not follow her, the aide said, "Ashley, you know what? Nina is waiting for you by the slide." When Ashley failed to move toward the slide, Nina called her, but she did not respond. Her aide commented, "Ashley, Nina is calling you." Then a classroom teacher approached the group and told Nina, "If you want Ashley, maybe you should walk over to her." Nina then returned to the row of tires.

Although Ashley sometimes needed the aide, the children might have worked out conflicts better on their own. For example, Nina may not have gone to the slide without Ashley if Ashley's aide were not present. Perhaps Ashley would not have stayed by the row of tires if her aide were not there and if Nina had not returned to the tires.

On other occasions, Ashley's aide facilitated positive interactions between the two girls. For instance, while the girls were swinging side by side, the aide suggested to Ashley, "Do you want to do a tummy swing? Nina's doing a tummy swing." Ashley proceeded to lie across the swing on her stomach as her friend was doing. This suggestion prompted Ashley to imitate a classmate. Most of the day, Nina had been attentive to Ashley, responding to and imitating Ashley's actions.

## REJECTION BY A CLASSMATE

The most aggressive attempt to promote a friendship between Ashley and a classmate was made by the mother of one of the students (Sandy) at the Sunshine Program. Unfortunately, the attempt was unsuccessful, perhaps because it was based on the mother's interests, rather than her child's. During Ashley's first month at the preschool, Sandy invited her to lunch. The invitation was probably Sandy's mother's idea, given that Sandy had never interacted with Ashley at school. At the next morning circle, Mrs. Addison asked Sandy's mother if Sandy would sit next to Ashley. Sandy's mother willingly consented, but Sandy was less enthusiastic and agreed only to sit on her mother's lap next to Ashley. For the remainder of the school year, Sandy stayed away from Ashley.

During my final visit to the Sunshine Program, Sandy approached Ashley, but the exchange was disconcerting. Ashley was playing with blocks and dolls. The aide suggested that Sandy build a tunnel along-side Ashley, and Ashley invited Sandy to play with her. Sandy ignored Ashley and her questions and talked only to Ashley's aide. Then, while

Sandy was building a house with blocks, Ashley asked her aide to make her house like Sandy's. The interaction continued:

**Aide:**    (Looking at Sandy) You want yours like Sandy's. You're neighbors.

**Ashley:**  Where's Sandy? What's she doing? What are you doing, Sandy?

**Aide:**    Aren't you going to tell her?

**Sandy:**   I'm not going to tell her.

At cleanup time, Sandy refused to put away toys near Ashley but tried to help another classmate put away her toys. The attempts to foster a friendship between Sandy and Ashley throughout the school year never succeeded. Perhaps the pressure from her mother to become acquainted with Ashley had been too threatening for Sandy.

## WHAT BLINDNESS MEANT TO ASHLEY'S CLASSMATES

There were frequent discussions about Ashley's blindness at the Sunshine Program. When the teachers talked with the students about blindness, they emphasized the things Ashley could do. They also discussed her special needs, which the students learned to accommodate. The children's understanding of Ashley's impairment developed over the months. They learned how Ashley used tactile and auditory cues instead of visual cues to learn about the world and were intrigued with the braille system that Ashley was learning at the BCP, often feeling the braille words.

The children used auditory and tactile cues to help Ashley understand what was going on around her. When Ashley approached the bathroom sink, Nina tapped on the step to signal Ashley to step up. While Hilary made dough for challah, she said to Ashley, "I'm making some for you," and touched Ashley's hand to let Ashley know she was being included.

Ashley did not always welcome nonverbal cues, however. In the following exchange, Ashley seemed to mistake Nina's intentions:

**Nina:**    (touching Ashley's shirt) I'm Nina.

**Ashley:**  Don't unbutton my shirt.

Ashley's own use of nonverbal contact was also difficult for some of her classmates:

**Ashley:** (approaching Andrea)

**Andrea:** (to the teacher) I don't want her touching me.

**Teacher:** Tell her.

**Andrea:** I don't want you touching me.

Sometimes the children's use of nonverbal behaviors revealed that they did not understand fully what it means to be blind. The children pointed toward objects, held out toys, and nodded to Ashley. Unless an adult was present to put their actions into words, Ashley was unaware of these nonverbal messages. Ashley's language and actions may have made it difficult for her classmates to understand that she could not see. Although Ashley was totally blind, she often appeared to be sighted, since her eyes were not disfigured and she oriented toward her partners and used gestures, such as pointing and offering objects. She also used the words *look* and *see*, which sometimes led to misunderstandings with her classmates:

**Donovan:** (approaching Ashley with a handful of jelly beans)

**Ashley:** Can I see?

**Donovan:** (putting jelly beans near Ashley's eyes)

**Teacher:** You have to put them by her hands because she sees with her hands.

Ashley and her classmates at the Sunshine Program often engaged in indirect interactions. Perhaps if her aide had not been so readily available, the children would have talked directly to one another. In the following exchange, Ashley and Melody were doing artwork at the same table inside the classroom while their classmates were outside:

**Ashley:** Why is Melody staying inside?

**Aide:** Ask her.

**Ashley:** Why is Melody staying inside?

**Melody:** Because I want to draw.

Inside the playhouse, Ashley was setting a table while her aide watched. Hannah came over and watched Ashley.

**Aide:**      Hi Hannah.

**Hannah:**   What is Ashley doing?

**Aide:**      You can ask her.

**Hannah:**   You.

**Ashley:**    I'm pouring coffee. You can't really have it. It's yucky.

# EVALUATING PEER INTERACTIONS

Ashley's caregivers evaluated her interactions with peers on the basis of their expectations for Ashley's mainstreaming experience and the norms they used to evaluate Ashley's behavior. Both of these factors are discussed in the following section.

## EXPECTATIONS FOR ASHLEY'S PRESCHOOL EXPERIENCES

Ashley was competent in her conversations with adults. She listened to their questions and comments, responded with appropriate language, asked for explanations when unable to follow their conversations, and creatively expanded on their ideas. She actively engaged adults in interactions and seemed to prefer their company to that of peers. She needed to develop skills that were important for peer interactions—skills that she could not master during interactions with her mother and teachers. To develop these skills, Ashley needed opportunities to interact with her classmates at both preschools.

The teachers at the Sunshine Program had two motives for wanting Ashley in their program. They wanted to learn more about blindness and they wanted their students exposed to individuals with special needs to teach them to be responsible and to help their friends.

The staff at the BCP focused on Ashley's needs. They taught her to follow instructions, to respect adult authority, and to make transitions. Although they recognized the importance of peer interactions, there was no appropriate partner for Ashley in the program. The instructor of the BCP had been willing to initiate a reverse mainstreaming program by bringing in nondisabled children of Ashley's age, but the Addisons chose to place Ashley in the Sunshine Program.

The staff at both preschools made sporadic attempts to foster interactions between Ashley and her classmates. They encouraged classmates to take Ashley's hand and lead her to an activity and informed Ashley of the location of her classmates. However, these efforts were not sufficient to increase significantly the number of interactions between Ashley and her peers.

## Norms for Ashley: Involvement with Peers

It is often difficult for both families and professionals to establish appropriate expectations for a disabled child. They frequently consider whatever a disabled child does to be exceptional. For Ashley and other disabled children who have the potential to be highly competent, inappropriate expectations may limit their achievements.

When I compared Ashley with her sighted classmates at the Sunshine Program, she appeared to be developmentally delayed. She engaged in few interactions with peers, but she often talked with adults; she engaged in too little group play and too much solitary play; she played too long at her favorite activities, but she played too briefly with peers; and she made few attempts to display her interest in and preference for any of her classmates. Staff at the Sunshine Program did not seem to be particularly concerned with the disparity between the social experiences of Ashley and the other children in the classroom.

# CONSTRUCTING EXPECTATIONS FOR ASHLEY

The teachers and aide at the Sunshine Program did not receive adequate pre- or in-service training to prepare them for working with a blind child. It was their first opportunity to work with a disabled child, and it was difficult for them to construct appropriate expectations for Ashley.

On several occasions, the staff discussed the importance of treating Ashley as they treated her classmates, yet the way in which they spoke to her reflected their ambivalent feelings toward her. For example, they used language that was similar to the language used with infants (Snow & Ferguson, 1977). When speaking to Ashley, they used proper names instead of pronouns, spoke in a high pitch and exaggerated their intonation, asked many questions, and often used baby-talk words. During an interview, the head instructor described Ashley as remarkable and more advanced and stronger than her classmates, yet she spoke to Ashley as she would to a toddler.

The instructors also had difficulty disciplining Ashley. One teacher recounted: "We kind of had a fight, Ashley and I. I'd say to myself, 'Oh no,' because there's this image I have that Ashley loves me. That was hard." (Kekelis, 1986b, interview on June 24, 1986)

Although this instructor may have wanted to be liked by all her students, she was swifter to set limits for the others and did less to avoid confrontations with the sighted students than with Ashley. For example, one morning, when the tables were covered with shaving cream that the children used to create sculptures, Ashley repeatedly spread her hands across the table and into her classmates' work. Despite frequent warnings from her classmates to stop, she continued to encroach on their play areas, and she greatly agitated her classmates. Observing the problem, the classroom teacher explained to the children that Ashley could not see where her space ended and theirs began. However, it seemed to me that Ashley was intentionally provoking her classmates. The conflict continued, and the instructor threatened to remove Ashley from the activity table, but she did not. Instead, she moved Ashley to another side of the table after it was vacated. If another child had acted as Ashley did, the child would have been removed immediately from the table and made to sit on a chair during time-out.

Even when the staff attempted to encourage Ashley to behave as her classmates did, they were not always successful. Ashley had difficulty making transitions from one activity and setting to another. She not only walked slowly, but she liked to stop along the routes to explore and talk about objects. Getting from one place to another was not a means to an end but an end in itself. As a result, Ashley was frequently out of sync with her classmates. She began activities after children had found partners and continued them long after her classmates had moved on to new tasks.

The staff and I developed a plan to help Ashley keep up with her classmates. Five minutes before transitions, Ashley's aide encouraged her to proceed to a new setting. The extra time enabled Ashley to participate in more activities with classmates, but the intervention was not entirely successful.

For a few weeks, Ashley refused to follow her teachers' instructions. For example, when it was time to wash up before snack time, she refused to stop the activity in which she was engaged. When given the option of obeying the rules or missing snacks, she chose to miss snacks and sit by herself while her classmates ate. On one occasion, she chose not to participate in a classmate's birthday party. (No other child in the class ever chose to miss snack time or a birthday party.)

When other students were removed from a group's activities for a few minutes because of their misconduct, they watched their classmates' activities and appeared upset not to be part of their peer group. In contrast, Ashley displayed no signs of dissatisfaction when she was unable to participate in snacks, religious ceremonies, or birthday festivities. During class time, she was not involved in peer activities to the same extent as were her classmates, and since Ashley could not see what she was missing, time-outs did not encourage her to behave more like her classmates.

## INTERACTIONS WITH SUBSTITUTE TEACHERS

On several occasions, Ashley's aide was unable to supervise her at the Sunshine Program, and substitute caregivers from within the preschool were provided. These occasions presented opportunities to observe interactions between Ashley and persons who were inexperienced in working with blind or visually impaired children.

The first substitute, Emily, engaged in constant conversation with Ashley. As a result, Ashley had no need to look to her classmates for attention and partnership, and her classmates had no opportunity to play or talk with Ashley. During the morning, Ashley broke a plastic fork while playing with clay. Observing the accident, one of Ashley's classmates found a replacement. She offered the fork to Emily and said, "Here's another for her." Emily was a go-between. Later, during snack time, the classroom teacher asked one of the children to pass a can of juice to another child. When the boy asked to whom he should pass the juice, Ashley announced that she wanted the juice. Unfortunately, Emily had anticipated Ashley's needs and had already served her juice.

A few weeks later, when one of the classroom teachers was absent, a substitute teacher, Jill, filled in. Jill also engaged in long conversations with Ashley that interfered with Ashley's participation in class activities. On a number of occasions, Jill talked to Ashley through her aide. At the start of the school day, Jill came up to Ashley and her aide and inquired, "How has Ashley been this morning? Is she enjoying herself?" Ashley's aide instructed Jill to talk directly to Ashley.

## FACTORS AFFECTING POSITIVE PEER INTERACTIONS

During the months of observation of Ashley and her classmates in both preschools, the following factors were found to affect Ashley's preschool experience:

- *Preservice and in-service training of teachers.* The staff at the Sunshine Program had never worked with a blind or visually impaired child and were uncertain of the goals and teaching approach to adopt with Ashley. It would have been helpful for them to have talked with the counselor who had worked with Ashley and her family during the previous three years. The counselor knew Ashley's strengths and weaknesses and may have been able to suggest ways to help Ashley become a more active participant in the program.

- *Priorities for Ashley's mainstreaming experience.* The staff at the Sunshine Program did not have a definite set of priorities for mainstreaming Ashley. Much of what they did limited the interactions between Ashley and her classmates because they did not realize the importance of these interactions.

- *Attempts to monitor Ashley's progress.* There was no systematic attempt to monitor Ashley's progress in the Sunshine Program. Short weekly meetings in which staff could discuss factors that had appeared to promote or impede positive social experiences should have been scheduled. Information gathered during these meetings could then have been used for the systematic design of activities, settings, and play groups that might stimulate peer interactions.

- *Communication with staff at both programs.* Although the instructors at Ashley's preschools were interested in each others' work, they never met. It would have been informative for the staff members of both programs to have observed Ashley in another setting and to maintain regular telephone contact. Ashley's instructors at the BCP could have helped the staff at the Sunshine Program develop more demanding expectations for Ashley. In addition, through such contacts, the staffs could have developed a preschool experience with continuity for Ashley.

- *Communication within the programs.* Staff at the Sunshine Program had opinions of each other's work that they did not openly discuss. By sharing their different perspectives, they could have improved their efforts to mainstream Ashley.

- *Less adult supervision of Ashley.* During much of her time at the Sunshine Program, Ashley was in safe situations in which she did not require constant supervision by adults. Perhaps Ashley's aide could have remained near enough to monitor Ashley and her peers but far enough away not to regulate them. If Ashley was alone more frequently at the Sunshine Program, she might have been more motivated to initiate interactions with her classmates.

- *Creation of a safe and predictable environment.* A classroom of 20 active children can be disconcerting for a totally blind child. No wonder Ashley was protective of her play area and materials. If play space had been arranged for Ashley in the corners of the room or in the loft away from the hustle of her classmates, Ashley might have found it easier to play with one or two classmates. Such an area could have been marked off with furniture or blocks and restricted to Ashley and one or two friends.

- *Reinforcement of interactions between Ashley and her classmates.* Ashley was often reinforced by adults when she was not interacting with classmates. Ashley may have approached her classmates more often if her caregivers had attended to and reinforced her when she was with peers rather than by herself. It would also have been helpful to model ways for Ashley to show her classmates that she wanted to be their friend. Interactions among young children present important opportunities to acquire language and social skills. For sighted children, these interactions require the minimal involvement of adults. For blind and visually impaired children, however, they require thoughtful planning and monitoring by classroom teachers and aides.

# CHAPTER 11

# Teaching Social Skills to Elementary and Middle School Students with Visual Impairments

Jane N. Erin

Learning how to solve problems related to socialization is an important element of education for students who are visually impaired because social skills can have a strong influence on success in employment and quality of life in adulthood. Students with visual impairments who attend public schools have regular contact with students who are not visually impaired, but their visual differences may create some obstacles in connecting and communicating with others. Because they do not have complete information about social interactions and must often exert extra effort to keep up with classes, they may concentrate on academic tasks without considering the effects of social skills on their ability to meet future goals. Students who are in specialized schools may experience a more individualized and adapted environment, but families and educators must find opportunities for these students to apply their social skills in settings where most students are not visually impaired.

The professional who works with students with visual impairments will find few relevant resources on social skills and visual impairment. Although social skills are widely discussed in educational literature, most writing emphasizes aggressive or resistant behaviors among students with mild disabilities who have cognitive or emotional disorders. Social difficulties for students with visual impairments are of a different type; they usually result from a lack of information about the visual aspects of social interaction, and they are reinforced by others' reluctance to establish and communicate appropriate expectations to a student with a visual impairment.

This chapter provides an overview of the general social characteristics of children from about ages 6 through 13 and the areas in which visually impaired students are at risk for incomplete skill development. Strategies for helping visually impaired students to develop appropriate social skills are described, along with suggestions for motivating activities for elementary and middle school students. It is important to keep in mind, however, that students are responsible for their own choices about socialization; but families and important adults can influence their experiences by modeling appropriate social behavior, encouraging students, and arranging opportunities for them to learn and practice their skills.

# TYPICAL SOCIAL DEVELOPMENT

## ELEMENTARY SCHOOL STUDENTS

Students between the ages of 6 and 13 not only master academic skills that allow them to express ideas more flexibly through the symbols of reading and writing, but they also develop the ability to view the world from the perspective of others. Their focus shifts from an adult-centered social context in which they work to gain the approval of loved and respected adults to a world in which the esteem of their peers gradually becomes more important. Their physical proficiency and increasing independence moves them out of the nurturing and protective preschool and kindergarten environment to one in which they are expected to compete, manage conflict, and manage failure and frustration as well as success.

Most elementary school–aged students have progressed to the stage of concrete operational thinking, allowing them to use basic logic, to think multidimensionally, and to understand social motivations. Personal competence, termed *industry* by Erikson (1963), is characteristic of children in the middle elementary years; conversely, the possibility of failure or *inferiority* is identified by Erikson as a significant threat to children at this age. During these years, an understanding of morality starts to emerge, and children's behavior is governed by established rules and routines in addition to the personal wants and needs that have influenced behavior at younger ages. Perspective taking has been developing in children in this age group; allowing them to understand that internal thoughts may differ from perceptible behavior and that others have personalities and ways of thinking that may differ from their own (Merrell & Gimpel, 1998). Children of this age become more concerned about establishing and maintaining friendships, and they expect friends to demonstrate loyalty and trust. They are more concerned about the opinions of peers, and the fear of rejection may influence their behavior.

As they mature, students' social behaviors become more controlled; they display fewer temper tantrums and fearful responses and less impulsive behavior. Students are able to describe and discuss feelings in greater detail and to engage in logical problem-solving related to social problems. They can identify and compare alternative ways of solving problems, and they recognize the advantages of communicating positively in social situations and withholding negative or egocentric perceptions.

In elementary school, the school culture becomes a major influence on social experiences. MacCuspie (1996) described the effects of school culture in a study of students with visual impairments who were integrated into mainstream classes, in which she observed students responding to a series of assumptions about culture. For these students, culture included artifacts, values, and assumptions that underlie the behaviors and interactions of students in a classroom. MacCuspie identified the major factors in elementary school culture as primary association with best friends, shared activities as the basis of friendship, initiation of interaction, refraining from close friendships with the opposite sex, association of unpopular children with others who were unpopular, class membership defined by similarities in dress and behavior, and support by best friends. Students with visual impairments might not have access to information about such cultural artifacts as clothing, accessories, or pictures of a popular singer or about when it is socially acceptable to enter a conversation. In this study, visually impaired students identified friends as those who would help them; however, this need for assistance is not the primary aspect of friendship for other students.

All these elements shape the experience of the elementary school student with a visual impairment. However, students with visual impairments have the extra challenges of gaining information about visual aspects of social interaction, such as gestures and clothing; of being aware of standards of personal appearance, which is based on limited or inaccessible visual information; and of developing self-esteem to oppose stereotypical attitudes about visual impairment.

## MIDDLE SCHOOL STUDENTS

Middle school students are increasingly empathetic, can think on an abstract level, and can make moral judgments based on values rather than external rules and consequences. Erikson (1963) views the core crisis during this period as *identity versus confusion*, as students work to develop a distinctive identity expressed through clothing styles, preferred activities, friendship groups, and personal goals. Adolescents can reflect on their own behaviors and interactions and can consciously plan to change behaviors, but the influence of peers is a strong force in shaping their behavior (Elias et al., 1997).

Adolescents are in the process of separating themselves from parents and the influence of family, and preferences for independent activities and time alone are typical. Interest in sexuality, dating, and intimate connections with others becomes increasingly important throughout the middle school years. Students explore ways of communicating with others whom they consider important, and they may play out their hopes for personal success and recognition through identification with popular students or famous people. Through this process, they become more realistic about the careers and lifestyles they may follow as adults.

Students with visual impairments are embarking on the same quest for independence and identity, but they often do so without a clear concept of the possibilities for adults with visual impairments. Adolescents who are visually impaired must have the strength to see beyond stereotypical views of blindness, some of which are expressed by neighbors, relatives, and teachers with whom they have regular contact. They must understand the implications of physical appearance on the impression they make on others, and they must make choices about their own clothing, hairstyle, and accessories based on feedback from others. In addition, they must develop the sensitivity toward communication from others that is required to initiate and monitor personal relationships so that they can make connections with others that may develop into intimate relationships. Social decisions of visually impaired adolescents are often based on limited information, but it is possible for them to be socially effective with appropriate opportunities for awareness and practice.

# SKILLS AFFECTED BY VISUAL IMPAIRMENT

Students with visual impairments demonstrate the same range of behaviors as any other cross section of students: some are talkative and some are quiet, some are demanding and others passive, some like to be with people constantly while others prefer more time to themselves. Whatever the student's personality, however, a visual impairment may affect his or her ability to receive some information about interactions with other people. For visually impaired students to be comfortable in relationships with others, they will need to make the best use of information that is available to them so that they can achieve an effective pattern of interaction.

## COMMUNICATION

The obstacles to communication experienced by students with visual impairments are subtle; they are related to the visual cues associated with communication as well as the discomfort others may have with the visual impairment.

### Nonverbal Communication

For a visually impaired child, the invisible aspects of communication may represent an inaccessible or limited source of information. However, making inferences from spoken language or asking others for information can supplement available messages, making the interpretation of information more accurate. Interventions at several levels can help students with visual impairments to learn about nonverbal skills.

The most basic intervention is to help the student with a visual impairment become aware of the use and types of nonverbal communication. Providing students with information about the types of gestures and body movements being used in standard conversation can make them aware of messages that supplement the spoken word. For young children, this may be as simple as knowing that people may pat their stomachs when saying "I'm hungry" or cover their faces when embarrassed. Students who can understand more complex communication should be aware that certain hand and arm movements, such as those referred to as "baton" symbols, add emphasis to an idea by creating the perception of force or movement. For example, a woman talking about returning a damaged piece of clothing to a store may move her open, flat hand down through the air when stating that the clothing is damaged, indicating that she's adamant about returning it. The hand movement has nothing to do with the specific situation, but it emphasizes the woman's intense feelings.

Adults or peers of students with visual impairments can mention these cues in casual conversation as a reminder that they are taking place along with spoken conversation. For example, the parent of a young blind child might comment, "That man was smiling when he asked if it was hot enough for us." This additional information helps the blind child understand that some messages are complex and that nonverbal information can conflict with what is said aloud. Sighted friends can briefly mention movements and expressions that are part of nonverbal communication during conversation to convey more information to a person who cannot see them. For example, it could be helpful to explain, "Sharon crossed her arms and looked sad when she said she liked her new school. I wonder if she has mixed feelings about it."

Students who are blind or visually impaired need to be aware of differences between movements and gestures that deliver a message in conflict with the spoken word (such as averting one's gaze or nervously weaving fingers in and out) and nonverbal signals that expand or support the spoken message (such as spreading the hands to indicate the length of a table). They must also realize that hand and body movements often accompany conversation in both formal and informal situations and that using appropriate gestures will help them be accepted and understood by others.

Learning to use nonverbal communication can take place through structured activities as well as in natural contexts. In early elementary school, games such as charades, pantomimes, or songs with body motions can provide the opportunity to practice nonverbal communication in a social context. For older students, participation in drama club or chorus can provide the context for specific feedback on appropriate nonverbal communication. Sometimes people are reluctant to provide feedback to older students about their appearance and physical movements, but it is important for visually impaired students to receive specific detail. This can be presented in a noncritical and informational manner by someone with whom the student is comfortable. Often, it is more appropriate to give this feedback in a private setting.

The following are some activities that can be fun and helpful in teaching visually impaired students about nonverbal communication skills.

## STRATEGIES FOR SOCIAL SUCCESS

# Teaching Nonverbal Communication

### For Elementary School Children

◆ Read a story that involves a variety of actions. During the reading, the children can use the gestures that go with the story. The reader can comment on effective or interesting gestures, or can suggest appropriate gestures for complex actions.

◆ Give a group of friends cards with an emotion word written in print and braille on each one, such as "angry," "delighted," or "disgusted." Have a student pick a card and try to show that emotion by using facial expressions. Sighted students in the room have to guess the emotion being portrayed. The same activity can be carried out with students using hand movements or whole body movements to show the emotion.

◆ Have a sighted student watch a speaker on a video or on television with the sound turned off and "narrate" the nonverbal communication. Ask the student who is blind or visually impaired to listen to the narration and describe what actions he or she thinks were going on or what the described expressions mean.

### For Middle School Students

◆ Invite an actor from a local theater to talk with students about body language and how the actor decides what gestures and actions to use. Have students participate in improvisations, with one student acting as a narrator to describe the body language of the participants.

◆ Have the student with a visual impairment work with a sighted partner to become aware of when he or she appears to be making eye contact or face contact. As the visually impaired student moves his or her face and eyes, ask the partner to says, "Now!" when the student appears to be making eye contact and paying the most attention to the partner. See if the student can maintain that same appearance while the partner talks about an experience.

◆ Have a student read aloud from a romance novel. (The poorer the novel, the more fun this is!) When the emotions of a character are described, have the students act out the character's actions and facial expressions. Select one participant to choose the best representation of the emotions described.

## Conversation

Understanding appropriate ways to enter, maintain, and leave a conversation is important for students with visual impairments. They need to realize that the use of visual cues is common practice and that they can substitute other ways of determining when to enter and participate in a conversation: Orienting head and body toward the speaker, using open hand gestures, nodding and smiling in response to others' comments are ways of indicating interest in a topic.

The occasional use of questions to gain information and maintain conversation is especially important to students with visual impairments. Some students ask too many questions or they ask questions that are inappropriate; other students are reluctant to request information because they feel it makes them appear dependent or vulnerable. Students who are visually impaired need to learn that questions are useful tools that can help them to understand experiences that cannot be seen. The appropriate and sparing use of questions can provide them with important information and it can also help others to understand what information is important to people with visual impairments.

Because students who are visually impaired may not be aware of objects around them, they may think of fewer things to talk about than their sighted peers. This can be of concern when meeting someone new; they cannot comment on the person's outfit or on a feature of the room in which they are standing. Practicing conversation starters may be especially important for an older student who must initiate conversation with peers, people in the workplace, or people who can provide directions or information in public areas. The following are some suggestions for helping students come up with their own conversation starters.

STRATEGIES FOR SOCIAL SUCCESS

# Conversation Starters

## For Elementary School Students

♦ Have a group of students think of different ways of greeting and saying good-bye to other people. Decide whether each example is formal, standard, or informal. Decide what level of conversation is appropriate when talking with the following people: a good friend; the friend of a parent; the cashier in the grocery store; a priest, rabbi, or minister; a peer you want to know better; a teacher; the school principal; a small child; your best friend's mother; a peer you do not want to get to know better; a salesperson at a technology fair.

♦ Ask students to listen to conversations among peers and adults and decide how the participants knew when it was appropriate to begin or enter a conversation. Have students interview older visually impaired students or adults about how they decide when to begin talking with others.

♦ Have students make a list of ten things to talk about with people they have just met. Ask students to role play starting a conversation about some of the topics on the lists. Discuss with the class how to know if a person is interested in the conversation.

## For Middle School Students

Suggest the following activities for middle school students with visual impairments:

♦ Write a questionnaire to survey other students about their interests and free-time activities (Sacks & Wolffe, 2000). Tally the responses to each question and decide what subjects are most interesting to other students and look at the answers given by boys and girls to see if they are different. Consider what subjects are more likely to be interesting to boys or to girls and what subjects are equally interesting to the two groups. Give the same questionnaire to students outside your school, for example students in a club or religious group. See if the answers from this group are different from those of students in school. After analyzing the questionnaires, make a list of subjects that students might be interested in talking about.

♦ Tape-record conversations of others (with permission). Listen to the recordings and decide when the topic of conversation is changed. Identify the person who decided to change the topic and how this person let others know that the topic was being switched. Pay attention to subtle changes of topic as well as sudden changes to a totally new subject.

◆ Ask visually impaired and sighted friends to describe flirting. How do they try to attract the attention of others when they are interested in getting to know them better?. Then, try role-playing behaviors that you think will increase attention from others; ask friends to supply feedback.

## INCREASING ASSERTIVENESS

From early childhood, children with visual impairments are often given extra guidance and instruction by others. Unfortunately, this may cause these children to distrust their own ability to make good decisions and to rely on others for important decisions. They may allow others to take control to please them and win them as friends. These children may not learn to assert themselves and to express their own wants and needs in a socially acceptable way. They may speak in a self-effacing manner that makes it clear that others are in control of the situation. These students develop a passive interaction style in which they are dependent on others to make decisions for them or to direct their actions.

Less often, visually impaired students are aggressive, attempting to exert physical or verbal control over others to get their way. Sometimes this occurs when a student is working to overcome a more passive style and becomes too demanding without considering others' perceptions. For example, a young person who learns his or her legal rights as a person with a disability may be quick to threaten litigation without trying to involve the other party as a participant in the solution. Students need to be aware that assertiveness means empowering all parties in an interaction.

In most situations, students will be more successful if they have learned to be assertive. This approach involves making their expectations known clearly and respectfully and participating in the process of solving problems. Assertive behavior is expressed through verbal and nonverbal behaviors that include body orientation and stance, voice volume, length of pauses in speech, statements of personal feelings and perceptions, and responses to others' feelings and perceptions. A person who is assertive can refuse or make requests, express feelings, and enter or exit conversations comfortably (Hargie, Saunders, & Dickson, 1994).

For visually impaired individuals, assertiveness increases their ability to request and refuse assistance appropriately, to provide information to others about their skills and abilities, and to make others comfortable in interacting with them. Assertiveness conveys a message that the student is confident and worthy of respect and encourages others to treat them as peers.

The following strategies may be used to help students who are blind or visually impaired learn skills to assert themselves in positive ways.

## STRATEGIES FOR SOCIAL SUCCESS
# Assertiveness Training

### For Elementary School Students

◆ Divide a group of friends or classmates into three groups: passive, assertive, or aggressive. Describe the differences between the three styles and provide examples. One person reads a scenario describing the following problem: "You are waiting in line to pay for a shirt in a department store. Someone steps in front of you and you hear them ask the salesperson to ring up their purchase." Each group must decide on a response that reflects their group assignment and demonstrate the response to the class.

◆ Discuss with students situations in which they acted passively. Discuss why they think they responded that way and what they could have done differently. Encourage students to think about whether someone else encouraged them to behave that way or if it was their own decision and why might they have behaved that way. Help students think of characters in books or films who act in passive, assertive, or aggressive ways. Discuss what happened to the character as a result of his or her behavior. Keep a list of the incidents, and ask students to add more examples during the school year.

### For Middle School Students

◆ Have students keep a journal of their social contacts for one week and document examples of passive, assertive, and aggressive behaviors. For passive and aggressive responses, have students work with a friend or mentor to find an alternative way of handling the situation. Suggest that the student participate in role plays in which the behavior is handled differently.

◆ Ask students to interview adults about their perception of assertiveness. Students might ask the adults to share examples of times when they acted assertively and discuss when, if ever, they believe that passive or aggressive responses are appropriate. The students can report their findings to their peers and discuss the question of whether assertiveness is always the most appropriate response.

◆ Introduce students to the broken record technique. This technique involves making a clear statement of one's goal and repeating the message until a resolution is reached (Pogrund & Strauss, 1992). Doing this turns attention to the goal without allowing deviation from the issue at hand and informs the other party that the problem has not been resolved. Give students an opportunity to practice it in a scenario in which they meet resistance in trying to accomplish something or think another person is taking advantage of them. Students can role play this technique until they master it.

## PARTICIPATING IN RITUALS AND ROUTINES

Participating in social activities and events depends in large part on being aware of the elements of the activity. The student who is blind or has low vision may have difficulty learning about the details of activities and therefore may be put at a disadvantage. For example, a student who is blind may know the words used by a television or radio commentator to describe a football game, but may not have a clear concept of how the players move during the game or where the goalposts are located. A child with low vision may be aware that church members go to the front of the church to take communion, but may not know that each individual stops and waits for the priest to offer the communion wafer.

Children experience a variety of routines and rituals. Some take place daily, such as reciting the Pledge of Allegiance and lining up on the playground. Other regular routines and rituals may occur less frequently, such as weekly religious services or scout meetings; and some take place infrequently, such as holiday rituals that occur once a year or family vacation routines. Infrequent routines may involve more preparation because the child may have forgotten his or her role since the last event, or the child's role may change with age and maturity. It is helpful to give children who are visually impaired opportunities to understand and prepare for events beforehand; for example, to examine the menorah before the first night of Hanukkah, to consider current popular characters for a Halloween costume well before the holiday, or to practice putting marshmallows on a stick before the summer camping trip.

To obtain the information needed to participate in an event, students who are visually impaired first need to understand what kind of information is inaccessible to them and then plan a way to obtain it. Also, students need to understand the sensory information that is received by others and be aware of what a sighted person can see, such as room decor and furnishings, facial expressions, groupings of people, arrangements of materials, and artifacts indicating level of formality (for example, understanding the difference between prewrapped plastic utensils at a meal versus a formal place setting that includes several forks and spoons). Students must be able to distinguish between information that helps them to participate appropriately (Are there designated seats? Where will the speaker be standing?) and information that may be a topic for conversation but is not essential (what pictures are on the walls or how many seats are in the room).

Then the student must plan a way to obtain the needed information appropriately, a skill that requires practice. Recognizing that the sound of a pencil or pen tapping, a door opening, or people standing up may be associated with actions or events that can prompt a visually impaired or blind child to ask appropriate questions ("Should I stand now?"), or to comment ("It sounds like more people have come on stage.") so that others will be aware of the need for more information. Use of appropriate and limited questions or comments will allow the individual to obtain the information necessary to participate in the routine.

Some rituals and routines involve components that are highly visual and may not be interesting to children who are visually impaired. A young child needs to understand what is involved before being offered the choice about whether or not to participate. When friends are attending the circus, for example, a child who is blind needs to know what the expectations are; for example, sitting in a seat for several hours and not being able to touch or move toward the people and animals. While there will be music playing and food for sale, there may be long periods of time in which the child will know what is happening only when others describe it. Adults might arrange a first experience of this type of event that is of limited duration and offers enough information for the child to decide whether to attend such events in the future. For example, it may be best to have a plan to leave the circus at intermission if the child's interest is waning.

The following strategies may be helpful for preparing visually impaired students for upcoming social events.

## STRATEGIES FOR SOCIAL SUCCESS

# Preparing for Events

## For Elementary School Students

◆ Have a group of friends or classmates describe three characteristics of a special event in their home or community. Ask other students to try to guess the event being described. For example, one person might give the clues: "We stay up late. Some people wear party hats. We sing 'Auld Lang Syne.' "

◆ Ask blind or sighted friends or classmates to take turns describing appropriate or inappropriate behavior in a social situation. The group gives a thumbs-up sign and shouts "Yay!" if the behavior is appropriate, or gives a thumbs-down sign and shouts "Boo!" if it is inappropriate. For example, if the speaker says, "Calling out your friend's name during a synagogue or church service," the group gives a thumbs-down sign, but if the speaker says, "Calling out your friend's name at a picnic," the group gives a thumbs-up sign. Assign one student to act as a reporter and interview another student about a family or community event or ritual. The reporter should be encouraged to find out about features of the event that might be visual and not immediately noticeable by students who are visually impaired; for example, Where do people sit during the event? Who makes the food? What kinds of clothes do people wear? Is it formal or informal?

## For Middle School Students

◆ Have a student who is blind or visually impaired visit a family or community event that involves an unfamiliar ritual, such as a religious service, local festival, or holiday event, accompanied by a sighted friend. Instruct the friend to record and document what he or she sees, while the visually impaired child reports on what he or she notices by using other senses. The students can then talk about how the rituals and customs are different from those they have experienced in their own families and communities. This will allow each student to understand how his or her partner gathers information and also broaden the students' understanding of various customs.

◆ Have a student prepare a tape recording for other students with visual impairments to tell them about a ritual or event that takes place in his or her family or community. The recording should describe customs or behaviors that the listener might not know about without seeing the people who are participating, for example, kneeling or standing during a religious service, eating foods in a certain sequence or combination, or sitting in a designated seat or area in a room. This provides experience in explaining and describing unfamiliar customs to others and helps the student to consider why families follow certain customs.

## Discussing Visual Impairment with Others

Students who are visually impaired need to understand the reactions of other people to visual impairment and to learn how to discuss their visual impairment appropriately. Most people welcome information that helps them interact appropriately with someone who is visually impaired, and a student who understands and responds to others' discomfort is more likely to be perceived positively.

Students need to be aware if their visual impairment makes them look unusual to others—for example, if a child's eyes move randomly or if a student has nystagmus, they need to know that they may look unusual to others. A student could practice a way to refer to the condition comfortably, for example, "You'll notice that my eyes move a lot, but I don't really see things in a shaky way—just blurry."

If a student with low vision has a condition that is not visible to others and decides not to mention it, he or she needs to consider how to address issues related to vision when they arise. For example, a middle school student whose friends are discussing plans for driving in the future needs to consider whether she wants to join the discussion as if she were going to drive, listen to others discuss their plans, or contribute from the perspective of a nondriver. Or, a student who cannot see store signs when shopping with others will need a way to locate a store if he decides not to ask for assistance. A student may be perceived as aloof and standoffish because she does not appear to make eye contact. A student's decision not to mention a visual impairment should be respected, but the student should be encouraged to consider the possible effects if he or she makes that decision.

At the early elementary level, a student needs to be able to describe what he or she can and cannot see. A simple explanation such as, "I can see people and what color they are wearing about 10 feet away, but I can't tell what expression is on their faces," may be enough information for people the child is meeting in a social situation. On the other hand, if the child is talking to a new teacher at school, the teacher will need to know if the child has sufficient vision to read print, use a computer, and find his or her own desk. Many teachers of students with visual impairments encourage their students to arrange a conference with new teachers at the beginning of the school year to talk about their visual impairment. By third grade, most students can take some responsibility for this kind of discussion, sometimes with support from the teacher of visually impaired students.

The student also needs to have a basic concept of the reason for his or her visual impairment and the effects of the impairment on vision. All students will meet people who misunderstand visual impairment or have false beliefs about its cause. Providing accurate information to the student will help him or her to counteract stereotypes or inappropriate cultural beliefs about visual impairment, for example that it is retribution for the behaviors of someone in the family. As the student gets older, he or she will be better able to provide a clear explanation of the impairment and its origin when he or she deems it necessary.

At the middle school level, students are usually mature enough to make independent decisions about how and when to talk about their visual impairment. However, students need to be aware of the possible outcomes of their choices in discussing or not discussing the disability. Students who are blind or visually impaired tend to receive too much assistance from others, but students with low vision often experience difficulty in obtaining appropriate assistance because others do not have clear information about what they need. Middle school students should be comfortable both requesting and redirecting assistance. It is also valuable for them to be able to serve as resources and mentors for younger students who have visual impairments. They need to be aware of sources for information, materials, and advocacy that will enable them to meet their own needs related to visual impairment. As they consider career choices, visually impaired students will have to discuss and describe the implications of their visual impairment for specific jobs.

The following strategies can help students of different ages become comfortable in talking about their visual impairment in various situations. See the Resources section at the end of this book for contact information for the organizations mentioned.

STRATEGIES FOR SOCIAL SUCCESS

# Discussing Visual Impairment

## For Elementary School Children

◆ Work with a student to plan a short presentation about his or her personal experiences with visual impairment. The student can practice presenting it to friends or classmates. If the student is anxious about giving a presentation to students in his or her class, suggest that he or she practice it first with younger students in another class. The presentation could include some of the following topics:

- a description of the visual impairment using glasses adapted to simulate the visual impairment

- a demonstration of low-vision devices such as a monocular

- a demonstration of braille

- a discussion of orientation and mobility techniques

◆ Ask students to write both a short and a long description of what they see. Have the student think about which description is most appropriate for different situations. For example, which is the best description to give a salesperson when asking for help reading a price tag? Which is best for a new friend in class whom the student will be seeing often? For a new math teacher? Talk about how to decide what information to give each person.

◆ Have students who are blind or visually impaired write a science fiction story about a piece of technology that would help them do things that they want to do, including a description of how the equipment would work and how they would use it.

## For Middle School Children

◆ Have students mentor a younger student who has a similar visual impairment. They can get help in finding the other student by asking their teacher of students who are visually impaired or by attending meetings of organizations for people who are visually impaired, such as the National Federation of the Blind or the American Council for the Blind. As a mentor, the student can share information they have learned about the visual impairment and talk about how they have responded to other people's reactions to the visual disability. They can write down some of their ideas in a letter or a list to help the younger student remember them.

◆ Have students search the Internet to find an organization that provides public information and advocacy materials about their specific visual condition. They can request materials from the organization and see if their own experiences are reflected in the materials. Students who are interested in contacting other people with the same condition can ask the organization for help.

◆ Assign students to interview working adults who are visually impaired about how they describe their visual impairment to prospective employers. The National Federation of the Blind or the American Council for the Blind can help find prospective people who students can interview, or students can use the CareerConnect Web site at www.afb.org/careerconnect. Students should prepare interview questions such as the following:

• When and how did you describe your visual impairment to your employer?

• How did employer react?

• What recommendations do you have for others with similar impairments who are applying for jobs?

Students may also interview employers about what they would want to know about a job applicant who is visually impaired.

◆ Have students maintain a file of contact information for people and agencies that can provide adaptations or information related to their visual impairment. For example, braille readers will want a list of local agencies that will transcribe braille materials, so that when they request brailled materials for a community event or religious service, the braille materials agency can help the student in obtaining it. This list should also include people or agencies that will repair or replace equipment that does not work.

## MONITORING APPEARANCE

One of the biggest challenges for students with a visual impairment is to monitor their own appearance and make choices about things that affect it. Because appearance is highly subjective and has such a strong impact on first impressions, students must understand the role appearance plays in how others react to them. If students do not have sufficient vision to observe the appearance of others and develop their own visual preferences, they may communicate an unintended message by the way they dress or by the expression their faces. (See also

Chapters 4 and 12 for perspectives on the importance of appearance in adolescence.)

Style of dress becomes increasingly important from upper elementary school and into middle school. Parents commonly make many clothing choices for first and second graders, and styles of dress are fairly standard at that age. By late elementary school, students more often choose their clothing based on the image they want to convey. For example, exposed midriffs, baggy pants, lacy dresses, and T-shirts with logos communicate something about the wearer, and it is often different from what adults may perceive as attractive. Starting in mid-elementary school, it is important for a child who is blind or has severe low vision to occasionally shop with young adults or teenagers of the same gender so that the visually impaired student can receive information about popular clothing. A babysitter, an older sister, or the college-aged son of a neighbor may be willing to go with an occasional shopping trip so that the student can become aware of the different styles preferred by different age groups.

Many of the messages conveyed by clothing and accessories are so subtle that others may overlook mentioning them to the child who is blind or visually impaired; yet these messages can contribute to a negative social image. For example, a student who wears baggy pants after his parent has ironed creases into them does not look the way the other boys do, and a 14-year-old girl who wears a T-shirt with pink dolls on it may not realize that her friends are now wearing shirts with rock musicians and movie stars imprinted on them. Decisions that may seem trivial to adults, such as tucking a shirttail in or leaving it out, wearing tight or loose pants, allowing underwear to show or covering it completely, or wearing flashy jewelry or natural beads, can make a difference in how a child is perceived by classmates in late elementary or middle school. Styles in hair, footwear, jewelry, book bags and backpacks, belts, and even notebooks and pens change regularly. Students with visual impairments need to remember to ask their friends about what is popular so that they can make decisions about dressing like their peers.

Many students with visual impairments are overweight or have limited muscle tone due to lack of physical activity. Students need to be aware that these physical characteristics can detract from their appearance and may cause others to react negatively toward them. Sometimes the advice of a fitness trainer or nutritionist can help them plan to reduce their weight and improve muscle tone, with the end goal of becoming more attractive and physically fit. Weight-related issues can be difficult to broach because people may often be reluctant to tell visually impaired students that they are seriously overweight; for example, congenitally blind students may be unaware of how stigmatizing extra weight can be in an appearance-oriented society. Visually impaired students who are not provided with this feedback may encounter some rejection and mistakenly believe it is the visual impairment that is causing others to avoid him or her. Discussions about weight and health issues should take place with the knowledge and support of the family, but the issue should not be ignored out of concern for offending the student.

Although it may seem artificial for students to attend to visual characteristics that may not be pleasing or interesting to them personally, they should be aware that appearance can influence others' responses. Feedback from one or two good friends about clothing, weight, and appearance can help students become aware of how they look to others and how they can project the impression that they prefer. The following strategies are designed to be used with visually impaired students to assist them in monitoring their appearance and recognizing the role appearance plays in their lives.

## STRATEGIES FOR SOCIAL SUCCESS
# The Importance of Appearance

### For Elementary School Students

◆ Have students select a trusted friend to act as a clothes consultant and to spend a few minutes with the visually impaired student every morning discussing their appearance when they get to school. Talk with the friend about the best ways to communicate information clearly and suggest ways to fix a problem. For example, the student can say, "Your belt is very tight and is up above your waist. Most people wear their belts really loose this year and let their pants go down a little. Look at how mine is."

◆ Assign students to interview people who work in various work settings and ask them to describe how people dress for work, including questions about whether anyone wears a uniform or other required form of dress and about how clothing varies among people in different job roles and between males and females.

◆ Assign students to interview their parents and grandparents about the fads, music, and clothing styles of their teenage years. Talk about how those compare to current music and clothing styles. Discuss why unusual fads become popular and why students might choose to wear the current fashions.

## For Middle School

◆ Invite a speaker from a human resources office to talk to students about dressing for an interview and how business clothing has changed over time. Discuss the appropriate types of clothing for different types of jobs. Encourage students to ask the speaker questions about how clothing and appearance might influence the decisions of a prospective employer.

◆ Encourage students to get involved in fitness training at a YMCA or other activity center with a friend or a group of friends. If appropriate, as a birthday or holiday gift, suggest that a family member pay for a session with a personal trainer who can give the student specific feedback on how to improve physical fitness and appearance. If the student is concerned about weight, a nutritionist might help plan appropriate meals based on the student's activity level.

## ESTABLISHING AND MAINTAINING FRIENDSHIPS

As students move from elementary to middle school, friendships become more flexible and less focused on the more rigid roles of best friends and friendship groups. (See Chapter 6 for additional discussion of friendships.) Students learn that they can have friends and acquaintances in different settings and contexts and that friendships can strengthen or diminish over time. The friendships of students with visual impairments, like those of their peers, are based on common interests and social roles (Rosenblum, 2000).

In elementary school, social interactions at school often center on gross motor play or ball games on the playground, which can present significant disadvantages to the student who cannot see well enough to locate friends or moving balls (MacCuspie, 1996). Kekelis (1988) describes a study in which one blind child's interactions increased when a play table was provided on the playground, allowing him to use smaller toys and materials in a controlled setting where other children could approach. Kekelis found that this student's interactions increased when there was less adult intervention. Even though toys that can be manipulated by hand allow children who are visually impaired to have more control, they also allow children to play separately and may reinforce the child's tendency toward solitary play. Therefore, it is important to select toys and materials that encourage children to interact. For example, a dump truck that hooks to a trailer, a shape box that allows several children to insert shapes simultaneously, or a model house large enough for several children to play in may encourage more social contact than objects like blocks or tiles that can be divided and used separately.

The student with a visual impairment may also have difficulty locating and identifying specific students with whom to establish friendships. Teachers may consider changing seating arrangements regularly to ensure that the student with a visual impairment gets the opportunity to sit near and get to know a variety of students. One teacher described by Kekelis and Sacks (1992) changed seating arrangements in her kindergarten class regularly. This allowed the student who was blind to have contact with different classmates, including those who were socially skilled and could draw the student into new circles of friends.

There may be activities in which students who are visually impaired cannot participate or from which they do not derive the same satisfaction as their sighted friends. In these cases, the friends will need to balance their different interests with their wish to spend time together. All friends have both common and differing interests. The teacher of students with visual impairments may need to remind students with visual impairments of this so that they do not feel rejected if a friend wants to do something that they do not enjoy. Most middle school students have groups of friends who socialize together. The visually impaired student who has a number of good friends has learned not to depend on just one individual for assistance, and the student can enjoy different activities with different friends. This visually impaired student can find ways to reciprocate when assistance such as transportation is needed.

Although sports and physical activities are popular ways for sighted students to spend leisure time, this is not as true for students with visual impairments. Adults who work with students with visual impairments may need to offer suggestions about physical activities that both sighted students and students with visual impairments can participate in together. Pfisterer (1983) developed a handbook of games and activities that can be played by groups of students in integrated settings. Among his ideas are floor volleyball (in which the volleyball is rolled rather than thrown), and partner activities such as Indian wrestling and trying to step on a partner's toes while holding hands.

The following are strategies that teachers may use to help visually impaired students develop friendships.

## STRATEGIES FOR SOCIAL SUCCESS

# Interaction with Friends

### For Elementary School Students

◆ Encourage students to spend free time using those materials and objects that the student personally enjoys and that invite participation by others. For example, an activity table on the playground where children can play jointly with building materials, trucks, houses, figures, or other manipulatives offers more opportunity for interaction than running games or using playground equipment.

◆ Talk to the classroom teacher about making cooperative learning part of the classroom routine. Cooperative groups can provide the opportunity for children to assist one another and take responsibility for accomplishing a task as a group. (See Chapter 8 for information about cooperative learning.)

◆ Help the student who is visually impaired to survey other students about how they spend their time. Ask each student in a class or group to make a list of the five things they like to do best in their free time. Have the visually impaired student make his or her own list. The student can pick something mentioned by other students that he or she would like to learn about, discuss how he or she could learn the skill needed to participate, and approach other students with the same interests to find ways of participating in the activity.

### For Middle School Students

◆ Encourage students with visual impairments to talk with adults and other children about how they met their close friends. Discuss with the students various places that they go where they could make new contacts with other students of the same age. Students can role play introducing themselves to new contacts, starting conversations with them, and communicating that they would like to get to know the person better. For example, to encourage future contact, a student might suggest another time to get together for a specific activity or invite several students to his or her home.

◆ Direct the visually impaired student to think of someone who is or has been a good friend. Then have the student make a list of things that the friend does that make the student feel good and that the student does that makes the friend feel good. Talk to the student about the importance of balance in a friendship, or have the student discuss this with a mentor or peer and ask how the other person has maintained that balance in their own personal friendships.

◆ Have students role play how to handle situations in which friends disagree, for example, in which one person wants to do something that a friend thinks is wrong or a scenario in which someone does not seem to want to spend time with his or her friend.

Have students find examples in books and videos of friendships that worked well and friendships that changed. Discuss why friendships may change and why they may remain strong over time.

# STRATEGIES FOR INTERVENTION

A number of structured strategies have been successful in increasing appropriate social behaviors for students who have visual impairments. Regardless of the specific strategy chosen, however, success is more likely when the instructional strategy is practiced in a real context, and if it is also taught and reinforced by the student's peers. For example, an auditory reminder for a student to stop body rocking will not be as effective if the teacher of visually impaired students only uses it during individual sessions and no one provides the reminder in the classroom. MacCuspie (1996) emphasizes the importance of involving students in the planning of their own social skills intervention, with attention to privacy issues, cultural variations, and appropriate methods of feedback.

## MODELING

Modeling, or observing and imitating the behaviors of others, is the way in which children typically learn social behaviors. Modeling can provide the student with the opportunity to observe how others manage a social situation. For example, a child who watches a parent and others wait in line at the grocery store learns that customers line up based on when they arrived at the checkout counter. Research has shown that modeling through direct observation or media (such as videotapes or audiotapes of a particular situation) is effective in modifying behaviors (Cartledge & Milburn, 1995). For a student with a visual impairment, planned modeling can provide more frequent exposure to social behaviors in a meaningful form. Cartledge and Milburn (1995) note that the first exposure to a modeled skill must include a rationale for the behavior.

For elementary school–aged children, stories and folktales can be used as a motivating way to explain social behaviors. For older students, it may be effective to present a scenario twice, once with a successful outcome and once with an unsuccessful outcome.

Depending on the child's age, cognitive level, and degree of vision loss, different forms of modeling may be motivating. For the younger child, modeling can involve the use of dolls or puppets. The use of a pretend character can add interest and allow the child to maintain distance from the behavior, especially if it is embarrassing or uncomfortable for the child to acknowledge. Use of media such as videotapes, audiotapes, television, or radio can also be effective for certain behaviors. Audio- or videotaped models can be replayed, allowing students to attend to certain features of the modeled behavior that they may not have noticed during their initial observation. For example, an audiotape of a conversation between a visually impaired student who needed a ride to the mall and a sighted friend could be replayed to allow listeners to focus on how the student mentioned her interest in shopping first, so that the friend offered her a ride before she had to make a direct request.

Books and stories can also provide models for effective social behaviors. Like tapes, they can be reread to review and reconsider the behaviors of the characters. Having children write their own stories demonstrating solutions to a social problem can encourage problem-solving in a safe, imaginary setting; it can be an effective way to try out behavior before transferring it to real situations.

Another effective modeling strategy is for students to observe peers when they are using a particular strategy. This strategy can be effective both as a role play and in a real situation. For example, a student who is reluctant to ask for assistance when shopping can observe a role play of a peer requesting assistance and then travel to a store with several friends to watch how they ask for help when needed. The student with a visual impairment might be assigned the role of an "undercover reporter" to gather information and examples of a particular social behavior in daily interactions of people. These observations may also remind the student that everyone requests assistance in public situations and that asking for help is often the most efficient use of time.

## Role Playing

Role playing involves structured and rehearsed interactions that can later be applied in real situations. For example, a student who wants to ask a teacher for a different seat in the classroom may practice making the request with the teacher of students who are visually impaired playing the role of the classroom teacher. A student who is reluctant to invite another student to join him for a hike or a concert might write a script for making the request and tape-record the rehearsal. A student who has difficulty telling others when she does not need assistance might role play the situation until she can comfortably explain that she appreciates the offer but does not need help.

Having practiced the words and movements associated with an interaction, an individual is more likely to be comfortable in the applied situation. Asking a girl for a date, requesting directions from another person, or making conversation with a new acquaintance can become more comfortable if the student has a chance to practice the skills aloud. If the student chooses to involve a friend or peer in the role play after learning a routine, it can be especially effective in creating a new scenario.

## PEER-MEDIATED INTERVENTION

The work of Sacks and Gaylord-Ross (1992) indicates that peer intervention was more successful than intervention by adults in encouraging the generalization of skills. Peer-mediated interventions involve one or more students who are the same age as the students with visual impairments (see Chapter 7 for a more detailed discussion). Sacks and Wolffe (2000) describe peer-mediated social skills training in which a sighted peer is instructed about the skills to be developed and, along with the teacher, identifies strategies for promoting social outcomes. For example, a visually impaired student who forgets to face others when speaking can develop a plan for a friend to give a little cough as a reminder to the student to turn toward the speaker when talking. The teacher may suggest ways of teaching but also emphasizes that the instruction is a partnership, not an interaction that places the peer in a controlling position. Frequent meetings and specific, constructive feedback are the key factors to success with this strategy.

A similar intervention, peer-supported social skills training, prepares a group of peers who have regular contact with the visually impaired student to be models for appropriate behaviors (Sacks & Wolffe, 2000). It is essential for the student with a visual impairment to understand and agree with this method and for several peers to rotate roles frequently so that the student learns from multiple models.

It is important for peers to be trained in the specific type of intervention to be used and for the intervention be limited to only the targeted behavior. The intervener and the student with a visual impairment both need to be aware of the behavior to be changed and the method to be used for changing the behavior. The relationship between the student and the intervener needs to be one of cooperation, not one in which the intervener is perceived as a helper, a role that may reinforce dependence. If possible, the student with a visual impairment can provide a service for the intervener, such as assistance with homework, to provide balance in their roles.

When undesirable behaviors are being reinforced by peers, peer programming can be an appropriate way of changing behavior. For example, a child who is blind who makes humorous noises in class may be reinforced by the laughter of peers. If peer programming is applied, the student with a visual impairment earns a reward for the entire class or peer group when he or she is successful in changing the behavior (Cartledge & Milburn, 1995). This method makes it advantageous for other students to support changes in the behavior of the target student, and it may additionally benefit middle school students by encouraging them to view change as a collaborative effort.

## MENTORING

Mentoring is also an important way of assisting students to learn appropriate social skills. (See Chapter 7 for a more detailed discussion of mentors.) The mentor should be an older student or adult who is visually impaired, and in most cases it will be most appropriate for the mentor and student to be of the same gender. Because visually impaired children in public schools may have little or no contact with others who are visually impaired, connection with a mentor who is visually impaired may provide opportunities to understand what experiences are common among people with visual impairments and how others have handled specific issues. Elementary school–aged students may not have a clear idea of how other people's reactions to them are related to their visual impairment; adolescents may discount guidance from parents or teachers because they feel that these adults can't understand the experience of a visually impaired person.

Although contacts with a mentor are usually initiated by the mentor or the adult who has made the arrangements, the student should be encouraged to initiate the frequency of the contact and the activities that are shared as the relationship develops. Shopping for clothing, attending concerts, having a meal at a restaurant, visiting the mentor's workplace, or sharing recreational activities are experiences that may combine enjoyable companionship with opportunities for the mentor to discuss his or her experience with visual impairment. A mentorship that is required or scheduled by parents or teachers can prevent the student from fully participating in the development of the relationship. A true mentoring relationship is satisfying to both the mentor and student.

The role of a mentor is to support and encourage a student. The relationship should be mutually satisfying and conversations or visits should be with the agreement of both individuals. The mentor is a guide for the student. He or she should facilitate and listen, not direct or discipline. The mentor should provide connections to new experiences and contacts with new people, but she or he should not take the place of peer friends or of parents. The following are some possible ways in which mentors may interact effectively with their student.

## STRATEGIES FOR SOCIAL SUCCESS
# Tips for Mentors

◆ Discussing personal experiences and solutions to problems posed by visual impairment

◆ Introducing leisure-time activities that are new to the student

◆ Inviting the student to accompany him or her during regular activities at work, home, or in the community

◆ Attending events and activities related to the student's career interests

◆ Introducing the students to others who have common interests or experiences that they might share with the student

◆ Listening and reflecting the student's concerns about personal difficulties

◆ Assisting the student in establishing goals and plans for how to achieve them

### ACTIVITY-BASED INTERVENTION

Activity-based intervention emphasizes social skills instruction that takes advantage of natural opportunities that occur in the regular classroom (Sadler, 2001). The teacher of students who are visually impaired, classroom teacher, or paraeducator serves as a coach or support during activities that the child has chosen, particularly during playtime or free-choice activities. Through prompting (verbal reminders) and shaping (decreasing prompts to improve independence), the child learns to use the appropriate skills in the real situation. For example, the visually impaired child might pretend to be a talk show host and act out ways of entering and exiting a conversation with several classmates who impersonate the guests on the show; the teacher might remind him, "Joe, how do you know this is a time you can talk?" Because the situation is motivating and the child applies the learning during real activities, the child can generalize the skills more easily. This model can be appropriately supported by a teacher of the visually impaired who is in the general education classroom infrequently; but it may have the disadvantage of not offering frequent enough opportunities to practice a particular skill (Sadler, 2001).

## BEHAVIORAL APPROACHES

Many aspects of traditional behavioral change can be applied to social learning. When deciding on interventions, it is important to target the behaviors to be changed and record data about the characteristics of those behaviors. The Antecedent-Behavior-Consequence method can be used to identify causes and reinforcers of behaviors and is an appropriate method for discovering the origins of social behaviors (Merrell & Gimpel, 1998). Like any behaviors, inappropriate social behaviors continue because they are reinforced. When educators recognize the reinforcers, they can better plan ways to change the behavior. Children who are visually impaired may respond to different reinforcers because of their visual impairment. For example, a child who is given a time-out for being uncooperative may actually enjoy the chance to get away from distracting sounds, and the child who rocks back and forth may continue to do so because the physical stimulation is more pleasant than the annoyance of the occasional mild reprimand he or she receives. Material reinforcers such as stickers may not be motivating to a visually impaired child unless the child views them as something that is valued by classmates.

When applying the principles of behavioral change, educators need to consider when and how often a behavior occurs, what causes it to continue, and what might discourage it. This approach may be effective with younger or cognitively disabled students who do not have a strong desire to please others or to be included in social groups within the classroom. It requires team members to consider what external reinforcers might be powerful enough to change social behaviors that are habitual or comfortable for a student. Different students may respond to different rewards; examples that have been effective with visually impaired students include listening to a favorite song or record, doing a classroom errand, earning a token toward a reward, receiving hand lotion with a good smell, sitting beside a favorite person, and playing a musical instrument. A structured plan of behavioral management also includes a plan for specific learning and generalization so that the behavior becomes a permanent part of the student's repertoire of responses.

## COGNITIVE APPROACHES

Cognitive approaches to changing social behaviors assume that the student can understand the difference between rational and irrational thoughts as well as the connection between thoughts and behaviors (Cartledge & Milburn, 1995).The individual must recognize both the events that affect the behavior and his or her own power to change the response. For example, a girl who is blind who is not assertive with her friends must recognize that she may be allowing them to impose their choice of activities during free time out of fear of offending them and losing their friendship. To change this behavior, the child first needs to consider the validity of the belief that others will stop liking her if she expresses her preferences. Then she needs to recognize what needs to be changed (agreeing to others' choices) and practice a substitute behavior (making a suggestion based on her own preferences). Practicing and testing the substitute behavior can help the student decide whether it is the best solution in the specific situation.

A cognitive approach empowers the child to make his or her own decisions and provides the child with a strategy that can be used when the situation arises. It encourages the student to think of a variety of solutions to a problem, consider the possible outcomes, choose the best strategy, implement it, and assess the outcome (Elias & Clabby, 1992). For students with visual impairments, taking responsibility for their own decisions can be a powerful force in contradicting the message from peers, teachers, and community members that others need to be responsible for them because they are visually impaired.

All of the strategies described in this section can be combined in planning for effective social change for the student with a visual impairment. The choice of strategies will depend on a variety of factors, including the age and mental ability of the child, the child's own preferences, resources available in the school environment, the time available for social intervention, and the nature of the behavior to be changed. Regardless of the method chosen, students who are visually impaired need to be active participants in their own social expansion, and it is important for them to recognize the benefits of increased social skills and more effective interactions.

## TEACHING SOCIAL SKILLS

Several factors affect decisions about how to teach social skills, but the primary factor is the individual student. Students need to understand how they can benefit from learning social skills, and as much as possible, they should be encouraged to participate in deciding what specific skills they want to learn. In addition, students may have personal preferences about a skill or intervention that needs to be considered in instructional planning. For example, a teacher thinks peer coaching would be a helpful strategy for reminding a student not to rock, but the student may feel that the issue is too personal and may not want others involved. The student's preferences need to be respected, although the teacher can provide the student with information about how involving another person could make learning easier. Helping visually impaired students learn how to make their own decisions needs to be a high priority because these skills will equip students to set and achieve future goals related to social behaviors. For this reason, it is important for students to make the decisions about if and how to involve others in the development and achievement of their social goals.

The extent of the student's participation and the type of intervention will also vary with a student's age and abilities. Younger students or students with cognitive delays may not understand that appropriate social skills result in approval or attention from others. For these students, using skills that have been taught needs to produce immediate positive results; for example, using "please" when making a request should result in receiving the desired item or eating a whole meal with utensils should result in having a favorite food. As a child becomes older, the reasons behind social responses can be explored and the child may want to learn about more complicated uses of social skills, such as how they vary in formal and informal situations or in interactions with people from different cultures.

## DETERMINING TEACHING STRATEGIES

### Involvement of Peers in Social Change

Involving the student's peers in the intervention is a critical factor in effecting change in a visually impaired student's social skills. Researchers have often noted that students with visual impairments spend more time with adults than their sighted peers (MacCuspie, 1996). Children with visual impairments may prefer to interact with adults because they are more predictable, usually follow established social rules, and can understand the implications of visual impairment. For these students to achieve social success, however, they need to establish skills that enable them to interact effectively with other children and to receive positive reinforcement from these social contacts. Therefore, it is important to involve other children in the development of social skills of the visually impaired student whenever possible. The selection of peers may be based on not only the specific skill and its application, but also on the preference of the student with visual impairments, the interest of peers, the existence of established friendships, the importance of older students as mentors, and the common interest of students in an activity.

As noted earlier, it is important that the peer involved in the intervention be encouraged to regard the interaction with the student with a visual impairment as a mutually beneficial contact that provides options for both participants to learn and change, rather than an interaction in which the peer dominates and is in control of the relationship. It is often assumed that the peers involved in an intervention program should be friends of the student with a visual impairment, but other options ought also to be considered. There are some benefits to involving peers who are not well acquainted with the visually impaired individual, including the peer's ability to be objective in the absence of a personal relationship with the student. Sometimes peers who are having academic or social difficulties exhibit increased self-esteem or responsibility as a result of their involvement as a peer mediator or coach.

### Setting

The setting or environment is also a factor in determining the type of intervention that is appropriate, and the setting in which the skills are to be used needs to be part of the planning for the intervention strategies. For example, teaching skills for interacting with new people cannot be taught in the regular classroom where all students know one another, and skills for planning social contacts during leisure time must be applied outside of school.

Sometimes, students who spend all of their school day in the regular classroom prefer not to participate in a social skills intervention that calls attention to their visual impairment; instruction in a separate setting can be considered in these instances. Practicing social skills in a middle school setting where there is contact with different students at different times of day may also require more planning for appropriate peer involvement. Students who attend specialized schools may serve as peer interveners for one another, but the methods and approaches may need to be adapted based on the peer intervener's degree of vision.

## Timing and Frequency

The frequency of practice and reinforcement will also depend on the skill to be taught and the student's level of proficiency. In general, students will learn and apply a skill more quickly when practice is more frequent. However, this must be considered with regard to the following factors:

- *Natural context.* In most cases instruction and practice should take place in the natural environment. For example, shaking hands is best practiced when there are visitors in the class to be introduced; asking for assistance can be reinforced when the student wants a human guide; and manners for a social event can be taught when a teenager is preparing to go to the prom or to a formal event such as a family wedding. If the opportunity for applied practice occurs infrequently (for example, if a student who needs to practice initiating conversations only has informal social contact with peers at lunchtime), more artificial opportunities may need to be created, such as inviting peers to the student's session with the teacher of visually impaired students.

- *Student's anxiety level.* Although anxiety is usually decreased by practice, frequent practice may not be tolerated until students are comfortable with the skill. In these cases, rehearsed practice strategies such as role playing may be used before applying the skills.

- *Student's learning characteristics.* Students who learn slowly or forget easily will need more frequent practice. In these cases, involvement of several peers and staff in the learning program may be necessary to create more frequent opportunities for practice throughout the day.

## TEACHING AND REINFORCING SKILLS

The process of learning social skills follows the same principles as learning to change any other behavior. The motivation to learn a new way of doing things must be stronger than the incentive to continue behaving in familiar ways. The learner needs a clear understanding of what new behavior is expected and how to do it. Then they need to practice it and receive specific feedback on their actions. This means that observation, modeling, and rehearsal will be important aspects of the change. The student needs adequate opportunity to practice the behavior until it is mastered, as well as a chance to generalize it by using it in the settings in which it will really be used.

## Motivators and Reinforcers

For a student who is visually impaired and has no additional disabilities, the motivators to perform social skills are the same as for other students: They want to be accepted, to have friends, and to fit in with peers. Changes in social behaviors may be reinforced by the experience of more satisfying social relationships. The opportunity to engage in varied social activities with friends and to have a more stimulating, positive social experience is the main objective of social learning. Ultimately, attention and positive responses from others should be sufficient to support behavioral changes. However, planned reinforcement for social behaviors may need to be included in the learning strategy to motivate students to make changes in their behaviors. For example, specific praise from peers and adults about the improved behavior can be a powerful reinforcer for the student to continue the behavioral change.

Students with multiple disabilities may not be as motivated to interact with others, particularly if they have severe developmental disabilities or autism (see Chapter 13). For these students, social situations may need to be accompanied by experiences that are known to be motivating for the child, such as preferred foods, vestibular activities like swinging or dancing, or listening to favorite music. Eventually the child will associate these desirable events with the company of other people. Reinforcers may also need to be provided while the desired behavior is taking place, particularly for children who have a very limited memory span. For example, a child who cries at the sound of a human voice might be reinforced by a primary reinforcer such as a food treat or a firm touch when he or she does not cry when someone is speaking. Eventually the frequency of the reinforcer can be decreased. Secondary (more abstract) reinforcers such as verbal praise or tokens saved for a privilege can be substituted as the child comes to associate the appropriate social behavior with a positive experience or result.

Educational team members need to be aware of what motivators will be reinforcing for particular students. Attractive clothing, for example, may have positive associations for a student who is blind and who is socially aware and associates clothing with compliments from peers and acquaintances, but it may not be intrinsically motivating for a child who has limited understanding of how clothing appears and how others value its appearance. Aspects of voice and suprasegmental (nonverbal) features of speech may have more important implications for students who are blind or visually impaired, who often base their impressions of others more on voice and less on physical appearance. In many ways, this may represent a more realistic perception of another person's personality and thinking for any listener, but visually impaired students need to be aware that sighted people frequently are heavily biased by physical appearance and that their first impressions are influenced more by appearance than by voice.

## Teaching the Skill

Like all new skills, social skills can be taught most effectively by a process that is clear and motivating for the learner. As already noted, it is imperative that the learner understand the goal as clearly as possible and that he or she be a part of the decision to change a particular behavior. If students with multiple disabilities do not understand the reasons for certain social skills, the behavior may need to be explained through demonstration and action; in this case, it is even more important that the desired behavior be specifically demonstrated and reinforced.

Many social skills can best be taught in the actual situation where they will be applied. This ensures that the student has both a need for the skill and an understanding of its context, as shown in the following example:

> While walking to class with her third-grade student who is blind, a
> teacher of students with visual impairments notices that when
> other students greet Joe, he shouts, "Who is that?" Some students
> identify themselves, but others just laugh and continue walking.
> The teacher suggests to Joe that he try returning their greeting first,
> saying, "Hi, how are you doing?" She explains that it might not
> always be important to know who every speaker is. They also discuss
> whether Joe would like to suggest to his classmates that they greet him

*by saying their name—for example, "Hi, Joe! It's Tim"—when they pass him in the hall.*

The families of students who are blind or visually impaired also need to be aware of the skills to be taught to the child. Some families may have different ways of looking at social interactions because of cultural background, and sometimes they may not have considered why a social skill might be learned differently by a child who is visually impaired. They also may not be aware that a student with a visual impairment should be expected to perform certain skills that seem visual, such as orienting toward others when speaking. When family members are aware and involved, they can encourage the child to practice the skill outside of school.

## Evaluating Outcomes

Changes in skills are more rapid and permanent if the student receives feedback about when the goal is achieved. This means that the student must know the desired outcome and be able to identify whether it has occurred. The following suggestions offer some ways in which students can evaluate their own success.

*Listen to what others say about role-playing scenarios.* After students participate in a role play, they might first share their own evaluation of how well they have addressed the skill. Then peers or adults can provide specific feedback about what elements of the role play were successful and which ones were not. After additional skills are addressed, then the student can reenact the role play to refine the skills, as in the following example:

> *Sharon, Peter, and Naomi role play a social conversation so that Sharon can practice entering the conversation appropriately. The first time they enact the scenario, Sharon approaches the others, orients her body, smiles, and nods while she is listening to Peter and Naomi talk about a concert they attended. But when she enters the conversation, she interrupts Peter and comments that she is looking forward to the pep rally that day.*
>
> *The four students who are observing comment that Sharon did a good job of showing that she wanted to talk with the others, but they suggest that she ask a question about the concert instead of beginning a new topic right away. The next time they try the scenario, Sharon does this and is able to gradually introduce a new topic.*

*Keep data about specific behaviors.* If a particular behavior is targeted, students need to know what the behavior is and how it will be measured. They can keep a list or tally of how often the behavior occurs. This may be easier to do when paired with a friend or acquaintance, who can keep documentation or let the student know that the behavior is occurring. Older students may even want to analyze the data about their behavior, by asking such questions as What is the average number of times I rocked in class this week? Did it decrease when my friend tapped his desk to remind me to stop? When he only gave the signal sometimes, was the rocking more frequent? The following scenario demonstrates how one student tracked his own behavior:

> *Jorge was a middle school student who wanted to get to know more girls. When he talked to girls, he would tell them all about himself. They would listen for a while and then say they had to go somewhere. If he asked them to have lunch with him or to take a walk, they always had a reason why they could not do it.*
>
> *In a peer-intervention meeting, two of Jorge's friends said that he should find out more about the girl and not talk about himself as much. They suggested he get to know some girls without asking them to do something with him right away. He agreed that for two weeks he would keep track of how many girls he talked with and that he would try to find out two things about each girl. He would keep track of the information in a notebook. When the peers met again at the end of two weeks, he found out that he had talked with 8 girls the first week and 15 the second week. The friends began to talk about which girls seemed most interesting and why. Then they set the next goal, which was to find the girls he liked best and talk to them again.*

*Talk to someone else about a social goal.* Talking to another person who understands the student's efforts in trying to change a behavior, whether a mentor such as an older student, a teacher or another adult, or a friend or classmate, can provide important feedback. As the student describes how he or she tried to change the behavior and why he or she thinks it did or did not work, the other person can listen and help the student to think about the best way of improving the skill. The following example shows how one student enlisted the support of a mentor:

> *Patty wants to be more assertive and to make decisions for herself instead of letting others tell her how to do things. She decides to practice doing this with her two sisters, who often say what they want and then tell Patty what they think she should do. One day they decide to go shopping and ask Patty if she wants to come with them.*

*Patty tells them she would like to go to the Southland Mall because she wants some new shoes. Her sisters say that they want to shop for dresses at the Eastside Mall and that there is no time to look at shoes. Patty agrees to go with them, but she does not enjoy the shopping trip because she feels that her opinion was not important.*

*Lauren, an older student who is also blind, listens to Patty tell about her experience. She asks Patty what she could have done when her sisters did not want to go to the Southland Mall. Patty realizes that she might have invited a friend to shop with her or said that she would wait to go shopping until there was time to look for shoes. She also realizes that she was responsible for her own resentful feelings because she decided to go along with her sisters even though it was not her choice. After talking with Lauren, she is also aware that she was successful in expressing her wishes and that being assertive does not always mean that she will get what she wants.*

Outcomes can be evaluated if the goal is clear to the student and to the individuals involved in the change process. While evaluation can take place through documentation, data collection, or spoken feedback, the student needs to be enlisted in taking responsibility for evaluating whether the goal has been met and establishing the next step.

## Generalizing and Reinforcing Skills

Mastering a new skill may take a long time. When a student learns a skill in one context, it is not thoroughly learned unless the student can apply the skill to another context. For example, being able to role play asking for assistance in a store does not mean the student can actually ask for help in a real store. Thorough learning must include the application of the skill in real situations, and students must be able to apply the skills in several contexts. If the skill is taught in a separate context, as it is with role playing, then a plan for trying it out in different settings to determine whether it is useful is also needed. In the following example, Paul is able to generalize his learning of specific skills to a real-life situation:

*Paul wanted to be more effective in using gestures while speaking in public. He worked with two friends and his teacher of visually impaired students to develop gestures that looked natural, and they discussed such factors as the meaning of an open hand versus a closed fist when speaking. They role played some short scenarios while Paul added the gestures he felt were appropriate.*

*When Paul was assigned a speech in his English class, one of his friends worked with him on the gestures and made a few notes when he delivered the speech. Because he was nervous when he gave the speech, he didn't use as many gestures as he had practiced. At one point he forgot his speech because he was busy thinking of the gestures. However, he received a grade of B and his friend told him that most of the gestures looked very natural. The next month, Paul participated in a play at church, following the same procedure for practicing gestures and using them in the play. He heard someone in the audience say, "It's hard to believe that boy is blind!" and he considered that a compliment on his use of gestures.*

A specific skill is more likely to be generalized if the student identifies the contexts in which he or she wants to use it. Even though a skill may be practiced apart from the real situation, students can be encouraged to investigate and observe how people in a real situation use the skill.

It is also important for students to understand that it is not unusual for people to feel some anxiety when they are trying out a new skill in a natural environment. Much of the discomfort stems from the switch from the practice environment to the real one; students need to understand that it takes time to become comfortable in the context of the real situation even if they are already at ease in the practice environment.

It is also important for students to periodically check their goals to determine which ones have already been met and which ones still need work, and to ensure that no regression has occurred. Peers can be enlisted to spot check for specific skills; for example, a peer could make sure the student is still using a specific gesture or is remembering to ask questions about other people.

## CONCLUSION

Visual impairment makes socialization more complex because students may not have access to information that can verify the feelings and responses of others; however, with appropriate feedback and practice, these students can become as socially competent and comfortable in social interactions as their sighted peers. Students with visual impairments demonstrate the same range of personalities and variety of social interests as other students. In elementary and middle school, visually impaired students need to learn about appropriate expressions of feeling, shaping their reactions to respond to others, and building long-term friendships and personal relationships. By the time they reach middle school, these students need skills to interact in larger groups and a larger variety of environments, to be aware that friendships can be fluid and unpredictable for all students at that age, to plan for future needs, and to learn about standards for appearance that affect how others respond to them.

As children mature, peers become increasingly important as a source of feedback and a reflection of social comfort. Although adults provide the foundation of social development, they become less important in motivating social activities as children grow older. Students who have learned the social skills to obtain the information necessary and take responsibility for making their own social decisions will ultimately be more comfortable in the workplace and in their personal lives.

# REFERENCES

Cartledge, G., & Milburn, J. (1995). *Teaching social skills to children and youth.* Boston: Allyn & Bacon.

Elias, M., & Clabby, J. (1992). *Building social problem solving skills: Guidelines from a school-based program.* San Francisco: Jossey-Bass Publishers.

Elias, M., Zins, J., Weissberg, R., Frey, K., Greenberg, M., Haynes, N., Kessler, R., Schwab-Stone, M., & Shriver, T. (1997). *Promoting social and emotional learning: Guidelines for educators.* Alexandria, VA: Association for Supervision and Curriculum Development.

Erikson, E. (1963). *Childhood and society* (2nd ed.). New York: Norton.

Hargie, O., Saunders, C., & Dickson, D. (1994). *Social skills in interpersonal communication* (3rd ed.). New York: Routledge.

Kekelis, L. (1988). Increasing positive social interactions between a blind child and sighted kindergartners. In S. Sacks, L. Kekelis, and R. Gaylord-Ross (Eds.), *The development of social skills by visually handicapped children.* San Francisco: San Francisco State University.

Kekelis, L., & Sacks, S. (1992). The effects of visual impairment on children's social interactions in regular education programs. In S. Sacks, L. Kekelis, & R. Gaylord-Ross (Eds.), *The development of social skills by blind and visually impaired students* (pp. 103–127). New York: American Foundation for the Blind.

MacCuspie, P. A. (1996). *Promoting acceptance of children with disabilities: From tolerance to inclusion.* Halifax, Nova Scotia, Canada: Atlantic Provinces Special Education Authority.

Merrell, K., & Gimpel, G. (1998). *Social skills of children and adolescents.* Mahwah, NJ: Lawrence Erlbaum Associates.

Pfisterer, U. (1983). *Games for all of us: Activities for blind and sighted children in integrated settings.* Victoria, Australia: Royal Victorian Institute for the Blind.

Pogrund, R., & Strauss, F. (1992). Approaches to increasing assertive behavior and communication skills in blind and visually impaired persons. In S. Sacks, L. Kekelis, & R. Gaylord-Ross (Eds.), *The development of social skills by blind and visually impaired students* (pp. 181–194). New York: American Foundation for the Blind.

Rosenblum, L. P. (2000). Perceptions of the impact of a visual impairment on the lives of adolescents. *Journal of Visual Impairment and Blindness, 94,* 434–445.

Sacks, S., & Gaylord-Ross, R. (1992). Peer-mediated and teacher-directed social skills training for blind and visually impaired students. In S. Sacks, L. Kekelis, & R. Gaylord-Ross (Eds.), *The development of social skills by blind and visually impaired students* (pp. 103–127). New York: American Foundation for the Blind.

Sacks, S., & Wolffe, K. (2000). *Focused on: Teaching social skills to visually impaired elementary students.* New York: AFB Press.

Sadler, F. (2001). The itinerant teacher hits the road: A map for instruction in young children's social skills. *Teaching Exceptional Children, 34,* 60–66.

CHAPTER 12

# Teaching Social Skills to Adolescents and Young Adults with Visual Impairments

Karen E. Wolffe

Although there has not been a great deal written about the importance of social skills in the lives of adolescents and young adults who are visually impaired, there is a substantial body of literature about the importance of social skills in the lives of adolescents and young adults with other disabilities (Elksnin & Elksnin, 1998; Evans, 1984; Hartup, 1992; Odom, McConnell, & McEvoy, 1992; Smith, 2002; Strain, Guralnick, & Walker, 1986; Vincent, Horner, & Sugai, 2002; Walker, Todis, Holmes, & Horton, 1988). In addition, there is considerable information about the importance of social skills in the lives of young people with disabilities who are making the transition from school to work and adult life (Cronin & Patton, 1993; Johnson & Wehman, 2001; Strain & Odom, 1986; Wolffe, 1996, 1997, 1999). The research about students with visual impairments serves to underscore the similarities while identifying the differences in these related populations (Erin & Wolffe, 1999; Huurre, 2000; Kef, 1997, 1999; MacCuspie, 1996; Sacks & Silberman, 2000; Skellenger, Hill, & Hill, 1992; Wolffe, 1999; Wolffe & Sacks, 1997; Wolffe, Thomas, & Sacks, 2000). What is agreed upon by all of these authors and those who address social skill development in the lives of young people without disabilities (Berne & Savary, 1993; Bloom, 1990; Fenwick & Smith, 1996; Harter, 1999; Ornstein, 1993) is that social skills are critical to life success.

This chapter builds on the information provided in Chapter 4 about the significance of social skills in the lives of adolescents and young adults (typically 14 to 25 years old) with visual impairments, focusing on research-based teaching strategies and learning activities to help this population develop positive social skills. Special attention is given to several social issues of special concern to young people with visual impairments: appearance, transportation, and relationship building, including dating. In addition, techniques for developing strong communication skills, including the use of assertiveness strategies, are presented.

Without good social skills, young people are at risk for loneliness and depression (Bee, 1997; Seligman, 1990; Seligman, Reivich, Jaycox, & Gillham, 1995). The best way to build friendships and develop long-term intimate relationships is by applying well-developed social skills. In addition to the importance of having friends and intimates for social well-being, it is worth noting that the best jobs—and, in fact, most job leads—come through a job seeker's personal network of friends and family (Azrin & Besalel, 1980; Bolles, 2003; Silliker, 1993; Wegmann & Chapman, 1990; Wolffe, 1997; Zadny & James, 1979). For young people with visual impairments, this is particularly relevant because research indicates that one of the consequences of visual disability can be difficulty in establishing multiple relationships (Kef, 1997; Mac-Cuspie, 1996; Rosenblum, 1997, 1998; Sacks & Wolffe, 1992, 1998; Sacks, Wolffe, & Tierney, 1998; Wolffe & Sacks, 1997). Research with adults who have disabilities has confirmed that most often they find their jobs through networks, the same path taken by adults without disabilities. The difference between disabled job seekers and those without disabilities is that disabled adults tend to have fewer people in their networks (Fesko & Temelini, 1997). Young people with visual impairments are at great risk of failing to establish strong, diverse social networks as a result of to their inability to easily observe individuals with whom they might like to establish connections, to travel easily to social venues, and to easily learn from observation of those around them about the critical components of appropriate social skills and how to apply them in social situations.

Certain themes recur throughout both anecdotal literature and research reports regarding the challenges that young people and adults with visual impairments face in the social milieu (Alexander, 2000; Hull, 1990; Kuusisto, 1998; Wolffe, 2000). Three of these themes are explored in the following sections: understanding how one looks in comparison to others and maintaining an attractive personal appearance, coping with the inability to drive and get around with the transportation options available to nondrivers, and learning to flirt and date in hopes of developing positive intimate relationships. These particular topics were selected based on previously cited research projects as well as studies that document the difficulty young people with visual impairment have with dating, and studies and articles that explore the concerns of many visually impaired adolescents and adults regarding the challenge of being nondrivers (Corn & Sacks, 1994; Corn & Rosenblum, 2000; Kirchner, McBroom, Nelson, & Graves, 1992; Marston & Golledge, 2003; Wolffe, 2000). Following a brief discussion of each of these themes, ideas are provided to help youngsters meet these challenges.

# PERSONAL APPEARANCE

## ASSESSING ONE'S LOOKS

As discussed in Chapter 4, assessing one's looks in comparison to others is not easily achieved without good vision. Therefore, young people with impaired eyesight need to have input from other people they trust (friends, family, and concerned helpers) with regard to both intrinsic personal appearance (face, hair, and body) and extrinsic appearance (clothing and accessories). They need to recognize that some problems of adolescence, such as acne and physical gawkiness, are common to almost all young people and not particular to them. As with all adolescents, youngsters with visual impairments need to know about appropriate skin medications and cover-ups for acne or other minor skin blemishes. Physical gawkiness is something that most people outgrow, and those who learn to smile or laugh at themselves often suffer little or no hardship during these awkward stages of growth.

Young people with severe visual impairments also need to understand that on occasion the outward manifestation of their disabilities may not be cosmetically attractive. For example, some eye conditions such as cataracts and retinopathy of prematurity may cause disfiguring cloudiness or shrinkage of the eyeballs. In hypertropia, one of the eyes deviates while the other fixates normally; with nystagmus, there is involuntary side-to-side or oscillating movement of the eyes, which can be disconcerting to normally seeing individuals; as a consequence of congenital glaucoma, a youngster may have an enlarged eyeball that is unsightly. If a teenager or young adult has disfigured eyes, he or she may wish to mask them with tinted glasses. It is rarely necessary to use dark lenses, which tend to promote stereotyping, but a light tint or glasses that darken in bright light may help the young adult feel more attractive.

Adults with low vision sometimes prefer not to wear cosmetic glasses if their vision is better without them. However, appearance is often of paramount importance for teenagers, and adults need to give teens permission to make their own decisions—unless their choices endanger them. Likewise, parents and adults involved with youths who have visual impairments may need to cease their attempts to get teenagers to use optical devices for the duration of adolescence; unless the device is inconspicuous, chances are it will not be used in public. While young people are in the throes of adolescence, typically one of their highest priorities is to look like their peers.

A study by Kaufman (2000) of the clothing-selection habits of 30 teenage girls (15 who were sighted and 15 teenage girls who were blind) pointed out the importance of fashion in the social milieu. As earlier researchers had indicated (Mangold & Mangold, 1983), Kaufman found that blind and severely visually impaired girls tend to rely on their parents more than on sighted girls when shopping and choosing clothing. As one might predict, they also relied more heavily on auditory sources of information (parents, radio, and audio books) rather than on visual media such as television, magazines, and movies for fashion information. Girls in this study who were blind also tended to wear less makeup and jewelry than the sighted girls. Only girls who were blind (3 out of the 15 visually impaired study participants) had help in applying their makeup. Although this was a small study, the results confirm that visually impaired girls rely heavily on their parents for fashion advice. Thus, the parents of a visually impaired girl need to look carefully at their daughter's acquaintances to determine what is fashionable or trendy and to help their child make clothing choices that are as much like her peers as possible. Dressing in styles and using accessories similar to those of their peers often helps teens assimilate into appropriate adolescent groups and, ultimately, into the social circles of the larger community.

In addition to helping teens and young adults with visual impairments understand what their peers are wearing, how they are styling their hair, and what accessories are popular, parents may want encourage their child to attend narrated (or audiodescribed) style shows and cultural events in which attire is detailed, meet with personal shoppers who can help them identify what colors and fabrics suit them best, and attend special classes (often offered through community schools or youth centers) that focus on grooming and etiquette. Special schools for students with visual impairments and rehabilitation facilities frequently offer short-term placements or weekend seminars that focus specifically on grooming and hygiene issues, such as shaving techniques, makeup application, hair styling, nail care, and so forth. These short courses or classes can be advantageous because they are designed to help students without good vision learn time-proven techniques for handling personal care issues. These courses frequently are taught by adults with visual impairments and may also be attended by visually impaired adults who make themselves available to share how they manage these issues and to answer questions. It is a great boon to adolescents and young adults—many of whom have never had personal contact with visually impaired adults—to have access to an adult role model (ideally of the same sex) who is willing and able to answer personal questions. The following are some specific suggestions for addressing appearance with adolescents who are visually impaired.

## STRATEGIES FOR SOCIAL SUCCESS
# Addressing Appearance

◆ Tell young adults with visual impairments what you like about them, but only compliment what you truly like; do not give untruthful compliments.

◆ Encourage young adults to attend community-based etiquette courses or modeling classes to work on posture and poise.

◆ Encourage young women to visit local cosmetics stores or cosmetic counters in department stores to get assistance from makeup artists in experimenting with makeup; encourage the use of personal shoppers, when possible, for both young women and men to determine what styles and colors suit them best.

♦ Invite a rehabilitation teacher to school to work with students one on one or in a small group of same-gender youngsters to teach grooming tips and techniques.

♦ Develop a list of books to recommend to students for leisure reading that includes fictional and nonfictional accounts of successful blind and visually impaired people.

## SMALL-GROUP DISCUSSIONS

Small groups, ideally facilitated by a counselor or teacher trained in group facilitation techniques can be formed to help young people with visual impairments learn how others see them. The group has to be offered in a safe, nonthreatening environment such as a teen club or school room set aside for such extracurricular activities. Peavey & Leff (2002) describe a small group in which adolescents with visual impairments and sighted peers discuss many issues of concern to the adolescents. They have achieved favorable results with structured trust-building exercises to encourage communication. The study warrants further consideration.

The author has facilitated a number of groups consisting solely of young people with visual impairments as well as groups with both sighted and nonsighted young adults. Both configurations can be successful if the group participants are comfortable with one another and the facilitator; are confident that their discussions will be kept confidential; and all parties, including the facilitator, are committed to actively participating in the discussions.

Some topics for guiding such a structured discussion might include:

• How others see me and what aspects of that might be important for me to consider: Do I want to be more or less like others see me? What do others see in me that I would like to change? What do others see in me that I would like to preserve?

• Five adjectives that describe how I believe others see me.

• Five adjectives that describe how I see myself.

• How I wish others saw me.

Two additional techniques that can be used successfully in small groups to elicit information about how individuals are perceived by others are the following:

1. Have each participant use their preferred medium (print or braille) to list five adjectives describing each of the other participants in the group. Collect the lists, have the descriptions for each participant compiled and transcribed by a third party, and then return the descriptive lists to the participants. Or, the participants can read their lists to each other; however, this technique requires a higher level of trust and comfort on the part of the participants.

2. Play the "Person-Out-of-the-Room" game, in which one participant (the listener) turns his or her back to the group while the rest of the participants discuss the person listening. The listener is not allowed to speak while being discussed—as if he or she were literally out of the room. In this activity, the facilitator needs to set the stage for the discussion by asking participants to share what they like about the person "out of the room." If anyone wants to share something that could be construed as negative, he or she has to give an example of the behavior that was perceived to be discomfiting.

Feedback about how their peers perceive them is often helpful for young people with visual impairments. Use of small-group discussion techniques can be advantageous for teens and young adults because they can often accept such feedback from individuals of their own age more readily than from authority figures. However, small groups are not the place to deal with potentially embarrassing personal issues; those issues are best dealt with in one-to-one counseling or teaching venues.

# DRIVING

Not being able to drive in a society that not only esteems driving but also views the acquisition of a driver's license as a rite of passage is a difficulty faced by totally blind and most legally blind individuals. In many states, individuals as young as 15 or 16 can secure a driver's license and begin to ferry themselves and their friends around in the community. For youngsters without the visual ability to drive, this can be a traumatic time, one that requires some problem solving to figure out how they can get away from their parents and family members to explore the community, be more independent and broaden their awareness about other people's lives. They need to become accomplished travelers using compensatory or alternative techniques such as a sighted (human) guide, cane skills, and, possibly, a dog guide. Youths who have some vision need to learn how to use appropriate optical devices, such as telescopes and bioptic lenses.

Travel is a significant issue for youngsters with visual impairments, one that affects a young person's life in many ways since the need to travel cuts across personal, social, and school-related aspects of one's life, including

- getting to and from everyday destinations such as home and school; other children's homes; school or home and the mall, theater, sports arena, or other venue for recreation and leisure
- being able to get to and from appointments and lessons (medical doctors, eye specialists, dentists, hairstylists, music lessons, ballet, sports, religious activities, drama, science, or other kinds of clubs and activities)
- meeting friends (picking them up or being picked up)
- running errands (dropping siblings off at their friends' homes, shopping for groceries or personal items, paying bills)
- dating
- working

Youngsters with impaired vision need to learn how to use both public and private transportation alternatives to driving cars. While they are still in school, it is important that their parents or caregivers work closely with orientation and mobility (O&M) instructors and encourage youngsters to practice learned travel skills in the community with family and friends as well as independently. When negotiating for O&M skills training on a student's Individualized Education Program (IEP) plan, both parents and students need to request training in the community on a variety of routes and using different transportation options, such as buses, trains, subways, taxis, shuttles, paratransit, and so forth. The greater a student's familiarity with different travel options, the better prepared he or she will be to use the available services, now and in the future.

Although driving a car is rarely an option for young people with severe visual disabilities, all students should be familiar with cars and the rules of the road. In fact, it is a good idea for visually impaired students to take, at a minimum, the classroom portion of standard driver's education courses. They will often be passengers in other people's vehicles, and it is important for them to understand the rules of the road and be aware of what is happening, even if they are not driving. Driver's education classes also often include computer simulations from which many low vision students can benefit. In safe locations with experienced drivers, students with visual impairments may appreciate the chance to get behind the wheel so that they have a firsthand sense of the experience of driving. If a driver's education instructor with an adapted car (dual controls) is willing, the instructor can show a student who is blind or has low vision some of the basics of driving just for enlightenment. This is not to suggest that anyone should be put in jeopardy; simply allowing a youngster the opportunity to briefly experience driving under safe conditions can help him or her gain insight into the task.

Youngsters with visual impairments also need to have some basic knowledge of automobile care and maintenance—for example, how to change a flat tire, how to put gas in the car, how to add oil and washer fluid, and how to clean the windshield. When riding with friends, one of the ways a youngster with a visual impairment can repay the favor is by pumping the gas or cleaning the windshield. In addition, car maintenance is an area in which youngsters with visual impairments can participate on an equal footing with their sighted peers. They can contribute in a meaningful way in their family or reciprocate for rides by learning to wash, wax, and polish a car; vacuum and wipe down the interior; and check fluid levels and tire pressure. Offering to help with gas money is another avenue for reciprocity.

In addition, many adults with visual impairments own cars that others drive for them, so knowing how to maintain a vehicle can be as important for them as for any other car owner. Finally, it is critical that visually impaired youngsters know where they are going and how to get there so that they can help the driver with directions. Visually impaired riders need to know not only the street address but also the route and significant landmarks to help the driver find their final destination (Wolffe, 2004).

It is essential for parents to understand the significance that learning to drive and the resulting freedom has for teenagers in Western society. Students with visual disabilities need to have some alternative rite of passage. One suggestion is a significant trip, whether across the country or across town to visit a friend or relative independently by bus, train, or airplane. If parents are helping a sibling to acquire a vehicle or paying extra automobile insurance to cover the sibling's use of a family vehicle, they might want to consider putting a comparable amount of money into an account earmarked for transportation expenses for the visually impaired child.

It is important for youngsters with visual impairments to understand and accept that it is unlikely that they will become drivers so that

**Figure 12.1**

# Evaluation of Transportation Options

1. List all the ways you can get to one place in the column on the left.
2. Score each method according to cost, time, and effect on independence.

> 1 = An advantage
>
> 2 = Neither an advantage or a disadvantage
>
> 3 = A disadvantage

3. Add the scores together and write the total in the column on the right.
4. Choose the type of transportation that has the lowest score, whenever it is possible.

**Activity:** *Attending a concert in the park*

|  | Cost | Time | Independence | TOTAL |
|---|---|---|---|---|
| Ride with a friend | 1 | 1 | 2 | 4 |
| Take a cab | 3 | 2 | 1 | 6 |
| Ask parents for a ride | 1 | 1 | 3 | 5 |
| Take the bus | 1 | 3 | 1 | 5 |

*Source:* Adapted from J. N. Erin & K. E. Wolffe, *Transition Issues Related to Students with Visual Disabilities* (Austin, TX: PRO-ED, 1999); K. E. Wolffe (2004), "Transitioning young adults from school to public transportation, in *EnVision: A publication for parents and educators of children with impaired vision, 8,* 7–9.

they can begin to identify and evaluate what transportation options are available to them in terms of convenience, cost, and impact on independence. One method of making sound decisions about available transportation options is to chart the options and analyze them. In this method, a numerical value is assigned to each method of travel according to the considerations of cost, convenience, and effect on independence; and the scores for each choice are tallied (see the example in Figure 12.1). This is an objective way for nondrivers to determine the most desirable transportation option available from an array of choices (Erin & Wolffe, 1999; Wolffe, 2004). An objective strategy such as this one gives back to visually impaired youngsters some of the control over the environment that they lose when they discover that they will be unable to drive. Another resource for exploring travel options is the curriculum *Finding Wheels* (Corn & Rosenblum, 2000), with lessons that can be infused into O&M training or community-based instruction in conjunction with work on other disability-related skills.

# BUILDING HEALTHY RELATIONSHIPS

## LEVELS OF RELATING TO OTHERS

Students with visual impairments need to learn how to communicate effectively and interact with people in the context of different kinds of relationships, from those with people they know well to those with strangers. An excellent vehicle for explaining the varying levels of relationships is the onion analogy.

In this technique, the teacher uses the onion as a model for the layers that exist in relationships. Students are asked to imagine holding an onion in their hands. The teacher describes the onion as pungent, round, and smooth with parchment-like skin, which could be sliced, if so desired, to make onion rings to be eaten in a sandwich or to be deep fried. Once the students have conceptualized an onion, the teacher asks the students to imagine the onion sliced in half. From the side they are reminded that it would look a lot like a target or the rings of a tree—small concentric circles of onion of ever-increasing size radiating out from the center. Then students are asked to assume that the onion under consideration has just five broad rings, each of which represents a different level of relationships with other people.

The outermost ring or layer represents the *public*. The public consists of all of the people one comes into contact with over time who are encountered briefly but are essentially unknown. This category includes people students pass on the street, people who attend the same school but are not known through class assignment or proximity, people who attend religious or community events but with whom students have only cursory contact. At this level of relating to others, the expectation is that individuals will be civil and polite. They might say "hi" or "hello" or "howdy," but it is unlikely that they would interact at any length or in more than a perfunctory manner with someone who is simply a part of the general public.

This is not to imply that rude or inconsiderate behavior is acceptable with this group. It is important that students understand that they may interact with people around them; for example, if someone asks for help—say, asking directions in an unfamiliar area—it is polite and caring to assist. Likewise, if they need assistance, it is appropriate and expected that they would solicit aid from anyone close at hand—even a stranger. However, students need to be cautioned about interacting with strangers and keeping personal information, such as one's full name, home address, or telephone number, confidential. They need to be taught to distinguish what communication is appropriate in situations where one is dealing with the public; for instance, when one is waiting for a bus, chatting with someone about the weather or asking what number bus is pulling up is appropriate, but sharing personal information is not.

The second level of relationships—or ring in the onion analogy—is the *acquaintance* level. In this category are the people whom students know only slightly; for example, people who attend the same school and share some classes, whose names they know and whom they would recognize at a school or community event. Conversations with acquaintances are generally chats about things one has in common (shared classes or team activities, for instance); or seasonal events such as Thanksgiving, Christmas, Hanukkah, spring break, and the like. Acquaintances are expected to exchange pleasantries—comments such as "Hi, how are you doing?" "What do you plan to do during spring break?" "Can you believe the amount of homework Mr. Wong gave us last Friday!" "Did you go to the game this weekend?"

The third ring of the onion is the *friendship* level of relationships. Students' friends are the people who are most like them, whom they find most interesting, whom they trust with their inner thoughts, about whom they care, and who care for them. Friends are people with whom they want to talk and share their ideas, feelings, joys, and sorrows. Students believe what their friends tell them to be more honest than information they get from the world at large. Friends are people who can be relied on to help out, and whose company is enjoyable. People at this level in relationships are often together—going to movies, going dancing, riding bikes, going to ball games, or dining out, for instance. In general, friends are available when they are needed or wanted. Friends are people with whom students may share their true thoughts or approach for a loan of money or clothing and help with transportation. They can discuss controversial issues such as politics or religion on which they agree or avoid those topics in order to maintain the friendship.

It is important to point out to students that as the rings of the circle get closer to the center, the rings in this onion analogy are growing smaller. Likewise, as people navigate the relationships in their lives, the numbers of people in their social circles decrease as they approach the center. Although the number of friends one has varies from person to person, the proportion is usually the same: people have many more acquaintances than friends, and there will always be many, many more people in the society at large than in one's acquaintance circle.

The next or fourth layer in relationships is known *as intimacy*. Intimates are those few human beings with whom people are the closest. Intimates are people one loves and trusts implicitly. In childhood, intimates are typically family members such as a mother, father, aunt, uncle, grandmother, grandfather, sister, brother, or other extended family members with whom intimacy is intellectual and emotional. When children mature and reach adulthood, spouses or significant others become their intimates. With sexual partners, there typically is a combination of physical, emotional, and intellectual intimacy. Other significant people who may occasionally become part of one's circle of intimates include priests, rabbis, or ministers with whom one shares a spiritual intimacy; and counselors or therapists with whom one shares emotional intimacy.

The innermost layer or ring of relationships represents the most private part of each person, consisting of information and feelings that are not typically shared with anyone else. For example, this ring contains one's most embarrassing moments, wildest fantasies, and most poignant concerns. Each person has a *private self* that no one else knows as well as that individual. It is important for each person to feel that he or she may have some secrets—private information or feelings—that do not have to be shared with anyone.

It is healthy to have relationships in all of the layers of the onion and it is healthy to have a private part to one's self. It is healthy to have enough friends to enjoy and care about over time and to recognize and acknowledge acquaintances. It is also healthy to be attuned to other people around you in the general public. The keys to relating successfully to others are recognizing in which layer of one's circle people are located and understanding how to help those with whom you want a different relationship to move through the layers—for example, from public to acquaintance to friend.

The following suggestions include ways for teachers, parents, and other adults to help visually impaired teenagers navigate the different levels of relationships.

## STRATEGIES FOR SOCIAL SUCCESS
# Techniques for Building Healthy Relationships

- ◆ Help young adults with visual impairments understand that getting to know better someone who is an acquaintance requires an exchange of information between the two people that is contingent upon the current level of the relationship. If the youngster is interested in developing a closer relationship with someone he or she doesn't know well, the kinds of information that can be solicited and shared are fairly superficial. For example, one can ask: "Where are you from?" "Where do you go to school?" "Do you have pets?" "What do you do for fun?" "Do you like (sports, shopping, theater, hiking, or the like)?" At this level of relating, one is not allowed to solicit, nor would one want to share, personal information (details about one's family or personal religious, political, sexual, or social preferences).

- ◆ Young people need to understand that true conversations are never one-sided. If they want to be friends, they have to listen as well as talk—and, it helps to remember what the other person has said in order to respond appropriately!

- ◆ Students also need to understand that friendship building requires more than chatting with people—one must be prepared to spend time with people doing things that they enjoy doing. They need to understand that inviting acquaintances to their homes or to activities such as ball games, movies, or shopping helps build friendships by demonstrating that one enjoys the other's company.

- ◆ Finally, it's important that students understand that people like other people who pay attention to them; and one of the ways they know that people are paying attention is when they compliment them on accomplishments or new acquisitions (clothing, hair styles, gadgets, and the like). Since visually impaired students may not realize when others have new things they are wearing or new hair styles, they have to pay attention to what others are talking about and ask questions if they need further input to know what's changed.

---

In addition to understanding healthy levels of relating to other people, it is important that adolescents understand not-so-healthy relationship development. Once students understand the five layers in the onion analogy, they can also recognize that people actually have layers within layers of relationships: for example, acquaintances that have just moved from the stranger level and acquaintances that are better known and likely to become friends; as well as friends, good friends, and best friends. Ask them to again picture the entire onion. Have them imagine themselves in the store picking an onion out from the rest of the stock to bring home. They would likely squeeze the onion to be sure it is firm. If it is not—if it is squishy—chances are they wouldn't choose that onion because it might be rotting. If it is soft or squishy—it is an unhealthy or icky onion. Relationships, too, can be healthy or unhealthy—firm or soft and icky. Relationships that develop over time as people discover one another's interests, values, abilities, and liabilities and accept each other in spite of differences are generally healthy relationships that can stand the test of time.

Healthy relationships require reciprocal exchanges of information and energy. Both parties must share information about themselves, and expend time and energy in fairly equal amounts with one another. Unhealthy relationships develop when people either spend too much time talking about themselves and not letting the other person share information about him- or herself, or don't share enough about themselves for others to feel comfortable with them. Using the onion analogy once again, the instructor can explain this concept with the icky onion. If an onion is icky (or a relationship is unhealthy), it is usually because the layers are not uniformly layered as in a healthy onion. In the first example, where the individual tells too much about him- or herself, the icky onion would have a huge center (private self) and small outer layers (public, acquaintances, friends, intimates). In the second example, where the individual doesn't tell others enough for them to get to know him or her, the icky onion would have small inner layers (acquaintances, friends, intimates, and private self) and a huge outer layer (public). Drawing graphic representations of these concepts (healthy and icky onions) with tactile marking fluid or puff paint or using a tactile graphic software program and enhancer can help students with visual impairments better understand this analogy of the layers of relationships.

## LEARNING ABOUT SEXUALITY AND INTIMATE RELATIONSHIPS

Human sexuality and learning how to develop intimate relationships present specific and significant challenges for adolescents with visual impairments, for a multitude of reasons. First, there is the challenge of gaining a full understanding of human sexuality without being able to see pictures or films that depict how people and animals procreate or witnessing actual events in nature. Finding good teachers for this content area is difficult. Many teachers don't want to teach human sexuality; they find it embarrassing or value laden and are uncomfortable with it. Parents may also find this a difficult area in which to provide instruction, often preferring to ignore the topic or to speak of it in vague or cryptic ways that may confuse children or fail to convey accurate information.

In the United States, unlike some other countries, the use of live models for instructing blind students in anatomy is not socially acceptable. Therefore, to teach children about the anatomy of both sexes, instructors must rely on dolls or inanimate objects that represent body parts. Examining plastic or inanimate objects is not the same as viewing pictorial representations or seeing real people in various states of undress, to learn about body parts and their functions. All told, teaching students with severe visual impairments about human sexuality is a challenge; and if the students don't learn about the subject from informed adults, they will learn in bits and pieces potentially inaccurate information from their peers. (Books and other recommended readings on this subject are included in the Recommended Readings section of this book.)

Coupled with the difficulty of gaining complete and accurate information about human sexuality is the sense that others often consider blind and visually impaired students inherently more vulnerable than their sighted peers. Granted there are elements of vulnerability in the lives of young people with impaired vision; however, the better informed they are, the less likely they are to fall victim to individuals who may try to take advantage of them. If they know what to expect in intimate interactions and they understand how to prevent unwanted intimacies, they are no more vulnerable than many of their age-mates.

Young people with impaired vision need to learn how to interpret overtures from others and how to accept or rebuff those overtures. They also need to learn basic elements of self-defense and rules of behavior that discourage misinterpretation of their intent. For example, girls need to understand that wearing skimpy clothing or see-through fabrics may be interpreted as suggestive or inviting of unwanted attentions. Boys need to understand that skintight jeans or swim trunks that expose their genitals may likewise attract unwanted attention. Young people with visual impairments need to learn how to dress and behave to attract the kind of attention that they desire and not encourage behaviors that they don't want. They need to learn what types of clothes and postures (standing, sitting, or lying prone on the beach or poolside) may be considered sexually open or leading and why.

Young adults also need to learn about mating rituals so that they can participate and not be hurt or abused in the process. They need to understand the rules and the consequences of breaking the rules; they need basic information about human sexuality, about safe and unsafe sexual practices; and they need to know what is acceptable in their families and social communities. In order to understand these issues, young people without good vision must hear from those who care about them what is acceptable sexual behavior, as well as how, when, and where that behavior can take place. They need to be aware of the terminology used for referencing private and public body parts in different environments; for example, the terminology used in a medical doctor's office is likely to be different from the terminology used with friends or intimates to describe body parts or bodily functions. They need to understand that there is usually safety in numbers, so that it may well be to their advantage to go out in small groups before going out with an individual unaccompanied.

## FLIRTING AND DATING

Dating, sexuality, and friendships are difficult for adolescents with visual impairments, at least in part because of the isolating nature of vision loss. It is easy for sighted classmates and contemporaries to be friendly, while it is extraordinarily difficult for a visually impaired individual to evaluate friendly overtures to determine the type of friendship intended. Learning how to flirt and recognizing when others are flirting can be tricky without good vision because so much of the flirting, courting behavior is visually based. Girls and boys look at each other with goo-goo eyes; how can that be explained to a youngster who has never seen? Coy or coquettish looks are often described as a glance through lowered eyelashes or an askance look rather than an eye-to-eye, straight look. Even if such looks can be described, how can young people be taught to produce or interpret them? For young people who are visually impaired, knowing how to emulate such feats is less important than understanding and interpreting them, particularly when such comments involve them, so that they can act accordingly.

Attracting desired attention from prospective partners is another challenge for youngsters with visual impairments. As noted earlier, it is hard for visually impaired youngsters to recognize that they are attracting attention or to communicate their interest in others, since much of the initial flirting that lets one teen know that another teen is interested is based on nonverbal communication. In addition, they cannot easily observe their peers evaluating prospective partners, how they pair up, or the impact these partner relationships have on others in the class or school. They will hear about these pairings, but may not capture enough detail to understand how to replicate the effort should they be so inclined.

## MEETING PEERS AND BUILDING RELATIONSHIPS

Determining who is available to date requires special efforts on the part of students with visual impairments to get to know the people in their classes, attend clubs with them, or participate in the same religious and secular activities. As discussed earlier, mixed discussion groups of sighted and visually impaired young people have proven effective in encouraging dialogue about issues faced by all teenagers as they attempt to establish relationships outside their immediate and extended families (Peavey & Leff, 2002). Meeting people with whom one might like to develop a more intimate relationship requires first meeting people, getting to know them and letting them get to know oneself, as suggested in the strategies that follow.

## STRATEGIES FOR SOCIAL SUCCESS
# Building Relationships with Peers

◆ Encourage students to attend the kinds of activities that their same-age peers are attending; for example, athletic events. If an activity is difficult to follow without vision such as baseball, suggest that the student bring a radio with an earphone so that he or she can follow the game while still socializing with friends at the game.

◆ Encourage students to take classes and develop skills that encourage their active participation with other students their age, such as woodworking, band, choir, or computer science.

◆ Encourage participation in local or neighboring community group activities (nature hikes, challenge course participation, walks or runs for various causes, collecting food or clothing for needy families, and so forth).

◆ Encourage student participation in student government, creative dramatics, the campus newspaper, and so forth.

In addition, young people with visual impairments can often benefit from opportunities at school to participate in group learning activities with other students. Cooperative learning activities can help students with social skills and developing relationships with peers because sighted and visually impaired students must interact to accomplish the group project, lest members of the group risk failing. (See Chapter 8 for a more detailed discussion of cooperative learning techniques and strategies.) Cooperative learning groups can set the stage for developing friendships outside of the group. Typically developing children are often in situations where they teach each other informally in the course of their everyday activities, often without trying to do so, and this is generally an effective way to learn. Hartup (1992) notes four types of peer teaching: peer tutoring, cooperative learning, peer collaboration, and peer modeling. In peer tutoring, a didactic transmission of information from one child to another takes place; usually the older or more knowledgeable youngster informs the novice or younger child. In cooperative learning situations, children work together (usually under a teacher's guidance and instruction) to solve problems, contribute to projects, and share rewards. Peer collaboration, on the other hand, occurs when children work together on tasks that neither can do on their own. Peer modeling is the transfer of information between peers by imitation. The first three types of peer teaching are well suited to helping youngsters with visual impairments develop or refine their social skills; however, peer modeling is more difficult because of the inherent difficulty children with visual impairments experience with observation.

Faculty who assign students cooperative learning projects help students with visual impairments mesh in the social milieu. However, the teachers assigned to work with students with visual impairments may need to set the stage for successful cooperative learning projects by working with their students to ensure that they know how to actively participate. Participation of visually impaired students can be maximized and enhanced if the students

- listen carefully to the teacher's instructions and determine what abilities and knowledge they can contribute to the project
- listen carefully to their peers to determine how they want to approach the project and determine what abilities and knowledge they propose to contribute to the project
- volunteer information to their peers about how they can and want to contribute
- demonstrate their competencies (by doing what they promise to do, by turning over their part of the work in a timely and accessible fashion, by assuming responsibility for an equal amount of work, and so forth)
- take credit and assume responsibility for the final product

Having friends who participate in cooperative learning experiences can make those experiences more fun and often makes the experience more productive and fulfilling. However, one of the advantages of cooperative learning is that new friendships may form as a consequence of involvement in such projects.

Peer tutoring may be helpful, but sighted tutors may not always be sensitive to the specific needs or concerns of adolescents with visual impairments, and it can be difficult to find tutors who are visually impaired due to the low incidence of blindness in the population. Therefore, concerned adults are encouraged to consider making an active effort to link teenagers with visual impairments with youths or adults with similar disabilities. Some of the special schools for students with visual impairments have short-term placement and summer programs in which older students mingle with younger students and a student who needs some shoring up of his or her social skills might find an able and willing tutor. Summer camps have long been a venue where children and youths with visual impairments can mix and mingle, and one of the benefits is that tutoring and role modeling are accessible and readily available in this environment.

Finally, adults with visual impairments are often willing to tutor young adults in the finer points of socializing successfully with both sighted and visually impaired peers. Consumer groups for people who are blind or visually impaired, such as the American Council of the Blind and the National Federation of the Blind, have local chapters and host annual conventions that abound with opportunities to meet other blind and visually impaired youths and adults (see the Resources section). Teachers and related service providers can often benefit from the experiences of these adult role models by either attending consumer conferences or making contact with visually impaired adults through public and private rehabilitation agencies, when possible. There are a number of successful, blind and visually impaired adults who are willing to not only mentor young people but are also willing to answer questions posed to them by service providers. The American Foundation for the Blind supports one such cluster of prospective mentors in the AFB CareerConnect database at www.afb.org/careerconnect. The CareerConnect database consists of employed adults with visual impairments who have volunteered to mentor other blind and visually impaired job seekers or youths who are in the career exploration process (see the Resources section for more information).

# STRATEGIES FOR REFINING SOCIAL SKILLS

A number of specific suggestions for building or refining social skills of young adults with visual impairments have been touched on throughout this chapter. This section focuses on broader strategies and techniques that can help refine social skills in the key areas of communication, including assertiveness skills.

## COMMUNICATION SKILLS

Communication skills are the foundation on which many of the higher-order social skills are built. Therefore, it is important that young people with visual impairments work diligently to improve their day-to-day communication skills. To accomplish that goal, they need to be encouraged to internalize some basic principles of one-to-one communication, which are outlined in the following sections. Although the described communication dos and don'ts assume that a friendship or intimacy level of relationship exists between speaker and listener, these basic techniques can be applied more universally in social dyads between acquaintances.

Ideally, these communication skills can be introduced to groups of students and practiced at school and at home. Teaching faculty may want to establish small mixed groups of sighted and blind students, as described earlier in this chapter, in which communication strategies can be discussed in a safe environment. Practice can easily take place in dyads (a speaker and a listener who give each other feedback) or triads (a speaker, a listener, and an objective observer who provides feedback) with faculty supervision. Teachers may also model these communication skills for students and then ask students to comment on how they think the skills would work for them.

## Communication Strategies: Dos

In communication between two people, there are specific behaviors that help convey that they are interested and involved in the conversation. The three communications dos described in the following sections are attending, listening, and responding.

*Attending.* If young adults want others to think that they are paying attention to what is being said, they must look toward the speaker to show they are attending, even if they can't see well enough to distinguish facial features. This may be a difficult concept to accept for an individual who is blind or severely visually impaired; however, it is a fundamental rule of communication in Western society. (This is not necessarily the rule in other cultures; for example, in some Eastern cultures such behavior might be perceived as rude or disrespectful.) Adolescents and young adults with visual impairments may need to be taught attending behavior such as the following:

- *Looking the speaker in the eye or orienting toward the speaker:* If the student can't see well enough to look the speaker in the eye, he or she must orient in the direction of the speaker by listening closely and facing toward the speaker. (If there is a large social gathering and someone is speaking using a microphone, it may be difficult for the visually impaired person to orient toward the speaker without assistance. In such a setting, it is appropriate to whisper to someone close at hand and ask where the speaker is located.)

- *Staying focused on the speaker:* Attentive listeners do not do anything but listen. They don't fiddle with their jewelry, hair, or papers; they don't look out of the window or at the door; they don't answer cell phones (they either let it ring or, better yet, turn it off when they are carrying on a conversation); and they don't fidget.

- *Moving periodically:* Attentive listeners don't sit frozen in place. They nod or shake their heads; smile or frown, depending on what is being said; shift forward in their seats or tilt their heads to one side and then back to center, and so forth.

- *Positioning one's body appropriately:* If the social pair or dyad is standing, the listener needs to stand as close as is comfortable for the speaker (Western society dictates approximately an arm's length between speaker and listener); if the social pair is sitting, the listener can lean in toward the speaker to indicate attentiveness.

- *Maintaining contact during the entire conversation*: Attentive listeners continue to face the person with whom they are communicating throughout the conversation.

**Listening.** Listening involves more than simply hearing what another person says. Listening requires the listener to take an active part in the communication dyad: hearing what is actually said and interpreting what the speaker is attempting to say or imply, as well as trying to understand how the speaker feels about what is being said. Skills for effective listening in a conversation may be taught to adolescents and young adults with visual impairments. For the listener the critical steps in this process include the following:

- *Listen for what is actually said*: Hear the words and remember them, at least the key points.

- *Listen for what is not said (sometimes called reading between the lines)*: Pay attention to voice intonation, inflection, and body language (if the listener can see well enough to do so). If the listener can't see the speaker's body language, he or she must listen for hints about body language: Is the speaker mumbling, talking to the floor, looking about anxiously, tapping his or her fingers or foot, or speaking through clenched teeth? A visually impaired person must pay close attention to subtle nuances of voice tone, modulation, pacing, punctuation, and presence to help understand how the person who is speaking feels.

- *Listen for the emotion or feeling behind the speaker's message*: Does the speaker sound happy, sad, angry, or fearful? Good communicators try to make inferences about how the speaker feels and then respond accordingly. It is acceptable to guess incorrectly; the speaker can always clarify the communication and how he or she feels. Most people want other people to pay attention to their feelings, and attempting to understand the speaker's emotions demonstrates that the listener cares about him or her.

- Determine the underlying message: If the listener is unsure about the message the speaker is trying to impart, he or she can get clarification by asking, "Do you mean___?" or "Are you saying ___?" or "Am I understanding you to say ___?" It is better to ask for clarification than to pretend to understand.

*Responding.* Communicating, carrying on a conversation, takes at least two people. Listening is only one part of the equation; when the listening has been accomplished, a response is in order. Good listeners respond in ways that indicate they have understood the speaker's message and can imagine how the speaker feels. The following are strategies that the listener can use to communicate this to the speaker:

- Paraphrasing what the speaker said.
- Restating or repeating a key point the speaker made.
- Asking questions about the content or message that the speaker conveyed.
- Reiterating what the listener believes the speaker was trying to say or what feeling he or she was expressing. Reiterating is different from paraphrasing; in paraphrasing, the listener is repeating back almost verbatim what one heard said. By contrast, reiterating involves listening to what's being said, synthesizing it and analyzing what the speaker is trying to convey, and then restating the message to the speaker to determine if one has indeed understood both what was said and what was inferred.

The listener needs to try and convey that he or she cares about the speaker as well as about what the speaker says.

## Communication Strategies: Don'ts

*Conveying Negative Messages.* Sometimes when people respond to communication from others that they find upsetting or disagreeable, they make the mistake of responding without thinking and conveying negative or hateful messages back to the speaker. Unfortunately, this kind of communication is especially likely to happen with the people who are closest, such as parents, partners, and best friends. When a listener disagrees with someone he or she cares about a great deal, he or she often reacts with comments such as, "What a stupid thing to do!" or "How could you say something so dumb?" Such negative or hateful messages may convey to the speaker that the listener does not esteem or trust him or her to say or do the right thing. Although people typically say such things in anger or when they are frustrated and are trying to capture the attention of the loved one and make him or her listen to reason, the recipient of such a message tends to close down and become defensive, the opposite of what is needed to maintain open, ongoing communication.

Some strategies to eliminate negative or hateful responses include the following:

- Listen carefully to the speaker's message and try not to impose value judgments on him or her. One way of doing this is by eliminating value-laden words such as "should," "ought to," "must," and "have to" that convey or imply one person's approach is right and the other's is wrong.

- Think before responding to another's message and carefully consider how the person is likely to answer.

- Try to frame the message in a positive way. For example, "I care about you and don't understand what you mean to say. From what you have said, I understand that you are angry with me, but that doesn't make sense to me. Can you help me understand what you are trying to say?"

- Try to respond to the message from a personal perspective based on how the message makes the listener feel; for example, "I feel hurt or angry when you speak to me in that tone of voice," rather than saying, "You're being rude and obnoxious!"

*Advising.* Sometimes a speaker will ask for the listener's advice, either overtly or subtly. For example, if a friend or family member says, "Don't you think I should tell so-and-so that I won't go to the prom with him?" the person is not asking for advice directly, but rather indirectly or subtly. A direct request for advice might sound more like "Whom do you think I ought to go to the prom with?" Giving advice can damage a friendship or close relationship, and students are well advised to avoid it. If the advice is bad, the recipient is likely to become irritated or angry and blame the advice-giver; if the advice turns out well or results in a positive effect, the recipient may continue to seek out advice anytime he or she needs to make a decision. The exception to this rule is when the speaker is asking for advice and the responder can give factual information. For example, if someone asks how many hours of credit are required to graduate from an academic program, the responder can give advice without jeopardizing the relationship. The following strategies for responding to a request for advice can help students determine what to do when a friend or family member asks for advice:

- When asked directly for advice, offer two or three ideas or thoughts on the subject. Don't indicate which ideas you think are best—let the other person decide. Assure the advice seeker that you believe he or she can make a good decision. If the person chooses a suggestion that you think is not the best option, simply be prepared to offer suggestions again if the idea doesn't work.

- When a speaker seems confused about what to do, instead of providing advice, try repeating or paraphrasing the message. This encourages the speaker to listen to his or her own words again and perhaps reevaluate the situation.

- When someone asks, "What do you think I ought to do?" respond by asking, "What are you considering?" rather than by giving advice. If the speaker says, "I don't have any idea," the listener may want to mention what he or she has seen others do in similar situations, share what he or she has done when faced with a similar dilemma, and brainstorm ideas that might work in the current situation. The key is to generate as many ideas as possible; not advise the speaker to do one thing, but to consider alternatives.

*Changing the Focus.* Many communication exchanges get muddled because the focus gets switched from the speaker and the speaker's message to something else. This is perhaps the most common communication pitfall. Sometimes a listener will shift the focus of a speaker's message to another topic entirely, effectively cutting the speaker off and taking over the conversation. For example, if a speaker is talking about what he or she did on a summer vacation excursion and the listener suddenly interjects a tale about what another friend did on a similar trip, the conversation is likely to veer off on this new topic, leaving the original speaker wondering what became of his or her original subject. Sometimes a listener will shift the focus from the speaker entirely. For instance, if the speaker is discussing a spat he had with his girlfriend and the listener interjects, "Why the same thing happened to me when . . ." By shifting the focus to himself or herself, the listener has usurped the speaker and likely left him or her feeling frustrated and possibly irritated. Some strategies that may help avoid the social quagmire that can result from shifting the focus from a speaker include the following:

- Do not respond to a speaker's tale with comments like, "The same thing happened to me." The speaker is more likely to want to continue the communication if he or she feels heard and understood, which means the speaker needs to complete the story. Leave your storytelling for another day or until you are sure the speaker has finished his or her story. No matter how similar your experience seems to the speaker's, each person's experiences are unique. Once the original speaker has completed his or her story, you can share your story and comment that a similar thing happened to you—the important thing to remember is to let the first story be completed before introducing your own tale.

- Attend to the speaker, listen to the story and, and respond to the speaker and his or her message. Don't get bogged down with insignificant details ("Who said that?" "Where were you when that happened?" "How do you know...?") and do not interrogate the speaker.

- Listen carefully and respond to the speaker's message. When engaged in a conversation, do not allow yourself to become distracted; do not daydream or fantasize about what you would say or do in similar circumstances; do not rush ahead and try to anticipate the story's ending. Pay attention and simply listen.

## ASSERTIVENESS SKILLS

Another important communication skill that can help adolescents and young adults in social settings, particularly when they need to advocate for themselves, is assertiveness. Although in a recent study (Kim, 2003), participation in an assertiveness skills training intervention did not evidence any statistically significant effect on students' social or assertiveness skills, descriptive data did show a slight increase in student-reported assertiveness scores from pretest to posttest. The researcher also noted that the intervention may not have been intensive enough to produce the results he had hoped to achieve. His primary concern was that the students often failed to complete their homework for the assertiveness class because they did not receive a grade or other tangible reward for their participation. In addition, the researcher correctly pointed out the difficulties inherent in applying a group experimental design as he did with a low-incidence population in which the small number of participants affects the statistical power of the study. Thus, although this research was inconclusive, teachers and parents are still encouraged to teach and reinforce assertiveness skills.

Assertive people are perceived by others as confident and self-assured. Assertive communicators convey their confidence by engaging others in positive ways. They communicate their needs and wishes without imposing them on others. They pay attention to how others receive their messages and make efforts to ensure that both the other people's needs and their own are being met. People who are assertive understand the impact of their behaviors on others and they strive to

**TABLE 12.1** A Comparison of Passive, Assertive, and Aggressive Communication Styles

| | Passive | Assertive | Aggressive |
|---|---|---|---|
| Characteristics of the communication style | Emotionally dishonest, evasive, self-denying, and inhibited | Appropriately emotionally honest, direct, self-enhancing, and expressive | Inappropriately emotionally honest, direct, self-enhancing at expense of another, and expressive |
| Your feelings when you engage in this communication style | Hurt, anxious at the time and possibly angry later | Confident, self-respecting at the time and later | Righteous, superior, deprecatory at the time and possibly guilty later |
| The other person's feelings about him- or herself when you engage in this communication style | Guilty or superior | Valued, respected | Hurt, humiliated |
| The other person's feelings toward you when you engage in this communication style | Irritation, pity, disgust | Generally respect | Angry, vengeful |

Adapted from R. E. Alberti & M. L. Emmons, *Your Perfect Right* (San Luis Obispo, CA: Impact Press, 2001).

make others feel comfortable while maintaining their own dignity and comfort.

An assertive approach is very different from either a passive or an aggressive approach to communicating one's wants, desires, and needs to others, as illustrated in Table 12.1. A passive communicator tends to avoid discussing his or her wishes and defers to others when it is necessary to advocate for disability-specific needs. On the other hand, an aggressive communicator makes demands on others rather than asking for assistance or explaining what it is that he or she needs. An assertive communicator lets others know what he or she wants or needs, but attends to other people's needs and wants as well. Students need to understand the purpose of using an assertive communication style: It does not mean that the assertive person always gets what he or she wants, but that the assertive person is able to express what he or she wants and feels and allows others the same courtesy.

Assertiveness skills can be taught, and frequently young adults are receptive to learning these skills so that they can communicate more effectively with others. Youths with visual impairments may need to receive specific instruction in assertiveness, as with many of the other social communication skills, because so many of the techniques used by assertive people are nonverbal and depend on body language and facial expression. Students learn these skills best by role playing, engaging in problem-solving scenarios, modeling, and receiving feedback from others related to their communication strengths and weaknesses. Examples from popular movies and television or radio shows can also help students understand the differences between assertive, passive, and aggressive communication styles and the consequences of using one style over another.

The following strategies describe basic assertiveness techniques and skills. Counselors, teachers, and other adults in the life of a visually impaired young adult can use and reinforce these techniques to assist young people interested in developing these skills.

## STRATEGIES FOR SOCIAL SUCCESS
# Assertive Communication Skills

♦ For blind or low vision students, maintaining eye contact or facial orientation toward a speaker is a skill that must be taught and reinforced by using auditory and tactile cues. If it would help to demonstrate physically, ask the student's permission before adjusting his or her orientation. It is important to let students know when they get this skill right.

♦ Students who are blind or visually impaired need to be taught to present a confident body posture, keeping their heads up (chin parallel to the floor or ground) and their bodies erect (shoulders in line with one's hips). They may need tactual or verbal cues to remind them.

♦ Teaching students to lean slightly toward and close, but not too close, to a speaker can help them convey an assertive attitude. Students may also need instruction on how sighted observers interpret certain nonverbal signals. For example, when someone folds his or her arms across the chest, it could indicate that the speaker is being aggressive—angry, unwilling to yield, or wanting to take control of a situation. If students are exhibiting body language that communicates an unintended message (such as standing with their heads down or facing away from a speaker) they need to be told how those postures may be interpreted by a sighted observer as either passive or disinterested.

♦ Appropriate gestures need to be demonstrated and taught using hand-over-hand or hand-under-hand techniques—for example, showing that palms up at shoulder height and raised shoulders indicates a question. It may help to let a blind student place his or her hands on the teacher's shoulders to feel how they are moved in such a gesture, if the teacher is comfortable with such an approach.

♦ Appropriate facial expressions also need to be taught through description or allowing students to feel sculpted images of the face or live models. Feedback from others about their own facial expressions is also helpful for visually impaired students. It can be very helpful to students to hear from teachers, family, and friends how their expressions are seen by others. Saying to a student, "You look so happy today," or "Your expression makes me think you are angry or unhappy," helps the student understand the importance of facial expressions and how to use them to convey feelings.

♦ Students need to be able to understand and interpret the different impressions made by speakers using a variety of tones of voice—from well-modulated tones (assertive) to screaming (aggressive), whining (passive), whispering (passive), or sarcastic (aggressive). The nuances of speech are what help most visually impaired people determine the subtext of communication from others, so mastering skills that involve the interpretation of voice tone and inflection are generally the easiest for visually impaired students who do not have hearing difficulties.

♦ The cornerstone of assertive communication skills is the honest expression of feelings, and visually impaired students must be taught how to state their feelings clearly. One method is to use "I messages," framing the issue in terms of how it affects one's feelings, taking the focus off what the other person has said or done—for example, "I feel frustrated when you don't come over on time," rather than, "You make me angry when you're always late." Students need to understand that "you" messages generally put others on the defensive.

♦ Although spontaneous communication is usually the most assertive, there are times when it is more appropriate to wait and share a message in private. Learning how to judge situations that are conducive to assertive communication is a skill that can be taught by modeling. For example, a teacher or parent might say to a child, "I chose to wait and share this feedback with you because I thought you would prefer to hear it when others were not present." This modeling of an assertive communication style lets the child know that the adult respects his or her privacy and it is possible the youngster will understand and emulate the adult's approach. This skill can also be taught through role playing. An instructor might give the student a scenario and ask him or her to act out one of the roles using either a passive, an aggressive, or an assertive communication style. Scenarios might include an altercation with a friend or relative, a dispute with a store clerk, a scheduled appointment with an employer to discuss a raise or promotion, and so forth. Typically, the instructor and any classmates who have observed the role play will provide feedback on the different approaches—what they liked and did not like, how the different approaches made them feel, which style seemed most effective, and why.

Assertiveness skills can be very useful in self-advocacy efforts and are much more effective than aggressive or passive behavior. When an individual uses an aggressive communication style, people tend to respond with anger or resentment. When someone attempts advocacy with a passive communication style, the effort tends to elicit irritation or pity. However, when an individual advocates with an assertive communication style, people tend to respond with genuine respect and listen closely to the message (Wolffe, 1998). Assertiveness also encourages others to support self-advocacy efforts because they feel comfortable with what is being requested rather than defensive or irritated.

Having good communication skills enables young adults with visual impairments to socialize effectively with other people and build strong, healthy relationships. The communication dos and don'ts described are especially helpful in strengthening friendships and intimate relationships, but can be used effectively to communicate a caring, open attitude to anyone. Likewise, the assertiveness techniques presented are most effective in situations requiring self-advocacy, but can be universally applied in communicating with others effectively.

The following strategies provide a short list of additional tips that can help young people with visual impairments in their communication efforts.

STRATEGIES FOR SOCIAL SUCCESS

# Tips for Socializing with Sighted People

- ◆ Recognize that as a blind person you will likely have to initiate most of the first-time interactions you have with sighted people. They are usually unfamiliar with blindness, and because they do not know what to say they typically say nothing at all! When you sit next to someone or stand behind someone in a line, you may want to say something like, "Hi. How are you?" If it is a safe environment, such as the school cafeteria, you may want to follow up with another question like, "Have we met?"

- ◆ Don't interrupt other people when they are talking. Wait until there is a natural lull in the conversation before you jump in. When you do jump in, stick to the topic under discussion. If you realize that you have interrupted accidentally, simply ask forgiveness with a simple comment like, "Oh, excuse me. Did I cut you off?" If you're not sure that the person speaking has completed his or her thought, ask, "Are you finished? May I jump in here?"

- ◆ Follow the two-minute rule: If you are engaged in a casual conversation, do not speak for more than two minutes—less is better—before passing the conversation to another. If you pause and the listener doesn't speak, ask a leading question such as, "What do you think?"

- ◆ When you ask other people questions, try to ask open-ended questions such as "What did you do?" "What are your thoughts?" "What do you like to do for fun?" rather than closed-ended questions that can be answered with a yes or no, such as "Did you go to the game?" "Do you like this song?"

## CONCLUSION

Social skills are crucial in the lives of young people in secondary and postsecondary settings. They need to build friendships and develop long-term intimate relationships to avoid loneliness and possible depression. In addition, having well-developed personal networks can help in the job search process.

The strategies discussed in this chapter work well with adolescents and young adults because they are cognitively mature enough to benefit from these approaches; they are not necessarily appropriate for younger children. Young adults with visual impairments can apply the communication skills detailed in this chapter to enhance the relationships they already have, develop new friendships, and build toward satisfying and more intimate relationships in adulthood.

# REFERENCES

Alberti, R. E. & Emmons, M. L. (2001). *Your perfect night* (8th ed.). Sanluis Obispo, CA: Impact Publishers.

Alexander, S. H. (2000). *Do you remember the color blue: The questions children ask about blindness.* New York: Penguin Putnam Books.

Azrin, N. H., & Besalel, V. A. (1980). *Job club counselor's manual: A behavioral approach to vocational counseling.* Baltimore: University Park Press.

Bee, H. (1997). The developing child (8th ed.). New York: Addison-Wesley.

Berne, P. H., & Savary, L. M. (1992). Building self-esteem in children. New York: Continuum.

Bloom, M. (1990). The psychosocial constructs of social competency. In T. P. Gullotta, G. R. Adams, & R. Montmayor. (Eds.), *Developing social competency in adolescence.* Newbury Park, CA: Sage Publications.

Bolles, R. N. (2003). *What color is your parachute?* Berkeley, CA: Ten Speed Press.

Corn, A. L., & Rosenblum, L. P. (2000). *Finding wheels: A curriculum for non-drivers with visual impairments for gaining control of transportation needs.* Austin, TX: Pro-Ed.

Corn, A. L., & Sacks, S. Z. (1994). The impact of nondriving on adults with visual impairments. *Journal of Visual Impairment & Blindness, 88,* 53–68.

Cronin, M. S., & Patton, J. R. (1993). *Life skills instruction for all students with special needs.* Austin, TX: PRO-ED.

Elksnin, N., & Elksnin, L. K. (1998). *Teaching occupational social skills.* Austin, TX: PRO-ED.

Erin, J. N., & Wolffe, K. E. (1999). Transition issues related to students with visual disabilities. Austin, TX: PRO-ED.

Evans, R. J. (1984). *Fostering peer acceptance of handicapped students.* Reston, VA: ERIC Clearinghouse on Handicapped and Gifted Children. (ERIC Document Reproduction Service No. ED262498)

Fenwick, E., & Smith, T. (1996). *Adolescence: The survival guide for parents and teenagers.* New York: DK Publishing.

Fesko, S. L., & Temelini, D. (1997). Shared responsibility: Job search practices from consumer and staff perspectives. In F. E. Menz, J. Effers, P. Wehman, & V. Brooke (Eds.), *Lessons for improving employment of people with disabilities from vocational rehabilitation research* (pp. 135–160). Menomonie, WI: University of Wisconsin–Stout.

Harter, S. (1999). *The construction of the self: A developmental perspective.* New York: Guilford Press.

Hartup, W. W. (1992). *Having friends, making friends, and keeping friends: Relationships as educational contexts.* Urbana, IL: ERIC Clearinghouse on Elementary and Early Childhood Education. (ERIC Document Reproduction Service No. ED345854)

Hull, J. M. (1990). *Touching the Rock: An Experience of Blindness.* New York: Pantheon Books.

Huurre, T. (2000). Psychosocial development and social support among adolescents with visual impairment. (Electronic doctoral dissertation, University of Tampere, Finland.)

Huurre, T., Komulainen, E. J., & Aro, H. M. (1999). Social support and self-esteem among adolescents with visual impairments. *Journal of Visual Impairment & Blindness, 93,* 26–37.

Johnson, S., & Wehman, P. (2001). Teaching for transition. In P. Wehman (Ed.), *Life beyond the classroom* (pp. 145–170). Baltimore: Paul H. Brookes.

Kaufman, A. (2000). Clothing-selection habits of teenage girls who are sighted and blind. *Journal of Visual Impairment & Blindness, 94,* 527–531.

Kef, S. (1997). The personal networks and social supports of blind and visually impaired adolescents. *Journal of Visual Impairment & Blindness, 91*(3), 236–244.

Kef, S. (1999). Outlook on relations: Personal networks and psychosocial characteristics of visually impaired adolescents. Amsterdam: Thelathesis.

Kirchner, C., McBroom, L. W., Nelson, K. A., & Graves, W. H. (1992). *Lifestyles of employed legally blind people: A study of expenditures and time use* (Technical Report). Mississippi State: Mississippi State University, Rehabilitation Research and Training Center on Blindness and Low Vision.

Kuusisto, S. (1998). *Planet of the Blind.* New York: Dial Press.

MacCuspie, P. A. (1996). *Promoting acceptance of children with disabilities: From tolerance to inclusion.* Halifax, Nova Scotia, Canada: Atlantic Provinces Special Education Authority.

Mangold, S., & Mangold, P. (1983). The adolescent visually impaired female. *Journal of Visual Impairment & Blindness, 77,* 250–255.

Marston, V. R., & Golledge, R. E. (2003). The hidden demand for participation in activities & travel by persons who are visually impaired. *VVIB, 97,* 475–488.

Odom, S. L., McConnell, S. R., & McEvoy, M. A. (1992). *The social competence of young children with disabilities: Issues and strategies for intervention.* Baltimore: Paul H. Brookes.

Ornstein, R. (1993). *The roots of self.* New York: Harper Collins.

Peavey, K. O., & Leff, D. (2002). Social acceptance of adolescent mainstreamed students with visual impairments. *Journal of Visual Impairment & Blindness, 96,* 808–811.

Rosenblum, L. P. (1997). Adolescents with visual impairments who have best friends: A pilot study. *Journal of Visual Impairment & Blindness, 91,* 224–235.

Rosenblum, L. P. (1998). Best friendships of adolescents with visual impairments: A descriptive study. *Journal of Visual Impairment & Blindness, 92*, 593–608.

Sacks, S. Z., & Silberman, R. K. (2000). Social skills. In A. J. Koenig & M. C. Holbrook (Eds.), *Foundations of education, Vol. 2: Instructional strategies for teaching children and youths with visual impairments.* (2nd ed.; pp. 616–652). New York: AFB Press.

Sacks, S. Z., & Wolffe, K. (1992). The importance of social skills in the transition process for students who are visually impaired. *Journal of Vocational Rehabilitation, 2*(1), 46–55.

Sacks, S. Z., & Wolffe, K. E. (1998). Lifestyles of adolescents with visual impairments: An ethnographic analysis. *Journal of Visual Impairment & Blindness, 92*(1), 7–17.

Sacks, S. Z., Wolffe, K. E., & Tierney, D. (1998). Lifestyles of students with visual impairments: Preliminary studies of social networks. *Exceptional Children, 64*(4), 463–478.

Seligman, M.E.P. (1990). *Learned optimism.* New York: Alfred A. Knopf.

Seligman, M.E.P., Reivich, K., Jaycox, L., & Gillham, J. (1995). *The optimistic child.* New York: Harper Perennial.

Sharma, S., Sigafoos, J., & Carroll, A. (2000). Social skills assessment of Indian children with visual impairments. *Journal of Visual Impairment & Blindness, 94*, 172–176.

Silliker, S. A. (1993). The role of social contacts in the successful job search. *Journal of Employment Counseling, 30*(1), 25–34.

Skellenger, A. C., Hill, M., & Hill, E. (1992). In S. L., Odom, S. R., McConnell, & M. A. McEvoy (Eds.), *The social competence of young children with disabilities: Issues and strategies for intervention* (pp. 165–188). Baltimore: Paul H. Brookes.

Smith, S. W. (2002). *Applying cognitive-behavioral techniques to social skills instruction.* Arlington, VA: ERIC Clearinghouse on Disabilities and Gifted Education. ERIC/OSEP Special Project.

Strain, P. S., Guralnick, M. J., & Walker, H. M. (1986). *Children's social behavior: Development, assessment, modification.* Orlando, FL: Academic Press.

Strain, P. S., & Odom, S. L. (1986). Peer social initiations: Effective intervention for social skills development of exceptional children. *Exceptional Children, 52*, 543–551.

Vincent, C. G., Horner, R. H., & Sugai, G. (2002). *Developing social competence for all students.* Arlington, VA: ERIC Clearinghouse on Disabilities and Gifted Education. ERIC/OSEP Special Project.

Walker, H. M., Todis, B., Holmes, D., & Horton, G. (1988). *ACCESS Program: Adolescent curriculum for communication and effective social skills.* Austin, TX: PRO-ED.

Wegmann, R., & Chapman, R. (1990). *The right place at the right time.* Berkeley, CA: Ten Speed Press.

Wolffe, K. (1996). Career education for students with visual impairments. *RE:view, 28*(2), 89–93.

Wolffe, K. E. (1997). *Career counseling for people with disabilities: A practical guide to finding employment.* Austin, TX: PRO-ED.

Wolffe, K. E. (1998). Transition planning and employment outcomes for students who have visual impairments with other disabilities. In S. Z. Sacks & R. Silberman (Eds.), *Educating students who have visual impairments with other disabilities.* Baltimore: Paul H. Brookes.

Wolffe, K. E. (Ed.). (1999). *Skills for success: A career education handbook for children and adolescents with visual impairments.* New York: AFB Press.

Wolffe, K. (2004). Transitioning young adults from school to public transportation. *EnVision: A publication for parents and educators of children with impaired vision, 8,* 7–9.

Wolffe, K., & Sacks, S. Z. (1997). The social network pilot project: A quantitative comparison of the lifestyles of blind, low vision, and sighted young adults. *Journal of Visual Impairment & Blindness, 91*(3), 245–257.

Wolffe, K. E., Thomas, K. L., & Sacks, S. Z. (2000). *Focused on: Social skills for teens and young adults with visual impairments.* New York: AFB Press.

Zadny, J. J., & James, L. F. (1979). Job placement in state vocational rehabilitation agencies: A survey of technique. *Rehabilitation Counseling Bulletin, 22,* 361–378.

# CHAPTER 13

# Teaching Social Skills to Students with Multiple Disabilities

Karen E. Wolffe and
Rosanne K. Silberman

Students with visual impairments come in all shapes and sizes, with differing abilities and different disabling conditions. Some students have vision problems alone, but many have multiple disabilities. Estimates vary, but some reports indicate that 50 to 75 percent of all students currently being served by teachers of students with visual impairments have additional disabilities (Sacks & Silberman, 1998; Silberman, 2000). These additional disabilities may include any number of syndromes, but some of the most common include learning disabilities, hearing disabilities, neurological disorders, cognitive impairments, and emotional disturbances. According to the American Printing House for the Blind (APH) Babies Count Project Leader, the largest group (23 percent) of infants who are referred for services from teachers of students with visual impairments are babies with cortical visual impairment (CVI), and many of these babies have additional neurological problems (Burt Boyer, personal communication, May 16, 2003). The second largest group of babies who are referred are children with retinopathy of prematurity (17 percent), and these infants, too, often have multiple disabilities.

Given that a minimum of 40 percent of the children in early childhood programs for youngsters who are visually impaired may have multiple disabilities, with similar or greater numbers among older students, it is essential that teachers and other service providers understand how best to work with these children and meet their needs. This chapter provides specific strategies and information to facilitate social skills instruction for students with multiple disabilities, in particular those whose additional disabilities require special teaching strategies and ongoing support services.

The importance of teaching social skills to students who are multiply disabled may not be immediately apparent to everyone. Although some people may believe that teaching such skills to students with multiple disabilities may in many cases be unnecessary or even unproductive, nothing could be further from the truth. Like other children who are visually impaired, children with multiple disabilities derive feelings of self-esteem and competence from engaging in satisfying ways with others. In addition, social skills instruction is vital for these students because social competence facilitates their inclusion in society at large. If students are able to master basic social amenities such as greeting others, smiling, and using social niceties like saying "please" and "thank you" and covering their mouths when they sneeze or cough, they will be better received in the community. When students display socially acceptable behavior, other people typically tend to be more relaxed and more receptive toward them. When they display socially unacceptable behavior, there are immediate social consequences: Children and adults alike are more likely to avoid them or feel uncomfortable in their company.

# STUDENT INTERVENTION CATEGORIES

Before discussing strategies for intervention, it is important to clarify the terms used in this chapter. Rather than attempt to categorize children according to their various disabling conditions or special education labels, the authors prefer to present a classification system that looks specifically at the individual student's need for intervention. Using this system enables the service provider—who may be a teacher, therapist, instructional aide, orientation and mobility (O&M) instructor, counselor, social worker, job coach, intervenor, or other helper—in determining how best to help students achieve their goals based on their functional abilities and needs. The terms *informational level*, *instructional level*, and *advocacy level* are used to describe children with varying needs; each term is discussed in the following sections. (For a more detailed presentation of this typology, see Wolffe, 1997; Wolffe & Johnson, 1997; Wolffe, 1998).

## INFORMATIONAL-LEVEL STUDENTS

The term *informational level* describes students who need only a minimal amount of assistance or intervention to acquire new skills and knowledge. Students at this level typically are good readers, listeners, and observers. Most can be given involved verbal directions and be expected to follow though with directives received. The majority of such students respond to the traditional content approach to teaching in which the facilitator lectures or leads discussions in curricular areas and students can apply what they have heard and seen in their lives. Students categorized as informational level learn by trying out new concepts in the environment and modifying them to suit their needs. They have the ability to generalize what they have learned in classrooms or clinical settings to new and different environments. They tend to be bright, creative, and motivated to learn.

Many students at the informational level who have visual impairments compensate almost intuitively for their disabilities, learning alternative strategies such as braille, use of optical devices, O&M skills, and other techniques to compete with their sighted peers. They learn and apply good social skills, self-determination techniques, and problem-solving skills. When they don't know how to accomplish a goal, they seek out assistance or information from others, including teachers and related service providers, friends or family members. These students seem driven to "learn for learnings sake."

Individuals with multiple disabilities, including visual impairment, can be informational-level students—Helen Keller was one. Students functioning at this level usually have strong cognitive skills and may also have positively challenging and supportive families and friends who encourage them and reinforce their efforts. With information about environmental cues, alternative techniques, and adapted tools and equipment from their families and service providers, as well as general academic and career education content, these individuals can live and work independently. They need very little external help, and the help they need is transitory. These students can and will succeed, in large part, on their own initiative.

## INSTRUCTIONAL-LEVEL STUDENTS

The term *instructional level* refers to students who are considered of average intelligence and need an average amount of intervention. Typically, students at this level require external motivation, such as grades, encouragement, and structured instruction from teachers as well as allowances, guidance, and nurturing from parents—they are not internally motivated or driven to learn and apply new skills. They need to receive direct instruction, rather than being able to learn on their own from books and observation—they are typical students. These students tend not to seek out learning experiences; rather they are drawn in by teachers who pique their curiosity. They can usually hear or see, read, write, and learn through observation; however, demonstration—doing an activity with them—is helpful. They can follow directions, but will benefit from the reinforcement of being shown and told how to perform.

Many instructional-level students respond best to process teaching, in which the teacher instructs students by showing them how to perform. Although they can learn through content teaching, in which the teacher presents information either through lecture or reading assignments, they tend to assimilate information best when they use it. Once a skill has been mastered, instructional-level students continue to refine and apply what has been learned in the classroom to their activities at home, in school, or in the community.

The majority of students with and without multiple disabilities are instructional-level students. They benefit tremendously from direct instruction and can typically transfer or generalize learned skills and knowledge into new or different situations and environments. Although such students need intervention and, like most people, benefit from learning throughout their lives, they do not need ongoing intervention or lifelong external support to survive. They are often encountered as traditional students with disabilities and rehabilitation clients (individuals without multiple disabilities) whose needs are time limited, as opposed to students or clients whose needs are extensive and likely to last throughout their lives. With instruction and practice, the majority of these students will ultimately live independently and work competitively without ongoing intervention from service providers.

## ADVOCACY-LEVEL STUDENTS

The term *advocacy level* is used to refer to the students who will require the most assistance. They are individuals who will always require help or advocacy from others to survive. Advocacy-level students typically are not able to live on their own, manage the complex demands of independent travel and daily living, or do academic or high-level intellectual work. These students require extensive support, typically throughout their lives, to survive and manage as independently as possible. Children and youths at this level function significantly below average in most areas of academics and daily living skills. They require intensive instruction, frequently on a one-to-one basis. Combinations of teaching methods will be necessary to teach such students the basic concepts that are the foundation on which higher-order skills are built. Instructions may need to be spoken, signed, written, pictorial, or offered in some combination of these approaches. Demonstration and coactive instruction (teaching a skill by doing the skill with the student; if necessary, using hand-over-hand or hand-under-hand guidance) may prove more effective than traditional instructional techniques such as classroom lectures, written assignments, and demonstrations.

Process learning is often used when working with advocacy-level students. Process learning involves teachers and students performing skills together in a natural environment whenever possible—for example, learning to use scissors by having the teacher sit beside the student and cut with the scissors while the child's hands are on the teacher's so he or she can feel how the tool is supposed to work; or learning to measure ingredients by standing or sitting beside a parent as he or she guides the youngster in using a knife to level a cup of flour. The traditional content or lecture approach, in which the teacher simply talks about a topic and the students read their textbooks for further edification, is typically too intellectually demanding of these students, who often cannot follow a lecture or read. If they do read, they are able to read only what is necessary for everyday functioning (such as their names, traffic or restroom signage, and warning signs). The majority of advocacy-level students have great difficulty generalizing information or skills learned in a classroom to different situations or environments, which is why their instructional needs are best met in natural environments whenever possible, rather than in schools or clinical environments.

Many students functioning at the advocacy level will be able to live and work in the community only with specific support, such as attendant care, communication specialists, job coaches or intervenors, supervised living arrangements, access to paratransit services, case managers, nursing care, and so forth. Although every advocacy-level student will not need all of these support services, he or she will need some kind of external support throughout life in order to be assimilated into the community and to actively participate in community-based activities.

Typically, students with visual impairments who need this kind of ongoing, lifelong support also have a cognitive impairment as one of their concomitant disabilities. Without average or higher-level cognitive skills, it is often difficult for an individual to compensate for vision loss and learn the alternative techniques (such as braille, use of optical devices, O&M, and such) that allow for independence in adult life. This does not imply that all students with visual and cognitive impairment are advocacy-level students. However, the more severe the cognitive impairment of a visually impaired student, the greater the likelihood that student will be an advocacy-level student in need of appropriate supports.

Students with visual and cognitive impairment are not the only students who may be considered advocacy-level students, however. For example, some children who are born totally deaf and totally blind may experience such severe environmental deprivation that they, too, would require ongoing supports throughout their lives to survive in today's quick-paced, complex, and intellectually demanding world. Some children with severe physical disabilities and visual impairment also may require ongoing supports for life; depending on their ability to coordinate and direct these needs, such as attendant care, these children may also be considered advocacy-level students.

This chapter focuses on interventions that are most applicable to advocacy-level students, as the strategies provided in earlier chapters essentially addressed students at the informational and instructional levels. Students who fall into the category of advocacy level are very different from their same-aged peers because they need extensive external assistance to succeed in social interactions with most of the people they will encounter throughout their lives. They may learn rudimentary social interaction skills, but they will need to rely on others to interpret the social nuances and subtleties of more sophisticated social interaction skills due to the severity and complexity of their disabilities. In many instances, these students will be nonverbal or, if they have language or communication skills, they will likely use alternatives to spoken language such as basic sign language or pictorial and symbol cues to convey meaning. Although these alternative systems may be deeply meaningful to the students, they may not mean much to a stranger. While advocacy-level students may be able to demonstrate communicative intent, they typically need an interpreter or an augmentative or alternative communication device, such as a communication board with tangible symbols, to convey meaning to another person.

Most people do not fall neatly into any one of these three levels; depending on circumstances and the demands placed on them at any given time, they may show characteristics of more than one level. For example, a person may be classified as advocacy level in most domestic, personal care, and vocational activities, but he or she may be at the instructional level when learning how to play the guitar. Or a person may be an instructional-level student in most areas, but be unable to learn how to perform basic mathematical functions and have to rely on an aide or attendant to help with shopping or other money exchanges. However, people tend to function at or near one specific level most of the time.

Instructional staff and families need to understand that most students with and without visual impairments, regardless of their primary level of functioning and need for intervention, learn best in environments where process learning is stressed (Wolffe, 1997; Wolffe & Johnson, 1997). Process learning is particularly important in the area of social skills acquisition, as students without good vision need to physically experience the nuances of social gestures to truly understand them. It is difficult to convert reading or hearing about shaking hands, for example, or smiling, frowning, or shrugging shoulders, into the physical process without actually doing it.

## LEARNING STYLES

When working with students with multiple disabilities, caregivers and instructional personnel must understand and accommodate the students' learning styles or channels—the combination of ways in which an individual learns best. Four primary learning styles—visual, auditory, tactile, and kinesthetic—are described in the following sections. Although the other senses—olfactory and gustatory, in particular—can complement learning, they are not usually primary learning modalities for teaching social skills and are therefore not discussed. However, it should be noted that many advocacy-level students may use their sense of smell or taste for identification purposes, for example, to recognize a person by his or her scent or an item by its taste.

### VISUAL LEARNING

Visual learners process information best when it is presented pictorially or in a printed format. With some vision, a child who is a visual learner can watch a social interchange and model that behavior. Waving "hello" or "good-bye" is an example of a behavior that a visual learner might observe and mimic. However, vision is not a requisite attribute for a child to be a visual learner. Sometimes children without vision still appear to be visual learners, inasmuch as they capture information best when they can picture it in their minds. This is often the case with adventitiously blinded children who were visual learners before losing their vision. For example, they may hear a description or look at a graph or chart tactilely, but the final processing that encodes the information happens when they visualize it in their minds.

## Auditory Learning

Auditory learners understand and remember information best when they hear it read or spoken to them—on audiotape or orally. They often learn jingles and information from listening to the radio, films, or television. It can be helpful to these learners for the teacher to repeat information verbally. For this type of learner, a verbal cue such as "say good-bye" or "wave good-bye" may be required for social behavior to be initiated.

## Tactile Learning

Tactile learners come to understand what is going on around them and how things work when they touch materials. They receive information through their sense of touch; hands-on, experiential learning may work best with these students. With the tactile learner who is visually impaired, for example, the teacher or caregiver may need to present a gesture, such as the thumbs-up sign, and allow the student to feel his or her hand so that the student can "see" the hand configuration tactilely.

## Kinesthetic Learning

Students who learn best kinesthetically need to move their bodies through the steps of a task and manipulate tools and items in order to understand them and their uses. These students usually enjoy movement and may like to be physically active. They may need to have their teacher literally move their hands in the motion of waving goodbye to understand how to perform it. With kinesthetic learners, the key is the manipulation of the body part in synch with the instructor (coactive movement); such students often benefit from either hand-under-hand or hand-over-hand demonstration.

Students with multiple disabilities who are functioning at the advocacy-level often benefit from instruction based on a combination of learning styles. For example, a tactile or kinesthetic cue such as feeling a ring or watch, coupled with an oral or signed name, may help the student recognize a classmate. Simple raised-line drawings, symbols, pictures, or marks to identify personal items likewise may help a student discriminate between his or her possessions and a classmate's. Learning styles have social implications for advocacy-level students because teachers need to recognize how students learn best in order to structure the social lessons presented, in much the same way that they would structure academic or vocational lessons.

Finally, it is important to underscore the critical need for consistency in presenting information to advocacy-level students. These students typically learn best when all the members of the interdisciplinary team and their families use the same techniques, the same instructional style, and the same vocabulary with them over time. Learning is also more likely to be successful when the behavior being taught occurs naturally in everyday activities rather than in isolation in a classroom or at home.

## BASIC PRINCIPLES

Throughout this book, the authors have shown why the acquisition and maintenance of social skills for students with visual impairments is challenging: These students cannot learn the social nuances of communicating and relating to others incidentally through vision. For students with multiple disabilities, including visual impairment, their additional disabilities may make inaccessible the alternative techniques often used by blind and low vision students to learn and practice social skills, such as careful listening or tactile exploration. Thus, children and adolescents with visual impairments and additional disabilities are at an even greater risk for social isolation, because they may lack the cognitive, physical, or neurological abilities to integrate social skills into their daily lives. Also, the nature of these students' disabilities may be more complex, requiring greater adult supervision, medical support, or external supports in order for them to experience real-life opportunities in their homes, schools, and the community.

These students with multiple impairments have a range of disabilities in addition to their visual impairments. They may include cognitive impairments, physical impairments, neurological impairments, auditory impairments including deaf-blindness, emotional or behavioral disabilities, and learning disabilities. The way in which these students acquire social skills may be affected by their learning styles and their cognitive and neurological abilities, as well as by the way others (families and professionals) interact and work with them. The acquisition of social skills in natural contexts is highly dependent on the implementation of consistent routines and expectations by teachers, classmates, and family members, in accordance with the following basic principals:

- The educational team must recognize the importance of social skill acquisition and make instruction in this area a priority in the student's IEP.

- Strategies for teaching social skills need to promote making choices within well-established routines throughout the day.

- Programs for teaching social skills must be consistent, so that the student learns that everyone in his or her educational and social circle, including family members, teachers, and peers, has the same expectations for social competence.

- Families, teachers, and peers must treat the student with dignity and in an age-appropriate manner.

- Families, teachers, and significant others must establish realistic expectations for the student's social performance at school, at home, and in the community.

- It is essential to consider the future environments in which the students will live and function when setting priorities for if and when specific social skills will be taught. Families and teachers need to determine what social skills are critical for the next living, training, or work environment.

Students with visual impairments and additional disabilities are often educated in noncategorical special education classes. They may receive support from a teacher of visually impaired students, an orientation and mobility specialist, or other instructors of vision-specific skills, but special educators with expertise in other disability areas, typically teachers trained to work with students who are cognitively impaired, manage the majority of their educational programming. Because these special educators may not have experience in methods of working with students who are visually impaired, they tend to rely on visual cues such as pictures or visual modeling to teach social skills. Alternative teaching modes, such as tactile cues, physical modeling of appropriate social behavior, and consistent verbal feedback from peers and adults, may be better suited for students who are blind and exhibit additional disabilities to enhance their ability to acquire and maintain a repertoire of socially appropriate behaviors. These students also require an organized and consistent environment in which to learn social skills. Repetition and practice are essential components for an effective social skills intervention program.

The educational team can ensure that opportunities are provided for students with visual and multiple disabilities for experiences that promote the use of social skills by emphasizing the following principles:

- Promote classroom placements where the teacher is organized and routine oriented.

- Provide opportunities for students to use social skills throughout their day in natural environments within the school and in the community.

- Encourage consistency in programming and expectations for appropriate behavior so that students can anticipate what will happen next throughout the day.

## SOCIAL SKILLS AND EARLY INTERVENTION

Teaching social skills to children and youths with visual impairments and additional disabilities is dependent not only on students' learning styles and abilities; numerous other factors contribute to the way in which these students develop socially competent behaviors and skills. Researchers have documented that early physical contact with family members and friends, as well as opportunities to interact with the natural environment through daily routines and activities, can enhance the child's willingness to explore and interact with others (Chen & Dote-Kwan, 1999; Fazzi, 2002; Ferrell, 2000). Young children with visual impairments and additional disabilities may experience sensory deprivation because they are initially ill or fragile. Families may have few opportunities to cuddle, touch, or play with their young children. The following strategies may help to reduce environmental deprivation and increase interactive activities for young children with visual impairments and additional disabilities.

STRATEGIES FOR SOCIAL SUCCESS
# Increasing Interaction for Young Children with Multiple Disabilities

- ◆ Include the child in environments where the family works, eats, and plays when at all possible.
- ◆ Talk to the child and explain what is happening in his or her world.
- ◆ When initiating a social interaction with the young child, pair a verbal cue with a tactile cue; for example, saying, "Hi, Lindsay, Mommy is here," while kissing the child on the forehead.
- ◆ Establish daily routines to help the young child predict the next activity.
- ◆ Create environments at home and in school that are calm, uncluttered, and predictable whenever possible. Too much visual or auditory stimulation can cause the child to withdraw or exhibit socially unacceptable behavior like screaming, pinching, kicking, or biting.
- ◆ Bring the child into environments where others are interacting (mealtimes, outdoor activities in the backyard or at the park, trips to the grocery store or other businesses in the community, and so forth).
- ◆ When appropriate, provide rough-and-tumble experiences like riding on an adult's shoulders and jumping or bouncing on a trampoline.
- ◆ For children who are hospitalized for long periods of time, investigate the use of massage to help the child continue to establish trust and rapport with others.

Social relationships that involve strong attachment and trust between a child and another individual, usually a family member or caregiver, are essential for creating emotional well-being and enhancing cognitive and communicative development. Vision and hearing are important to the formation of an attachment bond between mother and child. When children are born with visual impairments and multiple disabilities such as deaf-blindness, there are many challenges that affect their critical early interactive experiences: Mutual eye gaze between mother and child is either missing or distorted, and the infant is unable to recognize and respond to voices and facial expressions.

For example, the mother may not be able to interpret and respond to the child's nontraditional ways of communicating (such as moving his or her hands to show pleasure), and both mother and child may develop feelings of inadequacy and insecurity (McLetchie & Riggio, 2002). Futhermore, this interference affects the development of communication, trust, and social relationships that extend beyond the child into the outside world (Prickett & Welch, 1998, 1995; Silberman, Bruce, & Nelson, 2004).

## SOCIAL RELATIONSHIPS AND COMMUNICATION

Many students who are blind and have additional disabilities may exhibit a discrepancy between expressive and receptive language. These students may understand what people say to them but do not have the ability to express feelings, make choices, or express thoughts and ideas in a conventional manner. Their inability to express themselves verbally may be due to physical or intellectual limitations. They tend to express their communicative intent by the way they engage others behaviorally and these behaviors are frequently misinterpreted by others as negative or inappropriate responses, rather than as a means of expression and communication. For example, a child may express his or her dislike for a play activity by pushing away from an adult or peer, or may pinch or scream to let others know that the activity is not enjoyable. Other students may express feelings of excitement about sharing a game with a sibling by twirling around or exhibiting intense hand-flapping movements. While these behaviors may not seem socially acceptable, especially in natural contexts, they provide valuable information about the student's attempts at social communication, and they allow others to interpret the communicative nature of the student's behavior.

When engaging students with visual impairments who have additional disabilities and cannot communicate their social needs through expressive language, the following strategies may help to promote effective social communication.

### STRATEGIES FOR SOCIAL SUCCESS

# Promoting Social Communication and Expressive Language

♦ Observe the student in several different settings to determine how he or she typically communicates feelings, choices, and social intent.

- Recognize that behavior is communication. If students cannot communicate through expressive language, they will communicate through their actions (by smiling, nodding, pulling away, or pinching, for example).

- Acknowledge when the student is attempting to communicate a specific feeling or desire by describing the student's behavior verbally; for instance, "Oh, Susan, you're smiling. You must really like playing with Jennifer."

- Reinforce appropriate social behavior, physically and verbally, depending on the situation. For example, when a student is sitting in a wheelchair with his head up, the teacher might reinforce this behavior by saying to the student, "John, you look great when you hold your head up like that."

- Work with speech and language specialists to determine if augmentative or alternative communication devices can help the student in making social contact with peers and adults.

- Encourage students to make choices about the games or activities they like to play and with whom they wish to eat lunch, spend time, or go on an outing.

- Establish routines for eliciting appropriate social behavior across a variety of social situations and settings. For example, when students enter a classroom at the beginning of the school day, they engage in a series of social greetings with peers and adults ("Hi, how are you?" or "Hey, what's up?"). These initiations can be practiced with students with multiple disabilities and appropriate responses reinforced.

## CONVERSATION

Children with visual impairments and multiple disabilities will need to rely on others as supports to help them move from isolation to interaction, build positive, close relationships, and acquire knowledge about the world. Those with deaf-blindness can use touch, rhythmic movement, or facial expressions to convey their thoughts, emotions, interests, preferences, and dislikes (McLetchie & Riggio, 2002).

Many intervention strategies that are used to support the development of communication and social interactions of children who are deaf-blind evolved from methods developed by Jan van Dijk and colleagues in the Netherlands in the mid-1960s. The van Dijk approach is conversational and interactive and emphasizes following the child's lead and interests as a mutual relationship between child and partner is established and the child learns that he or she can influence the environment (Janssen, Riksen-Walraven, & van Dijk, 2003; Mac-Farland, 1995; Silberman, Bruce, & Nelson, 2004; van Dijk & Nelson, 1997). At first, the child and partner (parent, educator, or peer) take turns following each other's movements and actions in a give-and-take format. The conversation without words begins when the partner follows the child's lead, shares his or her interest, and joins the child in a familiar movement or activity that the child likes. The partner pauses and waits for a signal from the child to continue the activity. For example, a young girl is playing with a favorite ball, rolling it around and around in her hands. The adult sits beside her and offers another ball, which she picks up and explores, then sets aside and picks up her favorite ball again. The adult lets her play for a minute and then introduces another ball, one with a different color or texture or a bell inside. The girl sets aside her favorite ball and examines the new ball, plays with it for a moment and then drops it to retrieve the favored toy. The adult gradually increases involvement in the interaction—rolling new balls or bouncing balls as the child shows more interest. The adult may show the child two balls—the favorite and another—and let her choose one, then show two other balls (both new) and let her choose again. If she indicates pleasure in the game, by smiling or simply by attending to the activity, the adult continues to interact with the child. If she indicates displeasure, by pushing the balls or the adult away, the adult pauses and watches to see what happens and doesn't resume the activity until the child indicates that she's interested.

Pacing the conversation is important; many children with deaf-blindness or visual impairments with additional disabilities need about five to ten more seconds than their peers to process information and respond. By pausing, the adult or partner gives the child time to express that he or she is enjoying the activity. Through turn taking the child learns to accept, enjoy, and trust one or two people. These types of turn taking, interactive conversations set the foundation for relating socially to others.

When setting up such conversational opportunities, it is important to consider the child's visual and auditory functioning, as well as any physical disabilities the child might have. The child should be positioned within arm's reach and at eye level with his or her communication partner. Thus, a meaningful conversation with a child who is deaf-blind or one who is visually impaired and has additional disabilities is characterized by mutual attention, shared topic, common language, comfortable pace, turn taking, comfortable positioning, and mutual caring (McLetchie & Riggio, 2002; Miles & Riggio, 1999; see MacFarland, 1995, and Silberman, Bruce, & Nelson, 2004, for specific strategies that enhance communication and social interaction using the van Dijk approach).

## CONVERSATION BOOKS

For a child with visual impairments and additional disabilities that may include hearing loss or cognitive impairments, conversation books can provide another means to form social relationships with peers without disabilities. A number of authors have demonstrated how conversation books can be used as augmentative devices that are valuable in enhancing social interactions (Hunt, Alwell, & Goetz, 1991; Hunt, Farron-Davis, Wren, Horose-Hatae, & Goetz, 1997). In these models, students without disabilities are paired with a friend with multiple disabilities. The student without disabilities is taught techniques for maintaining a conversation by asking questions and making comments that their friend can respond to using the conversation book. The book may consist of pictures, drawings, photographs, tactile objects, or parts of objects from activities or routines. Conversation book pages can be used to convey a written message and questions related to the objects or symbols that encourage interaction. For example, a page might include objects such as beads with the attached message, "I like lots of beads. What do you like?" Conversation book pages can also be used to facilitate making choices related to participation in future activities, for example, choosing between photos of two classmates to choose with whom to play a computer game. They may also be used to form topics of conversations between the child and partner as they converse about activities the child has already experienced—for instance, a trip to the animal farm—or will experience in the future, such as a trip to the shopping mall (Miles & Riggio, 1999; Silberman, et al., 2004).

## AUGMENTATIVE COMMUNICATION DEVICES

A variety of augmentative communication devices can be used to enhance social interactions between students with visual impairments and multiple disabilities and students without disabilities. An augmentative communication device helps a person produce or understand speech. It can be as simple as a board with pictures or objects affixed such as soap, a toothbrush, a spoon, or a key representing a student's daily needs, or as sophisticated as an electronic speech synthesizer that can produce words. Selection of such devices depends on the student's needs, abilities, use of vision and hearing, and motor skills as well as the demands of the environment. Consideration of the size of the device may be based on whether or not the student needs a portable device and the number of symbols that can be displayed. Downing (2001) lists a myriad of devices in formats including a small book, large notebook, box, CD holder, videocassette holder, wristband, bracelet, small photograph album, and different voice output communication aids. The following are examples of how augmentative communication devices may be used for social interactions (Downing, 2001, p.152):

- An active fourth-grade student who is deaf-blind and has a hemiplegia form of cerebral palsy wears a wristband with a few symbols on it when he goes with his class for recess. He can point to the symbols to indicate which piece of playground equipment or activity he prefers.
- A tenth-grade student with low vision and in a wheelchair uses a notebook and a choice board that holds objects and parts of objects to make requests and to tell her classmates about herself. She also uses a BIGmack (a voice-output device) to call out to her peers because she cannot physically get to them easily.

Any number of appropriate objects or symbols can be attached to an augmentative communication device and used as symbols to promote social interaction and communication with students who have visual impairments and multiple disabilities including deaf-blindness. Symbols could be pictorial representations of objects, names written in print or braille, actual objects or parts of objects that relate to a student's daily routine (for example, part of a washcloth to symbolize going to the bathroom; a milk carton to symbolize going to lunch, or part of a swing chain to symbolize going out to recess). Caution is needed when selecting objects to make sure they are tactilely pleasing for students who have no vision; it is also important to note that miniature objects, such as a miniature school bus or a dog, which may be recognized visually by someone who is sighted, are often not meaningful when presented tactilely. Appropriate symbols for students who have some useable vision include photographs, colored pictures from magazines, black-and-white line drawings, or even the student's own drawings, if visually recognizable (Downing, 1999; Miles & Riggio, 1999).

## TECHNIQUES FOR STRUCTURING THE DEVELOPMENT OF INTERACTIONS

There are a variety of techniques that can be used to promote social interactions and friendships in neighborhood schools and classes attended by students with disabilities together with their typical peers. One such technique is known as MAPS—Making Action Plans, originally known as McGill Action Planning System (Falvey, Forest, Pearpoint, & Rosenberg, 2002; Forest & Lusthaus, 1989; Forest & Pearpoint, 1992; Pearpoint, Forest, & O'Brien, 1996; Vandercook, York, & Forest, 1989). MAPS is a process that involves a collaborative group consisting of the student with disabilities, classmates, and adults such as the classroom teacher, the teacher of students visually impaired, orientation and mobility specialist, speech therapist, and family members. The purpose of MAPS is to collect information about the student in order to brainstorm how to create an ideal day or schedule, design an action plan, and develop a vision for the student with the disability. By finding out what the student enjoys and wants for the future classmates have something to discuss with him or her and this can encourage socialization. The MAPS meeting is informal, with one adult serving as the facilitator (Falvey et al., 2002). The collaborative group attempts to answer as many of the following questions as possible:

1. What is a MAP and how is it used?
2. What is the student's background (history)?
3. What is your dream for the student?
4. What worries you about the future (nightmare)?
5. What words would you use to describe the student?
6. What are the student's strengths, gifts, and talents?
7. What are the student's needs or challenges?
8. What is the plan of action and who will be responsible for the steps in the plan?

Falvey, et al. (2002) and MacCuspie (1996) provide additional, detailed information about this technique, examples of responses to similar questions, and a discussion of how MAPS can be used with specific students to encourage social interactions.

Another process that can be helpful in facilitating friendships for students with visual impairments and multiple disabilities is a friendship awareness activity known as Circle of Friends (Falvey, et al., 2002; Forest & Lusthaus, 1989; Silberman, et al., 1998; Snell, et al., 2000). This activity involves gathering a group of typical students and the student with multiple disabilities (assistance is provided if necessary) and asking each person in the group to make a Circle of Friends diagram. This diagram consists of four concentric circles surrounding the individual participant's name in the center of the inner circle. The innermost circle represents *intimacy*; here the students fill in the names of those people they really care about and can't imagine living without. In the second circle, labeled *friendship*, students write the names of good friends. The third circle, *participation*, contains individuals students know less well (acquaintances) from organizations and networks with which students are involved (such as choir, scouts, reading group, music club). The outer circle, the *exchange* circle, includes those individuals who are paid by others or the student's family to provide services for the student (medical doctors, dentist, teachers, therapists, and the like). For an example of a completed Circle of Friends diagram for a student with visual impairment and additional disabilities, see Figure 13.1.

When the students have completed their diagrams, the facilitator discusses the value of peer support and brainstorms with the group about how nondisabled students can become part of the student with disability's circle of friendship and help him or her to become more involved with groups and activities. If the student with multiple disabilities is unable to complete a circle of friends diagram, this would be accomplished by a helper. The group facilitator could then discuss differences between the disabled student's diagram and those of the typical peers and use the discussion as a springboard to encourage the nondisabled students to help "populate" the disabled student's circle.

Using the circle of friends diagrams to determine where students have or need people in their lives is an ongoing process, and teachers need to continually play a role in facilitating social interactions and friendships (Silberman, et al., 1998; Snell, et al., 2000). The circle of friends activity may be most helpful in elementary school settings where a group of students is together for an entire academic year.

Figure 13.1

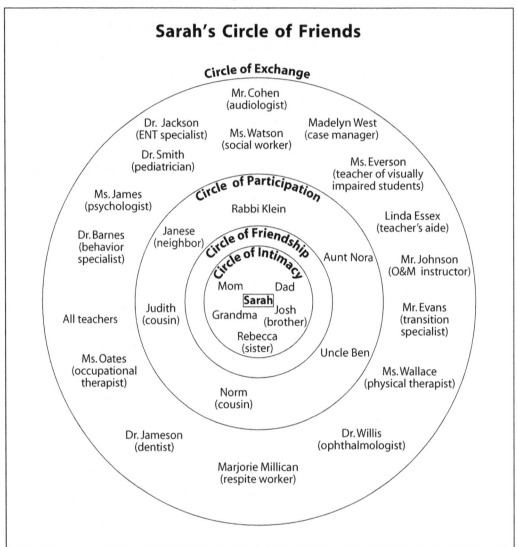

# FOSTERING SOCIAL INTERACTION IN THE SCHOOL SETTING

In school settings, there are three broad contexts within which social interactions occur: classroom-based activities, recess, breaks, and meal-times, and brief interactions in other settings such as passing other students in the hallways.

## CLASSROOMS

Within the classroom, the lead teacher plays a critical role in establishing an accepting environment. The most common types of social support that occur in classroom settings are access to others, information sharing, material assistance (students helping one another with desk work or class projects) and choice making (Kennedy, Shukla, & Fryzell, 1997). It must be stressed that simply placing a student with severe and multiple disabilities into general education settings in physical proximity to typical students does not necessarily ensure the occurrence of social interactions (Giangreco, Edelman, Luiselli, & MacFarland, 1997; Bishop, Jubala, Stainback, & Stainback, 1996). By engaging classmates in an activity such as Circle of Friends, teachers can help students get to know one another and facilitate social interaction.

All children, particularly those with visual impairments and multiple disabilities, need ongoing opportunities to have social inter-action with students without disabilities as well as instructional support to learn how to interact. In early childhood programs and during elementary school, teachers need to be facilitators, suggesting activities, directing children to play together, recommending the sharing of toys, and providing feedback and redirection when needed (Favazza, Phillipsen, & Kumar, 2000; Frea, Craig-Unkefer, Odom, & Johnson, 1999; Wolfberg, et al., 1999).

## Fostering Acceptance

All students need to feel a sense of belonging and equality and being an active participant in the social milieu contributes to these feelings. Teachers—both the general and special education teachers, including the teacher of students with visual impairments—play an important role in helping students with visual impairments and additional disabilities attain acceptance among their classmates, actively participate in their classes, and become involved in forming social relationships and friendships. Students with multiple impairments need opportunities to contribute in meaningful ways in order to enhance their self-esteem and earn their peers' respect. Teachers can suggest specific roles that students with disabilities can perform that put them in the position of contributing to their classes and assisting their classmates to enhance their image among their peers, such as holding doors open for others or collecting and distributing materials. For example, in a cooperative learning group studying Holland, a student with a visual impairment and additional disabilities might act as the recorder or timekeeper for each of the oral passages read by members of the group by using a vibrating or voice-activated kitchen timer (Downing, 2002). In a physical education class, the student with a visual impairment and multiple additional disabilities could serve as team captain, statistician, or equipment manager, or distributor of uniforms and towels in a basketball game (Bishop, Jubala, Stainback, & Stainback, 2000).

Teachers need to provide specific skills that will help students with visual impairments and additional disabilities to interact with their peers without disabilities. One group of skills is referred to as "pivotal skills," so-called because they allow students to participate in activities with their peers and have a central role in social interactions (Breen & Haring, 1991). A pivotal skill, for example, could be the ability to play a computer game by moving the cursor with the mouse or hitting the return key to advance the game to the next step. Once the student with multiple disabilities can do this, he or she can have a central role in playing the computer game with nondisabled students (Kennedy, 2004).

Other skills that need to be taught to students with multiple disabilities involve reciprocity during social interactions (see Chapters 4 and 12)—the equal exchange of social amenities between two individuals (such as responding "hello" to another student after that individual initiates a greeting), taking turns, initiating interactions, choosing activities, and complimenting another person. Students with visual impairments and additional disabilities may need to be taught when and how to act reciprocally in order to enhance the breadth and duration of social interactions. Teaching a student to say hello, to offer a toy or game to another student, or to ask another child if he or she wants to play increases the likelihood of ongoing interactions.

One of the most significant outcomes of social education is the establishment of friendships. Although friendships cannot be imposed, they can and should be encouraged by teachers and other adult team members because of the positive impact of friendships on the academic, behavioral, social, and communicative skills of most students.

Teachers, both general and special educators, need to facilitate interactions to make sure there is a balance of vertical interactions among the students, in which one student is in a dominant or instructional capacity, while the other student is the recipient, and horizontal interactions in which students share a common or equal role within an activity. For example, a student with multiple disabilities might have a vertical interaction with a peer tutor, while in another, more equal interaction, one student might cut pictures for an art history project and the other might arrange the pictures on a page (Kennedy, 2004).

Teachers also need to play a key role in teaching students interdependence (see Chapter 4), which can result in an increase in the frequency and quality of social interactions between nondisabled students and students with visual impairments and additional disabilities. Interdependence incorporates elements of both pivotal skills and reciprocity skills (Kennedy, 2004; Wolffe, 1998). The emphasis is on cooperation and collaboration between students; for instance, making smoothies for lunch is a joint activity with specific shared roles to achieve the outcome.

## Classroom Activities

Classrooms that use instructional groupings such as cooperative learning, small-group instruction, buddy systems, and learning centers tend to encourage more student interaction than classrooms that stress independent seatwork and large-group instruction led by the teacher (Johnson & Johnson, 1999; Putnam, 1998). Classroom-based activities that utilize cooperative learning groups as an instructional model provide numerous and varied opportunities for social interactions within the context of learning experiences that whole-class instruction does not permit (see Chapters 7 and 8 for more discussion of cooperative learning). Teachers place diverse students into small groups to complete a project or carry out a task and assign a different role to each member of the group. Roles in which students with visual impairments and multiple disabilities might participate using a variety of adaptive devices include recorder, checker, and runner. The recorder keeps notes when the group meets (using a tape recorder or note-taking device). A checker is responsible for keeping track of who is doing what and "checking off" the steps of the tasks as they are accomplished. A runner goes to pick up needed materials and brings them back to the group. Although each group member is responsible and accountable for fulfilling his or her assigned role, everyone offers support and solutions for the group whenever necessary. Within the elements of cooperative learning, students are taught social skills that are essential for collaboration; they help each other and provide feedback to achieve mutual goals, and they learn to share materials or information with the group (Johnson & Johnson, 1999; Silberman, Sacks, & Wolfe, 1998). Other classroom-based activities involve the use of targeted peer support to enhance social interactions and friendships between typical students without disabilities and students with visual impairments and additional disabilities, as discussed later in this chapter.

## RECESS, BREAKS, AND MEALS

Another important context for social interactions at school occurs during recess, classroom breaks, and meals. Communicative and social exchanges among peers can be targeted for instruction during these times. A student with a disability can choose both the type of activity he or she wants to engage in and with whom. For example:

> During snack time, Anna, a young girl with visual and motor impairments and limited verbal communication, uses a simple augmentative and alternative communication (AAC) device requiring minimal pressure to choose one of four messages. Each quadrant of the device is a different color so that she can use her limited vision to help her make her choice, and each one is paired with a line drawing representing a corresponding message. Anna is able to use her device with voice output to ask for more snacks or a drink as well as to talk to her peers. [Demchak & Downing, 2002, p. 82]

## UNSTRUCTURED TIME

Other social interactions at school occur outside of instructional time when opportunities to interact are much less structured, for example, at the beginning of class, toward the end of the class period, during the transition from one classroom to another, and during arrival or dismissal from school. For example, a student with a visual impairment and multiple disabilities may exchange social greetings, saying hello to half a dozen peers, when going from gym class to math class.

# ROLES FOR PEERS WITHOUT DISABILITIES

Students without disabilities can be helpful in supporting peers with visual impairments and multiple disabilities and can create and enhance opportunities for social interaction and potential friendships throughout the school day. Student volunteers are taught by the special education teacher how best to help students with multiple disabilities. Of particular value is the role the typical student can play in encouraging a classmate with multiple impairments to engage in a social interaction and to clarify communication attempts to other classmates. Downing (2002, p. 179) presents an excellent list of specific things peers can do to enhance the social interactions of students with multiple disabilities, including the following:

- Encourage the student to pay attention to the teacher or activity.
- Assist the student with mobility needs (for example, acting as a sighted guide or pushing a wheelchair).
- Help the student with moving and setting up equipment, tools, and materials.
- Learn and use the student's mode or modes of communication (such as sign language or AAC device).
- Sit beside the student for lunch, recess, or assemblies; serve as an appropriate role model.
- Make suggestions about what the student needs to say using an AAC device (for example, when ordering at a fast-food restaurant or responding to a school cheer).
- Design and make adaptive equipment or materials as part of a class.
- Brainstorm ways to include a classmate in a given activity.
- Be part of a telephone tree to call student at home.

Same-age peers or classmates may also be used to provide direct instructional support for students with visual impairments and additional disabilities in general education settings across a range of instructional situations, under the supervision of teachers or other members of the collaborative team (Kennedy, 2004; Snell, Janney, & Colley, 2000). (Chapters 7, 8, 11, and 12 discuss techniques for peers to act as tutors or provide other specific supports, which can be modified for advocacy-level students.) Same-age peers or classmates may provide direct instructional support for students with visual impairments and additional disabilities under the supervision of teachers or other members of the collaborative team (Kennedy, 2004; Snell, Janney, & Colley, 2000). Steps to creating and implementing such a peer support program include the following:

1. Use classroom announcements requesting volunteers to recruit peers without disabilities to serve as peer supporters.

   - Identify typical students who know or who have previously worked with students with disabilities.
   - Rotate opportunities among peers in the classroom.
   - Offer extra credit for students who serve as peer supporters.

2. After identifying peer supporters, select specific IEP goals for the peer to work on in the classroom with the target student.

3. Guide peers in creating adaptations that will enable the student with disabilities to access the general education curriculum along with his or her classmates.

   • Provide peer supporters with an outline of the types of adaptations that are appropriate and that will enable student with disabilities to access the general education curriculum along with his classmates.

   • Supervise the peer supporters in making the required adaptations for the student with severe disabilities.

4. Set up a regular schedule for monitoring the peer-support program.

5. Provide feedback to each student who participates in the program and obtain input on what works and what needs to be modified to make the peer-support program more effective.

In order for peer supporters to be effective, they need to be made aware of several adaptations that will enhance their interaction with students with visual impairments and multiple disabilities. They need to identify themselves when approaching the student with disabilities (for example, "Hey, Marc, it's me, Michelle. Want to go to lunch with me?"). By providing a verbal cue, the startle reflex of a student with low vision and severe physical disabilities may be reduced. Students without disabilities should also be taught to avoid using phrases that make visual references without explaining them, such as "put it here" or "go over there."

Nondisabled students need to be able to use the same modes of communication as their peers with multiple disabilities when interacting with them in order to feel comfortable initiating and maintaining interactions for a significant amount of time. When disabled students do not use speech to express themselves and communicate their thoughts and desires, interactions can become difficult and may be avoided. Students without disabilities may need to learn how to use their classmate's alternative communication system of pictorial or object symbols, how to converse with visual or tactile sign language, or how to make use of objects and touch cues for communication purposes (Downing, 1999). Faculty with skills in these areas (sign language or other alternative communication systems) can either offer after-school classes or provide individual instruction to peer-support volunteers.

# SPECIAL STRATEGIES AND ADAPTATIONS

## STUDENTS WITH VISUAL AND PHYSICAL IMPAIRMENTS

Visually impaired students who also have physical impairments often require assistance specific to their physical needs. The following strategies may be useful for teachers, professionals, families, and peers in helping to integrate these students in all environments—home, classroom, and community.

## STRATEGIES FOR SOCIAL SUCCESS
# Students with Visual and Physical Impairments

- Be sure that students have a system in place for communicating with others; if they are nonverbal, they may use an augmentative or alternative communication device, a communication board, or some other system. Learn about the device and how to efficiently use it to communicate with the students.

- If the student uses a wheelchair, be sure that materials and furniture are at the appropriate level so that the student can be included in group activities and social interactions.

- Let the wheelchair user decide who he or she would like to push the chair and encourage the student, if he or she is able, to invite that individual to do so.

- If a student is unable to reach out to others to shake hands, design an alternative technique and teach the student how to use it to engage others. If the student is able to reach out, but doesn't have the physical ability to grasp the other person's hand, he or she can still be trained in the process of shaking hands using the modified approach.

- Consider whether a student who is nonverbal and physically challenged would benefit from a system of written cards, similar to those used by deaf-blind students, to present basic information to strangers.

- Offer a student who uses a wheelchair interesting decals or toys that can be attached to the wheelchair tray or the chair itself to attract the positive attention of other students and perhaps elicit comments that could springboard into a conversation.

## STUDENTS WITH DEAF-BLINDNESS

Deaf-blind students may need specific strategies and materials in order to communicate, and teaching social skills to these students is often challenging. A respectful and comfortable way to greet a student with deaf-blindness is to use a friendly touch on the shoulder or back of the hand. Some students may require a firmer touch; therefore, it is important to observe the student's reaction and make sure he or she knows someone is there. People who interact regularly with a student who is deaf-blind should use a touch greeting in combination with a unique personal identifier, such as a ring, bracelet, key ring, baseball cap, or gesture or signing the first letter of one's name. In addition, it is critical to inform the student who is deaf-blind when someone is leaving, whether this information is communicated with a gesture, by signing, or by saying good-bye (McLetchie & Riggio, 2002). Classmates can learn to use body language, gestures, and objects or pictures to communicate with a peer who is deaf and has some useable vision (Downing, 2002).

Many children with deaf-blindness are averse to having their hands held, and they may withdraw from hand-over-hand assistance. For these students, their hands are their eyes; they are the tools for exploring their environment. A more effective and preferred strategy for exploring and introducing objects or topics is hand-under-hand touch (teacher's hand under the hands of the student). For example, the teacher might guide the student to a tactilely interesting piece of art and settle the student's hands to roam over the piece. The teacher then removes his or her hands so that the student can explore independently. This technique reduces passivity on the part of the student, is noncontrolling, and enhances the student's tactile experience. It becomes the tactile equivalent of the pointing gesture (Miles, 1998; Miles & Riggio, 1999; Silberman, et al., 2004). Some additional strategies for working with students with both visual and hearing impairments follow.

# STRATEGIES FOR SOCIAL SUCCESS

# Students with Visual and Hearing Impairments

- ◆ Be sure that students have a recognizable and recognized name sign and introduce them to others using their name signs.
- ◆ Include students in social interactions even if you are not sure that they fully understand all that is said. Do not engage in social discourse with others in the presence of deaf-blind children and leave

them out by not signing or vocalizing so that they can follow the conversation, if possible.

◆ If a child is congenitally deaf and you are not a fluent signer, find a fluent signer who can help you determine whether the child's efforts to communicate are recognizable. If so, work closely with an interpreter until you learn to communicate fluently yourself. If not, determine what the child's homemade signs mean according to family members, former instructional staff, or significant others. If the child is using homemade signs, couple those signs with the formal sign as you communicate with him or her.

◆ Encourage parents and other family members to use the communication system preferred by the child.

◆ Remember that most deaf-blind children and youths have either some residual vision or hearing or both. Use the most intact sense as a primary conduit for social interaction.

◆ Create a set of communication cards that the student may carry and use with the general public. The cards are used to facilitate an interaction that would otherwise be virtually impossible with someone who did not know the student. The cards might say things like, "I am deaf-blind and need help crossing the street," or "I am deaf-blind and need help finding bus number 10," or "I am deaf-blind and would like to buy a cup of coffee or a soda."

◆ Use available assistive technology. Teletypewriters or telecommunication devices for the deaf include a refreshable braille display, which can be used with cognitively able deaf-blind people to facilitate communication by telephone. Likewise, braille displays can make communicating by e-mail viable for individuals with severe visual and hearing impairments. Although no longer in production, a number of deaf-blind individuals continue to use Teletouch devices for others to communicate with them; these lightweight, portable devices have a QWERTY keyboard on the input side and a single braille cell on the receiving side. Other AAC devices may also be useful. The effectiveness of the device will be dictated by the needs and abilities of the deaf-blind person.

## TACTILE ADAPTATIONS

Other adaptations to be used with students who have visual impairments and multiple disabilities involve tactile presentations of materials. Classmates can be made aware that they can gently touch the student with a visual impairment in order to provide essential information. When giving an object to a student with visual impairments and multiple disabilities, the teacher or peer should put the object into the student's hands or on a table in front of the student and let him or her know where it is, rather than silently holding it in front of the student. For example, if a cooperative learning group is studying a model of an ear, one member of the group can guide the student's hand to the model so that the student with multiple disabilities will not miss vital information that is available to the rest of the group visually. Classmates can also assist peers who are blind and have cognitive or additional sensory impairments in moving around the classroom or from class to class by serving as sighted guides.

## STUDENTS WITH COGNITIVE DISABILITIES

Students without disabilities may need instruction to avoid talking down to their classmates with visual impairments and additional disabilities or treating them as if they were younger than their age, especially those who have cognitive disabilities. They also may need to be reminded to use age-appropriate games and to avoid holding hands when walking with peers past the primary grades. It is important for teachers to serve as role models for peers without disabilities who are likely to engage with a classmate with cognitive disabilities (Downing, 2002; Janney & Snell, 1996).

Teachers can use the following strategies to help students with visual and cognitive impairments acquire appropriate social skills, incorporating nondisabled peers as appropriate.

## STRATEGIES FOR SOCIAL SUCCESS

# Students with Visual and Cognitive Impairments

- Provide students with visual and cognitive impairments with external assistance as needed in making social connections with others through peer support or adult intervenors, depending on their level of cognitive impairment.
- Use techniques such as MAPS or Circle of Friends, and modify them as appropriate for the student.
- For students who have some vision, provide videotaped instructional materials for teaching socially appropriate behaviors. Videotaping the student during social interactions may also be helpful for the student.

◆ Consider augmentative or alternative communication devices to help students with expressive communication difficulties.

Finally all students need to be treated with respect, regardless of the severity of their mental challenge, and helped to engage in social interactions whenever possible. It is inappropriate to talk about or ignore an individual when engaged with others. Include the student or don't initiate an interaction in which the student is unable to participate.

# CONCLUSION

With appropriate supports and programming, students with multiple disabilities, including visual impairment, can acquire basic social skills and use them to build healthy relationships. The importance of social skills instruction for all children and youths with visual impairments, including those with additional disabilities, cannot be overstated. Developing positive self-esteem, building relationships with others, and socializing in inclusive environments are the essential elements that help students develop both the necessary skills and the feeling of confidence to participate to their maximum ability as full members of our society.

# REFERENCES

Bishop, K. D., Jubala, K. A., Stainback, W., & Stainback, S. (2000). Facilitating friendships. In S. Stainback & W. Stainback (Eds.), *Inclusion: A guide for educators* (pp. 155–169). Baltimore: Paul H. Brookes.

Breen, C. G., & Haring, T. G. (1991). Effects of contextual competence on social initiations. *Journal of Applied Behavioral Analysis, 24,* 337–347.

Chen, D., & Dote-Kwan, J. (1999). In K. E. Wolffe, (Ed.), *Skills for success.* New York: AFB Press.

Demchak, M., & Downing, J. (2002). The preschool student. In J. Downing (Ed.), *Including students with severe and multiple disabilities in typical classrooms.* (pp. 71–92). Baltimore: Paul H. Brookes.

Downing, J. E. (1999). *Teaching communication skills to students with severe disabilities.* Baltimore: Paul H. Brookes.

Downing, J. E. (2001). Meeting the communication needs of students with severe and multiple disabilities in general education classrooms. *Exceptionality, 9*(3), 147–156.

Downing, J. E. (2002). *Including students with severe and multiple disabilities in typical classrooms: Practical strategies for teachers* (2nd ed.). Baltimore: Paul H. Brookes.

Downing, J. E. (2004). Communication skills. In F. P. Orelove, R. Sobsey, & R. K. Silberman (Eds.), *Educating children with multiple disabilities* (pp. 529–561). Baltimore: Paul H. Brookes.

Falvey, M. A., Forest, M., Pearpoint, J., & Rosenberg, R. R. (2002). Building connections. In J. S. Thousand, R. A. Villa, & A. I. Nevin, *Creativity & collaborative learning* (2nd ed.; pp. 29–54). Baltimore: Paul H. Brookes.

Favazza, P. C., Phillipsen, L., & Kumar, P. (2000). Measuring and promoting acceptance of young children with disabilities. *Exceptional Children, 66,* 491–508.

Fazzi, D. (2002). Social focus. In R. L. Pogrund & D. L. Fazzi (Eds.), *Early focus.* New York: AFB Press.

Ferrell, K. A. (2000). Growth and development of young children. In M. C. Holbrook & A. J. Koenig (Eds.), *Foundations of education, Vol. 1: History and theory of teaching children and youths with visual impairments* (2nd ed.; pp. 111–134). New York: AFB Press.

Forest, M., & Lusthaus, E. (1989). Promoting educational equality for all students: Circles and maps. In S. Stainback, W. Stainback, & M. Forest (Eds.), *Educating all students in the mainstream of regular education* (pp. 43–57). Baltimore: Paul H. Brookes.

Forest, M., & Pearpoint, J. C. (1992). Putting all the kids on the map. *Educational Leadership, 50*(2), 26–31.

Frea, W., Craig-Unkefer, L., Odom, S. L., & Johnson, D. (1999). Differential effects of structured social integration and group friendship activities for promoting social interaction with peers. *Journal of Early Intervention, 22,* 230–242.

Giangreco, M., Edelman, S., Luiselli, T., & MacFarland, S. (1997). Helping or hovering? Effects of instructional proximity on students with disabilities. *Exceptional Children, 25,* 319–334.

Hunt, P., Alwell, M., & Goetz, L. (1991). Interacting with peers through conversation turntaking with a communication book adaptation. *Augmentative and Alternative Communication, 7,* 117–126.

Hunt, P., Farron-Davis, F., Wren, M., Hirose-Hatae, A., & Goetz, L. (1997). Promoting interactive partnerships in inclusive educational settings. *Journal of the Association for Persons with Severe Handicaps, 22,* 127–137.

Janney, R., & Snell, M. (1996). How teachers use peer interactions to include students with moderate and severe disabilities in general education classes. *Journal of the Association for Persons with Severe Handicaps, 21,* 72–80.

Janssen, M. J., Riksen-Walraven, J.M.E., & van Dijk, J.P.M. (2003). Toward a diagnostic intervention model for fostering harmonious interactions between deaf-blind children and their educators. *Journal of Visual Impairment & Blindness, 97*(4), 197–214.

Johnson, D. W., & Johnson, R. T. (1999). *Learning together and alone: Cooperation, competition, and individualization* (5th ed.). Upper Saddle River, NJ: Prentice-Hall.

Kennedy, C. H. (2004). Social relationships. In C. H. Kennedy & E. M. Horn (Eds.), *Including students with severe disabilities* (pp. 110–119). Boston: Pearson Education Inc.

Kennedy, C. H., Shukla, S., & Fryzell, D. (1997). Comparing the effects of educational placement on the social relationships of intermediate school students with severe disabilities. *Exceptional Children, 64,* 31–47.

MacCuspie, P. A. (1996). *Promoting acceptance of children with disabilities: From tolerance to inclusion.* Halifax, Nova Scotia, Canada: Atlantic Provinces Special Education Authority.

MacFarland, S.Z.C. (1995). Teaching strategies of the van Dijk curricular approach. *Journal of Visual Impairment and Blindness, 89*(3), 222–228.

McLetchie, B., & Riggio, M. (2002). Communication: Interactive relationships. In L. Alsop (Ed.), *Understanding deafblindness: Issues, perspectives, and strategies, Vol 1* (pp. 445–465). Logan, UT: Ski-Hi Institute.

Miles, B. (1998). *Talking the language of the hands to the hands: The importance of hands for the person who is deafblind.* Monmouth, OR: Western Oregon University: DB-LINK.

Miles, B., & Riggio, M. (Eds). (1999). *Remarkable conversations: A guide to developing meaningful communication with children and young adults who are deafblind.* Watertown, MA: Perkins School for the Blind.

Nevin, A. I., Thousand, J. S., & Villa, R. A. (2002). An overview of cooperative learning. In J. S. Thousand, R. A. Villa, & A. I. Nevin (Eds.), *Creativity and collaborative learning: the practical guide to empowering students, teachers, and families* (2nd ed.; pp. 325–348). Baltimore: Paul H. Brookes.

Pearpoint, J., Forest, M., & O'Brien, J. (1996). MAPs, Circles of Friends, and PATH: Powerful tools to help build caring communities. In S. Stainback & W. Stainback (Eds.), *Inclusion: A guide for educators* (pp. 67–86). Baltimore: Paul H. Brookes.

Prickett, J. G., & Welch, T. R. (1995). Adapting environments to support the inclusion of students who are deaf-blind. In N. Haring & L. Romer (Eds.), *Welcoming students who are deaf-blind into typical classrooms* (pp. 171–194). Baltimore: Paul H. Brookes.

Prickett, J. G., & Welch, T. R. (1998). Educating students who are deaf-blind. In S. Z. Sacks & R. K. Silberman (Eds.), *Educating students who have visual impairments with other disabilities* (pp. 139–160). Baltimore: Paul H. Brookes.

Putnam, J. W. (1998). *Cooperative learning and strategies for inclusion* (2nd ed.). Baltimore: Paul H. Brookes.

Silberman, R. K. (2000). Children and youths with other exceptionalities. In M. C. Holbrook & A. J. Koenig (Eds.), *Foundations of education, Vol. 1: History and theory of teaching children and youths with visual impairment* (2nd ed.; pp. 173–196). New York: AFB Press.

Silberman, R. K., Bruce, S., & Nelson, C. (2004). Sensory impairment. In F. Orelove, R. Sobsey, & R. K. Silberman (Eds.), *Educating children with multiple disabilities* (4th ed.). Baltimore: Paul H. Brookes.

Silberman, R. K., Sacks, S. Z., & Wolfe, J. A. (1998). Instructional strategies for educating students who have visual impairments with severe disabilities. In S. Z. Sacks & R. K. Silberman (Eds.), *Educating students who have visual impairments with other disabilities* (pp. 101–137). Baltimore: Paul H. Brookes.

Snell, M. E., & Janney, R. (2000). *Teachers' guides to inclusive practices: Social relationships and peer support.* Baltimore: Paul H. Brookes.

Snell, M. E., Janney, R., & Colley, K. M. (2000). Approaches for facilitating positive social relationships. In M. E. Snell & R. Janney (Eds.), *Teachers' guides to inclusive practices: Social relationships and peer support* (pp. 35–77). Baltimore: Paul H. Brookes.

Vandercook, T., York, J., & Forest, M. (1989). The McGill Action Planning System (MAPS): A strategy for building the vision. *Journal of the Association for Persons with Severe Handicaps, 14,* 205–215.

van Dijk, J., & Nelson, C. (1997). History and change in the education of children who are deaf-blind since the rubella epidemic of the 1960s: Influence of methods developed in the Netherlands. *Deaf-Blind Perspectives, 5,* 1–5.

Wolfberg, P. J., Zercher, C., Lieber, J., Capell, K., Matias, S., Hanson, M., & Odom, S. L. (1999). "Can I play with you?" Peer culture in inclusive preschool programs. *Journal of the Association for Persons with Severe Handicaps, 24,* 69–84.

Wolffe, K. E. (1998). Transition planning and employment outcomes for students who have visual impairments with other disabilities. In S. Z. Sacks and R. Silberman (Eds.), *Educating students who have visual impairments with other disabilities.* Baltimore: Paul H. Brookes.

# Appendixes

# Recommended Readings and Other References

This set of references supplies readers with a list of reference materials that will be helpful in supporting social skills instruction for children and adolescents who are blind or visually impaired, including those with additional disabilities. It includes listings of books and journal articles on social development in children, and the special issues of adolescents. A separate section presents resources on sex education. Finally, there is a list of videotapes, which can be helpful for sharing with family members as well as professionals.

## BOOKS AND PAMPHLETS

Anderson, S., Boigon, S., & Davis, K. (1991). *The Oregon Project for Visually Impaired and Blind Preschool Children* (5th ed., rev.). Medford, OR: Jackson County Education Service District.

Asher, S. R., & Gottman, J. M. (1981). *The development of children's friendships.* Cambridge: Cambridge University Press.

Blind Childrens Center (1993). *First steps: A handbook for teaching young children who are visually impaired.* Los Angeles, CA: Blind Childrens Center.

Bredekamp, S., & Copple, C. (Eds.). (1996). *Developmentally appropriate practice in early childhood programs* (rev. ed.). Washington, DC: National Association for the Education of Young Children.

Brookshire, B. (2001). *Loving Me: Secrets of Self Esteem.* Louisville, KY: American Printing House for the Blind.

Bukowski, W. M., Newcomb, A. G., & Hartup, W. W. (Eds.). (1996). *The company they keep: Friendship in childhood and adolescence.* New York: Cambridge University Press.

Chandler, P. (1992). *A place for me: Including children with special needs in early care and education settings.* Washington, DC: National Association for the Education of Young Children.

Chen, D., & Dote-Kwan, J. (1995). *Starting points: Instructional practices for young children whose multiple disabilities include visual impairment.* Los Angeles, CA: Blind Childrens Center.

Cooper, J. (1992). *For parents: How to develop your child's self esteem.* White Bear Lake, MN: J. Cooper Associates.

Cooper, J., & Harvatin, J. (1992). *Worry free parenting.* White Bear Lake, MN: J. Cooper Associates.

Corn, A., Cowan, C., & Moses, E. (1988). *You seem like a regular kid to me.* New York: AFB Press.

Corn, A. L., & Rosenblum, L. P. (2000). *Finding wheels: A curriculum for non-drivers with visual impairments for gaining control of transportation needs.* Austin, TX: PRO-ED.

Covey, S. (1997). *The seven habits of highly effective parenting.* New York: Simon & Schuster.

Covey, S. (1998). *The seven habits of highly effective teens.* New York: Fireside.

Crary, E. (1984). *Kids can cooperate: A practical guide to teaching problem solving.* Seattle, WA: Parenting Press.

Crary, E. (1990). *Pick up your socks . . . and other skills growing children need! A practical guide to raising responsible children.* Seattle, WA: Parenting Press.

Derman-Sparks, L., & ABC Task Force. (1989). *Anti-bias curriculum tools for empowering young children.* Washington, DC: National Association for the Education of Young Children.

Dinkmeyer, D., & McKay, G. D. (1990). *Parenting teenagers* (2nd ed.). Circle Pines, MN: American Guidance Service.

Downing, J. E. (1996). *Including students with severe and multiple disabilities in typical classrooms: Practical strategies for teachers.* Baltimore: Paul H. Brookes.

Elksnin, L. K., & Elksnin, N. (1995). *Assessment and instruction of social skills instruction of social skills* (2nd ed.). San Diego: Singular Publishing Group.

Erin, J. N., & Wolffe, K. E. (1999). *Transition issues related to students with visual disabilities.* Austin, TX: PRO-ED.

Everson, J. (1995). *Supporting young adults who are deaf-blind in their communities: A transition planning guide for service providers, families, and friends.* Baltimore: Paul H. Brookes.

Ferrell, K. A. (1985). *Reach out and teach: Meeting the training needs of parents of visually and multiply handicapped young children.* New York: AFB Press.

Glenn, H. S., & Nelson, J. (1989). *Raising self-reliant children in a self-indulgent world: Seven building blocks for developing capable young people.* Rocklin, CA: Prima Publishing.

Harris, J. M. (1989). *You and your child's self-esteem: Building for the future.* New York: Carroll & Graff Publishers.

Huebner, K. M., Prickett, J. G., Welch, T. R., & Joffee, E. (1995). *Hand in hand: Essentials of communication and orientation and mobility to your students who are deaf-blind.* New York: AFB Press.

Johnson, D. W., & Johnson, F. P. (1994). *Joining together.* Needham Heights, MA: Allyn & Bacon.

Lansky, Vicki. (1985). *Practical parenting tips for the school-age years.* New York: Bantam Books.

Levack, N., Hauser, S., Newton, L., & Stephenson, P. (1996). *Basic skills for community living: A curriculum for students with visual impairments and multiple disabilities.* Austin, TX: Texas School for the Blind and Visually Impaired.

Linder, T. W. (1993). *Transdisciplinary play-based intervention.* Baltimore: Paul H. Brookes.

Loumiet, R., & Levack, N. (1993). *Independent living: A curriculum with adaptations for students with visual impairments, Vol. 1: Social competence* (2nd ed.). Austin, TX: Texas School for the Blind and Visually Impaired.

Loumiet, R., & Levack, N. (1993). *Independent living: A curriculum with adaptations for students with visual impairments, Vol. 2: Self-care and maintenance* (2nd ed.). Austin, TX: Texas School for the Blind and Visually Impaired.

Loumiet, R., & Levack, N. (1993). *Independent living: A curriculum with adaptations for students with visual impairments, Vol. 3: Play and leisure* (2nd ed.). Austin, TX: Texas School for the Blind and Visually Impaired.

Lynch, E. W., & Hanson, M. J. (1992). *Developing cross-cultural competence: A guide for working with young children and their families* (2nd ed.). Baltimore: Paul H. Brookes.

MacCuspie, P. A. (1996). *Promoting acceptance of children with disabilities: From tolerance to inclusion.* Halifax, Nova Scotia, Canada: Atlantic Provinces Special Education Authority.

Manolson, A. (1984). *It takes two to talk.* Toronto, Ontario, Canada: Hanen Early Language Resource Centre.

Meighan, T. (1971). *An investigation of the self-concept of blind and visually handicapped adolescents.* New York: American Foundation for the Blind.

Morgan, E. (1994). *Resources for family centered interventions for infants, toddlers, and preschoolers who are visually impaired.* Logan, UT: HOPE, Inc.

Nowicki, S., & Duke, M. P. (1992). *Helping the child who doesn't fit in.* Atlanta, GA: Peachtree Publishers, Ltd.

Odom, S. L., McConnell, S. R., & McEvoy, M. A. (1992). *The social competence of young children with disabilities: Issues and strategies for intervention.* Baltimore: Paul H. Brookes.

Pogrund, R. L., & Fazzi, D. L. (Eds.). (2002). *Early focus: Working with young children who are blind or visually impaired and their families* (2nd ed.). New York: AFB Press.

Sacks, S. Z., Kekelis. L. S., & Gaylord-Ross, R. J. (Eds.). (1992). *The development of social skills by blind and visually impaired students: Exploratory studies and strategies.* New York: American Foundation for the Blind.

Sacks, S. Z., & Silberman, R. K. (Eds.). (1998). *Educating students who have visual impairments with other disabilities.* Baltimore: Paul H. Brookes.

Seligman, M.E.P. (1990). *Learned optimism.* New York: Alfred Knopf.

Seligman, M.E.P. (1996). *The optimistic child.* New York: HarperCollins.

SKI*HI Institute (1993). *A resource manual for understanding and interacting with infants, toddlers, and preschool age children with deaf-blindness.* Logan, UT: HOPE, Inc.

Smith, M., & Levack, N. (1996). *Teaching students with visual and multiple impairments: A resource guide.* Austin, TX: Texas School for the Blind and Visually Impaired.

Steveley, J., Houghton, J., Goehl, K., & Bailey, B. (1996). *Planning today, creating tomorrow: Guide to transition.* Terre Haute, IN: Indiana Deaf-Blind Services Project.

Swallow, R. M., & Huebner, K. M. (Eds.). (1987). *How to thrive, not just survive: A guide to developing independent life skills for blind and visually impaired children and youths.* New York: American Foundation for the Blind.

Trujillo, T., Tavarez, T., Rubald, T., & Roach, W. (Eds.). (1966). *I'm moving on: This book will help me as I move on into my community.* Santa Fe, NM: New Mexico Deaf/Blind Services.

Tuttle, D. W., & Tuttle, N. R. (1996). *Self-esteem and adjusting to blindness: The process of responding to life's demands* (2nd ed.). Springfield, IL: Charles C. Thomas.

Watkins, S. (Ed.). (1989). *The INSITE model: Home intervention for infant, toddler, and preschool aged multihandicapped sensory impaired children.* Logan, UT: HOPE, Inc.

Wolf, A. E. (1991). *Get out of my life but first could you drive me and Cheryl to the mall? A parent's guide to the new teenager.* New York: Noonday.

Wolf, A. E. (1995). *It's not fair, Jeremy Spencer's parents let him stay up all night!* New York: Farrar, Straus and Giroux.

Wolffe, K. E. (Ed.). (1999). *Skills for success: A career education handbook for children and adolescents with visual impairments.* New York: AFB Press.

# READINGS ON SEX EDUCATION

Because learning about human sexuality and intimate relationships can present significant challenges for adolescents with visual impairments, as well as their families and teachers, this section offers a number of helpful references on the topic Items followed by an asterisk * are available in braille through National Braille Press.

Bell, R. (1998). *Changing bodies, changing lives* (3rd ed.). New York: Vintage Books.

Camarena, P. M., Sarigiani, P. A., & Petersen, A. C. (1990). Gender-specific pathways to intimacy in early adolescence. *Journal of Youth and Adolescence, 19*(1), 19–32.

Dickman, I. R. (1975). *Sex education and family life for visually handicapped children and youth: A resource guide.* New York: American Foundation for the Blind.

Dixon, H., & Mullinar, G. (Eds.). (1985). *Taught not caught: Strategies for sex education.* London: Learning Developmental Aids.

Foulke, E., & Uhde, T. (1975). Do blind children need sex education? In *Sex education for the visually handicapped in schools and agencies . . . selected papers* (pp. 8–16). New York: American Foundation for the Blind.

Gravelle, K., Castro, N., & Castro, C. (1998). *What's going on down there: Answers to questions boys find hard to ask.* New York: Walker Publishing Company.*

Gravelle, K., & Gravelle, J. (1996). *The period book: Everything you don't want to ask, but need to know.* New York: Walker Publishing Company.*

Harris, R. (1994). *It's perfectly normal.* Cambridge, MA: Candlewick Press.*

Harris, R. (2002). *It's so amazing.* Cambridge, MA: Candlewick Press.

Heslinga, K. (1974). *Not made of stone: The sexual problems of handicapped people.* Leyden, Netherlands: Stafleu Scientific Publishing.

Mayle, P. (1981). *What's happening to me?* New York: Carol Publishing Company.

Mayle, P. (2000). *Where did I come from?* New York: Carol Publishing Company.

Miller, T. (1997). Social–sex education for children and youth with visual impairments. In *Proceedings of the International Council for Education of People with Visual Impairments' Xth World Conference: Stepping Forward Together: Families and Professionals as Partners in Achieving an Education for All,* Sao Paulo, Brazil, August 3–8, 1997. Available: www.icevi.org.

Scholl, G. T. (1975). The psychosocial effects of blindness: Implications for program planning in sex education. In *Sex education for the visually handicapped in schools and agencies: Selected papers* (pp. 20–28). New York: American Foundation for the Blind.

Torbett, D. S. (1975). A humanistic and futuristic approach to sex education for blind children. In *Sex education for the visually handicapped in schools and agencies: Selected papers* (pp. 29–34). New York: American Foundation for the Blind.

Van't Hooft, F., & Heslinga, K. (1975). Sex education and blind-born children. In *Sex education for the visually handicapped in schools and agencies: Selected papers* (pp. 1–7). New York: American Foundation for the Blind.

Welbourne, A. K. (1982). Sexual education of the blind adolescent. *Sexual Medicine Today*, 10–14.

## JOURNAL ARTICLES

Adolescence and early adulthood (1997). [Special issue]. *Journal of Visual Impairment & Blindness, 91*(3).

Beaty, L. A. (1991). The effects of visual impairments on adolescents' self-concept. *Journal of Visual Impairment & Blindness, 85*(3), 129–130.

Beaty, L. A. (1994). Psychological factors and academic success of visually impaired college students. *RE:view, 26*, 131–139.

Being blind and being a woman. (1983). [Special issue]. *Journal of Visual Impairment & Blindness, 77*(6).

Bush-LaFrance, B.A.C. (1988). Unseen expectations of blind youth: Educational and occupational ideas. *Journal of Visual Impairment & Blindness, 82*(4), 132–136.

Corn, A. L., & Sacks, S. Z. (1994). The impact of nondriving on adults with visual impairments. *Journal of Visual Impairment & Blindness, 88*, 53–68.

Dixon, J. M. (1983). Attitudinal barriers and strategies for overcoming them. *Journal of Visual Impairment & Blindness, 77*(6), 290–292.

Forest, M., & Lusthaus, E. (1990). Everyone belongs with the MAPS Action Planning System. *Teaching Exceptional Children, 22*(2), 32–35.

Foster S. L., & Richey, W. L. (1979). Issues in the assessment of social competence in children. *Journal of Applied Behavior Analysis, 12*, 625–638.

Freeman, R. D., Goetz, E., Richards, D. P., & Groenveld, M. (1991). Defiers of negative prediction: A 14-year follow-up of legally blind children. *Journal of Visual Impairment & Blindness, 85*(9), 365–370.

Freeman, R. D., Goetz, E., Richards, D. P., Groenveld, M., Blockberger, S., Jan, J. E., & Sykanda, A. M. (1989). Blind children's early emotional development: Do we know enough to help? *Child: Care, Health and Development, 15*, 3–28.

Hagemoser, S. D. (1996). The relationship of personality traits to the employment status of persons who are blind. *Journal of Visual Impairment & Blindness, 90*(2), 134–144.

Hartup, W. W., & Moore, S. G. (1990). Early peer relations: Developmental significance and prognostic implications. *Early Childhood Research Quarterly, 5*, 1–17.

Hatlen, P. (1996). The core curriculum for blind and visually impaired students, including those with additional disabilities. *RE:view, 28*(1), 25–32.

Head, D. (1979). A comparison of self-concept scores for visually impaired adolescents in several class settings. *Education of the Visually Handicapped, 10*, 51–55.

Howze, Y. S. (1983). The use of social skills training to improve interview skills of visually impaired young adults: A pilot study. *Journal of Visual Impairment & Blindness, 81*(6), 251–255.

Huurre, T., Komulainen, E. J., & Aro, H. M. (1999). Social support and self-esteem among adolescents with visual impairments. *Journal of Visual Impairment & Blindness, 93*, 26–37.

Kaufman, A. (2000). Clothing-selection habits of teenage girls who are sighted and blind. *Journal of Visual Impairment & Blindness, 94*, 527–531.

Kef, S. (1997). The personal networks and social supports of blind and visually impaired adolescents. *Journal of Visual Impairment & Blindness, 91*(3), 236–244.

Mangold, S., & Mangold, P. (1983). The adolescent visually impaired female. *Journal of Visual Impairment & Blindness, 77*, 250–255.

Matsuda, M. M. (1984). A comparative analysis of blind and sighted children's communication skills. *Journal of Visual Impairment & Blindness, 78* (1), 1–5.

Minter, M. E., Hobson, R. P., & Pring, L. (1991). Recognition of vocally expressed emotion by congenitally blind children. *Journal of Visual Impairment & Blindness Impairment & Blindness, 85*, 411–415.

Peavy, K. O., & Leff, D. (2002). Social acceptance of adolescent mainstreamed students with visual impairments. *Journal of Visual Impairment and Blindness, 96*, 808–811.

Pfanstiehl, M. R. (1983). Role models for high-achieving visually impaired women. *Journal of Visual Impairment & Blindness, 77*(6), 259–261.

Rosenblum, L. P. (1997). Aolescents with visual impairments who have best friends: A pilot study. *Journal of Visual Impairment & Blindness, 91*, 224–235.

Rosenblum, L. P. (1998). Best friendships of adolescents with visual impairments: A descriptive study. *Journal of Visual Impairment & Blindness, 92*, 593–608.

Sacks, S. Z., & Gaylord-Ross, R. J. (1989). Peer-mediated and teacher-directed social skills training for visually impaired students. *Behavior Therapy, 20*, 619–638.

Sacks, S. Z., & Wolffe, K. (1992). The importance of social skills in the transition process for students with visual impairments. *Journal of Vocational Rehabilitation, 2*(1), 46–55.

Sacks, S. Z., & Wolffe, K. E. (1998). Lifestyles of adolescents with visual impairments: An ethnographic analysis. *Journal of Visual Impairment &
Blindness, 92*(1), 7–17.

Sacks, S. Z., Wolffe, K. E., & Tierney, D. (1998). Lifestyles of students with
visual impairments: Preliminary studies of social networks. *Exceptional
Child, 64*(4), 463–478.

Stratton, J. M., & Wright, S. (1991). On the way to literacy: Early experiences
for visually impaired children. *RE:view, 23*(2), 55–61.

Welbourne, A. K. (1982). Sexual education of the blind adolescent. *Sexual
Medicine Today,* 10–14.

Wolffe, K. (1985). Don't give those kids fish! Teach 'em how to fish! *Journal of
Visual Impairment & Blindness, 79*(10), 470–472.

Wolffe, K. (1996). Career education for students with visual impairments.
*RE:view, 28*(2), 89–93.

Wolffe, K. E., & Sacks, S. Z. (1997). The lifestyles of blind, low vision, and
sighted youths: A quantitative comparison. *Journal of Visual Impairment &
Blindness, 91*(3), 245–257.

# VIDEOTAPES

Bricker, D. *Activity-based intervention.* Baltimore: Paul H. Brookes.

*Bringing out the best: Encouraging expressive communication in children with
multiple handicaps.* Champaign, IL: Research Press.

Can Do Series from Visually Impaired Preschool Services, Louisville, KY:
*Seeing things in a new way: What happens when you have a blind baby
Learning about the world: Concept development
Becoming a can do kid: Self help skills
Making friends: Social skills
Going places: O&M*

*Coactive signs: Introduction to tactile communication for children who are deaf-
blind.* Logan, UT: HOPE, Inc.

*Communicating with preverbal infants and young children.* Lawrence, KS: Learned
Managed Designs.

Derman-Sparks, L. *Anti-bias curriculum videotape.* Pasadena, CA: Pacific Oaks
College.

*Functional vision: Learning to LOOK.* Verona, WI: BVD Promo Services.

*Functional vision: Learning to SEE.* Verona, WI: BVD Promo Services.

*Getting in touch.* Champaign, IL: Research Press.

*Getting there: A look at early mobility skills of four young blind children.* San
Francisco: Blind Babies Foundation.

Helping your child learn series from BVD Promo Services, Verona, WI,
*Vol. 1: When and where to teach, Teaching self control, Teaching playtime skills*

*Vol. 2: What to teach, Teaching choices, Teaching dressing skills*

*Vol. 3: How to teach, Teaching with adaptations, Teaching mealtime skills*

Mangold, S., & Pesavento, M. E. *Braille literacy at work.* Castro Valley, CA: Exceptional Teaching Aids.

*Navigating the rapids of life.* Louisville, KY: American Printing House for the Blind.

Welch, T. *Hand in hand: It can be done!* New York: AFB Press.

# Resources

This resource guide offers readers a representative listing of organizations that are supportive of social skills instruction for children and adolescents who are visually impaired and those with additional disabilities. The resources are listed in categories: agencies and organizations; suppliers of books, braille, and other media; and camps and recreational organizations. For information on adaptive products and devices, readers can review the many catalogs that are available on request and online from specific companies and organizations. Readers are also encouraged to attend conferences of consumer and professional organizations for information from vendors and organizations.

Although the contact information for each organization was current at the time of publication, this information is often subject to change. A more thorough coverage of agencies and organizations serving people with visual impairments may be found in the *AFB Directory of Services for Blind and Visually Impaired Persons in the United States and Canada*, published by the American Foundation for the Blind, and constantly updated information is found on its Web site, www.afb.org. Similar information about U.S. agencies and organizations that serve people with disabilities is published in the *Directory of National Information Sources on Disabilities*, published by the U.S. Department of Education Office of Special Education and Rehabilitative Services.

# NATIONAL ORGANIZATIONS AND AGENCIES

The variety of organizations of and for people who have visual impairments listed in this section include national sources of information and referral, membership organizations for individuals who are blind or visually impaired, and organizations for professionals who work in the field of blindness. Also included are organizations that are not specifically focused on issues concerning visual impairment but that may be of related interest.

**American Council of the Blind**
1155 15th Street, N.W., Suite 1004
Washington, D.C. 20005
(202) 467-5081 or (800) 424-8666
Fax: (202) 467-5085
E-mail: info@acb.org
www.acb.org

Consumer group that acts as a national clearinghouse for information and has an affiliate group for parents. Provides referrals, legal assistance, advocacy support, scholarships, and consultative and advisory services to individuals, organizations, and agencies.

**American Foundation for the Blind (AFB)**
11 Penn Plaza, Suite 300
New York, NY 10001
(212) 502-7600 or (800) 232-5463
Fax: (212) 502-7777
E-mail: afbinfo@afb.net
www.afb.org

National organization devoted to expanding the possibilities of the ten million Americans who are blind or visually impaired. Since 1921, AFB has addressed the most critical issues facing the growing blind and visually impaired population, including independent living, employment, literacy, and technology. In addition to being a national information, consultative, and advocacy resource engaged in a wide variety of initiatives, AFB is home to the Helen Keller Archives, containing Helen Keller's correspondence, documents, photographs, and memorabilia. Headquartered in New York City, AFB maintains four National Centers in cities across the United States and a Governmental

Relations office in Washington, D.C. Publishes, books, videos, the *Journal of Visual Impairment & Blindness, AccessWorld,* and the *AFB Directory of Services for Blind and Visually Impaired Persons in the United States and Canada.* Also hosts the CareerConnect® Web site, which offers information about the range and diversity of jobs performed by adults who are blind or visually impaired for job seekers, employers, and professionals, and puts job seekers in touch with mentors in various fields.

**American Printing House for the Blind**
1839 Frankfort Avenue
Louisville, KY 40206-0085
(502) 895-2405 or (800) 223-1839
Fax: (502) 899-2274
E-mail: info@aph.org
www.aph.org

Official supplier of textbooks and educational aids for visually impaired students under federal appropriations. Promotes the independence of blind and visually impaired persons by providing specialized materials, products, and services needed for education and life. Publishes braille, large-print, recorded, CD-ROM, and tactile graphic publications; manufactures a wide assortment of educational and daily living products; modifies and develops computer-access equipment and software; maintains an educational research and development program concerned with educational methods and educational aids; and provides a reference-catalog service for volunteer-produced textbooks in all media for students who are visually impaired and for information about other sources of related materials.

**Association for Education and Rehabilitation of the Blind and Visually Impaired**
1703 N. Beauregard Street
Suite 440
Alexandria, VA 22311
(703) 671-4500 or (877) 492-2708
Fax: (703) 671-6391
E-mail: aer@aerbvi.org
www.aerbvi.org

Professional membership organization that promotes all phases of education and work for persons of all ages who are blind and visually impaired. Has a division that addresses the educational needs of infants and preschoolers, another that focuses on the needs of students with multiple disabilities, and an orientation and mobility division. Organizes conferences and workshops, maintains job-exchange services and a speakers' bureau, holds continuing education seminars, and is involved in legislative and advocacy projects. Publishes *RE:view*, a quarterly journal, and *AER Reports*, a newsletter, and has state or regional chapters in the United States and Canada.

**Blind Childrens Center**
4120 Marathon Street
Los Angeles, CA 90029
(323) 664-2153
Fax: (213) 665-3828
E-mail: info@blindchildrenscenter.org
www.blindchildrenscenter.org

Family-centered agency that serves children with visual impairments from birth to school age. Offers center-based and home-based programs and services to children who are blind or visually impaired and serves families and professionals worldwide through support services, education, and research.

**Council for Exceptional Children (CEC)**
1110 North Glebe Road, Suite 300
Arlington, VA 22201-5704
(703) 620-3660 or (888) 221-6830
TDD/TTY: (866) 915-5000
Fax: (703) 264-9494
E-mail: service@cec.sped.org
www.cec.sped.org

Largest international professional organization dedicated to improving educational outcomes for individuals with exceptionalities, students with disabilities, and/or the gifted. Advocates for appropriate governmental policies, sets professional standards, provides continual professional development, advocates for newly and historically underserved individuals with exceptionalities, and helps professionals obtain conditions and resources necessary for effective professional practice. Has a Division on Visual Impairments.

**Foundation Fighting Blindness**
11435 Cronhill Drive
Owings Mills, MD 21117-2220
(410) 568-0150 or (800) 683-5555
TDD/TTY: (410) 363-7139

Fax: (410) 363-2393
E-mail: infor@blindness.org
www.fightblindness.org

National organization that conducts public education programs and supports research related to the cause, prevention, and treatment of retinitis pigmentosa. Maintains a network of affiliates across the country and conducts workshops as well as referral and donor programs.

**Hadley School for the Blind**
700 Elm Street
Winnetka, IL 60093-0299
(847) 446-8111 or (800) 323-4238
Fax: (847) 446-9916
E-mail: infor@hadley.edu
www.hadley.edu

School that offers more than 90 distance education courses, including braille reading and writing, to eligible students free of charge. Also offers courses for parents of blind children and family members of blind adults.

**HEATH Resource Center**
**George Washington University**
2121 K Street, N.W., Suite 220
Washington, D.C. 20037
(202) 973-0904 or (800) 544-3284
Fax: (202) 973-0908
E-mail: askheath@gwu.edu
www.heath.gwu.edu

National clearinghouse on postsecondary education for individuals with disabilities. Serves as an information exchange about educational support services, policies, procedures, adaptations, and opportunities at American campuses, vocational-technical schools, and other post-secondary training entities.

**Helen Keller National Center for Deaf-Blind Youths and Adults**
111 Middle Neck Road
Sands Point, NY 11050-1299
(516) 944-8900
TDD: (516) 944-8637
Fax: (516) 944-7302
E-mail: hkncinfo@hknc.org
www.hknc.org

National rehabilitation agency that provides services and technical assistance to deaf-blind individuals and their families and maintains a network of regional and affiliate agencies.

**Howe Press**
**Perkins School for the Blind**
175 North Beacon Street
Watertown, MA 02172-2790
(617) 924-3490
Fax: (617) 926-2027
E-mail: howepress@perkins.org
www.perkins.pvt.k12.ma.us

Manufacturer of materials and equipment for reproducing materials in braille, including Perkins braillers and accessories, brailling slates and accessories, handwriting and mathematical aids, braille paper, measuring devices, games, and drawing supplies.

**International Association of Lions Clubs International**
300 22nd Street
Oak Brook, IL 60521-8842
(630) 571-5466
Fax: (630) 571-8890
www.lionsclubs.org

Community service organization that promotes diabetes awareness and education. Makes computer training available through individual Lions-supported and vocational facilities. Supports most of the world's eye banks, provides corneal transplants, promotes organ and tissue donation. Develops or supports programs to provide vision testing and screenings, and conducts special projects, such as those for low vision.

**National Association for Parents of Children with**
**Visual Impairments (NAPVI)**
P.O. Box 317
Watertown, MA 02471-0317
(617) 972-7441 or (800) 562-6265
Fax: (617) 972-7444
E-mail: napvi@perkins.org
www.napvi.org

Membership association that supports state and local parents' groups and conducts advocacy workshops for parents of blind and visually impaired children. Operates a national clearinghouse for information and referrals and holds national and chapter conferences.

**National Association for Visually Handicapped (NAVH)**
22 West 21st Street, 6th floor
New York, NY 10010
(212) 889-3141
Fax: (212) 727-2931
E-mail: staff@navh.org
www.navh.org

National organization that produces and distributes large-print read-ing materials; acts as an information clearinghouse and referral center; offers counseling to persons with low vision, their families, and the professionals who work with them; and sells low-vision devices.

**National Braille Association**
3 Townline Circle
Rochester, NY 14623-2513
(585) 427-8260
Fax: (585) 427-0263
E-mail: nbaoffice@nationalbraille.org
www.nationalbraille.org

National membership organization that offers continuing education courses for those who prepare braille, and provides braille materials to persons who are visually impaired.

**National Dissemination Center for Children and Youth with Disabilities**
P.O. Box 1492
Washington, D.C. 20013-1492
(202) 884-8200
TDD/TTY: (800) 695-0285
Fax: (202) 884-8441
E-mail: nichchy@aed.org
www.nichcy.org

National organization that provides information on disabilities in chil-dren and youths; programs and services for infants, children, and youths with disabilities; IDEA, the nation's special education law; No Child Left Behind, the nation's general education law; and research-based information on effective practices for children with disabilities.

**National Eye Institute Information Center (NEI)**
National Institutes of Health
31 Center Drive

MSC 2510
Bethesda, MD 20892
(301) 496-5248
Fax: (301) 402-1065
E-mail: 2020@nei.nih.gov
www.nei.nih.gov

Federal agency that finances and conducts research on the eye and vision disorders, supports training of eye researchers, and publishes materials on visual impairment.

**National Family Association for Deaf-Blind**
c/o Helen Keller National Center
111 Middle Neck Road
Sands Point, NY 11050-1299
(800) 255-0411
E-mail: nfadb@aol.com
www.nfadb.org

Volunteer-based national network of families focusing on issues surrounding deaf-blindness.

**National Federation of the Blind**
1800 Johnson Street
Baltimore, MD 21230
(410) 659-9314
Fax: (410) 685-5653
E-mail: nfb@nfb.org
www.nfb.org

Consumer organization that maintains affiliates in all states and the District of Columbia and works to improve the social and economic opportunities of blind and visually impaired persons. Evaluates programs and provides assistance in establishing new ones, funds scholarships for blind persons, and conducts a public education program. Its divisions include the National Organization of Parents of Blind Children.

**National Industries for the Blind**
1310 Braddock Place
Alexandria, VA 22314-1691
(703) 310-0500
E-mail: info@nib.org
www.nib.org

National organization that operates, through the Javits-Wagner-O'Day (JWOD) Act, a federal procurement program enabling people who are blind or otherwise severely disabled to have meaningful employment opportunities. NIB and its more than 80 associated agencies employ more than five thousand people who are blind nationwide. Provides on-the-job training and sponsors the unique Business Leaders Program designed specifically to prepare individuals who are blind for careers in business management.

**National Information Clearinghouse on Children**
**Who Are Deaf-Blind (DB-LINK)**
c/o Teaching Research
Western Oregon State College
345 North Monmouth Avenue
Monmouth, OR 97361
(800) 438-9376
TDD/TTY: (800) 854-7013
Fax: (503) 838-8150
E-mail: dblink@tr.wou.edu
www.dblink.org

Federally funded service that identifies, coordinates, and disseminates, at no cost, information related to deaf-blind children and youths from birth through 21 years of age. Helps parents, teachers, and others by providing them with information to foster the skills, strategies, and confidence necessary to nurture and empower deaf-blind children.

**National Organization for Albinism and Hypopigmentation (NOAH)**
P.O. Box 959
East Hempstead, NH 03826-0959
(603) 887-2310 or (800) 648-2310
E-mail: info@albinism.org
www.albinism.org

National organization that offers information and support to people with albinism, their families and the professionals who work with them. Operated by members on a volunteer basis and funded primarily by dues and contributions of its members.

**Office of Disability Employment Policy**
**U.S. Department of Labor**
200 Constitution Avenue, NW
Washington, D.C. 20210
(202) 376-6200 or (866) 633-7365

TDD: (877) 889-5627
Fax: (202) 693-7888
www.dol.gov/odep/

Federal agency that provides national leadership by developing and influencing disability-related employment policy as well as practice affecting the employment of people with disabilities.

**Office of Special Education and Rehabilitative Services**
**U.S. Department of Education**
400 Maryland Ave., S.W.
Washington, D.C. 20202-7100
(202) 245-7468
www.ed.gov/about/offices/list/osers/index.html

Federal agency that oversees education, employment, and community living for people with disabilities by supporting programs that help educate children and youths with disabilities, provides for the rehabilitation of youths and adults with disabilities and supporting research to improve the lives of individuals with disabilities.

**Prevent Blindness America**
500 East Remington Road, Suite 200
Schaumburg, IL 60173
(847) 843-2020 or (800) 221-3004
PBA Center for Sight: (800) 331-2020
Fax: (847) 843-8458
E-mail: infor@preventblindness.org
www.preventblindness.org

National organization that conducts a program of public and professional education, research, and industrial and community services to prevent blindness. Services include screening, vision testing, and disseminating information on low-vision devices and clinics. Has a network of state affiliates.

**Texas School for the Blind and Visually Impaired (TSBVI)**
1100 West 45th Street
Austin, TX 78756-3494
(512) 454-8631 or (800) 872-5273
TDD/TTY: (512) 206-9188
Fax: (512) 454-3395
www.tsbvi.edu

School for the blind that is a major source for published curriculum guides, and supports an excellent Web site that offers a variety of information and resources for professionals, parents, and others associated with programs for people who are blind or visually impaired.

## SUPPLIERS OF BOOKS, BRAILLE, AND OTHER MEDIA

**American Printing House for the Blind**
See listing under National Organizations and Agencies

**Descriptive Video Service**
**Media Access Group at WGBH**
125 Western Avenue
Boston, MA 02134
(617) 300-3600 or (800) 333-1203
Fax: (617) 300-1020
E-mail: access@wgbh.org
www.wgbh.org/access

Alternate media producer of accessible videos and DVDs for people who are blind or visually impaired.

**JBI International**
110 East 30th Street
New York, NY 10016
(212) 889-2525 or (800) 433-1531
Fax: (212) 689-3692
E-mail: admin@jbilibrary.org
www.jewishbraille.org

Library that provides large-print and audio books as well as magazines on cassette and in braille. Produces educational materials in braille, large print or audio for students of all ages. Provides counseling for families of children who are blind, visually impaired, and reading disabled. Has an outreach program in the greater New York area (including Nassau and Suffolk counties) and in South Florida for elderly Americans dealing with the traumatic effects of age-related vision disease such as macular degeneration, cataracts, glaucoma, and diabetic retinopathy, and for seniors who cannot read standard print because of a physical disability.

**Kenneth Jernigan Library for Blind Children**
**American Action Fund for Blind Children and Adults**
18440 Oxnard Street
Tarzana, CA 91356
(818) 343-2022
E-mail: twinvisionkjl@aol.com
www.actionfund.org

Service agency that maintains a free lending library of braille and Twin Vision books for blind children and publishes and distributes a free weekly newspaper in braille internationally. Has a widespread campaign of public education, administers a program of scholarships and financial and other specialized assistance to individual blind persons, conducts seminars about blindness, and provides information to senior citizens to help them deal with vision loss in their later years. Operates the National Center for the Blind, a manufacturing facility, which also houses the International Braille and Technology Center for the Blind, a facility where people who are blind or visually impaired can learn about and evaluate the various kinds of computer-access devices available for them.

**National Braille Press**
88 St. Stephen Street
Boston, MA 02115
(617) 266-6160 or (888) 965-8965
Fax: (617) 437-0456
E-mail: orders@nbp.org
www.nbp.org

Publisher and on-demand producer of braille materials.

**National Library Service for the Blind and**
**Physically Handicapped**
Library of Congress
1291 Taylor Street, N.W.
Washington, D.C. 20542
(202) 707-5100 or (800) 424-8567
Fax: (202) 707-0712
TDD/TTY: (202) 707-0744
E-mail: nls@loc.gov
www.loc.gov/nls

Federal agency that conducts a national program to distribute free reading materials in braille and on recorded discs and cassettes to blind and visually impaired persons who cannot use printed materials.

Operates a reference section providing information on reading materials for disabled persons.

**Recording for the Blind and Dyslexic (RFB&D)**
20 Roszel Road
Princeton, NJ 08540
(609) 452-0606 or (866) 732-3585
Fax: (609) 520-7990
E-mail: custserv@rfbd.org
www.rfbd.org

National organization that lends tape-recorded textbooks and other educational materials at no charge to blind and visually, perceptually, and physically impaired students and professionals. Recording is done in a network of studios across the country.

**Seedlings: Braille Books for Children**
14151 Farmington Road
Livonia, MI 48154-4522
(734) 427-8552 or (800) 777-5882
E-mail: seedlink@aol.com
www.seedlings.org

Publisher of low-cost braille books for children.

# CAMPS AND RECREATIONAL ORGANIZATIONS

The organizations in this section are just a few of those that offer recreational activities directed at students with visual impairments. Participating in recreational activities is an important way for students to interact socially with others, is beneficial to health and physical well-being, and enhances their self-esteem. In particular, attending a well-run camp for children who are blind or visually impaired, some of which are listed here, gives students who are visually impaired the opportunity to meet peers with visual impairments, to learn from the experiences of older individuals who are blind or visually impaired, and to develop and use new skills.

**Boy Scouts of America**
**Special Needs and Disabilities**
1325 West Walnut Hill Lane
P.O. Box 152079

Irving, TX 75015-2079
www.scouting.org

National organization that develops and coordinates an effective scouting program for youths with disabilities and special needs, using all available community resources.

**Camp Allen**
56 Camp Allen Road
Bedford, NH 03110-6606
(603) 622-8471

Provides a quality outdoor recreation program for individuals with developmental and physical disabilities.

**Christian Record Services**
**National Camps for Blind Children**
4444 South 52nd Street
Lincoln, NE 68516
(402) 488-0981
Fax: (402) 488-7582

Provides camping programs for individuals whose corrected vision is no better than 20/200.

**Girl Scouts of the U.S.A.**
**Services for Girls with Disabilities**
420 5th Avenue
New York, NY 10018-2798
(212) 852-8000 or (800) 478-7248

Membership organization dedicated to helping all girls everywhere build character and gain skills for success in the real world.

**Pennsylvania Lions Beacon Lodge Camp**
114 SR 103 South
Mt. Union, PA 17066-9601
(814) 542-2511
Fax: (814) 542-7437

Camp for children and adults with special needs including blindness, deafness, and many other physical and mental challenges.

**Space Camp for Interested Visually Impaired Students**
Dan Oates, Coordinator
West Virginia School for the Blind

P.O. Box 1034
Romney, WV 26757
(304) 822-4883 or (540) 539-8768
E-mail: scivis@atlanticbb.net
www.tsbvi.edu/space

A weeklong camp that takes place at the U.S. Space and Rocket Center
in Huntsville, Alabama, coordinated by teachers of visually impaired
students. Programs are designed for students in grades 4–6, 7–9, and
10–12. Students learn about aviation and space travel and experience
simulated missions and can select from astronaut training or pilot
training.

**Vacation Camp for the Blind**
500 Greenwich Street, 3rd Floor
New York, NY 10013
(212) 625-1616
E-mail: Camp@visionsvcb.org
Camp site:
111 Summit Park Road
Spring Valley, NY 10977-1221
(845) 354-3003

Recreation and rehabilitation facility for people of all ages who are
blind or visually impaired.

**United States Association for Blind Athletes (USABA)**
33 North Institute Street
Colorado Springs, CO 80903
(719) 630-0422
Fax: (719) 630-0616
E-mail: media@usaba.org
www.usaba.org

National membership organization that provides training for blind
and visually impaired athletes for competition in sports such as cycling,
goalball, judo, powerlifting, skiing, swimming, wrestling, and 5-A-side
football.

# Index

# F

# G

# About the
# Contributors

**Sharon Z. Sacks, Ph.D.,** is Director of Curriculum and Professional Development at the California School for the Blind, where she was previously Assistant Superintendent. She was formerly Professor and Coordinator of the Teacher Preparation Program in Visual Impairments at California State University, Los Angeles. She has worked in the field of education and rehabilitation of blind and visually impaired individuals for almost 30 years as a resource and itinerant teacher of students with visual impairments, a home counselor for the Blind Babies Foundation, and a coordinator of teacher preparation in moderate and severe disabilities at San Jose State University. An executive editor of the journal *RE:view* and, with Karen Wolffe, co-editor of the *Focused on ... Social Skills* series of videos and study guides, she is also co-editor of *Development of Social Skills by Blind and Visually Impaired Students: Exploratory Studies and Strategies* and of *Educating Students Who Have Visual Impairments with Other Disabilities.* She has presented and published widely throughout the United States and abroad in the areas of social skills instruction for students with visual impairments, transition programming for students with visual impairments and multiple disabilities, psychosocial implications of low vision for students and adults, and issues related to braille literacy. Dr. Sacks is past president of the Association for Education and Rehabilitation of the Blind and Visually Impaired.

**Karen E. Wolffe, Ph.D.,** is Director, Professional Development and CareerConnect® at the American Foundation for the Blind and a distance education instructor at the University of Arkansas at Little Rock and has engaged in private practice as a career counselor and consultant in Austin, Texas, since 1992. Previously, she was a faculty member in the Department of Special Education at the University of Texas in Austin and directed the Job Readiness Clinic, in addition to being on the faculty of the Hadley School for the Blind. She is the author of *Career Counseling for People with Disabilities: A Practical Guide to Finding Employment*, co-author of the *Transition Tote System*, and editor of *Skills for Success: A Career Education Handbook for Children and Youth with Visual Impairments*. She also co-authored *Transition Issues for Students with Visual Disabilities* and is co-editor of the *Focused on . . . Social Skills* series of videos and study guides. She has published numerous articles and book chapters and presented frequently in this country and abroad on the importance of career education, social skills development, transition issues, employment opportunities for people with disabilities, and literacy in the workplace.

**Lizbeth A. Barclay, M.A.,** is Coordinator of Educational Assessments in the Assessment Program of the California School for the Blind in Fremont, where she was previously a teacher of the visually impaired and an orientation and mobility specialist. She has contributed to *RE:view* as well as the book *Collaborative Assessment: Working with Students Who Are Blind or Visually Impaired, Including Those with Additional Disabilities*. Ms. Barclay is a member of the boards of Northern California Association for Education and Rehabilitation of the Blind and Visually Impaired and California Transcribers and Educators of the Visually Handicapped.

**Jane N. Erin, Ph.D.,** is Professor in the Department of Special Education, Rehabilitation, and School Psychology at the University of Arizona at Tucson. She served as editor in chief of the *Journal of Visual Impairment & Blindness* from 1998–2001 and is a former executive editor of *RE:view*. She is author of *When You Have a Visually Impaired Student with Multiple Disabilities in Your Classroom: A Guide for Teachers;*

co-author of *Visual Handicaps and Learning;* co-editor of *Diversity and Visual Impairments: The Influence of Race, Gender, Religion, and Ethnicity on the Individual* and *Visual Impairments and Learning;* and has written numerous articles, chapters, and presentations. Dr. Erin previously held presidencies of state and local chapters of the Association for Education and Rehabilitation of the Blind and Visually Impaired (AER) and the Council for Exceptional Children in Arizona and Texas, and she is the recipient of the 2000 Margaret Bluhm Award and the 1996 Mary K. Bauman Award for contributions to education in visual impairment, both from AER.

**Judith Lesner** is the Supervisor of Residential Programs at the California School for the Blind in Fremont. The Region 6 representative for the National Association for Parents of Children with Visual Impairments, she has published in *CTEVH Newsletter, Awareness, Mouth* magazine, and the Blind Babies Foundation Newsletter. She has received the Parent Advocate Award from the Northern California Association for Education and Rehabilitation of the Blind and Visually Impaired and the 2002 Josephine L. Taylor Leadership Institute Fellowship Award.

**Susan LaVenture** is Executive Director of the National Association for Parents of Children with Visual Impairments (NAPVI) in Watertown, Massachusetts. She lectures student groups at Harvard Medical School and elsewhere on the role of parents in children's development, education, and medical care; consults on the development of organizations and programs serving families of blind and visually impaired children throughout the world; and serves as an advocate for parents of visually impaired children, speaking throughout the country and all over the world. Ms. LaVenture is the editor of NAPVI's quarterly magazine, *Awareness,* as well as the books *Childhood Glaucoma: A Reference Guide for Families; Equals in Partnership: Basic Rights for Families of Children with Visual Impairment or Blindness; In Celebration of Grandparenting: For Grandparents of Children with Visual Impairments;* and the forthcoming *A Parents' Guide to Special Education for Children with Visual Impairments.*

**Sandra Lewis, Ed.D.,** is Associate Professor and Coordinator of the Program in Visual Impairment at Florida State University, Tallahassee. She is a member of the board of directors of the Council on Exceptional Children Division on Visual Impairments and previously served as Executive Editor of *RE:view;* chairperson of Division 17, Personnel Preparation, of the Association for Education and Rehabilitation of the

Blind and Visually Impaired (AER); and president of the Florida chapter of AER. Dr. Lewis has worked as an educator of individuals of all ages who are blind or visually impaired and has published and presented widely on the education and assessment of visually impaired students.

**P. Ann MacCuspie, Ph.D.,** is Director of Programs for Students with Visual Impairments of the Atlantic Provinces Special Education Authority (ASPEA), Halifax, Nova Scotia, Canada and an honorary adjunct professor at Mount Saint Vincent University in Halifax. She is a member of the board of directors of the Canadian Braille Authority and was previously on the boards of the Association for Education and Rehabilitation of the Blind and Visually Impaired (AER), the Canadian Council for Exceptional Children, and the National Coalition for Vision Health. The author of *Promoting Acceptance of Children with Disabilities: From Tolerance to Inclusion; Technology Handbook for Teachers of Students who are Blind or Visually Impaired;* and *Access to Literacy Instruction for Students who are Blind or Visually Impaired: A Discussion Paper;* as well as many articles, book chapters, and presentations; she is also an executive editor of *RE:view.* Dr. MacCuspie was the recipient of the 2005 ASPEA Distinguished Service Award and the 1996 Excellence in Education Award from AER.

**L. Penny Rosenblum, Ph.D,** is Adjunct Assistant Professor in the Department of Special Education, Rehabilitation, and School Psychology at the University of Arizona in Tucson. She is co-author of *Finding Wheels: A Curriculum for Nondrivers with Visual Impairments for Gaining Control of Transportation Needs.* Dr. Rosenblum has published a book chapter and various articles in the *Journal of Visual Impairment & Blindness* and has presented papers at a variety of conferences.

**Rosanne K. Silberman, Ed.D.,** is Professor in the Department of Special Education at Hunter College of the City University of New York, where she coordinates the graduate teacher preparation programs in blindness and visual impairment and severe disabilities, including deaf-blindness. She is co-editor of *Educating Students Who Have Visual Impairments with Other Disabilities* and *Education Children with Multiple Disabilities: A Collaborative Approach* and has written extensively in chapters and articles as well as made numerous presentations on students who have visual impairments with other disabilities. Dr. Silberman is a member of the board of trustees of the New York Institute for Special Education and the advisory board of DB-LINK and a consulting editor for *Deaf-Blind Perspectives* and *Focus on Autism and Developmental Disorders.*

She is past president of the Council for Exceptional Children Division on Visual Impairments and the recipient of the 2002 George E. Keane Award for Distinguished Service and Contributions to the Field of Blindness and Visual Impairment from the New York State Association for Education and Rehabilitation of the Blind and Visually Impaired.

**Mary Zabelski, M.A.,** is Director of Educational Services at the Chicago Lighthouse and President of the National Association for Parents of Children with Visual Impairments. She has contributed to *RE:view* and *Awareness* and made numerous conference presentations.

CPSIA information can be obtained at www.ICGtesting.com
Printed in the USA
BVOW09s0808290815

415319BV00004B/28/P

9 780891 288824